WHEN BASEBALL
WAS STILL KING

ALSO BY GENE FEHLER
AND FROM MCFARLAND

Center Field Grasses:
Poems from Baseball (1991; paperback 2012)

Dancing on the Basepaths:
Baseball Poetry and Verse (2001)

I Hit the Ball!
Baseball Poems for the Young (1996)

When Baseball Was Still King

Major League Players Remember the 1950s

Gene Fehler

McFarland & Company, Inc., Publishers
Jefferson, North Carolina, and London

LIBRARY OF CONGRESS CATALOGUING-IN-PUBLICATION DATA

Fehler, Gene, 1940–
When baseball was still king : major league players remember the 1950s / Gene Fehler.
        p.   cm.
Includes index.

ISBN 978-0-7864-7065-5
softcover : acid free paper ∞

1. Baseball — United States — History — 20th century.
2. Baseball players — United States — Anecdotes.
I. Title.
GV863.A1F44 2012   796.357 — dc23   2012018147

BRITISH LIBRARY CATALOGUING DATA ARE AVAILABLE

© 2012 Gene Fehler. All rights reserved

No part of this book may be reproduced or transmitted in any form or by any means, electronic or mechanical, including photocopying or recording, or by any information storage and retrieval system, without permission in writing from the publisher.

Cover illustrations © 2012 Retro Clip Art

Manufactured in the United States of America

*McFarland & Company, Inc., Publishers
Box 611, Jefferson, North Carolina 28640
www.mcfarlandpub.com*

Contents

Preface 1

ONE. When It All Begins   3
TWO. Minor Leagues and War Years   12
THREE. Men in Blue   38
FOUR. Playing Fields   49
FIVE. Skippers   61
SIX. Joe and Mickey, Ted and Stan   82
SEVEN. The First Time   95
EIGHT. I Remember Him!   103
NINE. Swinging the Lumber   133
TEN. The Hurlers   145
ELEVEN. A Little Bit of Money   164
TWELVE. Now That Was a Moment!   170
THIRTEEN. Trades   198
FOURTEEN. Injuries   208
FIFTEEN. Outside the Lines   219
SIXTEEN. Team Play   229
SEVENTEEN. Endings, Wishes, Regrets and Joys   243

Appendix: The Players   257
Index   267

For John Creighton and Lew Frosch, and others from The Park, who lived '50s baseball with me — and for Polly, my forever best friend, with love

Preface

The 1950s—the decade considered by many to be one of baseball's finest. The last decade in which there could be absolutely no argument as to which sport the words "the National Pastime" called to mind.

In those years shortly after World War II, the hundreds of players who had missed time because of the war were back on the playing fields, and except for a relatively small number involved in the Korean War, each team was at full strength once more.

Among the more than two hundred players who made their big league debuts in 1950 and 1951 are such notables as Mickey Mantle, Gil McDougald, Clem Labine, Vern Law, Jimmy Piersall, Chico Carrasquel, Frank Thomas, Dale Long, Bob Turley, Gus Bell, Bob Nieman, Charlie Maxwell, Jim Lemon, Lew Burdette, Jim Busby, Whitey Ford, Jackie Jensen, Joe Adcock, Dick Donovan, Billy Loes, Billy Martin, Irv Noren, Johnny Logan, Roy McMillan, Pete Runnels, Bob Friend, and Willie Mays. The years that followed would soon bring Mathews and Aaron, Killebrew and Haddix, Kaline and Banks, Don Larsen and Hoyt Wilhelm. Add to these and so many others the greats who began their careers in the '40s and whose most productive years still lay ahead—and we have a list of names that will live forever in the minds and hearts of all who love baseball's rich history.

Between 1993 and 2003 I was privileged to have conversations with more than ninety former major leaguers from the '50s and to receive written recollections from many others. This book contains more than 1,078 separate items—their stories and comments, their moments remembered. Forty-two of these items appeared in two books published by Sports Publishing (*Tales from Baseball's Golden Age*, 2000; and *More Tales from Baseball's Golden Age*, 2002).

Some of the players, like Jimmy Bloodworth and Bobby Doerr, were just finishing up long big league careers at the time; others like Dick Hall and Milt Pappas, were just beginning careers that would extend into the 1970s. One player, Tim McCarver, would last until 1980. The focus of this book, however, is squarely on the 1950s; most of the quoted comments deal directly with moments from that decade, and all have some connection to the game as it was played then. Chapters one and two, for instance, deal with the start of the players' careers. Their years in the minors—often pre-'50s—not only were instrumental in preparing them for the major leagues but left vivid memories of those days when they first sensed that their childhood dreams were within reach. The book contains only a handful of other non-'50s items, such as the pennant race in 1949, which was the beginning of the great Yankee run of five straight World Series championships, from 1949 to 1953.

Many of these men have, alas, passed away since our conversations. But perhaps, as Joanna Walls, wife of ballplayer Lee Walls, wrote me after her husband's death, their baseball life has not ended: "Lee went to live in baseball heaven. He is with his buddy since high school and roommate, Don Drysdale; fellow Dodger Leo Durocher; and fellow teammate, manager and friend, Billy Martin. I'm sure they are playing cards, golf or going over the hitters."

CHAPTER ONE

When It All Begins

When do they begin, those big league dreams? As an infant, tossing a baby bottle to the floor? As a toddler, rolling a ball across the room? As a youngster, playing catch with Dad? Perhaps in school, recognizing that you can hit a ball farther than anybody else your age, or throw a ball harder, or run faster. Perhaps for some, dreams don't begin until that day a scout spots you and shows interest. In some cases, they might truly begin only with that first minor league season, when you find without question that you have what it takes to play in the majors. It might be that first big league game, that first step onto the field, when you find yourself one of the select few among the millions who wish they were in your place, but who never were, and who know they never will be.

I was signed by Detroit as an outfielder in the sandlots of Birmingham. They pigeonholed my contract and didn't send it in, and I later signed with Andalusia, which was in the Class D Alabama-Florida League. They signed me and it beat the Detroit contract in and made me the property of the Andalusia ballclub. They weren't affiliated with any major league club. *[That year, 1938, Trucks pitched, going 26–5 with a 1.25 ERA. His 418 strikeouts — in 273 innings — are the second highest total in the history of professional ball. He struck out 20 in his first game. He pitched two no-hitters that year, winning one of them 1–0, getting the game's only hit in the 9th inning and scoring the game's only run.]* After that season Detroit bought my contract from Andalusia for ten thousand dollars, as a pitcher. At that time there was an abundance of ballplayers. They had like a hundred Class D teams. *[In Trucks' first minor league season there were 261 minor league teams, and, with an estimated average of 20-man rosters, over 5,000 active minor leaguers at any given time.]*
— **Virgil Trucks**

I pitched a no-hit game in local baseball, then the following year *[in 1941]* I pitched two one-hitters in amateur ball again, and because of these accomplishments the local scouts were anxious to give me a chance to see what I could do. I did get two chances, one with the Cleveland Indians organization, which I didn't make out. Then I went to the Red Sox organization, and they signed me up within the same week.

I was twenty-five when I broke into pro ball. That's old. And my object was just to get the experience and see how professional baseball players lived because in my youth professional baseball players were my idols, particularly Babe Ruth. That's going back in history. And whatever happened was cream on the top of the bottle.

— *Joe Ostrowski*

When I was sixteen I went down and worked out with the Dodgers at the parade grounds in Brooklyn, and Clyde Sukeforth was throwing batting practice. You got three swings and three throws from the outfield, and I hit one ball over the fence and they called me back to hit some more. I guess I got about twenty or thirty swings at least, and I hit maybe seven or eight out of the ballpark or off the wall. That's how I originally signed with the Dodgers.

I was sixteen when I started with the Dodgers in 1945, with Thomasville, North Carolina. I only played a few games, and they released me. *[Lennon played 12 games, hit .204.]*

Then the following year the Dodgers invited me down to Maryland in spring training. They brought me in a hardware store, I believe it was, like in the back room with a little light there hanging down, and they signed me to a contract there.

— *Bob Lennon*

I lived in Maryland, but my mother and I rode a Greyhound Bus up to Appleton, Wisconsin, when I was fifteen years old. The Cardinals had a tryout camp there for three days, and my cousins up there talked me into going out and trying out, and I was scared to death. They had 300 kids the first day and they cut it down to 100, and the last day it was 50, and then we had a game.

They called three of us in and said, "We're going to be in touch with you next spring."

I was only fifteen. I said, "Aw, I'll never hear from those guys."

The next spring, in Maryland, about March or April, here comes a guy knocking on the door from Pennsylvania, and wanted to sign me to a Cardinal contract. I signed for a hundred fifty bucks a month. That was 1944. I went away in June, after my junior year in high school. I played until September, came back and finished my senior year and took off again the next year and never even waited around for my diploma. My mother picked up my diploma.

— *Johnny Klippstein*

I got released twice my first year, 1946. I went to Albany, Georgia, for a tryout with the Cardinal farm team, and signed a contract for a hundred dollars a month. They sent me home after two weeks. I think it was just as well that I got released, because I don't think I could have lived on a hundred.

I went to a tryout camp out at Fredericksburg, Pennsylvania. Me and about four other kids hitchhiked our way out to a tryout camp, and I got signed up and sent to New Iberia, Louisiana. I was there about two weeks and I was sent home again *[King pitched one inning, giving up 1 run on 1 walk and 3 hits.]*

You wonder why people give you an opportunity to do things sometimes. Somebody did, a guy named Roy Dissinger gave a chance to go play again. And I finally made it with the lowest league there was in baseball, the Alabama-State League. *[In 1947 King went 8–11 with Geneva, at the age of 19.]* I kind of hung around there and learned how to pitch. I think the best thing was that I was playing with older people, some guys who had just come back from the service and wanted to try to continue their career in baseball. They were about 27–28 years old. The catcher I was throwing to was 29. Those guys had some wisdom. I got more knowledge playing with them than I did playing any place else.

I think it just changed my whole career. Listening to older people was, I think, the best thing that happened there. In those days, with a lot of older guys in the minor leagues, you could pick people's brains.

— *Nellie King*

I always wanted to play ball. My father was an ex-semi pro pitcher, and so I was brought up with baseball.

I was signed by the Yankees *[in 1946]*. I relieved in a semi-pro game up here and there happened to be a Yankee scout there and he liked the way I threw the ball so he asked me if I'd like to go down to New York and work out with them, and I told them "Yeah."

I went down to New York and pitched some batting practice and everything and they signed me.

— *Bob Keegan*

[After an outstanding college career at Western Michigan University, he was signed in 1954 as a bonus baby, thus having to stay on the big league roster for two years.] Signing a bonus contract was probably beneficial because they had some money in me so they gave me some opportunity to be around the big league club. The disadvantage was that it was difficult to play on a team that was a contender, which we were with the White Sox.

I had a year to go in school, so I had a figure that I set. If they met it, I'd forgo that last year, and they met it. I signed a three-year contract.

— *Ron Jackson*

I was 29 years old when I started in professional ball. I was dissatisfied with my job. I longed to play baseball.

I was playing semi-pro ball in Galveston County, and a scout asked me, "Just tell me about the ballplayers in this territory. We're looking for a guy that can play the outfield and pitch a little bit in a Class C league."

I just ran down every ballplayer, in Galveston County, and when we got down to the bottom line, I said, "There's only one ballplayer in this whole area that would fill that bill, and that's me." So I guess I was guilty of scouting my own self. *[In 1950, at the age of 29, Murff debuted in A ball with a 17–4 record. Five seasons later, in 1955, he was 27–11 in Double A with a 1.99 ERA and 28 complete games. Parts of the next two seasons were spent with the Braves. After his career, as a scout he signed many future major leaguers, including Nolan Ryan.]*

— *Red Murff*

I came from a little town in Montana, and believe it or not they were baseball-minded up there. My dad was a pitcher in his day, playing semi-pro ball. That's all I ever thought, I just wanted to be a baseball player, even since I can remember. So I stayed with it, played American Legion ball and then went on to college, and enjoyed it. There haven't been too many major league players from Montana. The summers were short, the winters were long. It wasn't too conducive to baseball. *[Plews signed with the Yankees in 1950.]*

— *Herb Plews*

Dad was pitching semi-pro baseball. He pitched twice a week for different teams, and he'd get twenty-five dollars from each one of them, and he was making fifty dollars a week, plus his barbering. He was doing his barbering business too. And then when he'd pitch a real good ballgame, sometimes, he said, they'd pass the hat and instead of getting twenty-five dollars that day he might get fifty or sixty. So he didn't go and play professional baseball because he had a family — I wasn't born then — but he had my two older brothers, Frank and George.

He had to do what he could make the most money at, so Dad was managing a baseball team that George and Frank played on when I was just a little boy, and he kept right on managing the semi-pro baseball team as I came up. I was a catcher back then in semi-pro.

Dad was a great influence on all of us.

— *Skeeter Kell*

Lou Meggy, who was the running guard for Red Grange at Illinois, decided to start an American Legion team.

He said, "Well, who's going to pitch?"

"Well, Upton can throw hard, we'll let him pitch."

"Okay."

I pitched every inning of every ballgame, and seventeen innings against Sockem Post in St. Louis, who had Yogi Berra, Joe Garagiola, Whitey Ford on the ballclub. Bill Essie, the Yankee scout, came up and wanted to sign me right after.

I said, "Oh no, I have to finish high school."

He came down at the end of the season *[in 1944]* and signed me. I said, "Mom, they're going to give me money to play ball."

— *Tom Upton*

I originally was supposed to sign with the Boston Red Sox. My father and Mike Ryba grew up together. And Mike, I recall, called the house after the Red Sox and Cardinals played in the '46 World Series. I was writing letters back and forth to the Red Sox organization and was invited to the Dodgers' camp unsigned, waiting to hear from the Red Sox.

And my first game — I'm playing on the Dodger B team in Vero Beach, we were playing Scranton, and Mike Ryba is managing the Scranton club. He called me over after an inning or two, and said, "Are you Bill Hunter from Indiana, Pennsylvania?"

I said, "Yes, I am"

He said, "I've been waiting for you for three weeks in Cocoa Beach."

I said, "Well, I've been waiting to hear from you, too."

He said, "Have you signed?"

I said, "I signed yesterday."

He said, "There's an awful lot of players in the Dodger organization."

I said, "Mr. Ryba, if I have it, I'll get there. And if I don't have it, it wouldn't make any difference what team I'm with."

He said, "Good luck to you." That was how I ended up in the Dodger organization. *[Hunter spent five years in the minors, 1948–1952, and was traded to the Browns in October 1952.]*

— *Billy Hunter*

If a player was halfway decent, the scouts would see him. When I graduated from high school, the Giants offered me five hundred dollars to sign, and I said, "No, I'm going to Swarthmore, to college."

I played in a semi-pro league, the Susquehanna League. I played for Hickory, which was a little town near Aberdeen. My recollection of the Aberdeen team in that league was that half the team was named Ripken. It turned out later it was only three, I think.

Then I went on to play in Massachusetts a couple summers in a summer college league, and did pretty well there, especially pitching. By the time between my junior and senior years in college, virtually every club had contacted me at that point. They'd make me an offer, and when I asked for too much money I got a "don't call us, we'll call you" kind of answer from them. So finally I chickened out and I signed for Pittsburgh *[in 1951]*. Branch Rickey was their general manager. One of his daughters went to Swarthmore, so I was sort of drawn to him anyway.

— *Dick Hall*

Here it was, my first year in big league baseball with the World Series pennant winner, 1945. But that was when the rules were such that you could sign guys before they're out of high school. Detroit, at the end of World War II didn't really have a farm system to speak of, and they had no regular decent place to send me, and they'd spent a little money on me to sign me, so they kept me with the big league club. They were short of pitching, too, and basically I was just around. I was at Buffalo just three weeks, I think, in 1945. But I mean here it was, first year in pro ball, at seventeen, being on a World Series winner.

— *Art Houtteman*

Joe Engels, with Chattanooga in the Southern Association, sent me a contract in 1944 for two hundred and seventy-five dollars a month. I signed it and sent it back and went over there for spring training.

When I was in Chattanooga, the Cubs offered the Washington organization a hundred thousand dollars, which was a lot of money at that time, but they turned it down because I'd had so much publicity that year Washington had to bring me up. I probably should not have been up with Washington in 1946. I'd only played pro ball in '44 and '45. *[Coan was brought up in '46 to the Senators after hitting .372 for Class A Chattanooga. He had his first .300 big league season in 1950.]*

— *Gil Coan*

I signed out of high school at 17 years old and was a very skinny kid. I was almost 6'2" and about 138 pounds. I got to the major leagues at 6'2" and 198. The first pitch I threw professionally I crossed the catcher up and hit the batter in the chest.

At seventeen, I didn't have any idea what my potential would be. By '57, in the Texas League, I kind of matured. I got up to 198 pounds, and I started throwing the ball hard for nine innings. I was 20, going on 21, and I said, "Hey, I might have something."

Up until then I was just enjoying myself.

But someone had seen my potential. Probably my scout, Lefty Phillips. He was the guy who signed Drysdale the next year behind me. I played against Don in high school. He was six-four, five, gangly, you know, awkward. He didn't really throw all that hard in high school either. *[Sherry signed with Brooklyn in 1953.]*

— *Larry Sherry*

My signing bonus of $67,500 from the White Sox was the highest ever up to that time — for about two weeks, I think, when Paul Pettit signed for $100,000. I turned down a lot more money with the Yankees. My father and my high school coach were of the opinion, and rightfully so, that the fastest way to the major leagues was not with the Yankees, it was with a struggling team. I never looked on my contract as a negative. It was a wonderful start for a kid from Oklahoma who had probably not had five dollars in his pocket at one time up until then. I don't believe anyone would ever say that I backed off or didn't hustle or didn't work hard because of the money. Marty Marion once said the only other person that he saw work so hard or hustle as much was an ex-teammate of his named Enos Slaughter. But there were some negatives. I was the one that always got picked on by the rival fans, especially early.

When I signed with the White Sox *[in 1951]*, they had hardly no one in the organization that I had to beat out. Red Wilson finally did come out of the organization, but I think I signed just about the same time he did. Both of their major league catchers, Phil Masi and Gus Niarhos, were in their mid-to-high thirties by that time, both getting toward the end of their career. So it seemed like, "You'll be in the major leagues within two years if you sign with the White Sox. It might take you five or six if you sign with the Yankees." Well, that part of it was true, I was in the major leagues in a year and a half. Not with the White Sox, but I was in the major leagues. *[Porter was playing with the Browns at age 19.]*

— *J.W. Porter*

In 1950 I was given a $100,000 signing bonus by the Pirates, which was the highest up to that time. I signed out of high school. I made up my mind when I signed that I would work harder than anybody else, and I did, and that seemed to subside any jealousy or any resentment.

— *Paul Pettit*

Catching the Cardinals' veteran catchers was a bit intimidating at first, with me being just out of high school. These pitchers had better stuff than anybody I'd ever caught before, and to some degree it overwhelmed me physically. I mean, these guys were tearing my glove off.

Two and a half a months before that I was catching high school pitchers, who never signed professionally. So you can imagine what kind of difference it was for me, trying to master some of the stuff that Bob Gibson threw, or Marshall Bridges, or Larry Jackson. Guys like that. *[In 1959, as a 17-year-old, McCarver hit .360 for Keokuk in 65 games. He hit .357 for Rochester in 17 games. He went 4 for 24 in 8 games with the Cardinal. His first full-time season with the Cardinals was 1963.]*

— *Tim McCarver*

Baseball was something that I couldn't get away from. I was always throwing something. My mother said, "You threw your bottle farther than the other kids, so I knew you were going to be a ballplayer."

I guess I inherited a love of baseball from my father. I have to say he loved the game as much as I did. He would talk about seeing a major league baseball game in Cincinnati or St. Louis when he was a young man. And I asked him jillions of questions about this. "Tell me about it. What'd they look like?" He thought they were special.

— *Red Murff*

I was offered a contract by Cleveland. George Susce lived up the street from me, and his boy and I were pretty good friends. *[Susce had been a catcher for Cleveland and others; he was now a Cleveland coach. His son George pitched in the big leagues from 1955 to 1959 and went 22–17.]* But I wanted to play in my home town, so I called Pittsburgh and said, "Mom and Dad have a mortgage on their house." I think it was about thirty-two hundred dollars. I said, "If you pay the mortgage on the house I'll be more than happy to sign." I never did see the money; it went right to the mortgage company; it paid the house off for Mom and Dad. *[Thomas was 18 years old when he signed in 1948.]*

— *Frank Thomas*

I was 17 when I signed with the Tigers in 1944. They sent me to Jamestown in Class D for $100 a month. Hey, I thought that was a lot of money; I would have played for free. I could hardly believe they were actually paying me to play ball.

I was in the minors for five years before I came up with the Tigers. One of my biggest thrills was to play in Detroit, my hometown, in front of many of my boyhood friends and my family.

— *Joe Ginsberg*

Back when I was in school I just loved to play baseball. I was 15, 16 years old when I was playing with 25–30 year old guys, playing at the semi-pro level in New York City. So I knew I must have been as good as the older guys, but again, it wasn't my intention to play professional baseball, because I never knew anything about it until I got into it. I came out of high school and really didn't know what I was going to do with my life. I went to school to become an electrician, and the next thing I knew I was playing baseball. *[Malzone signed with the Red Sox in 1947.]*

— *Frank Malzone*

'51 was my first year in pro baseball. I was 18 years old. In '52 I had a great year *[with Waycross in the Class D Georgia-Florida League]*. I pitched 297 innings in a 140 game schedule. I led the league in hits given up, I led the league in walks, I led the league in strikeouts, balks, wild pitches. I led in everything except ERA. My ERA was 1.39. Another guy had a 1.37. I had 265 strikeouts, and I walked 180 something. I could throw hard. I threw it in the high 90s.

— *Taylor Phillips*

I graduated from high school on Friday night in 1944 and joined the ball club in Milwaukee with Charlie Grimm as manager on Saturday. Then I was in the service in '45 and '46. In '49 I played at Beaumont in the Yankee organization, before I was drafted by the Browns, and I played every inning of every ballgame down there. I led the league in triples and stolen bases. The triples were actually doubles stretched into triples. I was pretty fast. I went back to the Yankee organization in '52 and they sent me to Washington. That's when I decided to retire *[at age 26]*.

— *Tom Upton*

When I signed in 1950, you could sign with anybody. The only thing was, if they paid you over six thousand dollars in bonus *[actually four thousand]*, you had to stay with the parent club for two years. *[The "bonus baby" rule was abolished in 1965.]* In fact, Koufax sat on the Dodger bench for two years because he had got a sizable bonus to sign. All he did was throw batting practice and mop up. I faced him in '55 when he was just wild as a buck, bounced his curveball halfway up there, and threw it about a hundred miles an hour.

And then to see the finished product — I saw that finished product in Vero Beach. He threw for about thirty minutes — he had three pitches, fastball, curve, and change, and he could put them all in tea cups. Unbelievable.

But I think I got fifteen hundred dollars to sign, and was signed to a Class B contract. When I went back to spring training after I'd signed, I had to beat out twelve first basemen to make a Class D ballclub. I mean, they had minor league teams in every town in the United States. I think the Giants must have had twelve or fourteen minor league teams then.

But one thing it did, it gave a person a chance to develop. Nowadays, if you don't hit the ground running and you're not really producing in a couple years, three years, you're gone.

— *Gail Harris*

Back when I started out there were more opportunities for young players because there were so many farm clubs. The Cardinals alone had about thirty-six. A kid with potential got a chance to play *[in 1941]* and prove himself.

I was only one hundred thirty pounds, but I could run and catch the ball, so I got a chance. Today I probably wouldn't have got signed.

— *Chuck Diering*

When I was 17 years old I played in the same town with Bobby Hazel in South Carolina. Me and him got picked to play in the all-star game between North Carolina and South Carolina. That's when I felt I might have a chance to get into pro ball. Right after that game — North Carolina beat us 2-1 — a scout from the Boston Braves came down to my house and signed me. My dad had to sign with me. I signed for three thousand dollars. About a day or two later Cincinnati came by and offered me thirty thousand dollars. They signed Bobby. That was in 1950. I missed four years during the Korean War. *[In 1950, their first years of pro ball, Taylor, at age 17, hit .301 in Class D ball, and Hazel, at age 19, hit .313 in Class A ball.]*

— *Sammy Taylor*

When I was 16 years old I had already worked out with the Red Sox in Virginia and with the Yankees in Norfolk. And the Dodgers had me all up to Bear Mountain in West Point. They had spring training in the fieldhouse at West Point. I was up there working out with them. My dad had to sign my contract for me at 16 years old. I came back to high school the next year. *[Flowers signed with the Red Sox in 1945.]*

— *Ben Flowers*

As a teenager I used to go out and pitch batting practice with the New Orleans Pelicans, which was a St. Louis Cardinal farm club, and Ray Blade, the old Cardinal manager, was then managing the New Orleans ballclub, and Branch Rickey would come down, and another fellow on my high school team, Ray Yokem, he and I used to go out and throw batting practice to them, and Rickey used to get behind the cage and watch what we were doing, and also giving us the sign when to throw a curveball and so forth. I was pretty much interested in the Cardinals until some of the fellas that had signed with the Cardinals told me, "Mel, if you get another offer, go to them. Don't go with the Cardinals"— because the Cardinals had too many farm clubs at that time and you're pretty much known as a

number, not a name, so that kind of discouraged me from signing with the Cardinals. And a little bit later I was pitching a ballgame, and a Red Sox scout was in the stands, Hugh Montague, and he saw me pitch and I struck out 17 on that day. He became interested and he and Herb Pennock came in to talk to me and of course I signed with the Red Sox *[in 1941]*.
— *Mel Parnell*

Paul Kritchell of the Yankees wanted to sign me when I was sixteen years old. Well, my mother said no. My dad had died when I was two. I was a junior in high school. My mother said I was going to graduate first. I said, "Mom, I'll come back and graduate."

I couldn't believe I was going to play and get paid to play baseball. My mom said, "Jim, you can't go play. You won't stay a week. You'll be back." At that time I couldn't stand to be away from home. I had to sleep in my own bed at night.

I said, "Mom, this is what I want to do." The funny thing is, I never did get homesick. I think that was just my destiny. *[Greengrass signed with the Yankees in 1944.]*
— *Jim Greengrass*

Chapter Two

Minor Leagues and War Years

Minor leagues. The stepping stone. In many cases, like a stone that skips several times before reaching its target. Most major leaguers in the '50s spent several years working their way through the minor leagues, experiencing the bus rides, low pay, less than ideal clubhouse and hotel conditions. Many had to wait their turn, hoping for that break that would bring them to the majors, and then hoping they could take advantage of that break. Many had outstanding seasons in the minors that they could, for one reason or another, never duplicate once they reached the major leagues.

Many players had the start of a promising career interrupted by World War II. Others had a promising career curtailed by being in the wrong organization, one that already had its full measure of first basemen or catchers or outfielders. Some found a perfect way to close out their career by moving from the majors to the Pacific Coast League, considered by many to be a third major league. To many players, that journey through the minor leagues was filled with many good moments.

In the minors they had some clubhouses where you had one shower, one stream of water for 25 guys. That was usually in the visitor's clubhouse.
— *Bob Smith*

It wasn't that it was a big hardship to play, 'cause we enjoyed it. I enjoyed it when I broke in Class D ball *[with the Giants in 1950]*. I enjoyed the bus rides and everything else, 'cause it was just a bunch of young guys just trying to get up the ladder a little bit in baseball, living the best we could in those conditions. There were a lot of long bus rides, but that was just part of it. Sometimes you play a game and get into a hot bus and go eight or nine or 10 hour ride to go into another town and have a ball game. It wasn't the best conditioned as far as putting up at hotels and all.
— *Gail Harris*

Sometimes in the minors, in the small towns, we weren't appreciated by some of the local boys because the girls would want to go out with some of the ballplayers.
—*Jack McMahan*

Two. Minor Leagues and War Years

What I remember most about my minor league years are those gol-darn bus rides, station wagon rides.

— *Wally Westlake*

It was pretty tough riding those buses in the minor leagues. Lots of times you were riding overnight and then playing a game as soon as you got into town, which made it pretty tough, but when you want to get to the top you just ignore that stuff and try a little harder to try to get out of that atmosphere and get up to the big boys. It was a great experience. I think it's something all kids should experience, start at the bottom and come to the top.

— *Mel Parnell*

The conditions in the minor leagues were not always too good, but it was the best place to play baseball at the time. And you'd stand on your head and let them pour hot lead in your butt if you could get to the big leagues. That was the ambition of most of the ballplayers.

Our conditions were not monetarily enriching, but we always had good fans if we tried hard. If you try hard, you always have good fans. You don't even have to win for them.

— *Red Murff*

I loved the minors. I thoroughly enjoyed it, honest to God. If you didn't love it, you'd never stay in baseball, because it's a tough business.

I think when I came up we were getting twenty dollars a day or twenty-five dollars a day meal money. Down in the minor leagues, you were getting a buck or five. You still got to eat, whether you're in the major leagues or the minor leagues. That always got me. "Well, you're not as hungry in the minors." That always fascinated me.

You always rode buses, you washed your own jocks and things like that. You were on your own. After the game sometimes there wasn't any water, or the pump didn't work, you get on the bus half soaped up, you put your uniform on, you keep it on. I never slept in a hotel the first year I played ball. In the Alabama State League we drove and came right back.

— *Nellie King*

Facilities in the minor leagues were bad. Clubhouses were very poor. In those days mainly your clubhouses were wooden. You had wooden lockers, and the shower facilities were dirty, filthy. You only had a couple showers, you had to wait for the next guy to get in and out.

— *Chuck Diering*

The living in the minors was the worst part, worse than the travel. You'd get in the places where you didn't have good air-conditioning. You get the heat in the summertime you wouldn't get a good night's rest. You'd just have to cram your pillow in the window and lay your head up in the window and hope you'd get some outside air. Halfway breathe. Many the time I'd wet my sheet, wrap up in it and hope I went to sleep before the sheet dried.

— *Tom Wright*

Clubhouse conditions in the minor leagues were terrible *[in 1944]*. The lower you went, the tougher they were. You paid your dues in those minor leagues. We had rats running around and everything else in some of those clubhouses. It wasn't very nice. Some of the buses wouldn't make it from town to town. You wound up pushing them up hills and things like that. You'd have to play a doubleheader in the same uniform.

It was tough to play in the minor leagues, but we loved it anyway. We knew the ultimate, that if you got to the big leagues, that's when you got the nice uniform, the nice clubhouse. We thought that five thousand dollars was a lot of money, and that was the minimum then. And if you made ten, why Geez, you were an established player.

— *Joe Ginsberg*

When I started *[in 1946]*, there were 48 leagues — eight teams in a league. So that's about 3,500 players playing in the minor leagues. And there were only 16 teams in the big leagues, so there were a lot of people at the bottom You could still play baseball and make two-three hundred dollars a month, work in the off season. If you were making three-four thousand a year you could survive. It was fun and a lot of guys did that, in small towns, had their own team.

— *Nellie King*

Sometimes when you're young and you do silly things you don't get much chance to play much longer. You're out of the lineup. There were enough minor league teams in the fifties to support minor leaguers so they could play four or five years in the minor leagues before they played in the major leagues. They would learn their trade and get more experience, and by the time they got to the big leagues they didn't make a lot of minor league mistakes.

— *Paul Pettit*

Back in the thirties, forties, and fifties they had more minor league clubs, and as a result they of course had more players to compete against. They used to keep sending you back down to the minor leagues for more seasoning. That's all you heard, "You gotta go down for one more year, one more year."

The Dodgers, back in those days, had three Triple A clubs and two Double A clubs, plus they probably had 20–25 other farm clubs at lower levels. Brooklyn would win the pennant or be contenders in Brooklyn, and then all three Triple A clubs would either win pennants or be contenders and the Double A clubs would win or be contenders. You'd see guys go back — they'd hit .330 or .340, they'd go back to Double A again. There were a lot more good ballplayers out there and the club could control you for about ten years before they had to let you go. It was a difficult time for a lot of guys to make the major leagues who were good enough to play here, but there just wasn't the opportunity.

— *Bobby Malkmus*

A lot of players of my era were major league material but they never got a chance because we had an awful lot of minor leagues. Minor leaguers had to wait for guys like Pee Wee Reese to retire before they got their chance. You had Class D, C, B, A, AA, ad AAA before you came to the majors. And even Mr. Rickey used to say it took five years to become a major league ballplayer. I skipped classes each year. I went from D to B to AA to the majors. *[Abrams started D ball in 1942.]*

— *Cal Abrams*

Two. Minor Leagues and War Years

I had some good years in the minors. My first year *[1938]* I hit .330 when I played in D ball, and the next year I went to D ball again. I hit around .300 and they upgraded me to C and I hit about .340 there. Then I went to A ball. I spent two years there and I went to Toledo in Triple A. I was hitting about .375 or something like that and then I finally got in the big leagues.

— *Al Zarilla*

There were a lot of good players in the minors who never got much of a chance to play in the big leagues. There was one year when the sportswriters in the East were quoted as saying that if the Newark Bears were in the American League they'd finish second to the Yankees. *[In both 1941 and '42 Newark won the International League pennant by 10 games over Montreal.]* There were so many players that, like in the Coast League, would have 130 RBIs and 45 home runs, and maybe at the end of the season they'd go up to the major league club and sit on the bench for about a week, and then they'd let him pinch hit, and he'd strike out on a curveball or get a fastball blown by him, and they'd sit him down for another three or four days and then give him another at bat, and they'd get him out. And then they'd send him back and say, "This guy can't hit the curve," or he can't do that, and this guy would go back, and maybe for ten consecutive years would have a hundred RBIs or more in the Coast League or the American Association or maybe the International League. This guy would give you a hundred RBIs. And if you were the Yankees or the Cardinals or the Dodgers or whoever you were, if you took him up there and stuck him in his position and left him for a season, he'd give you a hundred RBIs, he'd give you 30 to 40 home runs. But they never got a chance.

We had a player in Seattle late in my career, Joe Durham *[Durham got 202 big league at-bats with the Orioles and Cardinals; he hit .188 with 5 home runs. Durham led the Piedmont League in stolen bases in 1953. In 1954 he led the Texas League in triples and drove in 108 runs. In 1957 he hit .391 in 50 games with San Antonio. After the '57 season, Durham had only five more big league at-bats.]* I hit behind him for two or three years. I know how he could hit. Gosh, the guy was phenomenal. He went up three or four times. He didn't get to play. And they'd send him back, and say, "He can't hit the curveball." Well, I'd sit in the on-deck circle and I watched him hit a lot of curveballs. And hit them a long ways. You just had to be in the right place at the right time, just like Jerry Coleman, when he got my shot with the Yankees.

— *Jim Dyck*

When I went to spring training with the Yankees in 1950, being born and raised in the West Coast, San Joaquin valley in California, I never had the opportunity to see a major league baseball game. I went to spring training in St. Petersburg and was able to play in the first game I ever saw. Even though it was an exhibition game, it was a major league game against the St. Louis Cardinals. I was able to pinch hit and got a base hit and scored a run, so I was really enthused about it. That was really a highlight at that point in my career.

— *Bill Renna*

I spent the last year of the war in Rochester, New York. I hooked on with a Navy team Everybody else was a former major leaguer. I was a first baseman, but I saw that the Red Sox first baseman Tony Lupien was on first, so when they asked me what position I played, I gave them the right answer. I said, "I'm an outfielder."

— *Pete Milne*

I played down in Texas, and the Texas League was a heck of a good league in 1950. We had to ride the buses and everything, but at nineteen who cares? You're out there doing some of the things you like to do. We didn't make a lot of money, but you didn't care about the money.

— *Bob Friend*

I played with a semi-pro team in the Federation League, but it was what you'd call a semi-pro team in Fort Worth, Indiana. We were good enough that we went to the National Federation League Tournament in Youngstown, Ohio, in the fall of 1943. There were a lot of scouts at a national tournament. I had a good series, pitched pretty well and played other positions and hit well, and when the thing was over, we won quite a lot of games. We didn't win the thing, but we did pretty good. After we were finished, the managers at our break-up meetings said that the scouts of four different teams had come to him, and they were offering me a contract to sign and play minor league ball with their ballclubs. I was pretty thrilled about that.

My first year of pro ball, 1944, was a mighty important year in my career. First of all, I'd never known anybody that made a living playing ball, I didn't suppose that I could either. But here I go into professional baseball, and the first year fine things happen. *[In 1944 for Newark in the Ohio State League, Garver led the league in innings pitched, strike outs, wins (21) and ERA (1.21), while batting .407.]* Really, from that year I developed confidence that I think put me in good stead for the rest of my baseball life. I figured that I was good enough to be there. You have to have some confidence in yourself, and that year developed that. I could hit the ball, so the first year I played I pinch hit a lot and I played some other positions once in a while.

I never had any serious thoughts of playing any position other than pitcher, once I got started in professional ball, because I was a successful pitcher most of the way, and once you get to the big leagues, you better not monkey with it. But I was a good hitter as a kid. When I played for that Fort Wayne team, I was not the best pitcher on that team. I was probably the third best pitcher. So I played a lot of different positions. I played outfield and third base. And we played the touring black teams. There was some tremendous talent touring around, playing with the Indianapolis Clowns and Birmingham Black Barons and people like that. So I got to play against some people who really should have been in the big leagues.

— *Ned Garver*

I signed with the Yankees and played three years in their organization. I played with Mickey Owen and I really learned a lot of baseball from him. He was in his early forties, and he was still catching Class D baseball then. So he was still active.

My second year I played with Mayo Smith in Birmingham. And then later on Mayo coached Detroit and the Phillies. There again was a fine coach.

In fact, I thought maybe there were better coaches in the minors than what I saw in the big leagues. My third year here in Triple A ball in Denver was with Ralph Houk. We all know the kind of fellow he was, so I was pretty fortunate to have played with those kind of men.

— *Herb Plews*

When I went into Denver in the American Association, our manager Ralph Houk came over to me and said, "You're with a good ballclub. We'll get you four or five runs, you know. You'll win a lot of ballgames."

The first start I had was against Omaha, against a colored pitcher named Barnes. I shut them out for nine and a third innings, hung a curveball and got beat 1–0. Houk said, "What can I say?"

I was back in Denver the next year and me and Barnes got tied up again. This time I shut him out and had 8 strikeouts.

— *Ben Flowers*

I started in 1943 and I only played part of a year. Then I went in the service and I didn't get out until '45. I went to Manchester, New Hampshire, in the New England League in '46, and that's where I played against Don Newcombe, Roy Campanella and all that group that the Dodgers later brought up. In '47 I was at Jersey City and '48 with Jersey City and Minneapolis, and then in '49 I was traded to Memphis. The White Sox called me up at the end of the '49 season. I had never been inside a major league ballpark until I was actually able to play in one in the major leagues.

The next year I was invited to go to spring training out in California. I think I was the fifth left-hander on the ballclub that year, because they had Billy Pierce, Bill Wight, Mickey Haefner, and a bonus player by the name of Jack Bruner. I didn't think I even had much of a chance of making the ballclub, but I had a real good spring training, and luckily I ended up staying with the White Sox that year. *[Cain started 23 games in 1950, completing 11, and going 9–12. The only White Sox pitcher with a winning record was Luis Aloma, 7–2. Aloma's 4 year big league career ended in 1953; his record was 18–3. He pitched a shutout in the only big league game he started, in 1951.]*

— *Bob Cain*

If you go back to the St. Louis, Pittsburgh clubs and Dodger clubs — Branch Rickey was with all those teams — his idea was to sign ten players for a thousand dollars apiece, and sell one for a hundred thousand and have maybe one or two get to the big leagues, and then sign ten more. And that's the idea of building your minor leagues.

When I joined the Dodger organization, there were nineteen Dodger farm clubs. We had 700–750 ballplayers in spring training, and you signed as many as you could. I came up the normal way. came up step by step. I went from C to B to A to Double A to Triple A to the big leagues, back to Triple A, then back to the big leagues. It took me four and a half years. By then I was a seasoned player. I could fundamentally do the things I was supposed to do at the major league level.

— *Larry Sherry*

In Spartanburg, South Carolina, we won the pennant *[in 1947]*; it was a Class B league. The fans were just absolutely great in that part of the country. I stayed on a little hotel on the main street. It had a big old brass rail across the front, a bunch of rocking chairs on it, and everybody in town would come by and say hello and sit down and talk you in the morning. A couple of little old ladies had a little breakfast shop there in the hotel, and they took care of me like I was one of their sons. I ate good.

We're playing a ballgame against Knoxville late in the season. Old Dale Alexander was their manager. I'm hitting hot against him and he was stood on the top step of the dugout and said, "Hit him in the ear!" They threw at me every time I came up to the plate, sometimes twice. And I got hit about five or six times by that ballclub until I crippled up their second baseman, third baseman, and I ran over their first baseman. Finally the pitchers refused to throw at me anymore. But I was killing them. And the more they'd throw at me, the more I'd hit against them.

— *Pete Milne*

I played in the minor leagues parts of three years, '45 to '47. I can't tell you a thing most of my coaches did for me, outside of being a friend and wishing me well. One of my big league pitching coaches, who had a great reputation, would tell me, "Well, you're having trouble with your fastball, we've got to work on it." Well, that would be about the extent of the coaching. He didn't have any suggestions.

— *Art Houtteman*

I was a catcher as a young kid growing up in American Legion and high school, and I went to spring training as a catcher with Cleveland. In 1947, my third year of pro ball, I was catching in the Texas League for Oklahoma City and we'd had about five shortstops come and go all year. A guy would come and play two or three weeks, and they'd let him go.

Our manager, little Pat Ankenman *[a 5'4", 125 pound infielder]* — he had played in the Cardinal organization — asked me if I'd ever played shortstop, and I told him no. He said, "Well, would you like to play it tonight? If you don't play it I'm going to have to activate myself."

So I said, "Yeah, I'll play it."

I played the last 25 games, and went back to spring training the next year as a catcher with Cleveland. Lou Boudreau said he'd had some good reports on me as an infielder and wanted to know if I wanted to play there, and if I didn't like it I could go back to catching. That was the best thing for my career, because I became a much better hitter. When I was catching I never did weigh over 175 pounds, especially when we got into hot weather. And as soon as I stopped catching, I matured and filled out and became much stronger. I would have made it as a catcher, but I don't think I would have been as decent a hitter as I wound up being. *[Boone hit 151 big league home runs and batted .275 over his 13 year career.]*

— *Ray Boone*

I played two years in Japan. I liked it because I'm 6'3" and the people there, being mostly shorter, thought I was something special.

— *Lee Walls*

In the minors there was a third baseman, Packy Rogers. He was tough. A scrappy guy. He'd stand in the base path when you were coming around third and make you make a circle around you and slow you up. He blocked third base on me one time with a throw coming in. He stepped up in front of me, thinking I was going to go around him. I just knocked him over in the coach's box. He got up and came over to me and said, "Nice play, kid. That's the way to play the game." That's the way you played in those days. You played rough and tough.

— *Jim Greengrass*

In 1949 I was the Most Valuable Player in the International League with the Dodger's top ball club. *[Morgan hit a league-leading .337, had a league-leading 38 doubles, 19 home runs and 112 RBI for Montreal.]* We had a tremendous ball club. We had guys going up to the Dodgers all summer, guys coming back, and we won the pennant by eighteen games or something. One time one of the players on an opposing club told me, "Gosh, I hate to see a player go back up to the Dodgers from your club because they send two back that are better than he is."

— *Bobby Morgan*

In 1955 I was with Buffalo in the Tigers' organization. After our season ended I was picked up by the Cardinals and I went up and won a game. The next spring I had the best spring training of any pitcher down there, and we had Harvey Haddix and a bunch of good pitchers. I gave up one run in about eleven innings. I got back to St. Louis and I was a starting pitcher with them. I was in high heaven. It didn't last long. Frank Lane ended up trading me and Harvey Haddix to Philadelphia. I got sent back to the minor leagues. *[Flowers won only three big games but spent parts of 13 seasons in the minors with a 100–98 record.]*

— *Ben Flowers*

There were some mighty strong leagues. Harvey Haddix spent several years in Columbus when he should have been in the big leagues, but the Cardinals had all those left hand pitchers. They had Howie Pollet and Brecheen and Lanier and where's Haddix going to break into that starting rotation? *[The Cardinals also had lefties Al Brazle and Cliff Chambers. Haddix came up to the Cardinals in 1952 after winning 42 games in three seasons at Columbus of the American Association. In his first full big season, 1953, he was 20–9.]*

— *Ned Garver*

In 1958 I was one of those guys that figured he was going to get sent out. But I pitched pretty well and actually made the club. The Dodgers had at least four pitchers with sore arms: Newcombe, Bessent, Roebuck, and Roger Craig. They'd been on the '57 Dodgers in Brooklyn. And Drysdale and Koufax were in the six month service.

So there was a big hole in spring training, so I was given every opportunity. I think I pitched something like 26 innings and gave up one run. What they said is that you pitch yourself off the club. They'll keep running you in there until you screw up. If you don't, you might make the club, so that's what happened.

— *Larry Sherry*

I was a thirty-year-old major league rookie, thanks to being shuffled around in the talent-rich Yankee farm system for ten years. Before my career was over I had been on the All-Star team at every level D, C, B, A, AA, and all 3 AAA Leagues, and also, as a thirty-year-old rookie, was chosen on *The Sporting News* all rookie all-star team of 1952.

The Yankee policy in those years was to not trade or sell their players, just hang on to them until they were needed upstairs. My brother, Art, a left-handed pitcher in the Yankee chain, was locked in at the AAA level and finally quit in frustration at not getting a shot with the Yankees. Ten years later he was officially released.

— *Jim Dyck*

I went to Evansville of the Three-I League as a catcher *[in 1941]*, but shortstop was my favorite position. Evansville is where I met Warren Spahn and Litwhiler. We had quite a ballclub with Spahn pitching and a few other topnotch men. They had a number one catcher, and when two shortstops got hurt the manager asked me if I ever played the infield, and I said, "Sure. I started as a shortstop."

From there I came up the next year as an infielder with the Boston Braves when Stengel was manager. About the middle of May they had some catchers hurt, and they asked me if I'd catch batting practice. From then on I started to catch, and I kept catching the rest of my career. Probably it's a good thing because it kept me in the league a little bit..

— *Mike Sandlock*

I was in the service and I got out and played in Minneapolis in '52 and then the Giants brought up Dusty Rhodes from Nashville so they sent me down to replace him. So I was playing in and out in '53, and I think I hit about 24 homers.

Then in '54, the first week or so, Larry Gilbert, the Nashville owner, and his son Charlie had me come out every morning and they changed my batting stance. I was a stand up straight hitter, held the bat high, and I used to have trouble with the high fastball. So he lowered me into an open stance, and really into a crouch, holding the bat kind of flat back where I lowered the strike zone, and then I would come up kind of out of that and I was able to handle the high ball. And I went on to lead the league in hitting and everything else *[led in hitting, .345; runs, 139; hits, 210; home runs, 64; RBI, 161].*

Then the following year I come up with the Giants the end of that year and they beat Cleveland four straight, but I wasn't eligible to be in the World Series. I pinch hit three times for the Giants. I went oh for three. I hit the ball good twice. The guy made a diving catch in right field. So I went oh for three that year. The next year they sent me out opening day, '55.

— *Bob Lennon*

I pitched a couple one-hitters in the minor leagues. Once the first batter up beat out a ball to first base and they never got another hit.

— *Don Liddle*

I started at the bottom, Class D in Mansfield, Ohio *[in 1940]*. I went there after I got out of high school, and I was scared to death. The manager was a rough, tough guy and he had me scared to death. I went in there and he said, "Where do you play?"

I said, "I'm an outfielder," and he said, "Go out and play third base."

Christ, it didn't take him long to find out I wasn't a third baseman. But I was only 17 years old. I'd never been away from home or anything.

I enjoyed the minor leagues. We had a lot of fun. I was fortunate to lead four leagues in hitting before I got to the big leagues. In the minors I hit .398, .394. Then I choked up and hit .344, and in the Coast League I hit .385. Then I got to the big leagues and Boudreau said I couldn't hit. He found out later I could when I played against him.

— *Gene Woodling*

After I knew I couldn't stay in the major leagues because of my arm injury, I went to the minors to try to make it back as an outfielder/first baseman. I learned how to play the outfield by luck. I had a teammate who liked to hit fungoes. He used to hit fungoes to me by the hour in Salinas. I learned to catch the ball in all different positions, going away from the infield, catching balls over my head. I used to play this guy for Cokes. After a while, he would always owe me the Cokes because I'd never drop a ball.

— *Paul Pettit*

I broke into the minors in '51 in June, when I got out of high school. In the minor leagues we traveled by bus. In the major leagues, it was a big deal, we traveled by train. If you're a young boy, at age 19, it was like night and day. We had our own private cars, dining cars and sleeping cars. And everybody treated you fantastic. Of course, the buses weren't so hot, because invariably on our longest trips they would always break down. In retrospect, when I look back, the bus rides with all those guys, they were fun. They weren't too comfortable, but it was a lot of fun.

— *Ted Kazanski*

One time we were coming out of spring training, going to barnstorm north. We went to a town in Georgia and checked into a hotel. Our train was pulled off on a siding somewhere. It was not a very nice hotel and I can recall saying, "I'm not staying here, I'm going to go back and sleep in the train." Some of the hotels we had to stay in were not the greatest in the world.

It was like night and day, the difference between the majors and minors. You traveled by bus all night, got up, played the next day, didn't make a lot of money, didn't get a lot of meal money. You could change in a locker room that may not be bigger than a kitchen. But you didn't know any better, and you didn't care. You were playing baseball, something you enjoyed, and never complained about those things, because everybody else did it.

— *Dick Gernert*

In the minor leagues, and in spring training, especially in the Dodger chain, boy, you worked on the fundamentals all day — what base to throw to, what you're going to do with the ball when you get it, different situations. If the ball's hit to you, you know exactly where you're going to go with it.

And then you play a ballgame too, during the day, but you'd be up at eight o'clock in the morning, go to the auditorium and Fresco Thompson or one of the other minor league managers or coaches would get up and talk. They always stressed fundamentals. Even sliding. You'd go to the sliding pit for a half hour and learn how to slide.

— *Bob Lennon*

In those days they only had eight clubs in each league, and the minor leagues were strong. If you faltered at the major league level there was always somebody at the Triple A level to take your place. So there was an urgency to perform well, and every time you went out there your job was on the line, especially when you weren't a star. It was your living.

— *Tom Ferrick*

I think there was a big difference between the high minors and the big leagues. In the big leagues, every day you'd face a good pitcher. In the minor leagues, that's not true. Some days you're going to face a guy that's not that outstanding. But in the big leagues, every day you ran out there there was someone that was tough.

— *Ted Kazanski*

I got thrown at a lot. Like they say, you hit off your butt a lot. I never got hit in the head, thank God, but I've been hit all over the right side from the shoulder on down to the ankles. But it was part of the game then.

Big Bill Taylor was at Nashville one year, and I was hitting in back of him, and he hit a home run off a guy. I came up, and the pitcher knocked me down, and then I got up, and he knocked me down again, and then the next one, I just threw my bat on the ground — skidded it out there at him, and we rolled around out there for a while.

One time in Toronto I hit a home run, and the pitcher knocked me down my next time up. I hit another home run, and then the next time up, he knocked me down again. Then I hit one off the center field fence for a double. He turned around to me and said, "Aw, I give up." *[In 1954 with Nashville of the Southern Association, Lennon had 64 home runs, 161 RBI, 139 runs scored, 210 hits, and batted .345.]*
— *Bob Lennon*

I come so close to quitting after the first two years. They made me a relief pitcher in Class C and D ball. The next year, '48, I was at Pawtucket, Rhode Island, and they wouldn't give me any more money because all they'd tell you was that your win and loss record was no good. Well, I was being used late in the ball game — I'd go in there with us in the lead, he wouldn't use me if we were behind. But I'd go in there in that eighth or ninth inning and try to save, and back then relief pitchers weren't even thought of for that.

I was very down in the dumps and my wife and I had had a child, and I came home. I wasn't make enough money to support them. I asked for money to go back to Pawtucket and I happened to run into a guy that gave me a break. That was Rip Collins, the first baseman from the Cardinals, the old Gas House Gang, was managing Pawtucket. Hugh Wise had been there the year before, and they changed managers.

I had sent some contracts back. He called me, and I told him one of the reasons. I said, "Well, they made me a reliever, they won't pay me any money, and I've got family to take care of, and I can't live away from home on the money they're giving me," and he said, "Well, I can get you fifty dollars a month more money."

Well, back then that was quite a bit really. And he promised me that if I could pitch nine innings, I could start. He said, "You'll have to take my word." I said, "Well, I've been told that before, Rip. They send me down to the bullpen every ballgame that eighth inning." He said, "I won't say I won't relieve with you, but if you can go nine innings, you can start."

And my wife put it to me in a funny way. She said, "I'll put up with doing without, Don, if — I don't want you to quit when later on in your life you think, 'Did I quit too quick? How far could I have gone and everything?'"

And I said, "Well, all right, I'll try it one more time." I went to spring training, and Rip started me. In fact, he and I together, about the middle of the season, went to Hartford.

I had 11 and 2 at Pawtucket, and he started me. *[Liddle went 8–5 at Hartford, a combined 19–7 in 1949.]* So it made a big difference. You know, some pitchers can relieve, and some can't. Later in my career, I could do both. But it seemed for my attitude I had to start one now and then or I got my daubers down, I don't know. I did both in the major leagues.
— *Don Liddle*

Originally I signed with the Dodgers *[in 1948]* and spent five years in their minor league system I was one of the many heir apparent to Pee Wee Reese's job. Carrasquel was one of those people who left a year or two before I did to join the White Sox. My last couple years as Vero Beach as a minor leaguer in the Dodger organization, my roommate was Don Zimmer, who was also heir apparent to that job, so we used to argue all the time about who was going to get sold or traded. I kept telling him that he was two years younger than I was and his bat was a little more proficient than mine, so it didn't take a rocket scientist to understand that I would be the one going and he would be the one staying. Of course that's the way it ended up. We both ended up going back to Double A for the second year, both of us being Most Valuable Players in our prospective leagues — he was with Mobile and I was at Fort Worth. After that second year in Fort Worth I was sold to the St. Louis Browns. That was 1953 and Satchel Paige and I were the representatives to the All-Star team that year from the St. Louis Browns.

— Billy Hunter

I played almost three years in the minors, and I made the All-Star team in each league. I was Rookie of the Year in the International League. I needed that minor league experience. No way I could have gone straight from college into the major leagues. But the minor leagues were fun. *[Jackson started in the minors in 1948.]*

— Randy Jackson

We had Class D ball. Gosh, you played under lights that you were scared to even go down on a ground ball. You'd get killed, you know. You'd travel with buses where you'd ride two and three and four hundred miles between teams. You'd get in there late in the afternoon and play that night. But I found, really, I found as much difference between Triple A and the majors as far as quality of play as I did between Class D and Triple A ball.

There's just a big difference between Triple A and the majors. Triple A, you play a four game series, you've generally got two good pitchers, two fair pitchers, and one reliever. In the majors you play a four game series, you've got three good ones, one pretty good one, and at least two or three relievers. So you're looking at good pitching all the time. That's even evolved more with the relief specialists.

But back when I played you had your Hoyt Wilhelms, you had your Clem Labines; these were pretty good relievers.

— Gail Harris

I started in 1941, and '42, and then I went into the service for three years. I came back in '46 and finished in '53. It's hard to say how it affected my career. Others who went into the service too might have beaten me out.

— Joe Ostrowski

After I hit those 64 home runs for Nashville in 1954, I guess that's what people expected of me. Even more so when I hit 31 in the American Association the next year. In 956 I got off to a good start with Minneapolis and the Giants brought me back up. I was playing in and out, I'd get a chance to play, then I would not play for a while. I went on a little hitting streak, six or seven games, then they took me out again and sent me back to Minneapolis.

I said, "Well Geez, when I was hitting good you took me out of the line-up."

Chub Feeney was the general manager for the Giants. He said, "Well, you weren't hitting home runs. We brought you up here to hit homers."

I said, "If I could hit a home run any time I wanted I'd be making a million dollars."

— Bob Lennon

The biggest difference between the minor and major leagues was probably the meal money. You went from eating hamburgers to steaks and ribs.

Also, clubhouse conditions were very poor in the minor leagues. I remember one where you had room for about twelve guys in the locker room, and the showers weren't clean. The water wouldn't drain; you'd be standing in ankle deep water with scum on the floor. So when we could we would try to shower at the hotel, but on getaway nights we had to shower there. We had to get right on the bus and travel.

— *Bobby Malkmus*

I won 21 games one year in the minors with Zanesville. Ray Boone was our catcher. And we had Joe Tipton and Cliff Mapes. That's about the only three that went to the big leagues with me later on. Boone was a good catcher in the minor leagues, and when he went up to Cleveland they made a shortstop out of him.

I spent six years in the bus leagues, the minor leagues. I thought I learned my craft pretty good. I started out when the meal money was fifty cents a day, and went to the top to play in the World Series, and what more can I say. *[Kuzava's first year in the minors was 1941.]*

— *Bob Kuzava*

I was just a young squirt, and I was playing baseball and enjoying it, and I had no idea as the year went along that I was even having that kind of year. Then as the stats came out, I led the league in almost every department. I didn't give the statistics a thought at the time; I was just playing baseball and having a good time.

[In 1945, playing for Chattanooga in the Southern Association, Coan was named Minor League Player of the Year. He led the league with 201 hits, 40 doubles, a league-record 28 triples, 16 home runs, 37 stolen bases, and a .372 batting average. His 117 RBI were 3 short of Ted Cieslak's 120. His 126 runs were one short of Cieslak's 127. Coan also had a 38-game hitting streak.]

— *Gil Coan*

I had a fabulous first year in the minors and was doing even better my second year. *[In Porter's first year he hit .302 for Waterloo with 95 RBI in 117 games. In his second year he was hitting .340 for Colorado Springs, with 57 RBI in 66 games.]* In 1952, the White Sox came out of nowhere to become a good team for the first time probably since 1919, since the Black Sox. *[Since 1926, the White Sox had never finished any closer than 16 games out of first.]* Bill Veeck wanted me for the Browns, and the White Sox were only about five games out of first. Frank Lane thought Jungle Jim Rivera, the center fielder with the Browns, was the answer. They get Rivera, they could push the Yankees, maybe even catch them. In those days the "have" teams, like the Yankees and the Red Sox, etc., would really take advantage of the "have-nots" and almost use them as a farm system.

Well, Veeck said he would not make the deal unless I was thrown in. Frank Lane claimed he didn't want to include me, but he felt he had to if the White Sox were going to do anything. So I was in the deal going to the Browns, and Rivera went to the White Sox. Well, the irony of the trade was that at the end of the season the White Sox finished third, 14 games out. The Browns hadn't given me a penny to sign, it was the White Sox that gave me all the money, so what do the Browns immediately do? My first game in the major leagues was as a center fielder.

Never had seen center field in my life. I had played a few games in left field and a few games in right field. Every big strong guy does, you know, at one point or another, in high school, Legion, or wherever. But center field is for the fastest. The Browns were hurting, though, for a halfway decent defensive outfielder who could run a little bit. And Clint Courtney, who could do nothing but catch, was having a Rookie of the Year year. *[Courtney hit .286 in 119 games, but Harry Byrd of the Athletics was named Rookie of the Year with A 15–15 record.]* So they said, "Jay, how about trying center field." Well, that started the "what position to we play?" situation, which lasted through my whole 18 year career.

And now Veeck is losing money and starts making deals. He traded me for Virgil Trucks and sold Trucks for a hundred thousand dollars. And he made half a dozen trades like that.

So now I go to Detroit for Trucks. They have their own bonus catcher, Frank House. In fact, he'd come along and probably signed for a little more than I signed for, and he was their baby. They got me in a trade, and they were happy to have me, but now I've got to win a job in the outfield, or win a job at first base. Both were off positions for me.

The utility end of it got me to the big leagues, maybe, kept me for there for awhile, but I like to think if I had stayed in the minor leagues as a catcher and continued to do well, and get comfortable back there, get to where I was known as a good defensive catcher, I was going to hit enough to stay in the major leagues a long, long time as a catcher. But I had never caught enough to become an everyday catcher for somebody, because there was always somebody else there who was either their guy or a more experienced catcher, so I wound up hanging on and playing all the positions.

— *J.W. Porter*

Most of the clubs wanted to sign me as a pitcher. I always played both in the field and pitched in college and semi-pro and up in New England in the summer. I hit pretty well. Branch Rickey sort of figured that I had potential as a hitter and a fielder, and he figured an everyday player was more valuable, so he was one of the few clubs that looked at me as a fielder. And because I liked him anyway, I went with that.

In winter ball, between my second and third years, I started pitching again. That league was the caliber of a middle minor league or something. But we only played four games a week, on the weekend, so we carried only four pitchers. So I told the manager, "Look, I used to pitch a lot in college and semi-pro. Come Sunday and we're out of pitching, I might be able to pitch a few innings and maybe hold them. You'd have nine hitters in the lineup." So he tried me out.

The first game I pitched real well—five or six innings, and gave up maybe three hits, and one of the scouts saw me. The next spring training they tried to make a switch hitter out of me. That didn't work, so they said, "Let's try making him a pitcher."

So my fourth year of ball, 1955, they sent me to Lincoln, which was Class A then. We had a five man starting rotation. I would play left field four days and the fifth day I'd pitch. I was batting fifth and playing every day. In the minors and Mexico I hit decent. I played outfield one year in Pittsburgh in '54 and didn't hit much. *[Hall played 102 games in the outfield for the Pirates in 1954, hitting .239 with 2 home runs.]* But I was a better pitcher right off than a hitter, so I ended up pitching.

— *Dick Hall*

In the old days, when you came up, other than with the Yankees, I'd say, a young kid would come up to spring training with the top club and most of the guys wouldn't talk to him, they wouldn't help him, because he might take your job away. I think Stengel changed all that when he had his pre–spring training camps.

I remember the first one I went to in Phoenix, Arizona, in 1951. I was nineteen years of age, and they had this instructional school for the young phenoms that they'd signed or guys that had been in the organization. That was really instruction, and you got to be with the guys that were in the major leagues, and I think that probably some of the things that Stengel taught us then helped me advance to the majors in one year whereas it would probably have taken me three years.

— Andy Carey

After I got out of the service I went to spring training with the Braves in '46 and I lasted until Opening Day, and Southworth told me that they were sending me to Indianapolis to learn how to play shortstop.

I told him, "Billy, I know how to play shortstop. I was signed as a shortstop."

But if they want to get rid of you, they want to get rid of you. So I went down there and the first thing I did when I got off the train was to pick up a paper to see how the shortstop was doing, and looked at the averages and I said, "Holy Cow." The shortstop was hitting .375. So I didn't know how I was going to break into that line-up.

About two days later the shortstop got hurt and I got into play. I was hot right off the start and he never got back in there again. I was fortunate to lead the league in hitting — I led it in total hits and triples — and *The Sporting News* gave me the award as Minor League Player of the Year, so that gave me the break to get back up to the Braves again in '47. So I played from '47 to '52, then they went to Milwaukee and I went with them.

— Sibbi Sisti

In 1956 I was with Wichita in the American Association. Chet Nichols, a left-hander with the Milwaukee Braves, got hurt. I got called up to the big leagues, and it scared the daylights out of me. Man, goin' to the big leagues, they got good ballplayers up there. It just goes to show you, you put an average ballplayer in with a good team, you know, he can be pretty good. That's the way it was.

My record in '56 was 5 and 3. I was runner up to Frank Robinson for Rookie of the Year. I hurt my arm that winter in Winter Ball in Puerto Rico, and next year I guess I could say I had a decent year, I won 3 and lost 2 and I had an ERA of 5 something. I gave up 10 runs one night in one inning in Brooklyn. I never did figure out what my ERA would have been if I hadn't. But I was there competing. I was blessed to be on a team with some good ballplayers.

— Taylor Phillips

In doubleheaders in the Coast League, they used to have a nine inning game and then a seven inning game.

— Bobby Doerr

I enjoyed the Pacific Coast League. They had a lot of older ballplayers that had been in the majors or they had played quite a while in the Coast League. You might recall that the Coast League not too many years before that had ideas of becoming a third league, so they had players in that league that made more money in that league than they made in the big leagues. So they stayed instead of going to the big leagues.

— Ron Jackson

I played in the Texas League and the Western League. Really, the Coast League was the best league, even compared to the big leagues. I mean, for conditions. It was always cool at night. You didn't have a lot of rain, not a lot of rain outs. You had nice towns, you had good fan appeal, and you flew everywhere. I enjoyed that.

In the Western League, you had two leagues. You had the East, which was Des Moines and Omaha and Lincoln, then you'd go West and you had Denver and Pueblo and Colorado Springs. Well, when you get out West, that ball really jumps. In the East it was a pitcher's league.

And the Texas League, it was just hot. Hot and muggy, but I was young. You lose a lot of weight during the course of the season because you sweat so much, but heck, I enjoyed them all.

— *Elvin Tappe*

The Coast League was my first full year *[1949]* in ball, and it was exciting. The swimmer Esther Williams threw out the first ball for us in Los Angeles, opening day against San Diego. They had some big names out there, a lot of guys that were good players then, and some of them eventually came up, like Minoso and Easter, and had big years in the big leagues. It was a hell of a league out there. Every Sunday was a day doubleheader, and every Monday was off all season long. And every Tuesday was a night game. So you had Sunday night, Monday, Monday night, and Tuesday off. It was great for the players.

I played with Billy Schuster. Talk about your loosey-goosey guys. He was with the Cubs for awhile. He was the shortstop when I was the second baseman. I was making four hundred fifty dollars in Los Angeles, my starting salary there for Triple A. I got off to a big start, I was hitting four hundred after the first month or something, and Billy Schuster asked me what I was making and I told him.

He said, "Geez, is that all you're making?"

He took me right upstairs to the president of the Los Angeles Dodgers office, knocked on the door, marched me in — I think it was Pants Rowland, I'm not sure — anyway, he walked in there and said, "This kid is hitting four hundred blah blah blah, and he's making four hundred fifty bucks. I told him he's not making enough money."

And I'll be a son of a gun, the guy raised my contract to six hundred dollars and made it retroactive to the start of the season. I thought Bill Shuster was the greatest guy I ever met.

— *Wayne Terwilliger*

I agree with those who say the Coast League was like a third major league. Guys that didn't play out there probably wouldn't believe that, but you had a lot of the big league players that preferred to play out there, because they lived out there, and a lot of those players made more money in the Coast League.

They had guys like Bob Dillinger, great players. When you face line-ups like Luke Easter and Minnie Minoso and Suitcase Simpson and Al Rosen and Max West and Jack Graham — that's just one team. They had big league players scattered all over the league. Really a good quality league. It could have easily been turned into a major league at that time.

— *Cal McLish*

People ask me about the Coast League compared to the National League or American League. We had teams out there as good, probably even better, than some of the clubs they have in the major leagues today. To me, the traveling in the Coast League was great; we flew every place. We played a week in each town. Monday was off for traveling, but it was great. You've got all the big towns, like Sacramento, Seattle, San Francisco, Oakland, Hollywood, LA, Portland . They're great towns.

— *Mike Sandlock*

There were a lot of former major leaguers in the Coast League. It was a tribute to that league, I guess. I guess the people out there liked to get to see players that formerly played in the big leagues. The weather was nice. I was with Seattle and that was a beautiful part of the country. They gave me an opportunity to play first or the outfield. I was doing everything in the world to get back to the big leagues.

I know the Cardinals had been interested in me, and I told Dewey Sorianto, "Don't sell me to the Cardinals. I've been to St. Louis one time, and it's hot enough down there." But I would have gone, I guess, if those were the only folks who were interested in me. But when the Yankees inquired about me, I stuck up a deal with them and wound up making more that year out there and coming back to the Yankees than I'd made my previous year in the big leagues. So it turned out okay.

— *Tommy Byrne*

The Coast League was a good league. You didn't have that razzle-dazzle schedule like you had in some of those other leagues. The pitching was good out there. We had clubs out there that were probably better than some of those in the big leagues. I played in Oakland, and the weather was cool and you stayed strong all the time.

— *Spider Jorgensen*

I loved the Coast League because you spent a week in the same town. And you flew, with every Monday off. It was better than the major leagues in terms of the schedule. You were off from Sunday afternoon until Tuesday night. You got so spend more time with your family. A lot of guys refused to go back to the majors because they were making more money in the Coast League than they were making in the majors.

— *Jim Greengrass*

I finished up my career in the minor leagues. I played in the Pacific Coast League in Hawaii. It was a beautiful spot to play. We had long home stands, and on the mainland we'd be gone maybe two weeks at a time. Harry Kallas, who became a broadcaster for the Phillies, was the one that did our games in Hawaii.

— *Herb Plews*

There were a lot of ex-major leaguers playing in the Triple A level, like in the Pacific Coast League. Heck, they paid them good, too. We weren't making a lot of money in the big leagues. Good Lord, have mercy. My first major league contract, in 1948, called for thirty-five hundred dollars. The minimum was five, so I got five thousand dollars. Well, Judas Priest, those people in the Coast League were making a lot more money than that. So they didn't want to go to the big leagues. They could play out there in nice weather, not so much traveling, and make more money. Oh, there were a lot of guys played at Triple A level that were mighty, mighty fine. Then, too, there were guys that played at the Triple A level that when they got their shot at the big leagues they couldn't do a whole heck of a lot because they'd maybe have one weakness. And the major league pitchers could deal with that.

— *Ned Garver*

The Coast League was nicer than the major leagues. You'd go into a town and you'd play Tuesday night, Wednesday night, Thursday night, Friday night, Saturday afternoon, double header on Sunday. Every Monday was off. You'd go on the road two weeks, you were home two weeks. You'd fly everywhere when you went on trains at the big league level. Other than Sacramento and Portland, all those towns that were in the Coast League are in the major leagues today.

In 1956 when we won the pennant, we had a great club. *[Los Angeles won 107 games and finished 16 games ahead of Seattle. Steve Bilko led the league in batting, runs, hits, RBI, and home runs.]* We had Bilko, Mauch, and Casey Wise, George Freese. We had Drott, Hillman, Fodge. I caught. We had Speake, Bolger, Wade. We'd go two, three weeks and wouldn't lose a game. We were beating everybody. My folks came out to visit me, they were there twenty days and never saw us lose. That was my favorite year in baseball. The season lasted two weeks. I mean, that's the way it felt. Bob Scheffing was our manager. He was a great, great manager.

— *Elvin Tappe*

The year that stands out most for me was '56. It was so peaceful out there, and by God, you knew you were going to win.

We had one of the finest ballclubs that I'd ever played on. *[With Los Angeles in the Pacific Coast League in 1956 Wade hit .292 with 20 home runs.]* In fact, we could have beaten probably over half the big league clubs. We had Bilko at first, Gene Mauch at second, Casey Wise at short, George Freese at third. Bob Speake in left. I was in center. And Jim Bolger in right. Our outfield was voted one of the top outfields because of our speed. All three of us were actually center fielders. You couldn't shoot a ball between us. If our pitchers got the ball in the air and kept it in the ballpark, it was caught.

— *Gale Wade*

The Pacific Coast League was like a third major league at that time. Ryne Duren was out there. Sam Chapman lived out there and he played for us at Oakland rather than go back and play in the big leagues. He was a great defensive outfielder. One of the best defensive outfielders I've ever seen. *[Chapman played 11 years in the big leagues between 1938 and 1951 and hit .266 with 180 home runs.]*

But we had the best minor leaguers. Chuck Connors played down there. He and I played on the All-Star team in 1953. We beat the major league all-stars after the season. You know the magazine *Look*, which was a popular magazine then. "They would pick the all–Pacific Coast League All-Star team, I was picked on it three years in a row with Oakland. Mel Ott was the manager when I went out there—and by the way, he was the manager with the Giants when I went up. Augie Galan was his coach. *[Galan played 16 seasons, 1936–1949, in the big leagues, hitting .287 with 100 home runs and 123 stolen bases.]* They were both out there.

The bigger towns, like Oakland and San Francisco and Los Angeles—they had two teams in the Los Angeles area and two teams in the Bay area—had tremendous rivalries. On the weekends we drew forty or fifty thousand people. It was just as close as you could get to playing in the major leagues. The facilities were great. In fact, when I went out there in 1952, I was amazed, because we were the first teams that flew, strictly flew to all our destinations. It was great. Playing conditions were great.

— *Pete Milne*

When I was with the Browns, Bill Veeck would be out there at the ballpark and take that leg off, that plastic leg he wore, that fiberglass thing, and he'd put one of those buckets of beer under each arm and you'd see him jumping out in the bleachers from the dugout. Hell, he'd be buying people beer, sitting there chewing the fat. He was a beautiful man. Later, when I was in the Coast League, I was pitching one night against L.A. in Los Angeles, and I could hear this guy up there near the press box when I was warming up, just before I was going to take a breather and then go out to the mound. I wouldn't look up there, but the guy was really after me, you know, he had a real foghorn voice. I finished warming up and kind of glanced up there, and this guy was waving to me. It was Veeck. It turned out we beat them 1–0. I hit a home run into centerfield off a knuckleball pitcher. He came down to the clubhouse, he and the Mrs., and we went out and had dinner after the game. He was something else.

— *Tommy Byrne*

In the Coast League I batted against Ryne Duren. He pitched for Seattle, and our first trip North, it was drizzling rain. He wore glasses that looked like the bottoms of Coke bottles. And the catcher squats back there, and he's talking, trying to keep me from concentrating. He said, "I don't even know why I'm putting this finger down, he can't even see my hand."

And Duren is squinting. He's standing out there, and he looked like a big gorilla out there, raking the ground. And he could throw, oh, man, he could throw aspirin tablets. I got out of the box and I'm thinking, "I know I paid my insurance." But you didn't have helmets then. So if you got hit between the horns with one of those pitches they're just going to bury you, that's all there is to it. But this guy's out there, the steam's coming off him, 'cause he was sweating, and his glasses were fogging up. He'd done thrown a couple up against the screen. He did that on purpose, I think. There was a guy I hated to hit against.

— *Pete Milne*

I'm glad I quit when I did. A guy I played with in Savannah and Ottawa were sitting together on the train one night and he said to me, "Skeeter, when you feel like you've gone as far as you can go, find you a profession and don't stay around and be a baseball bum." He said, "I'm not trained to do any kind of job. I go in the summer and make good money and live good, and then I go back home in the winter and just do what I can to make a living and get by. I don't have any choice but stay with it, but you're young, and when you see you're not going to go any farther, it's time to make a change." I saw that at the end of the '54 season.

— *Skeeter Kell*

I hurt my shoulder in 1956. I pitched a lot during my career, and maybe if I'd told the manager that my arm hurt, then I would have been able to play a little longer. *[The injury forced McMahon's retirement at the age of 27.]*

But I was afraid if I told them, they would find somebody else. Things were a lot different than they are today. *[While McMahan appeared in only 34 major league games with an 0–5 record, he pitched in 249 games in seven minor league seasons, going 50–39 with an ERA of 3.65.]*

— Jack McMahan

Played with Sal Maglie, "The Barber"— mean on the outside, gentle on the inside. Don Mueller — most underrated right fielder in the league, a tough out. Stan Musial"— the nicest guy in an enemy uniform beating a pitcher's brains out. Gil Hodges — even the Giants liked and respected this man wearing the Brooklyn uniform. Fans ask me: "After a 17-6 record compiled in 1951–53, what happened to Al Corwin?"

No papers reported my arm troubles and in those days no one complained, we just kept pitching.

— Al Corwin

My life changed dramatically after my sixth game in 1960. I came down with bursitis, and inside of three years I was home carrying the old lunch bucket. That just about sums up my mediocre career, but I am grateful the good Lord gave me the chance. I enjoyed everything while I was there.

— Jerry Casale

In 1964 I hurt my arm in the White Sox organization pitching to Tony Perez in the Coast League. I broke a good curveball off and it was like my elbow was like to come off. It still hurts.

— Taylor Phillips

I'm certainly thankful for my years in baseball, but my career was cut short by an arm injury. I had a great start, two twenty-game years right to start with — the leading pitcher in the American League in '46 and such and all, and hold a number of major league records that stand still today.

But then I hurt my arm out in Cleveland in a night game in '47. It was nothing-nothing, I think I was pitching against Red Embry in Municipal Stadium in a night game. I think around the seventh inning George Metkovich, who'd been a teammate with the Red Sox and now was with Cleveland, was batting with the bases loaded. I think I had a count of two and two on him and I was really going to break him off a low inside curveball. I really got up on top of it and cracked down and I struck him out. But I felt at the time I did something — sprained it or something. I didn't think a whole lot about it really at the time. We went on to win the game. Bobby Doerr hit a home run in the top of the ninth and we won it. Of course, about all they did then to you after the game was to put rubbing alcohol on you and tell you to put your jacket on.

We went on a Pullman that night to Chicago. The next day I went out to throw and I just couldn't get my arm up. That was the start of my trouble. I rested for a couple of weeks and came back. I pitched pretty fair, but it just never was the same again. So I do remember that specific incident. As a player, you regret that happened, but those things happen to anybody. Unfortunately it happened to me at that stage of my career. I came back and went back to the minors and eventually did some pretty effective pitching and hitting too in Triple A in Louisville and then went back as a pitching coach for the Red

Sox for five years. Then I came here to Cleveland, Mississippi and was baseball coach at Delta State University for twenty-six years. That was a very enjoyable and rewarding experience, coaching the young men and being part of their lives. Maybe if I hadn't hurt my arm and had pitched longer, the coaching career never would have opened up.

— *Boo Ferriss*

My whole career was hindered by the fact that I had a bad back. I had to wear a corset. And God, I was going to all the chiropractors in the country. I can only be thankful that I even played. So I'm thankful for that, but there were days I wish I wasn't out there. *[In the 1940s, Marion played the most games of any big league shortstop, 1,383.]*

But anyway, I struggled through it. But take Mickey Mantle, for instance, who was a great, great ballplayer. He was taped up his whole career. So a lot of people played with pain. I didn't play much with the Browns because I wasn't able to play *[in his final two seasons]*. My legs were hurting, my back was hurting.

Let me tell you something about playing. If you're playing shortstop, and the ball goes by you, and you know in yourself you should be catching that ball, you've had it. Your legs give out first. Nobody has to tell you.

— *Marty Marion*

I broke my leg in the first inning of the last game of a home stand. We were leaving that night to go to Minneapolis after the game and Herbie Plews had led off with a single, and on a hit and run play I singled to right. When they made the play at third base I tried to go to second base and I was out by about twelve feet. And I tried a slide I had never tried before, throwing your feet away and going away with your hand, and my front spike caught, and I just slid right over my leg and broke the inside ankle bone and two places on the outside. My toes were coming out where my heel is. It was like a rifle shot. Houk, you know he had been a commando in the Second World War, and he came out and just turned and walked away. Johnny Pesky was there and Darrell Johnson — anyway, it was the end of baseball for me that year.

The broken leg had a big effect on my career. It did in that I felt like once it healed that I was moving as I had before, but everybody that saw me play said that I was a step slower and so forth. And then they traded me to Kansas City just prior to the '57 season. I was there for a year and a half and went to Cleveland. Had shin splints in spring training in '59 and they sent me to San Diego, which was their Triple A club. I don't know whether it was that heat or whatever, but my shin splints were gone in two days. I played every game of the season in '59. They moved me over to second base, and I was the all-star second baseman and was 30 years old and led our club offensively in about four categories, and they sold my contract to Toronto. And I told them to put me on the voluntary retired list.

I said, "If I can't get back to the big leagues with the kind of year I had in San Diego, I couldn't do any better in Toronto, and I would be thirty-one."

— *Billy Hunter*

I spent a couple years with Chicago and then went over to Washington. Calvin Griffith gave me 28 days. I needed 28 days in 1956 to get my retirement in. At that time you had to have five years, and I lacked 28 days, so he called me back up. Charlie Dressen was the manager and he'd told Charlie I was going to spend my time, so Charlie got mad at me, took it out on me. So I went all spring and didn't go to bat or nothing else. He was upset 'cause he was told I was going to stay. Anyhow, we played New York, the first pinch hitter asked for was me, "Wright, get your stick." The boys on the bench knew what was going on all spring and let out some blasts at him. I got my time in. Then I went back to Birmingham and finished up there.

— *Tom Wright*

I was with Detroit from the beginning of the *[1967]* season until just before Memorial Day when I was released. Mayo Smith called me in and said, "John, I haven't had a chance to use you much here. Suppose we send you down to Toledo and I'll bring you back in September."

I said, "Mayo, I've been here, this is my 18th year, I don't want to go to the minor leagues. I'm going home."

When I got home, I was in shape, so I thought, "Well, I'll send a telegram to the Cubs." I was living outside Chicago, so I sent a telegram to Durocher and asked him if I could come out and he could watch me throw. I said, "I'm in shape, maybe I can help you the rest of the year."

I never heard from him. Dutch Leonard, I guess, ran into him a couple months later down in St. Louis, and Dutch said, "Hey, did Klippstein ever come out and try out?" and he said, "No, he never came out to the park. I never heard from him."

So I guess he was waiting for me. I figured when he got the telegram, he would give me a call. He had my phone number and everything. Or somebody would have got in touch with me. But I was 39 years old, and though I wasn't tired of playing ball the traveling and being away from home had run its tool, I think.

— *Johnny Klippstein*

In 1959 I hurt my shoulder. I guess it was a rotator cuff, but in those days they didn't know what it was. It was, "Rub it in the dirt and see you later." When I hurt my shoulder, I lost that extra stuff that I'd had, and I was just another journeyman type pitcher from then on.

— *Don Ferrarese*

The year I quit, the Athletics sold my contract to Havana, Cuba. Johnny Lipon was playing for Havana then in the International League, and that was when they were having all that uprising down there. Johnny was a friend of mine, and he called me and tried to get me to come down there and said we could room together in this big hotel-apartment building that had drug stores, kind of like a mall. It had restaurants and drug stores and everything inside of it. You had to stay in that; you couldn't get out of it because they were having all that trouble down there. Johnny wanted me to come down; he played shortstop and me second, but I didn't like to be away from my family for two weeks, much less leaving them for all summer.

— *Skeeter Kell*

They sent me to Indianapolis in August of '58 and I didn't do very well there. But the next year they wanted to send me back to Indianapolis, and I told them I'd quit before I went back there, to sell me to Rochester *[Triple A, International League]*, so they made a deal with Rochester. And I came here and I led the league in wins. I won 18 and lost, I think it was 11.

I thought I would get a shot with the Cardinals, who were operating the ballclub at that time. I went to spring training, but they told me they decided to go with the young guys. I was forty years old at the time, and a starting pitcher, never a relief pitcher. So I came back to Rochester, and I think I won 7 and lost 9 the next year. And then I was out.

— *Bob Keegan*

My last year was 1957. I wasn't doing as well as I should have. I wasn't pitching as regularly as I probably needed to. I was thirty-two years old and wasn't going to be getting any younger, and Baltimore might spend the time with the younger ballplayer, so I didn't prolong it.

I didn't stay in baseball after my playing career. I had to go out and get a job, make a living. The money you got in baseball then seemingly was a lot compared to the guy working eight-to-four but by the same token there wasn't a whole bunch left over, so I had to work all my life.

— *Art Houtteman*

I got a late start. I got caught in World War II. I had to spend three years and three months in the Navy. That's 18, 19, 20, and 21—years that I should have been throwing a baseball. Being in the Navy, I played a little bit of softball on the islands, very little. Then when I did come back, it took me awhile to get up there.

I was getting toward the age that you be retiring before I ever got up there. I struggled a long time getting there, but I finally made it.

— *Don Liddle*

I was in World War II for three years. I signed with the Braves in '42, a minor league contract, then I went in the Marine Corps for three years, so I didn't get my first full year in 'til 1946. I was in the minor leagues about five years before I got a chance to go with the Braves.

I don't know if the war had much effect on my career. I got a little slow start. I had malaria when I was over in the Pacific, and that first year back wasn't worth much. I was sick most of the time with malaria. I was fortunate that I went out when I was 18 years old. I got out when I was 21. I didn't play in the service at all. I was in the Marine Corps. We didn't have any room for any of that stuff. So it didn't affect me too much.

But I played with some guys that were like 27–28 years old, they had gone when they were 24, 25, and they lost a lot to it — they lost three years, and it seemed to affect them.

— *Ernie Johnson*

I was in the Army from 1942 to '45. Then in '46, I came out — that's when the Dodgers signed Robinson. He signed as a shortstop, but he played second base at Montreal. I played third; Lew Riggs came in later on. He was a good hitter that Brooklyn sent down. Al Campanis played short. Jackie played second and Les Burton played first.

We had a good ballclub. We would average about seven runs a game. Herman Franks was our catcher. I probably learned more baseball from him than person I ever played with. He was just a good catcher and did a lot of things. *[Franks played 190 games in parts of six big league seasons, batting .199. He was a big league manager for seven years, finishing second four times with the San Francisco Giants, and third, fourth, and fifth with the Cubs.]*

I hurt my arm in spring training in '48. I don't know what the hell happened to it, but I couldn't throw, so I got scuffed off to St. Paul, and we won the playoffs — we got in the Little World Series in '48. We played the Montreal club, which was the other Brooklyn club.

Then in '50 I went to the Giants and the middle of the year I went to Minneapolis, and we went to the Little World Series there. Bert Haas was on that club, a good hitter, and Ray Dandridge was on that club in Minneapolis. The next three winters I played in Havana, Cuba, in the Cuban League. We won the pennant three years in a row. The fourth year we didn't. After the fourth year they traded all us guys out and got some younger blood in there.

I was with the New York Giants in 1951, rooming with Bobby Thomson. Then in the middle of '51, at the All-Star break, they sold him to Oakland in the Coast League, and I finished up my career out there with the Oakland club.

I got bounced around pretty good.

— *Spider Jorgensen*

I was really in my very prime at 26 or 27. I was going into my 28th year when I was called back into the service in Korea. And that really took most of what I had away. I had flashes after that, but I ended up mainly a utility player. The only regret I have is that I never will really know if I would have sustained what I did the first couple years. You always wonder about those things.

But when I look back — I've been in this business over fifty years, I've played on eight championships, six World Championships. I've been a broadcaster for over thirty years. How can I complain? I'm one of the favored few to be around this long.

— *Jerry Coleman*

The war came right at the prime of my career. I played in '42, when I was twenty years old, and I lost the next three years. That was the time of my life when I was probably the strongest, ran the fastest, threw the hardest. In training, down in Texas, they had a base team, and we played other bases down there. Johnny Sain was on another team. We played maybe a twelve game schedule. That was the only ball I played.

I came out of the service after the season was over in '45 and I hadn't played any ball to speak of in three years. My brother Art and I were both sent to Quincy in the Three I League. It was like I had forgotten everything I learned. We had a manager there that really was hard to get along with, so we jumped the ballclub, went home. We both just said, well, we guess we'll just find another career.

At that time Frank Lane was the director of the Yankee farm system. We got a phone call from Frank, and he said, "You come on up, I want to talk to both of you." So we went up to Kansas City, where the Kansas City Blues were playing in the American Association. Frank didn't think we'd given ourselves a fair chance. He talked us to going to Joplin, in the old Western League, and play one season at least, and give us a chance to get our feet back under us. We got to Joplin and the whole thing just switched around for me. It was like I'd never missed a game. I always thank Frank Lane for keeping me in baseball.

— *Jim Dyck*

I was in the service '44, '45, and came back in February or March of '46. I played ball at Norfolk for about three months in 1944. I was in a Destroyer pool and I'd gone to school and taken all the navigation and all stuff about the armor on a destroyer and everything.

While I was there in Norfolk they saw me out working out one day, just exercising in that big gym they had there in Norfolk, in the Naval Training Station. The baseball coach wanted to know what I was doing working out with those people, and I said, "Weill this is part of our training."

He said, "How would you like to pitch for the Naval Station?"

I said, "Well, I don't know. I'm getting ready to be shipping out pretty soon, as soon as I finish these courses." Because normally they bring those ships back in and do a little work on them and they switch officers around and give them a month or two off and then send a new crew on — not all new crew but they'd put on a few rinky-dinks like myself.

Well, they got in touch with the Bureau of Naval Personnel, so I played for maybe two and a half months on that team. Just as soon as that season was over, the honeymoon was over. They sent me out. I went to Brooklyn Navy Yard and picked up my ship and I was gone. I enjoyed that duty. It was interesting. But there wasn't much green grass out there.

— *Tommy Byrne*

I didn't play ball in the service. I wasn't a name ballplayer at the time, still a minor league player, and most of the guys like DiMaggio and Feller and those guys got to play on some service teams. But I didn't, just went in the army and served my hitch. I don't think about how it might have affected my career. It was a growing period. I was 18 or 19 when I went in the army, but there were guys that did lose a lot of time. Take Ted Williams now, he missed five years in the Marine Air Force and those probably would have been his most productive years. DiMaggio was another one.

Well, most of the players that were established major leaguers that went in the service, those were their best years, really. You're talking about early twenties or middle twenties, but, hey, think of the poor guys that went over there and didn't come back. So count your blessings.

— *Bob Kuzava*

I was in the service for three years in World War II.

I was in boot camp and they said, "Lieutenant so-and-so wants to see you," and I thought, "Christ, they must want to send me to the moon already." And they said, "We're going to have a team, we'd like to have you play." I spent the damn war playing ball.

— *Wally Westlake*

I signed in 1936 and went to Pensacola my first camp with the Giants, and then the next year we went to Havana. I was always on the Giants' roster, and I had some success until I hurt my arm. Then when my arm wouldn't come back they released me, and I pitched two years of semi-pro ball before I came back, so I was 26 when I finally made it to the big leagues with the Athletics.

In 1941 everybody was at strength. There weren't too many people in the service. *[Number of major leaguers in the service: in 1941, four; 1942, 71; 1943, 219; 1944, 342; 1945, 384; 1946, 23.]* I think Bob Feller and a few others went off early. So the strength of the league was still pretty strong. But they started to drift back, and a lot of people hadn't played baseball during the war years, and the problem was, could they get in condition quick enough and have enough left to sustain. They had a ballplayer in Washington who I think was a great ballplayer by the name of Cecil Travis. Prewar he was a pretty good ballplayer; [when] the wartime came along he was almost at an age they didn't want to send him overseas. He was in the Army. He was a great player, a shortstop, lifetime average was .314. All of the sudden the Battle of the Bulge came on, and it was an emergency, so they took a lot of the people out of the United States, and sent them to the Battle of the Bulge. Cecil got involved in that, and he managed to get his feet frost-bitten, so when he came back in '46 he couldn't perform at the level he did before, and he had to drop out of baseball. But he was Hall of Fame caliber before that.

I got to play ball during the war. I was 27 when I enlisted in the Navy in December of '42. I went up to Great Lakes for my boot training for I think thirteen weeks. My unit was getting ready to get put on board ship when a sailor came over from main camp in Great Lakes and said that Mickey Cochrane was the commander up there and he had the baseball team, and he sent this young man over to see whether I wanted to play baseball.

We had a big league ballclub. We entertained the sailors. We traveled through the Midwest, entertaining. Then they sent us all overseas. I went to Hawaii and then I went to Guam. We played an Army-Navy World Series in Hawaii—we beat the Army, and after that was over they sent us to the forward areas with the two teams. We went all over the South Pacific. I was stationed on Guam. We had Johnny Rigney, Johnny Vander Meer, Schoolboy Rowe, Billy Herman. All the Navy personnel were sent to the forward areas and we performed down there. I didn't get back until after the war was over.

I came back from the service in 1945. I was 30 years old. Of course, I missed the three years, but everybody missed; I have no complaints. I was still owned by Cleveland. I went to spring training with them in '46 and from there I bounced around with different clubs—the Cards, the St. Louis Browns, the Washington Senators twice, and finally the Yankees, and then I bowed out.

— *Tom Ferrick*

Chapter Three

Men in Blue

It's all but impossible to sit through an entire game without disagreeing with an ump on at least one call. A fan's disagreement is usually public and vocal. Sometimes a player's disagreement is a private one, seen and heard only by the participants, and often the fans are treated to the sight of umpire and player, coach, or manager going jaw to jaw, chest to chest.

We've all seen such confrontations, yet many players go through an entire career without being booted from a game. Some even admit to liking umpires. Some umpires are respected for the way they call the game, some barely tolerated. Some are aloof; some like to joke with the players. It's unlikely, though, that an umpire exists who is not well-remembered by at least one player for that umpire's role in a particular game.

[How much did Boggess love the game? Well, as an infielder and catcher, he spent 21 years in the minor leagues, then umpired in the NL for 18 years. He had every umpire he worked with autograph a baseball and had the baseballs buried with him when he died in 1968.]

Dusty Boggess was just a good old boy. We'd have run-ins with him and he'd take a stopwatch out like he was a train man. He'd show you that watch and say, "I blew that play, I missed it. Now you can argue with me five minutes."

Well, how can you argue for five minutes with a friend who admits he blew the play? The only thing you can do is just turn around and walk away.

— *Elvin Tappe*

I was playing shortstop one day at the end of my career, and there was a double play hit to the second baseman, and of course I ran over to second base, caught the ball and fired it to first, and Dusty Boggess said, "Out, out, double play." So I went back to shortstop, and Dusty went back behind second base, and he said, "Hey, Chuck."

I said, "Yeah, Dusty, what do you want?"

He said, "I'll tell you what, next time you better touch second base, because I'm going to have to call him safe." He was nice about it. That was Dusty Boggess, a real nice guy.

— *Chuck Diering*

[Vinnie Smith, an NL umpire from 1957 to 1965, and the plate umpire for Harvey Haddix's 12 perfect innings on May 26, 1959, was responsible for one of Frank Thomas' five big league ejections.]

Vinnie Smith was umpiring second base, and I was the runner on second. Dusty Boggess was behind home plate. The pitch came in and the guy foul tipped it, and Smoky Burgess trapped the ball. Boggess called it strike three.

I said to Vinnie, "You saw that."

He said, "Yeah."

Then I said, "Now if they say he caught the ball clean and you go in there and agree he caught the ball clean I'm going to tell you you don't have a gut in your body."

Sure enough, he goes in there and he comes back out, and they call the guy out. I said, "Hey, Vinnie, you know, I told you I was going to tell you you don't have a gut in your body."

He said, "I'll show you I don't have a gut in my body," and he threw me out of the game.

— *Frank Thomas*

I got thrown out of games twice. Once was in New York by Ed Runge. I was on first base and they threw a ball over to Moose Skowron. Moose tagged me, but he really gave me a pretty good push and knocked me off the bag, and then he tagged me. They called me out.

— *Ray Boone*

[The only person to be elected to the baseball, college football, and pro football Halls of Fame, Cal Hubbard, at 6'3" and 250 pounds, was an imposing figure.]

Umpires appreciated the people who didn't give them a hard time. I learned that early and I got along well with all umpires. I got thrown out of one ballgame the whole time I was up in the major leagues, and that was intentional. Cal Hubbard, the old football player, was umpiring, and we were losing pretty bad in Washington one day, and it was hot and I told Cal, "Couldn't you get me out of here?" and he said, "Well, argue with me a little bit and I'll get you to the showers." So he did.

— *Gil Coan*

Cal Hubbard was a great big guy, and a good umpire.

I'm pitching a game in St. Louis one night and I'm having my problems, can't get them out, and about the fourth inning they bring in somebody else. I'd been arguing with Cal all during the game, and as I leave the field, I walk by home plate and tell him, "Cal, you were terrible tonight. I never saw you miss as many pitches as you did tonight. That's the worst I ever saw you umpire."

He says, "Sid, my night must have been better than yours, because you're leaving and I'm staying."

— *Sid Hudson*

Cal Hubbard stopped a game I was pitching and called the manager out there. He could see I wasn't feeling too good and probably shouldn't be out there, but in those days you didn't want to be relieved unless you had to. But anyway, he called time and got the manager out there and suggested that they ought to get somebody else in there, and they did. But the umpires, if you treat treated them right, they treated you right.

— *Ned Garver*

[A National League umpire from 1941 to 1965, Jocko Conlin was elected to the Baseball Hall of Fame as an umpire in 1974.]

Jocko was umpiring third base and I was playing third *[20 of Litwhiler's 1057 big league games were at third base]*. Walker Cooper was the hitter. He hit a blue darter just over my head. I threw my glove hand up and the ball hit the glove and took it right off my hand. Walker winds up on first base. Beans Reardon, the umpire behind home plate, yells, "Three bases! Three bases!" He thought I threw the glove at the ball.

Jocko is standing right by me, and he says, "Danny, did you throw that glove at the ball?"

I said, "Hell no, it tore it right off my hand."

He says, "That's the way I saw it. Watch this." He goes in and tells Beans Reardon, "Walker Cooper goes back to first base or you're going to see me walk up those steps right there in center field. I'm going right up to the clubhouse."

Beans Reardon sends Walker back to first base. Jocko was quite a guy.

— **Danny Litwhiler**

We're playing in the Polo Grounds and it's pouring rain. Ninth inning, bases loaded, three-and-two on me, and they're beating us by one run. The Barber, Sal Maglie, is pitching, and everybody's screaming in the rain, and Sal threw a curveball three-and-two. I knew it was high. The ball went over my shoulder and down into the catcher's mitt, and this is the way Jocko Conlin called it: "Strike three, let's get out of here, it's raining."

I turned around and said, "Jocko," my face pouring with water, "tell me the truth."

He said, "You know it was a ball, but let's get out of here."

And that was the end of that. To me, there's such a significance to that. The fact that this man could tell me this. Jocko, with certain Irish feeling about him — to me, it was like the Irishman and the Jewish man were getting together.

I was very relieved, and I said, "Oh, ha, it was a ball, so I would have walked and tied the score."

— **Cal Abrams**

I doubt I could pitch with today's strike zone because I threw a lot of high pitches. I could pitch in Chicago. I could pitch anywhere Jocko Conlin was behind the plate. That was day games, and that was his home town. He wanted to get the hell out of there and go home.

— **Taylor Phillips**

I lost my cool one day in Yankee Stadium with Joe Paparella. He's behind the plate. I actually got very vocal and I probably said some things — there's some words you can use in baseball, like "horseshit" to express how you feel about how he's calling the pitches — you know, you can say words that will catch their ear, and make them mad as hell although you're not calling them those real bad names. You're trying to make an impression on them.

Yogi was catching, but for me to go all the way up to home plate to get after an umpire about a pitch — I didn't want to see Yogi get thrown out. I didn't want to get thrown out myself. But Yogi tried to walk around me, and took his mask off and started toward the mound like I was supposed to follow him. And I wouldn't follow him. Casey come running out there. He didn't say a word, he just stood there listening to us. Finally I got a little, not

what you might say embarrassed, but I figured I'd said my piece, and I just walked away, but slowly toward the mound. Paparella didn't run me, I couldn't believe it.
— *Tommy Byrne*

I was in St. Louis. Bill Jackowski was the umpire at third base. A guy was going from first to third. The throw came in and I tagged him, and he was out. Bill called him safe. I jumped up, not really to argue with him but just to kind of question it, and as I jumped up, I bumped him. And that was a no-no. I was gone for three days. Bill and I laughed about it in front of the hotel the next morning. He said, "You can't touch the umpire."
— *Ted Kazanski*

[Obviously, making accurate ball strike calls is an umpire's most difficult and most important task. How good was Larry Goetz, a 22-year National League veteran?]
Larry Goetz was probably the best ball and strike umpire in the game. He was slow and deliberate. The ball would hit the catcher's glove and go bang! and then he'd say, ... "Striiiike," or ... "Balllll." He'd never call it right away. He looked at it, thought about it, and then made the call. I always said if my life depended on it, I would want Larry Goetz to call the balls and strikes for me.
— *Danny Litwhiler*

On this particular night I was throwing little bitty baseballs and putting the ball where I wanted to throw it. I think I'm painting the black, but Goetz is calling it a ball. About the third time he called it a ball, I came off the mound and I started toward home plate, and I got something to say, and my catcher Andy Seminick, our Mad Russian, came out there and met me.
He said, "Hey, stop. Don't argue with this guy, he'll throw you —."
And Larry Goetz was right behind Andy, and he said, "You — get back on that mound and pitch. It was a ball."
So I went back up there, and I did the best I could do.
The next day Goetz came to me and said, "Hey, Bubba, I want to talk to you."
I said, "Okay." I know I won the ball game; otherwise, I would not have talked to him.
He said, "Let me show you what's happening out there. Coming off the rubber your left foot is going too far to the left, and when the ball gets to home plate, you're looking at it from the first-base side. It looks like a strike to you, but the darn thing is three inches outside. I will not call it a strike."
So I went back over it and looked at it, and you know, the guy was right.
— *Bubba Church*

We had good umpires in our league. I had respect for all the umpires. I wouldn't argue with them. One time I said, "Aw shucks," and they said, "Oh, golly, Tom must be mad. He's cussing."
— *Tom Upton*

I hated an umpire who would call you out on strikes and the next time you came up he would say, "I think I missed that one."
I really didn't want them to be that honest with me.
— *Randy Jackson*

[Iron men? We think immediately of Gehrig and Cal Ripken, Jr. But Bill McGowan, an AL umpire from 1925 to 1954, reportedly worked 2,541 consecutive games over a 16-year period. He died two months after umpiring his final season.]

Bill McGowan was the best umpire I ever saw. He was great. I've seen him many a time umpiring at first — you only had two in those days, you know — he'd be umpiring at first base and maybe the runner would take off trying to steal a base and he'd run right with him, slide right with him into second.

Many a time I've him when he was umpiring the bases and be standing behind the pitcher and you're in a little jam and he'd say, "Hey, Sid, let's see you get out of this now. Show me something."

— *Sid Hudson*

One time in my rookie year *[1953]* McGowan was behind the plate and he called strikes on me that I thought were high. So I stepped out of the box. I didn't turn around, I just reached down for some dirt and I told him, "It's a lousy call. You guys are all the same, you've been missing these high pitches on me. I can't believe it."

Irv Noren, when I came back to the bench, said, "Geez, Bill, don't get on this guy, he'll heave you out of the game. He doesn't like guys to talk to him like that."

I said, "I didn't really show him up." In other words, if you turn around and look at him and say something, it kind of shows him up, but if you're not looking at him, why, not everybody in the park can see that.

— *Bill Renna*

Ray Scarborough, a pitcher on our club, was one of the best bench jockeys in baseball. Scarborough was on the umpire pretty good one day. McGowan came over to the dugout and he and Scarborough got into a heated argument. He threw his ball and strike indicator at Scarborough. It went underneath the players' bench, and when it did Scarborough was on all fours, on his hands and knees, down there to get that ball and strike indicator. So he comes up with it, and Bill McGowan, the umpire, says, "Give me that ball and strike indicator."

Scarborough says, "Like hell I'll give it to you. You'll get it from the league president." So Scarborough sent it into the league office, and I think McGowan got in trouble for that.

— *Mel Parnell*

[Bill McKinley was one of the most highly regarded ball and strike umpires. In the majors from 1946 to 1965, he umpired in 2,977 games, including four World Series and three All-Star games.]

The Browns were playing at home against the Red Sox, and I guess it was about the tenth or eleventh inning. I threw a ball right down the middle for strike three, and how in the hell McKinley said "ball" I don't know. I got a bit vocal. He came out to the mound and started mouthing off and I said, "Well, it's about 94 out here, 95, and I've been working hard all day. Maybe you're getting tired but I'm trying to win the game. How about going back behind home plate?"

The batter swung at the next pitch and popped up, and we got out of the inning.

I came off the mound and I was going right to the dugout. I wasn't going to say anything to McKinley. But he wanted the last word, and he met me at the foul line. He said something to me and without thinking I took my three fingers and just drove them right into that breast protector and said, "That's where the pitch was."

And I just kept right on walking. If there had been a big crowd there, he might have really popped it to me right there.

— *Tommy Byrne*

I only got kicked out of one game. Jim Honochick was the culprit. We were playing in the tenth inning. A three-two pitch bounced and hit home plate. He called me out and I said a few choice words and he finally threw me out.

— *Don Buddin*

An event on my first day in the big leagues *[1949]* almost ended my career right then. One of the sportswriters asked me for a ride home. And while we were riding home, he was writing the box scores for the game that we just played, and I'm thrilled that I'm playing with the Dodgers.

He said to me, "Cal, you just came up from the minor leagues. Can you tell me what the difference is between major league and minor league umpires?"

So while I had my hands on the steering wheel I just shrugged my shoulders and I said, "Ehh." Like that. "Ehh." Which to me meant, "Everybody's got two eyes, it's either a strike or a ball. Ehh. You know, nothing."

Well, I picked up the newspaper on the way to the park the next day, and it said, "Cal Abrams blasts major league umpires."

Now, I'm leading off, and the umpire-in-chief Larry Goetz, I'll never forget that man — when he yelled, the veins on his throat stuck straight out, and he scared me, actually, I would jump — and he said, "Play ball." And I get up to the plate, I'm tickled to death, and I'm getting into the groove more or less, becoming accustomed to being a big leaguer, and he says, "You better swing at anything that's down near your feet or close to you or over your head or behind you, because they're all strikes."

Suddenly my arms, my legs, went like jelly. I couldn't even hold that little bat. And I didn't turn around, because in those days you didn't turn around to an umpire and yell at him. Today you can punch him and it doesn't mean anything. You're fined fifty thousand, so you write a check, what's the difference?

But I said, "Mr. Goetz, what are you doing to me?"

He said, "What did you tell that reporter who asked you about the umpires, in the major or minor leagues?" I said, "Mr. Goetz, all I said was 'Eh.'" He said, "That'll teach you to open your goddamn mouth."

— *Cal Abrams*

Larry Goetz was a great big tough-looking guy. In Cincinnati my first year *[1949]* the pitcher threw a ball pretty close to neck high. There wasn't any question about it. I didn't even think about it. But Goetz called it a strike. I can remember standing there a minute and saying to myself, "Did he say a strike?" I stepped out of the box and looked at him funny, and I didn't even get a chance to say anything. He told me, "Get back in that blank-blank box and hit. Just like that. That's all there was to it. I said, "Okay." I didn't get thrown out. I got thrown out of a game only one time, by Lon Warneke.

— *Wayne Terwilliger*

I found out that if I got a little bit of wax shoe polish on my fingers and then got out to the mound and took the rosin bag, I had a sticky finger. It just helped the rotation on the ball. Now, there was an umpire named Lon Warneke who had pitched for the Cardinals; he knew what it was like out there. Lon carried me into a higher dimension. He said to me, "Ever heard of olive oil? Just picture a glove in your hand and fold your hand around it. Put about four drops of olive oil in the crease, down there on the heel of your hand, and then go out there and sprinkle some rosin on it."

And you ain't seen nothing like it in your life. I've got pictures in my den right now where my fingers are so black from the rosin and the olive oil. You can do anything you want to do with the ball.

— *Bubba Church*

[Al Barlick umpired for 27 years, including a record seven All-Star games. In 1953 Pittsburgh catcher Mike Sandlock was 38, nearing the end of a long pro career.] It was about 118 degrees in the shade in Pittsburgh. We were playing the Brooklyn Dodgers, and Al Barlick was the umpire. The pitcher was John Lindell, the Yankee outfielder who was enjoying a second career as a knuckleball pitcher. I was catching. It was about 80 feet to the backstop, and during the game I went back a few times, chasing John's knuckleball, sweating like anything. Everything the Dodgers got their bat on was a base hit. They scored seven or eight early runs and we had to change pitchers.

In about the sixth inning we go out and I come back behind the plate. Barlick and me are both soaked. Barlick says, "You forgot your apron." I had to go back to the dugout for my chest protector. My uniform was so heavy from sweating I didn't even realize I didn't have it on.

Then, all of a sudden, I see John Lindell sitting up there in the stands and he's got what I call a lollipop. You know, something that's got a head on it. He's sitting up in the stands with a nice clean shirt, and I think, "Oh boy, that's where I probably should be sitting, right next to him."

While water's sopping out of my shoes because of perspiration, I'm thinking hard, trying to trump up some way to get kicked out of the game.

Hodges is hitting. A good close pitch comes over the plate, and Barlick calls it a ball. I didn't turn around. I just said, "Barlick, does the strike zone change with the color of the uniforms?" and boy, he flew out from back there and swept home plate, and he stuck that little broom right in front of my nose and said to me, "You're not going anywhere."

That's the way it ended up. He wouldn't let me get out. He knew what I wanted.

— *Mike Sandlock*

We had some great umpires, which the best I thought was Al Barlick. Al's the only guy that ever really was going throw me out of a ballgame. The reason being he called a balk on me one day for not stopping. And I told him I thought I'd stopped, and I said, "In fact, I'm sure I did."

He said, "I'll tell you what. I've given you twenty seconds, twenty-five seconds to speak your piece. I'm getting paid to umpire this ballgame and call it the way I see it. As far as I'm concerned you balked. Get back on the mound and let's play ball."

This is the way Barlick controlled a ballgame. He wasn't one of those guys that you say one word to him, he'd throw you out. He let you have your speech. He'd tell you why and then you'd get back to playing ball. Everybody respected him, because he was always hustling. He was an excellent umpire, and he was always right there to make the call.

— Johnny Klippstein

Al Barlick was behind the plate in a 17-inning game. In the ninth we were behind by three runs, and I hit a three-run homer to tie the game. It was a particularly hot day in the later part of July. In extra innings it seemed like everything just shut down. Nobody could get a hit. It just went on and on and on. Every time I'd come up to the plate, Al would say, "You're the cause of this mess. I'm going to get you."

I said, "Well, let me hit, Al. Maybe we can get it over with." But I had to leave the bench ready to swing at anything.

We won it in the 17th when our pitcher Harry Perkowski was on second base and Roy McMillan got a base hit in right center field, and Harry came chugging around third and I know to this day that Barlick would have called him safe no matter what. That game was over when he turned third base. It was a close play, but he made it anyway. He was safe.

I met Barlick years later and he said, "Greengrass, I've been looking for you. You remember that 17-inning game in Cincinnati when it was about a hundred and twenty in a shade and you tied it up in the ninth?"

I said, "I remember. If you'd let me hit in extra innings maybe we'd've got it over with sooner."

— Jim Greengrass

I really respected Al Barlick. When I first came up I slid into second base I jumped up and was ready to say something, and he said, "Earn your letter first" or something along those lines.

— Frank Thomas

Two umpires I loved behind the plate were All Barlick and Dusty Boggess. I didn't think they gave me anything, but they didn't take anything away. Umpires had to be consistent, and they were. On the pitch right at the knees, they called the same pitches balls and the same pitches strikes. Other umpires, they'd call one pitch a strike and you'd throw the same pitch a little later and they'd call a ball.

— Don Liddle

I was a bad loser. I hated to lose. I got chased around 18 times in the Southern League in 1952, but only got chased once *[in 1960]* in the big leagues. Eddie Vargo got me. I got suspended two days and fined a hundred dollars on a play at the plate in Philadelphia. I tagged a guy out in the ninth or extra innings. We were the visiting team. Vargo called him safe. I chewed tobacco, and somehow he ended up with freckles all over his face, and his white shirt had brown spots on it. Dick Groat got fined twenty-five and Don Hoak got fined twenty-five and Fred Green, the pitcher, got fined twenty-five, too. But I got the worst. I still have the telegram.

— Bob Oldis

Nestor Chylak and Larry Knapp, when you had a confrontation, they were man enough to say, "You know, I might have missed a call and you might be right." And that was the end of it. Some other guys were kind of persistent, when they missed a call or missed some play they were just arrogant and just saying they were right.

— *Ted Lepcio*

I thought Nestor Chylak was one of the fairest umpires. Even if it was a goof. Let's face it, nobody's going to be a perfect umpire. At least he would come back and say, "You know, I think I did screw that one up." At least he let you know, and let's play ball. He never tried to even it out either. He was just one of the best at battling and trying to be a real good umpire.

— *Jim Landis*

[Bill Summers umpired in the AL from 1933 to 1959 and was behind the plate in six All-star games.]

I just missed seeing history made.

One day in Yankee Stadium, I thought we had Gil McDougald struck out, and Summers called it a ball. I turned around to argue and he kicked me out. After I was gone, McDougald singled on the next pitch.

Then Mantle came up. I was on the runway when I heard the cheering, but I didn't get a chance to see the home run Mickey hit, the one off the top of the facade in right field in Yankee Stadium.

— *Lou Berberet*

I remember hitting once with Ed Runge behind the plate. The ball was outside about six inches. I took it. He called it a strike.

I said, "That ball's outside, Ed."

He said, "You take another one, it'll be a strike too." At least he told me what to expect.

— *Don Buddin*

I played ball for twenty-one years, and never was thrown out of a game. The first manager I had in baseball was Rabbit Powell, he was a little outfielder. I think he had played with Boston. Rabbit told me, "You know, you can get away with saying things to an umpire if you don't turn and face him. If you're at bat and he makes an obviously bad call, you don't have to turn around. Just say, 'Jesus Christ, ump. How can you miss that one? Let's bear down, I only get three.' Stuff like that." I just kept that in mind all through my career.

And Jo Jo White had told me down in San Antonio, "You can't help the team sitting on the bench. Don't ever do anything to get kicked out of a ballgame."

So I never did.

— *Jim Dyck*

All the umpires treated me fantastic. They bent over backwards to help me, maybe because they knew I was just a young kid. I remember times when the catcher would run out to the pitcher to talk to him, and the umpire would say to me, "Now you watch for this, he's going to throw you this now."

They were great guys.

— *Ted Kazanski*

I didn't give umpires much trouble. I became more arrogant when I became a manager than I was a player. I was a very nice kid when I was a player. But when I became a manager,

I couldn't play so I got mad at everybody because they didn't do things the way I wanted them to, you know.

— *Marty Marion*

I found out that every time you moved up a league as a player, the good umpires would move up too. And they have the same ambitions in their field as baseball players do in a baseball player's field. They want to go to the top.

I was never an umpire–baiter. I managed one year of baseball and got thrown out of a ballgame one time. I never got thrown out of a ballgame as a player. I just felt like I could do my job and I hoped he could do his, and if they were missing pitches, I would say, "Hey, don't dribble that strike zone like you're playing basketball with me, kind of level it out and I'll try to get in there with you."

He'd have something smart to say. But I had the ability to throw control pitches, and when they didn't call one pitch a strike, then I'd move it into the area that they would call it a strike. Oh, I'd growl at him, but I didn't want to show one up, because I felt like we were all in this program together.

— *Red Murff*

One day in Little Rock I slid into third and the umpire called me out. Anyway, I thought I was safe, and I came up with my hands and I scooped a lot of dirt with them. It went right in his eyes, right in his face, and he was spitting. I apologized to him. He was a nice guy. He didn't throw me out of the game.

He said, "I know you didn't do that on purpose."

— *Bob Lennon*

I had played a long minor league career by the time I got to the big leagues. In my first game, when I took my position at third base and I got ready to play the first hitter, a voice behind me said, "About two steps to your right, kid."

I moved over two steps to my right, and the batter hit a ground ball right at me. I didn't turn around, I just said, "Thanks a lot, ump.

I went to play the next hitter, and he said, "You'd better get over in the hole a bit." So I moved a little bit to my left, and he just steered me around the whole ball game. Finally I said to him, "Geez, this is nice when you've got an umpire behind you telling you where to play. Why are you doing that?

He said, "We've got the word on you. We'll take care of you."

— *Jim Dyck*

We always figured the National League umpires gave the low pitch more than the American League because in those days the National League umpires operated with the inside protector and stood over the inside shoulder of the catcher. The American League umpires used the balloon and they of course operated over the catcher and they could see the high pitch and they'd call more high pitches than they would low pitches. The low pitch was a little tougher for them to see, so we always felt like the strike zone was lifted in the American League where the pitcher would get more high pitch strikes.

— *Billy Hitchcock*

I was thrown out of a game in the big leagues twice. One time there was a swinging bunt down the third base line. I let it go foul and I picked it up and the umpire called it fair. I said, "Ask the third base umpire." He said, "I don't have to ask the third base umpire. It was fair." We argued, and the next thing you know I guess I said something I wasn't supposed to say.

The other time was when an umpire called me out on a three-two pitch. I said another couple things that I wasn't supposed to say. But only twice in thirteen years, so actually I wasn't the kind of guy to get thrown out a lot.

— *Joe Ginsberg*

The only game I ever got kicked out of was in the Eastern League. The game was played about thirty miles from my home town, Addison, New York. About all of Addison was there. The umpire called me out twice on pitchers over my head. The second time he called me out I just dropped the bat at home plate. The bat just rolled down and hit his foot. I was walking back toward the dugout. He came charging up behind me and he said, "You're out of here, Greengrass, you're out of here!"

I turned around and I was really mad at that point of the game and I said, "What do you mean? What did I do?"

He said, "You threw that bat at me!"

I said, "Hell, if I'd thrown that bat at you, you wouldn't be standing here talking to me."

— *Jim Greengrass*

We had a lot of confrontations with umpires, but they always won. It didn't make any difference what it was, they won. That's important. If they don't keep law and order, the game wouldn't be so good. We had a great bunch of umpires. They might throw you out of a game, but the next day they'd forgotten and you started new. There was a good relationship between the players and umpires. Leo Durocher was kind of rough on them, but you know, they really enjoyed him. I had one umpire tell me one time, "I enjoyed umpiring when Durocher was playing. There's never a dull minute." So you see, they got a kick out of it too.

— *Jimmy Bloodworth*

You could say something to the umpires back then, and they'd say, "Okay, Max, I made a mistake. Just forget about that." That's the way we went. I never got thrown out of a ballgame in the big leagues.

— *Max Lanier*

Chapter Four

Playing Fields

In 1950, the following major league teams played in these parks:
  National League — Brooklyn Dodgers, Ebbets Field; Boston Braves, Braves Field; Chicago Cubs, Wrigley Field; Cincinnati Reds, Crosley Field; New York Giants, Polo Grounds; Philadelphia Phillies, Shibe Park; Pittsburgh Pirates, Forbes Field; St. Louis Cardinals, Sportsman's Park (renamed Busch Stadium, 1953).
  American League — Boston Red Sox, Fenway Park; Chicago White Sox, Comiskey Park; Cleveland Indians, Municipal Stadium; Detroit Tigers, Briggs Stadium; New York Yankees, Yankee Stadium; Philadelphia Athletics, Shibe Park; St. Louis Browns, Sportsman's Park; Washington Senators, Griffith Stadium.
  The 1950s saw five teams change cities, and thus ballparks.
  1953: The Boston Braves to Milwaukee (the Braves at County Stadium).
  1954: The St. Louis Browns to Baltimore (the Orioles at Memorial Stadium).
  1955: The Philadelphia Athletics to Kansas City (the Athletics at Municipal Stadium).
  1958: The Brooklyn Dodgers to Los Angeles (the Dodgers at Memorial Coliseum).
  1958: The New York Giants to San Francisco (the Giants at Seals Stadium).
  As of 2012, major league baseball is played at only two of those 1950s parks: Wrigley Field and Fenway Park.
  During the 1950s, some different parks came into play. How much did the park affect the play? Is there a difference in how one hits or pitches or fields? Is there a difference in the grass? the speed? the heat? the mental approach? the fences? the wind? the fans? Forty years from now, will today's players recall the particulars of their parks as vividly as those men who stepped onto the Polo Grounds and Sportsman's Park and the other distinctive fields of their era recall theirs?

One difference in playing the outfield from the minor leagues to the major leagues was that a lot of times you were three-quarters surrounded by upper decks, and that wind would get down in there and blow the ball in different directions, and that's something you had to learn. You had to watch the wind and watch which way it was carrying the ball from you, 'cause it would get you turned around in a minute.

— *Tom Wright*

I loved pitching in Fenway Park. I had some of my best games right there. It was such a compact ballpark and had great atmosphere. And those great Red Sox fans, they're right there on the field, almost with you.

I always felt that Fenway helped you more than it hurt you. Those pop flies go out of there pretty quick, but a lot of hard hit balls bounce off that wall so fast that the outfielder can hold the hitter to a single or no more than a double while in other parks the ball would be gone. That wall kept a lot of balls from being home runs.

— *Boo Ferriss*

I don't think my hitting approach changed from one ballpark to another. In Fenway you use the wall, but it hurts you as far as home runs go. Everybody thinks it's a home run hitting ballpark, but it's not. Really, the wall is more for doubles hitting. You look at the records — almost everybody that's played at Boston has a high double production. The wall stops a lot of balls that would be home runs in other ballparks, especially if you're a line drive hitter.

— *Frank Malzone*

I enjoyed in Chicago and Cleveland, they were big ballparks. You could gamble a little bit with some of your pitches, where in Fenway you couldn't because of the short distance. You could make pitches with one or two out. You could let the guy hit the ball. If he hit it out, shake his hand at home plate, he did it. You could be a little more at ease pitching there.

Every pitch had to be a good pitch at Fenway or you were out of the ballgame. A five run lead at Fenway meant nothing because of that short left-field wall and the lack of foul territory. The lack of foul territory in Fenway just gave the batters another shot at you because not many foul balls were caught.

— *Mel Parnell*

Playing shortstop at Fenway was a lot different than playing at other ballparks. On a base hit over third base you had a wall behind third base. You had to go out in left field to catch any ground balls to save them from being doubles. You had to go out to help the left fielder.

— *Don Buddin*

When you played shortstop in Fenway you had to watch where that little place jutted out from the stands behind third base. When the ball was hit down the line, you had to hustle over there to keep the guy from going to second base, while in other ballparks you knew it was going to be a double down in the corner and you'd be going out for the relay.

— *Milt Bolling*

Oh, boy, I would have loved to have played for Boston, with that little short porch out there in left field. I was really a dead pull hitter. I had good power, but I hit so many balls that curved foul just before they got over the fence. Marty Marion said to me, "God, if you'd played in the Polo Grounds, you'd of broke Ruth's record." I hit so many that just missed that left field pole by about four feet and be about forty feet in the air yet. *[The second deck down the left field line at the Polo Grounds was only 250 feet from home plate.]*

— *Jim Dyck*

One regret I have is trying to adapt my game to Fenway Park, trying to pull the ball. In the minors I hit more to the alleys in left and right center. I was expected to pull the ball more in Boston.

— *Dick Gernert*

Fenway Park was always great to hit in because of the low stands. You didn't have the shadows come in like you did in those double deck stands, and the wind was always prevailing pretty much to left field, center field. You could see the ball good all the time. Most of the parks were oriented pretty much for left-handed hitters. They were all pretty much short on the right field fences. Fenway Park was the only one that had the short left field. I hated to play in Yankee Stadium. There was always shadows there in the day games, and we played to big crowds so they took the tarp down in center field, so you were always looking at the white shirts in center field. You had to hit it a ton to hit it out in left field. It was always a big fly ball out where in most any other park it would at least get to the fence.

— *Bobby Doerr*

My favorite ballpark was Fenway, no doubt about it. It had that big, green, wonderful wall. It was like a magnet. I did very well in Boston. I was a pull hitter, and the balls I hit that were big, big outs in Yankee Stadium would have been home runs or up against the wall in Boston. It would certainly have improved my average and my home run production. Any right-handed pull hitter in Yankee Stadium was dead. They had that big Death Valley. Career-wise, I'd probably have been better off playing in Boston all my life. But looking back on the history of it, who can say he wouldn't want to be in a World Series? At least with the Yankees I was fortunate enough to have played in four, and was eligible for five.

— *Andy Carey*

I think the reason I was one of the more successful left-handed pitchers in Fenway was that I pitched in tight. I think the right-handed hitters came into that ballpark seeing that left-field fence they had one thing in mind, hitting the ball out of that ballpark. So I tried to keep the elbow as close to their body as I could, keep them from having their arms extended because if they're extended that's where they get their power.

Most left-handers coming into Fenway try to keep the ball away from the right-handed hitter. In doing so it's fine if you can keep that ball consistently on the outside corner, or just off the outside corner. But when you miss inside you were right down the middle of the plate, and that's when you got hurt. I threw a lot of breaking stuff too because of that. I never threw much above the knees. That's where I got the nickname Dusty. I always thought that in keeping the ball down, out of the line of vision, the hitter sees the top of the ball. For that reason he's hitting a lot of ground balls. In my ten years at Boston I only had a hundred and five home runs hit off me, even in that small ballpark. Which averages out to about ten and a fifth a year.

— *Mel Parnell*

Boston was hard to play in because of the short fence. It seemed like you never had enough runs there. You could score six runs in the first inning, and you weren't safe. Most left-handed pitchers didn't like to play there because Boston loaded with right-handed hitters. The lefthanders would really take their lumps when they'd walk into Fenway Park.

— *Joe Ginsberg*

In Yankee Stadium it's really a thrill to walk out in front of the crowd and pitch a ballgame. You were proud to be out there. There was something different about that park.
— *Carl Scheib*

Yankee Stadium was a good park to pitch in, as long as you kept the ball out of right field. Even right-handers could hit the ball in the seats in right field. Left field was 301 down the line, but then it went out real fast. In the alleys you could run forever to catch up to a ball. DiMaggio, had he played some place else, would probably have hit a lot more home runs than he did, but he'd hit a 400 foot out.

The tradition there was something awesome. And the fact that a mediocre ballplayer like myself was playing on the same team as all these stars was really a thrill.
— *Randy Gumpert*

I liked to pitch in Yankee Stadium, as long as you could keep the ball away from the two sidelines, 'cause it was short down in left and right field. But center field was huge. The mound was good, and you had a little more incentive maybe trying to beat the Yankees than you did some of the other clubs. 'Course Washington, Griffith Stadium was a huge park. You'd just throw that high hard one and let the outfielders go get them. There's no use pacing yourself I don't think. You go as hard as you can as long as you can. If you run out of gas, why somebody's got to come and help you.
— *Sid Hudson*

I thought Yankee Stadium was tough to play in because of sun elements and the shape of it. My God, you'd have to go four hundred and forty feet in the ballpark to shag down a ball, or try to shag it down. It was just an odd-shaped ballpark.
— *Jim Landis*

Yankee Stadium was great to play in, no doubt about it. When you walked into Yankee Stadium for the first time as a rookie, it was very impressive, because you'd see those statutes out in dead center field when they had them there — there was Babe Ruth and Lou Gehrig and the monuments.

When you went into Yankee Stadium, you just said, "Well, I'm a big leaguer now," because that's where it all started as far as we were concerned.
— *Joe Ginsberg*

In Yankee Stadium Stengel had those handkerchief-wavers up there, trying to hide the ball from you with that white background.
— *Tom Wright*

When you walk into Yankee Stadium, you're in awe.
The House That Ruth Built.
You could just reflect back on all the different players that had played there, Hall of Famers. It was just something else, particularly for a kid who was raised on the Coast and had never been in a major league town before.
— *Bill Renna*

Ebbets Field was quite a place to play because the fans were right on top of you. You don't have much room, not much foul territory or nothing else. And the fans were rabid there. Dodger fans were very vocal and really rooted for their home team all the time. A lot of times they'd have a bunch of guys walking around with instruments blowing—it was a circus atmosphere there a lot of times.

— *Pete Castiglione*

[*Third baseman Randy Jackson was traded in 1956 from the lowly Cubs to the pennant-winning Dodgers.*]

With the Cubs, when you come to Ebbets Field you're about two runs behind before you even walk to the plate, because of the crowd and the intimidation of playing there, and the teams they had. You know, back in the fifties, the Dodgers had fantastic players. When you switch and you come over there, it's like old home week. Everybody loves you and you love everybody, and you feel like you're the one that's intimidating other teams when they come in because of the closeness of the fans, and the fact that most of them had about forty-eight cards in their deck. They were a little short on cards.

And they had the band, it was about the only place you had something like that. It was really a fun place to play, particularly if you're winning. And I wasn't used to winning with the Cubs, so this was quite a change.

— *Randy Jackson*

It was tough to pitch in Ebbets Field. And they had some great hitters. All I remember is the flag always flying out. But I had pretty good luck there. I was a right-handed pitcher, and the Dodgers were mostly right-handed power hitters, so I had a little edge going into there. But not much.

— *Bob Friend*

When I got my first look at the Polo Grounds I thought, "My gosh, I've never seen such a ballpark. I felt like a little ant, it was so huge. Hornsby pushed me, and he said, "You're the fastest guy I've got. I want you to play center field."

In batting practice I went out all the way to the center field wall and looked in. The batter looked like he was about four inches high. I didn't make any errors or anything, and caught three or four balls, and I played center field the rest of the seventeen games I played at the end of '52.

— *Jim Greengrass*

At Baltimore the fans were great, in Pittsburgh the fans were super, but there will never be a fan like the Brooklyn Dodgers. The Brooklyn Dodger ballpark, Ebbets Field, was so small behind home plate that while you were hitting you could talk to people in the stands. You could have running conversations, and that's what made it a close-knit family-like operation. The fans respected you, and they loved you. Even if we lost ten straight games in a row, they would still fill that ballpark.

— *Cal Abrams*

Playing in the Polo Grounds was great. It was almost five hundred feet to the keyhole in center field, and that's where the clubhouse was. After the game, you'd go the whole length of the Polo Grounds to get to your dressing rooms. One team dressed on one side, and the other team on the other side. I hit an inside-the-park home run right in the keyhole. Snider at that time could really run. You really had to hit a ball hard for it to roll that far, because they had a heavy turf.

You go into play at St. Louis at that time, at old Sportsman's Park, and that outfield and infield were so hard you couldn't hardly stick a spike in it. They had that bunch of rabbits. Every team in the league that's had running ballclubs, they had a grass field that's just as hard as a rug, to take advantage of their speed. And when you're playing with a club like the Giants were, depending on the long ball, they had it all softened up. The infield was soft, trying to slow up the rabbits. The outfield was soggy to try to slow down the speed that was going to be used against you.

In Sportsman's Park you could lay down a bunt so easy, 'cause it wouldn't go out of bounds. It wouldn't trickle off and go out of the base path, you see. But in the Polo Grounds nobody hardly ever bunted.

— *Pete Milne*

In the Polo Grounds they had a cutout in dead center field, and back in that cutout they had a statue of John McGraw. I hit a ball back to that statue one day that Willie Mays went back in that cutout and caught. I was standing on second base when he caught the ball. That's probably the longest ball I ever hit.

Dead center field was no man's land there in Pittsburgh with Virdon out there roaming around catching those balls.

— *Jim Greengrass*

The ballparks are different. If Mickey Mantle played at Ebbets Field, he would have broken Babe Ruth's home run record. The Polo Grounds was a strange park. The lines of the football stadium itself were very shallow, but it dips out very strongly because it is a football stadium. I hit a grand slam home run there — I call it a Chinese home run — off Ruben Gomez. He threw me a sinker ball on the outside, and I flipped the bat down toward the outside part of the plate, and it lofted the ball and it just nicked the upper stands in the Polo Grounds. The upper deck extended over the playing field, and if it touched any part of that, it's an automatic home run.

Bobby Thomson's home run, in any other park, would have been an out, but being that it was so close to the foul line, it went right through to the lower deck.

— *Cal Abrams*

I enjoyed playing in Chicago, because it was day baseball, and I thought that was great. It was nice being able to string two weeks together where you didn't have a night game in there somewhere. I think it makes you maybe appreciate the game a little more. It's pretty tough sometimes, when you're playing night, day, night, day, night, night, day, you know. It's a little different, upsets the pattern, and is not the best for family life or even for feeling good going to the ballpark.

— *Johnny Klippstein*

All the visiting teams hated to come to St. Louis because we had a ballpark that the Browns and the Cardinals both played on, and it was in pretty bad shape. We called it The Old Rock Pile. If you could play there, you could play anywhere.

By about June 1 we didn't have any grass on the field. Because two teams played on it, it was always worn out. But it was a good place to play for the St. Louis Cardinals, and pretty tough for the guys who came in there because we were used to the field and the heat.

— *Marty Marion*

Four. Playing Fields

There was a great contrast in fields between Cincinnati and St. Louis. That infield in Crosley Field had real black rich soil underneath that grass, which would deaden any ball hit on the ground.

In St. Louis where both the Browns and Cardinals played, there was no time to work on the field because when one club went away the other club was at home. The field there was like concrete. The Cardinals always had a fast running ballclub, and on a base hit to the outfield they knew that they had to get the ball into second or otherwise that guy's going to keep going. An opposing outfielder would maybe jab at the ground ball coming out to him, and the Cardinals would just keep right on running.

Once when I was playing second base in St. Louis I was playing real deep on the grass because a left-handed hitting pitcher was up, and the second bounce bounced over my head for a single. That gives you a rough idea how hard the ground was. The guys came up with more strawberries sliding on that hard dirt.

— *Sibbi Sisti*

The old St. Louis Brown ballpark was terrible. It actually had cracks in the dirt, it was so hard.

— *Wayne Terwilliger*

You'd go into St. Louis when the Browns and the Cardinals were both playing in the same park, the grass was all dead and the infield was rough and they'd just drag it with a mat. It was really a challenge. In the clubhouses there wasn't room to hang up anything.

My favorite ballpark? Just any of them that I could get my uniform on and get to play in I enjoyed.

— *Jimmy Bloodworth*

There was a concrete wall on the terrace in Crosley Field. The terrace gradually leveled off in right center field. So you had to learn how to go up that bank. If you weren't conscious of that bank you'd take a step and the next thing you knew you'd buried your face into the ground.

Hornsby taught me how to play that terrace in Crosley Field. Every day of my life when we were in Cincinnati Rogers stood in back of shortstop and hit balls against that wall, a hundred a day. He'd holler out, "Hey, you getting' tired yet?" and I'd holler back, "No, come on, hit some more."

Rocky Bridges and Roy McMillian were my roommates, and we'd get out there about ten o'clock and we'd throw batting practice to one another. But who'd already be sitting in the dugout in his uniform? Rogers Hornsby. Every day. He'd let us take our batting practice and then he'd get that sack of balls and say, "Come on, Jim." He'd put a guy on third base and I'd field the ball and throw to third base.

I had so much practice with that terrace I could field a ball off that terrace and throw to second blindfolded. One of my biggest thrills was one afternoon big Hank Sauer hit what he thought was a double off the left center field wall. I played that carom off that bank and fired to Temple at second base. Hank was giving that kind of long-legged jog into second like he knew he had a stand-up double. Temple turned around and showed him the ball and said, "Look what I've got, Hank."

Hank went into a fit. "There's no way that ball...." He threw his hat on the ground.

The whole place just went crazy. He swore that Temple must have had that ball in his pocket. All that practice out there, that one play was worth it all.

— *Jim Greengrass*

I loved to pitch in St. Louis; they had great fans there. And pitching in the heat in St. Louis was right down my alley, I loved the hot weather. In fact, we had a meeting one day on the road and Branch Rickey said, "Max Lanier and Enos Slaughter ain't worth a hoot 'til it gets hot weather."

I loved hot weather 'cause we could win ballgames there because other players come in there and you could tell they were getting tired about the middle of the ballgame, a lot of the pitchers especially.

— *Max Lanier*

You bet it was warm in Washington. You were lucky if you had a little window fan for your apartment. You never stopped perspiring from the minute you got up in the morning and all night long. By the time you finished a doubleheader, goodness sakes, you were pretty tired.

The players didn't care much for doubleheaders, because in Washington we played Saturday night games, and then you had to come back and play a Sunday doubleheader, and goodness sakes, that was really hard. If it rained a little bit during the doubleheaders and you had a rain delay, you were there from nine-thirty, ten o'clock in the morning until eleven at night. I don't know if the fans liked that, but the players didn't.

— *Herb Plews*

Briggs Stadium in Detroit was a hitter's ballpark. The background was good, the prevailing wind went out more than it came in. In other words, you hit a ball there, you get out of it what you did to it.

Some places you could hit a ball real hard and it just wouldn't carry. For example, in St. Louis. They had a short right field, but the air was so heavy that the ball never carried like it did in other places. So you'd hit a shot and it would get out there and die, and you couldn't believe the thing stopped so quick when the same shot in New York or Detroit would be in the upper deck.

— *Art Houtteman*

In Baltimore, before they put the fence inside, it was ridiculous. It was actually a big bowl. It wasn't a good hitters' park. The lines were very short. And this fools a lot of people. The least amount of balls a player hits will be down the line. If a ballpark is short in left and right center, that's a good hitter's ballpark. Down the line don't mean that much. Of course, foul territory means a lot too, and Baltimore every time you hit a ball in the air it would stay within catching range.

— *Gene Woodling*

Wrigley Field was a great field to play in, except the background. They used to have the white shirts in center field, and pitches thrown out of the white shirts, especially by a pitcher who could blow that ball and you didn't know where it was going part of the time — you had to be loose up there.

— *Danny Litwhiler*

In Philadelphia there were some loud lungs in the stands. I know of one guy, he liked my name, and he would draw out all the syllables in that big voice of his.
— *Wayne Terwilliger*

I remember going into Philadelphia, and they had a leather lung. I didn't know it at the time. But we're working out before the ballgame, and this leather lung out in left field gets all over me, and gives me all up and down, you know, and the guys are looking at me and kind of grinning, and I figured this guy greets all the rookies that way. "What do you think? You think you're a major league ballplayer?" and all this kind of stuff. They had their characters, the different ballparks.
— *Pete Milne*

I used to love to play in Crosley Field. I liked to play on a soft infield. When you're an infielder, the only thing you look at is, "How good is the infield?" Are there bad hops? Crosley Field was great. I never did like to play in a ballpark that had too hard an infield, except St. Louis; I knew where all the bounces were.
— *Marty Marion*

My favorite ballpark was Shibe Park. Ebbets Field was another. And Wrigley Field was a great field to play in, except the background. They used to have the white shirts in center field, and pitches thrown out of the white shirts were tough to hit.
— *Danny Litwhiler*

We had a situation in Philadelphia where the fans were throwing coke bottles and beer bottles at Gene Woodling, and all of a sudden he was throwing them at the umpire. He said, "These guys are going to hit me. Stop this. This is ridiculous." And we went out of there with bats in our hands, because the fans got really unruly.
— *Andy Carey*

There were two parks I liked to pitch in, but for different reasons. I always enjoyed pitching in Milwaukee because I think it was laid out in a way that was fair to left and right handed hitters. I think it was about 400 feet to center field and 365 or so up the alleys and 330 something down the line, which I think is a pretty fair ballpark. *[404 center, 376 power alleys, 320 lines.]* And also the fans were great there. It was just a ballpark that was easy access to get in and out. Nice clubhouse. Everything about it was just a pleasure to play there.

But the park and the mound that I liked best was in the old Polo Grounds. They had some kind of a dark clay dirt that you just got great traction out there pitching. It was just great to throw off that mound. Not only that, but there was I think about 80 feet behind home plate back to the screen, so naturally a lot of balls that were popped up were caught. In other parks, those guys would have another swing coming. The down side, was, of course, the short lines, down the left and right field line where you could get hurt sometimes. A guy swinging late and maybe dropping one in 280 feet for a home run.
— *Johnny Klippstein*

I prided myself on my defense, enjoyed being in charge in the outfield. I loved the challenge of learning the grass, of playing the ricochets off the short wall in right at Ebbets

Field — a crazy, broken up park — and off the corrugated sheets of metal at the top of the fence at Shibe Park; of playing the ball that dropped straight down off the screen in front of the pavilion in right center at Sportsman's Park.

Forbes Park was big, about 450 to center. You had to make sure the ball didn't get past you for a sure triple, maybe even a home run until they brought the fences in — Kiner's Corner.

Another park with all kinds of room in center was Baltimore, where I made one of my greatest catches. Mantle hit one that kept going well over four hundred feet, and I caught it in the bushes in right center. Later, manager Paul Richards said of how far away from the plate I was when I caught the ball: "They had to send a taxi cab to get him."

At Wrigley the winds and ivy made it a tough outfield. So did the grass, always in bad shape from playing football there. Comiskey was a tough center field; the park was built on a dump, and center field was built low, so low that sometimes I could see only the top half of the hitter, like playing uphill. Sometimes fog would set in and I couldn't see the hitter at all. The terrace at Crosley Field was a challenge. One day I forgot about it when I went back for a fly ball. My spikes caught on the incline and I fell on my back. My legs flew up in the air, and while I was sprawled on my back the ball came down between my legs. I made the catch.

Detroit's sprinkler system kept it mostly wet, muddy. Yankee Stadium had the best grass of any field; in Sportsman's Park it was hard to grow grass because of the heat.

Defense was different then. Players had to learn when and how to leap into unpadded concrete walls. Natural grass cut down on ground rule doubles, made for more plays at the plate with runners trying to score from first on a double. Bad hops, unpredictable caroms, non–symmetrical fields all made for some interesting baserunning situations; they created more excitement for the fans, back when defense was more of an art.

— *Chuck Diering*

I didn't like hitting at Forbes Field. Oh man. That's a good ride in a limousine.
— *Sammy Taylor*

I didn't have a good enough arm to play center field. And the other part of it was that left field was so big in Washington and I could cover a lot of ground out there. It was 400 feet down the left field line. It was a big, big area out there, and I did a pretty good job out there covering that big left field. I played deep 'cause I could come in real good, but I couldn't go back well. I liked to play in Yankee Stadium because of that short right field porch out there for left-handed hitters. I guess Detroit's ballpark would be my favorite overall, though. It was a good hitter's ballpark, and it was more or less uniform down each line and it was always in good condition. Old Sportsman's Park in St. Louis was a bad ballpark. Municipal Stadium in Cleveland was just like being out in the boondocks somewhere because it was so big. They put that fence inside there in later years, but there wasn't much background in hitting there. The Cleveland ballpark's playing surface was as good as anybody's but there was no background, to me, where I could pick up the ball. 'Course the pitching staff made it hard for anybody to get base hits.

— *Gil Coan*

I think Detroit is the best baseball town out of all of them I've been in. The fans seemed to stand behind the club. In St. Louis the field wasn't too good and you had the hot and humid days there, and they had the short right field fence. But another place that was real bad to pitch in, and it seemed like every time we'd get there it'd be so hot and humid, was Washington. Washington had a high right field wall, but it wasn't nearly as high as the one in Boston. I know Boston usually is a nightmare for a left-handed to pitch in. I had pretty good luck pitching there because they had so many of the free swingers, you know, the right-handed power hitters, Vern Stephens and those that I seemed to have pretty fair luck with.

— *Bob Cain*

I thought old Shibe Park was a good ballpark to hit in. Not Cleveland. In Yankee Stadium, what you had to do is make sure you had to pull the ball. You hit the ball in left center or right center, you're dead there. You had to get the ball from where the left fielder or right fielder played to the line, then you're okay.

— *Dick Gernert*

I liked to pitch in Comiskey Park. It was probably considered a pretty good-sized park, they had to hit the ball pretty good to hit it out. I didn't like the dad-blamed small parks — make a good pitch and fool somebody, but he'd still hit it the opposite field or something, and bingo. Or like Boston, hit a little pop fly and it'd be over the wall down left field. Or in Yankee Stadium, you'd pull it down the line. It was not very far. And in St. Louis we had a pretty short right field fence.

— *Ned Garver*

Once upon a time when we played baseball we used to keep our gloves on the playing field. Because when you run out after three outs, you pick up your glove, and you're ready to play.

— *Cal Abrams*

The type of gloves we used were small, and they had the big heel on them with the felt.

We wore those stupid old flannel woolen jobs. They were big and baggy with all that cloth flopping around, and if you perspire a lot and hit the dirt with those woolen jobs it's just like you've got two more tons you're carrying around with you.

— *Sibbi Sisti*

It was in, I guess, about 1950 when the first changes that I recall came into gloves.

Dave Philley, an outfielder with the White Sox, came out there one day with a big old web built in between his thumb and the first finger of his left hand. It was just a great big net. Well, pretty soon after that they put a rule in that you could have just so much area between those two fingers.

— *Gil Coan*

You couldn't dive for a ball, except a perfect ball, because the gloves weren't really that good. We caught the ball in the center of the palm. We didn't have much of a web in those days. There was a web, but you didn't catch the ball in the web. One thing we really stressed is making two-handed catches.

— *Danny Litwhiler*

Until sometime in the fifties the team leaving the field would leave their gloves on the playing field while they were hitting. I think Hank Greenberg was the one who instigated getting the gloves off the field. *[A 1954 rule prohibited leaving gloves on the field.]*
— *Wally Westlake*

Until the fifties the defense would leave their gloves on the playing field. I can't think of any particular situation where it affected the outcome of a game, but once in a while an infielder would go back for a pop fly and trip over a glove or else a ground ball would hit a glove.
— *Billy Hitchcock*

It was in, I guess, about 1950 when the first changes that I recall came into gloves.

We were taught to use two hands. In the outfield, we fielded ground balls just like infielders. You charge the ball and then you get set and go down and stay down just like an infielder.
— *Gil Coan*

Chapter Five

Skippers

Do the players make the manager, or does a good manager account for those few extra games that make the difference between a second and first division finish, or that can carry a team to the pennant? What makes a good manager? Should he be a disciplinarian? a pal? a public relations man? a brilliant strategist? a psychologist? a teacher? a risk-taker?

While only a handful ever seem to get more than token credit for a team's championship, headlines annually flash the names of several fired managers who are scapegoats for a team's failure to win a championship. Here is a switch: Instead of the managers making out the line-up, we'll see — though the players' recollections — a line-up of managers and some of the things they're remembered for.

The good managers emphasized and drilled the players on fundamentals, that's the important thing. And you've got to do it every year, no matter how long you play. If you played twenty years, you've got to be drilled on fundamentals every year. 'Cause once you stray from the fundamentals, that's when they get in trouble. I'm talking about your hitting, your fielding, and everything. It's so simple, it's scary, you know what I mean?
— *Pete Milne*

I was blessed to play with some wonderful managers: Connie Mack, Lou Boudreau, Jimmy Dykes, Bucky Harris.

Connie sent me in to pinch hit one day after I'd been catching for eight innings. That was in his later years when his mind was failing. *[This was in 1950, Connie Mack's 50th, and last, year of managing. He was 87 years old.]*
— *Joe Tipton*

I played under Stengel for three and a half years with the Braves. He was a great guy as far as I was concerned, though, because he was talking baseball all the time. We'd get on the train and travel from one city to another — it seems like Phil Masi and myself were a couple of his pets because he'd always park himself in a seat on the train and be talking baseball all the time. He helped me considerably, me being a young kid. He talked about the mental approach, like thinking what to do before you get the ball. He gave us all these little inside tips that were new to me.

— *Sibbi Sisti*

I thought Casey was crazy at first. He was a likable guy, he was easy-going, and he ranted and raved and he carried on. He was pretty much outspoken on the bench when we'd get behind, and when we'd get ahead he was kind of quiet and unassuming. And if we were behind or close in a game in the 7th, 8th, or 9th, he'd get up in the dugout and start running up and down the dugout and throwing left hooks. It was out of this world; he was trying to shake everybody up.

I think he really realized what the game was all about after we won the pennant and the World Series in 1949. I think he smelled the glory or he smelled the desire of the players that had been there, passed on through the older guys. Some of the fellas felt like he was doing things kind of half backwards sometimes, putting left-handed hitters up against left-handed pitchers and vice versa. It was kind of strange when we had all that talent on the bench, but sometimes it paid off.

Some of the guys said, "Well, by God, we're going to win despite him." I'm serious. Some of the older guys were thinking that. I never thought that. I never paid any attention to him as long as we won. But after we won that year, I think he found out what the Yankees were all about. He had had his career of losing, I guess. He went on and did a heck of a job. He was a good public relations man for baseball and for the Yankees.

— *Tommy Byrne*

Stengel really knew his baseball. I mean, he took you right in the rookie camps; he took you right from the dugout and told you what to think about all the way from the pregame warm-ups to the on-deck circle and batting and everything. He was really thorough; he had a whole system, and his coaches presented what they had to offer — the pitching coaches, with Jim Turner and the catching coaches with Bill Dickey. They were much more thorough than any other of the ballclubs.

— *Lou Berberet*

People ask me about whether Casey was a good manager, and I say, "Hey, I can't argue with success." There's a lot of books on the Yankees back in that era, and every one of them says that Bauer and I wanted to kill Casey. That's a bunch of baloney. It's just like the Old Man said — we called him the Old Man — when he brought me to the Mets in '62.

He told the writers, "When me and him was over on the other side and everybody said I didn't like him and he didn't like me, now I just want to clear the air — how in the hell can I hate this guy? All he got mad at me for, he wanted to play. I ain't gonna hate any ballplayer wants to play every day."

But, you know, you win five pennants and five World Series in a row with Casey and all of a sudden they say Bauer and I wanted to kill him? That's ridiculous. I can't argue with success, I'll guarantee you.

— *Gene Woodling*

One day I was out there pitching pretty good and getting them out rather easily, and we'd gone five or six innings and we had about a five run lead. Well, between about twenty pitches and ten foul balls, I walked the bases loaded. With one out Casey sent Jim Turner out to talk to me. Yogi and I are out there at the mound as Turner comes out, and he's taking his time, we can hear them gloves poppin' down in the bullpen. I said, "Well, it looks like Turner wants to kill a little time." And Yogi said, "Yeah, it sounds like it, doesn't it."

Turner walked up out on the mound and said, "How do you feel?"

And I said, "Well, pretty good. I've got good stuff, I'm still all right."

He said, "Let me ask you something. Are you throwing to spots?"

Well, with a five run lead you generally don't normally go to that much trouble to pitch to spots. I looked at Yogi and I looked at Turner, and I said, "Well, I don't know, but I think I've hit every spot up there."

He got real red in the face, and he turned around and walked back to the dugout and Yogi started back to the plate. I watched him all the way in the dugout, and he sat down next to Casey and I watched Casey say something to him and Turner wouldn't answer him. Casey probably wanted to know, "What'd he say?"

A couple pitches later somebody hit into a double play. They didn't score any runs and I walked off like we really knew what we were doing. I went in the dugout and got a drink of water and sat down next to Turner. He got up and walked away from me because he was afraid I was going to ask him something, with Casey hearing it. Casey was a real comedian, but he got real serious too, when the game was going on. I was always serious, but it's kind of hard to stay serious a hundred percent of the time. You have to be a little wacky even to go through that kind of ordeal.

— *Tommy Byrne*

Stengel knew the game very well. I used to think playing against the Yankees that Jim Turner and Crosetti ran the team, but that was not the case. Stengel, unlike Weaver, who, used to use stats all the time and so forth, I said Stengel used a crystal ball. He had it in his head. This was before computers. He knew the game quite well and of course had all kinds of talent. He would look down the bench and say, "Get a bat," and about four guys would jump up.

I used to marvel at him in talking when he had a press conference. You know, he never used anybody's name. That boy, or whatever, but the press loved him in New York. He was especially interesting in World Series time. You'd gather around the table in the press room or whatever and they were six or eight deep around the table just listening to him with his stories.

A lot of times Casey was one of those fellows that stayed up 'til all hours of the morning, yet he was at the ballpark or in the dining room before any of the players were. I recall one day in Cleveland we were having a doubleheader and it looked like Casey was asleep on the bench, but something happened on the field and he was up out of his seat and up those steps — in fact, he banged his shin on one of those steps, and he had that little limp anyway. It didn't appear that he was in the game when it was going on, but he didn't miss a whole lot.

— *Billy Hunter*

Casey was tough to play for; he made you pay attention. They made him out to be a clown. But when that ballgame started — he knew what was going on, and he knew how to get the best out of his ballplayers. He got on Bauer and me, but some other people he'd leave alone. That's part of managing. If you're handling twenty-five temperamental people, you've got to know how to do that, and a lot of managers are in trouble right away 'cause they don't know how to do that. You don't have to know how to teach them how to play ball, or they wouldn't be in the big leagues.

— *Gene Woodling*

We had a tremendous fight when Clint Courtney was traded from the Yankees to the Browns *[after the 1951 season]*. In a game at Sportsman's Park he went into Phil Rizzuto at second base and knocked Rizzuto about ten feet, and that emptied both dugouts. I ran over, trying to be peace-maker. I was holding Courtney and the Old Man *[Stengel]* came up and said to Courtney, "You shouldn't do that," — got real mad and just took a poke at him. Popped him right in the mouth.

The Old Man was upset about Courtney hurting one of his players. I don't think Rizzuto got knocked out of the game, but he certainly got hit awfully hard. The Old Man ran right out there to protect him.

— *Andy Carey*

One time I was in Chicago and I was batting against Billy Pierce. He always gave me a hard time, even though he was a lefthander. He could throw the ball hard, he had a rising fastball. So I'm up and first base is open with a man on second base. I'm just trying to make contact. I took a couple swings and Stengel came out to talk to me. He thought with first base open Pierce might nibble, not give me something good to hit because he didn't care if he walked me. Stengel wanted me to know that and not swing at a bad pitch. That's how much he was into the game.

— *Bill Renna*

Casey Stengel and I both knew what my role was, and he always knew I was sitting there, not one of those guys who said "Play me or trade me." I knew what the situation was, and where we were going as far as pennant winners. I accepted that. Casey knew that, so we got along well.

One time we were playing a doubleheader and we're out of pitchers the second game, and I'm down in the bullpen by myself and he called up, and I said, "Casey, what do you want? We're all out of pitchers."

He said, "I just wanted to know, how are you? If you've had a tough day."

— *Charlie Silvera*

Stengel was grumpy, distant, brilliant. My feeling about managing goes into four categories: you have to understand your players or you can't manage, obviously; you have to understand your front office and know what they want from you with your players; you have to understand the fans — that's part of your job, too; and man, you better understand the media. Stengel understood all these things, and that's why the Mets hired him as manager because he distracted people from the terrible abilities of the Mets and made sort of a folk hero of that team.

— *Jerry Coleman*

Stengel was a lot smarter than a lot of people thought. He double talked and he did these and those and all that stuff, but he was very much aware of the talents that he had. He knew how to utilize them. In fact, that was really one of his big attributes, I think, the fact that he could use the different people in the areas that they really were much better. He platooned a lot of people. They didn't like it, but they ended up on pennant winners.

He wasn't hard to play for. He didn't scream and holler. He just sat back, and he had his coaches. But he would get up and yell once in awhile. But he knew how to handle people. That was one of the reasons he was so successful.

— Bill Renna

I was pitching against the Athletics one day *[in 1951]* at Yankee Stadium. It was in the fifth inning, and we had them 5–2. With two outs, after a bunch of foul balls, I walked the bases loaded. Gus Zernial is coming up to hit. Well, Casey came running out of the dugout, and he hadn't even crossed the chalk line yet and he's waving to the bullpen for the right-hander.

I said, "Wait a minute! Wait a minute!" I'm yelling at him. You know, I felt great. I had good stuff. They couldn't hit it, so that's the only reason we hadn't got them out. They'd just walk after they fouled off pitches.

And he says, "No, I'm going to make a change. I'm going to make a change."

I said, "Change, my ass." You know, I very rarely got mad out there.

He said, "Give me the ball."

I said, "No, I'm not going to give you the ball." And I kicked the rosin bag halfway to second base. And he's following me, see, he's going up on the mound, now he's going down the mound, and we're halfway to second base.

He says, "You know why I'm taking you out?"

I said, "Heck, no. It was nothing-nothing when we started and we're winning 5–2 now."

And he said, "I'm afraid you're going to hurt somebody." He thought that was funny, but it wasn't funny to me. I had already hit four guys, and I had hit Ferris Fain twice. But the point was, he said that jokingly, thinking that would be something to cool me down a little bit.

And I saw this pitcher coming in — Fred Sanford, coming in from right field — and he was halfway between Hank Bauer and Jerry Coleman and I threw the ball over Coleman's head and it hit Sanford right at the belt.

I said, "Did you see that, Casey?"

He said, "Yeah, I saw it."

And I said, "It was a strike." And I walked off the mound. Well, when I walked off the mound, then he got real angry. I went in and sat down in the dugout. It's got numbers where the guys hang their jackets, you know, and 37 is where he'd sit. Well, I sat in his place, and he gave Sanford the pep talk. When he came in from the mound, I wouldn't get up. He sat down right next to me, and I didn't say anything and he didn't say anything. After a couple or three pitches, Zernial doubled and tied the score.

After that inning was over, I went on in and took my shower and listened to it on the radio. It went on to the 11th inning and we got beat. Everybody came in there pretty much upset that we blew the game. Casey yelled to Pete Sheehy, the clubhouse man, "Call everybody in the center of the clubhouse."

Casey went in and threw his hat down. He had his shirt half-buttoned, unbuttoned, his pants half down, and he was mad. But this was good. You know, you've got to get upset. He looked around at everybody and he said, "The next time I go to the mound and make a pitching change, the guy I'm taking out, we'll both walk in together." And I didn't get the inference to that, other than the fact that I did act like an idiot.

But what probably happened was that the fans evidently applauded some for me when I came off the field, maybe because I was showing my butt, I don't know. But then when he came in, they obviously booed; but sitting back in the dugout, I didn't hear it. I mean, ballplayers don't think of that, or don't hear that, you know, but Casey could hear it. And he was telling me in a nice way that we weren't going to do any of that crap again.

But Casey was a good man. We got along fine. He was left-handed and I understood him and he understood me.

— *Tommy Byrne*

When I was with the Mets, Casey made out the line-up one time *[in 1962]* — Gil Hodges was our first baseman — we looked up and wasn't nobody at first base. I told our pitcher, Roger Craig, "We ain't got no first baseman. Where's Hodges?"

So here comes Casey up there at the plate and said to the umpire, "Let me see your line-up card." He looked at it and said, "You know, my mind ain't on this side of the river, it's on the other side of the river." He had Moose Skowron playing first base, and Gil Hodges couldn't go out there until they changed the line-up.

— *Sammy Taylor*

It was a hot day in New York — it had to be a hundred degrees — and Casey was managing the Mets and he fell asleep in the dugout. He was sleeping along, and all of a sudden he heard the crack of the bat. It woke him up and he started applauding and said, "Well fellas, that's the way to go, hitting the ball —" And we had to tell him, "Casey, that's not us, that's the other team running the bases."

But Casey was about 75 years old then and naturally, things happen like that when you get to be 75, I guess. But he was good for a laugh every time. He'd be with those sportswriters, and he'd drink with them all night if they wanted to, and he would tell them stories until the wee hours. Casey was something else.

— *Joe Ginsberg*

On the plane if Casey would catch somebody not asleep he'd sit down and he'd start talking baseball. He got me one day before I got to sleep and he and me talked all the way from New York to Los Angeles. When we got there I had a little more knowledge than I usually had. He sure knew his baseball.

— *Sammy Taylor*

I played for Rogers Hornsby the year or two I was down there in St. Louis *[1951-52]*, and I'll tell you what, I was crazy about him. He was a hard-nosed guy, he loved to win; that was the nice part of being with that club. He was probably one of the greatest of the right-handed hitters, but I don't think he put too much pressure on his players. If anything, he maybe should have put on a bit more.

I think Bill Veeck probably wanted him to play certain players, and Hornsby wanted to do it the way he wanted to do it, and I think they had a little misunderstanding. There was a petition started among the players to try to get rid of Hornsby. I think everybody signed it except myself and somebody else, and I don't even know who that was. *[In 1952 Hornsby was 22-29 with the Browns, a .431 winning percentage, before being replaced by Marty Marion, who went 42-61, a .408 percentage.]*

I felt like Hornsby was a hard-nosed baseball man. If you don't have the talent, it's hard to beat some of those clubs. But I think he tried to do a good job, I really do.

— *Tommy Byrne*

In those days there were two or three places where the blacks had to stay in different hotels, so it wasn't unusual for us to pull into a city and we'd have a bus waiting for us to take us to the hotel, and it would be one of those hotels where Satchel Paige wasn't allowed. I generally sat up pretty close to the front of the bus. One day — I think it was in Chicago — Satch pulled up alongside the bus in a big black Cadillac, and Hornsby was sitting up there looking down at him, and Satch rolled the window down and stuck his hand out and gave Hornsby a little wave goodbye. I could hear the comments Hornsby made inside the bus. They weren't very nice.

— *Jim Dyck*

Rogers Hornsby was the manager when I went to the Browns in '52. He wouldn't stick up for his players, sort of like second guessing, it seemed to me. Like a time I missed the ball in Chicago, ran into the shade with my sunglasses down after a pop fly. The ball disappeared, of course, by having my sunglasses down, and he took me out of the game.

I'd go get on the team bus early, but we'd have some guys sit in a lobby and read their books, magazines, papers, and that stuff until time to go. If the time to go was ten o'clock, they'd wait until ten o'clock. They'd look at their watch and read until that time and go out. Well, Raj would get on the bus early and he'd tell the driver, "Come on, let's go. I'm here, they ought to be." So they're go off and leave some guys. So that was building up, you know. The manager doing you that way and all.

One day in New York there was a pop fly down the third base line and a fan reached and messed with the ball. The third baseman couldn't catch the ball. Hornsby didn't stick up for the player at all. He just said, "Get back on the field!"

The players called Veeck. He came into town the next day and that was the end of Raj. The boys had a plaque made: "The greatest thing since the Emancipation Proclamation."

— *Tom Wright*

When I got to the Browns in 1952, Rogers Hornsby had been fired just hours, or it might have been days, before. When I walked into the clubhouse the first time, there was a trophy sitting there that the team had given Veeck.

A great big trophy, almost as tall as I was, inscribed by all the players on the team: "Mr. William Veeck, the Greatest Move Since the Emancipation Proclamation."

That's what they thought of Mr. Hornsby.

— *J.W. Porter*

I played for one of the greatest ballplayers, batters, Rogers Hornsby. Now here was a man who really came from the rough neighborhoods, a rough and tumble sort of a guy. He thought nothing of walking through the tunnel toward the ball park, under the stands, coming out to practice or hit or whatever, and instead of going into the latrine or the bathroom that they had just made underneath the stands, he would urinate right on the walls. Spray everybody, hit their shoes, whatever.

He was from the old school.

— *Cal Abrams*

Bud Podbielan was pitching for us in Ebbets Field *[in 1953]*. Had a pretty good ball game going. At the start of the sixth inning, we've got them 6 to 3. The first guy up gets a handle base hit, one of those balls that had eyes and nobody could make a play. He walked the next guy. The next guy got a broken bat single to load the bases. Nobody out. Rogers Hornsby would never the dugout to go out to the mound to talk to the pitcher. All he would do was lean over on the bench and point to the bullpen and tell him to come in and he'd go out there to get the ball and the pitcher would come in to the dugout. But this time he got up off the bench — I was playing left field and I watched it. He walked out and talked to Bud.

Bud told me this later: he asked Bud, "How you feeling Bud? You getting tired?"

Bud told him, "Get your ass back in that dugout. I'm going to finish this game."

Raj just said, "All right, it's yours," and he walked back to the dugout.

Three hours later the damn game ends, we lost 16 to 7. He let Bud pitch every inning of it. After the game Rogers was sitting in the clubhouse when a writer came in and ran across the clubhouse and knelt down in front of Raj and said, "Raj, what the hell did you leave Podbielan there that long for?"

Rogers came off that stool, fifty-seven years old, grabbed the writer and picked him up and shook him. He said, "You son-of-a-bitch, don't ever come back in my clubhouse again." He carried him to the door and threw him out. I thought, man, don't mess with Hornsby. And Rogers never let him back in the clubhouse. The writer wrote in his column about dissension in the clubhouse. There was no dissension. Bud knew what he had done. Bud knew he was wrong.

— Jim Greengrass

With the Cubs *[in 1958]* I got to know one of the best people I ever met in my life over there. I really adored him. He was like a grandfather to me. Rogers Hornsby. That was one of the greatest thrills of my life, just to be sitting on the bench with Rogers Hornsby. He was the hitting coach over there. When he was managing at Cincinnati, the pitcher begged him to let him stay in one more hitter and the guy hit a grand slam off him. From that time, he told the umpire to send a guy in and send that guy off. He wouldn't go out to talk to the pitchers. He was a compassionate man, you could talk him into anything, but he would never leave the bench after that.

— Taylor Phillips

Hornsby was a little different sort, because he didn't associate with people much, and so playing for him was kind of different. But I liked everybody else that I was playing for, to beat the dickens. If you were a square shooter, and did the best you could and went out there when it was your turn, they liked you all right. I didn't have any trouble.

But Judas Priest almighty, Harry Craft was a guy, if he said, "Try to run through the wall," I'd a tried it. Those guys — Harry Craft, Bucky Harris, and Hutchinson, they were good to play for.

— Ned Garver

Pitchers really would have had trouble making good managers years ago because of the bunting, the hitting and running and all the finer things involved that managers like the Durochers and Darks and Mauchs can understand, those kind of guys that really got into the game a little bit deeper than pitchers did. A manager has to know the opposition and know what your guys can do, not just the words — actually know it.

— Cal McLish

The Yankees sent me to Beaumont in the Texas League in 1952. Harry Craft was the manager. He was a great outfielder, and he taught me to play the outfield. They tell me he played the shallowest center field of anybody. He taught me how to get a jump on the ball. I'd been playing third base, but I got to where I really loved it out there. In 1952 I hit about .280 but I had a hundred RBI's. At that time the Yankees needed a pitcher to win them about four games at the end of the season. They were looking at Cincinnati's Ewell Blackwell. Rogers Hornsby, who managed Cincinnati, and Gabe Paul, the GM, were out scouting the Yankee minor league teams.

They saw me play. Hornsby told me, "I saw you play, I knew you could hit." *[Greengrass his 22 home runs and 16 triples that season.]* I hit two home runs that game. But what he liked about me, I got a base on balls and ran to first. He loved guys who hustled.

They called Harry Craft about the trade and told him they wanted me to report, and he told them, "He has 97 RBI's. I'd like him to get a hundred before he leaves. Looks better than ninety-seven." Harry called me to the office and said, "When you get that one hundredth RBI, you just come into the dugout and keep right on goin'." I packed all my stuff every day, three or four days, and then I hit a three run homer. When I got in the dugout, of course everybody was cheering and hollering and all, and I shook everybody's hand and I got to Harry and he said, "Good bye, Jimmy. Good luck to you, buddy. You can do it."

— *Jim Greengrass*

Billy Southworth had a great expression: "You can catch more flies with honey than you can with vinegar." That's the way he treated his players. He was always nice to everybody, and he was very successful.

— *Marty Marion*

The best manager I played for was Billy Southworth. He started right in spring training. Everybody had to learn how to slide. In fact, I didn't really learn how to slide until I got with him. Everybody had to know how to bunt. The first inning, if the first two guys got on, Musial was bunting. Everybody bunted. And nobody said anything about it. He was great at playing for one run. He convinced me that if you can bunt and you can slide, you're going to win ballgames. We constantly went over the fundamentals. That was his success. He believed in teaching.

The thing that ballplayers didn't like about Southworth, and I didn't like it either: every night at twelve o'clock he's knocking on the door to see if you're in. Heck, he knocks on the door and about half an hour later whoever wanted to be out would be out anyway. But a lot times in the summertime it's hot and you're worn out and you finally get in a hotel that's comfortable — we didn't have air-conditioning in those days, we were up on the fortieth, forty-second, third, fourth floor, and it was fairly cool up there with the windows open — and you get sound asleep about nine-thirty or ten o'clock, and here at twelve o'clock bang, bang, bang, to see if you're in. Then you can't sleep all night.

— *Danny Litwhiler*

I had respect for a manager. I never tried to second-guess him. All I ever thought about, really, was to pitch good enough to make this guy like me so he'll pitch me some more.

Of course, you sensed it when a manager gave you the impression that he didn't think you were good enough and he'd give the ball to someone else that you felt wasn't any better.

But I ran hard, I practiced hard. I competed when I went out there. My objective with a manager was always to make him like me well enough that he would pitch me some more.

— *Cal McLish*

The first year I managed the White Sox we had a pitcher named Dick Donovan. He was a pretty good pitcher, and a good hitter. I used to use him as a pinch hitter. We were about to win the pennant, and he had an appendicitis operation about one month before the season was to end. We were in first place, and he was my star pitcher. When we had his operation, we went down. *[In 1955 the White Sox finished five games out of first; Donovan went 15–9. His career record was 122–99. He hit 15 home runs.]*

He was the type of pitcher that when you walked out to the mound, he'd say, "No, no, Marty, you can't take the ball from me, I'm not going to give it to you."

I'd say, "Give me that ball, Dick, you're through."

He was just such an intense pitcher, a competitor, and when he became sick with his appendicitis, the Chicago White Sox, instead of finishing first, finished third. That's how important he was to us. Something like that happening to a player can make the difference between a great manager and a bad one.

He was very superstitious. When he'd come in from the field, he'd lay his glove on a certain spot. Nobody better touch that glove. Pick up a towel, nobody better touch it.

— *Marty Marion*

One of the great things about baseball is its strategic moves. I was part of one of those moves back on opening day of 1955 with the Washington Senators. I was used as a pinch runner for a pinch runner. It all happened when Pedro Ramos, our team's fastest runner, pinch ran for our catcher — Mickey Grasso or Clint Courtney, I don't recall which.

On a base hit Ramos went to third base.

Charlie Dressen, our manager who was also coaching at third, called time and brought me in — with the kind of speed that got me exactly no steals in seven years — to pinch run for Ramos. I stayed in the game and caught the rest of it.

After the game the sports writers wanted to know why Dressen used a pinch runner for a pinch runner. He said, "I wanted someone running on third who understood English."

I guess speed isn't everything.

— *Bob Oldis*

I came up young, and then I got sent back to the minor leagues, and really, I was just starting to mature then, and I learned the most baseball in Toronto, playing for Charlie Dressen.

— *Ted Kazanski*

I enjoyed Fred Haney a lot. He was our manager when we won in Milwaukee *[1957]*. If you did your job — say you got in a ball game and the game was lost, but you got somebody out for two or three innings, he didn't lose sight of that. He'd walk by your locker and say, "Nice going, big guy."

It wasn't like you had to be a star to be on his team. He treated everybody the same way.

— *Ernie Johnson*

I liked Fred Haney. He knew I loved to work. I was never a guy that liked to sit around. When he said, "You're going to work today and tomorrow," well, that gave me what I wanted, and I gave him what I got. I could always remember every pitch thrown to every batter and what they hit and what they didn't hit and where we lost the ballgame. If we lost, I walked the streets trying to figure out where I made a mistake, if the game was close. Did we make the wrong pitch, or what?

— *Mike Sandlock*

I thought Bucky Harris was an excellent manager. He was a step or two ahead in a ballgame all the time. The nicest guy to play for, and he'd treat you like a human being. I guess another reason I liked him was because he gave me a chance to pitch.

— *Sid Hudson*

Bucky Harris was my favorite manager. He was with Washington for several years while I was there. He had a philosophy that he never expected any more out of a player than he had the ability to give, but he expected one hundred percent of that. A lot of managers expect a singles hitter to go up there in the ninth inning when you're tied or one run behind and hit a home run. That just doesn't work.

— *Gil Coan*

Bucky Harris was a nice fellow. As long as he had his coffee he was all right. He drank coffee by the gallon. He was an all-right manager, but he was a little bit too easy-going. He just never really put his foot down. But I liked him. He didn't bother the ballplayers. He just kind of sat there and watched the ballgame.

— *Randy Gumpert*

I liked Bucky Harris. He was at New York before Stengel came there *[managed the Yankees in 1947 and '48, winning a World Championship in 1947]*. He was a no-nonsense guy, but he knew his baseball. He was smart. Before I was even around he was what they called "the Boy Wonder" at Washington. He managed over there like in 1925 *[managed the Senators 1924–1928, 1935–1942, 1950–1954 — managed 29 years in all with five different clubs]*.

With Washington he was the kind of guy that everybody liked. On Opening Day we'd have a meeting and he'd say, "Hey, we don't maybe have the best ballplayers in the league, but you'll get no complaints from me if you give me a hundred percent every day." He said, "I know you're going to make physical errors, but you shouldn't make mental errors."

I'd go out and bust my butt, get beat maybe 2–1, and he'd come in the clubhouse and pat me on the back and say, "Hey, you pitched a great game. Get 'em next time." So you wanted to go out there and do well for him.

— *Bob Kuzava*

Oh man, Bucky Harris was one of the great guys, a really nice guy. He was a great ballplayer — a second baseman himself— and he took a lot of interest in me and really helped me. He'd sit on the bench and I'd look in at him and he'd move me around on the hitters. A lot of people thought I was smart. Hell, it was Bucky Harris who was moving me around. He probably taught me more than anybody. He'd talk to me a lot about how to watch the pitchers and how to raise up on my toes just as the pitcher got ready to throw. He taught me to watch the ball, whether it's going to be outside or inside, to get a good jump. I wasn't fast, but I was quick. For the first two or three steps I was wide open, so I could cover pretty good ground by getting a good jump.

Skipper Sawyer at Philadelphia and Bucky Harris were both the fatherly type. They wanted to see you do good. They were always willing to help, and if you'd have a bad day, they'd come by and say, "Well, it's part of the game. Don't worry about it. Tomorrow's another day." They'd take the pressure off you. That's one thing I appreciated about those guys.

— *Jimmy Bloodworth*

Mike Higgins was easy going, real easy going. Too easy sometimes. I liked him. I named my son after him, so he must have been pretty nice.

— *Don Buddin*

The most brilliant manager I was ever around was Paul Richards. Paul knew more about the game, the ins and outs. He started things like the double switch. If Ted Williams was at bat, for example, and a right handed pitcher was pitching in the ninth inning, and he wanted a left-handed pitcher to pitch only to Williams, he wouldn't take the right hander completely out of the game. He would put him in left field, knowing Williams wasn't going to hit a ball to left field, or even at third base, knowing Williams wasn't going to deliberately hit a ball to third base. So a left-handed pitcher would pitch to Williams. You've got Vern Stephens or Jackie Jensen or somebody like that following, so he can bring back the right-handed pitcher and not have to use another right-handed pitcher. He had the right-handed pitcher in there already that he wanted in there.

— *J.W. Porter*

Paul Richards would walk out of the dugout very calm, one pants leg up and the other down, and he was questioning the umpire's birth from the time he walked out of the dugout 'til he walked back.

— *Gail Harris*

Paul Richards was my first *[major league]* manager. I feel Paul was probably one of the smartest managers, because he knew how to handle a pitching staff. And we had a pitching coach, Harry Brecheen. Unbelievable. I was very fortunate. But every time Harry would talk to you and Paul came over, Harry would stop and Paul would take over. As soon as Paul left, Harry went back through it again. Those two men were very instrumental as far as my career was concerned.

Paul was just superb in handling the pitchers. Actually, on the Baltimore pitching staff, back in the late fifties, when I first went there *[in 1957]*, we had four pitchers that were just twenty or twenty-one years of age, and back then it was just totally unheard of that you had a starting staff that was that young. You go to the minors, you get your seasoning and play down there four or five years and then when you're ready they bring you up. Paul Richards really changed the history of baseball by putting us four guys out there.

Paul Richards had the foresight and the guts to do what he did with pitching, and it revolutionized the game. Even my own teammates gave me hell when I came up at the age of eighteen. "What are you doing here? I had to play six years in the minors before I got a chance, and here you are —"

But I thought, "Paul Richards saw something in me, and I'm not going to let him down."

I admire Richards for having the guts to do what he did, plus the fact that he was excellent with pitchers.

— *Milt Pappas*

Paul Richards baited the umpires just unmerciful, cussed them out and got on them all the time, and he'd get kicked out of the game, and I didn't think that was good for the club. When you're a low place club, you need all the breaks you can, you don't have to have the umpires mad at you.

— *Chuck Diering*

My first big league manager was Paul Richards [*of the 1956 Orioles*]. My personal experience with him was that some people need pats on the back, some people need a kick in the butt, and my personality was not good for his personality. For instance, I would pitch a game and then after the game I'd have to go out to the bullpen. Harry "the Cat" Brecheen was my pitching coach. When I was traded to Cleveland, Harry's comment to me was, "You must have felt like you were getting out of jail." Richards made me more tense than relaxing me. When I got to Cleveland, Joe Gordon took over for Bobby Bragan, who got fired. Gordon's comment to me was, "Here's the ball, throw the damn thing. You won 18 games in Triple A. I've seen you pitch before. Just throw it and don't worry."

— *Don Ferrarese*

I learned it the hard way — the Paul Richards Sliding Method — my first year of professional ball, 1954, just out of college, playing with the White Sox. I hit a ball off the right center field wall. My legs called "triple" all the way, and I did a hook slide into third base. I was there in time, but when my foot went past and over the bag I was out, costing me a chance at a rare triple.

In the clubhouse after the game Coach Luman Harris summoned me to Manager Paul Richards. Mr. Richards came right to the point. He said a hook slide is good for two things: first, to break my so and so leg; second, to slide past the bag. From now on he wanted to see me slide feet first, straight at the bag, then should I slide too far I'd be sitting on the bag.

As a player I was, perhaps, too hardheaded. But in this instance he got his point across: I never did a hook slide again.

— *Ron Jackson*

Pitchers just accepted the fact that it was the manager's decision to take you out of the game. The only one time I made a mistake, I was beating Detroit in Detroit, 2–1. I was pitching a pretty good ballgame, but I was getting a little tired. Lopez came out in about the eighth inning, and I told him I was getting tired and he took me out. Gerry Staley came in and we lost the ballgame, so I never should have told him I was tired.

I always felt as though Lopez held that against me, because sometimes they think you want to get out of there. I was just telling the truth. I should have said, "No, I'm all right."

— *Bob Keegan*

Al Lopez was a great manager. I feel later in his career, trying to please the public, the front office, and the players for so many years, it took a little toll on him. But while everything was really there, he was a great manager. He knew how to handle the personnel. I think his main asset was being able to handle people. You know, you kick one guy in the butt, and you pat one guy on the back. I think he did that very well. He knew my personality, especially when I was young. Who knows, if it hadn't been for him I might have been carrying a lunch bag right away.

— *Jim Landis*

I was responsible for beating Cleveland in a game in 1954 in a Sunday doubleheader. I was up seven or eight times and I had four hits or so, one of them a home run. The ironic thing was, a couple years later, Al Lopez, who had managed the Indians in 1954, took over the White Sox. I would say if there's one thing Lopez did, he remembered everybody. He remembered how they hit and where they hit, and against certain pitchers. He could move players around according to the pitcher and the hitter, and had an outstanding knack for moving players to where the hitter was going to hit. He told me that he didn't remember me, so it was sort of the beginning of our relationship.

— *Ron Jackson*

I don't think there's any question but that Al Lopez was the best manager I ever played for. I don't think there was anybody close. He had the respect of the players. He was a gentleman, and he played the type of baseball that was required by his players. When he managed Cleveland, he had power. When he had speed with the White Sox, he won with speed. And he was a great handler of pitchers. I can't think of any negatives on Al Lopez.

— *Bob Shaw*

1958 was my most disappointing year. I had a winning record in '57 and pitched a no-hitter, and the next year I didn't start one ballgame. Early Wynn came over from Cleveland, and he was Lopez' pet, he couldn't do anything wrong. All managers have their pets. But I thought I deserved the chance anyway, after having a winning year the year before. *[After going 10–8 in '57, Keegan started only two games for the White Sox in '58 and pitched 10 games in Triple A. In '59 for Triple A Rochester Keegan completed 15 of 31 starts with an 18–10 record.]*

— *Bob Keegan*

I thought Al Lopez was an outstanding manager when I played with him in 1955. He would be the best of the managers I ever played for, and I played for quite a few.

— *Ralph Kiner*

If I had to pick one manager, I'd say Al Lopez hands down. He knew the game, he was a good strategist, but his real strength was in the way he handled you. When you screwed up he had a way of talking to you without really screaming at you or getting mad. He'd just talk to you, and man, he'd make you want to crawl under the grass.

— *Wally Westlake*

Just watching such a class person as Al Lopez and the way he went about managing the ballclub, just in a really professional way, had a lot to do with the way you produced. You can't take away anything from Al Lopez as far as minuses as a manager. He was plus in all departments of managing, and plus as a human being. He could dictate a ballgame by just looks, just the way he looked at you. He didn't have to say anything to you. He was a quality manager.

— *Ray Boone*

Gene Mauch and I were together at Los Angeles one year *[1955]*. He turned into a really, really good player in the Coast League, and that brought him back to the big leagues. He played a year with the Boston Red Sox. And like he said, he became a good ballplayer after his body gave out on him.

But he did, he was a good ballplayer. *[Mauch had 1,080 minor league hits with a career average of .291. Mauch became a Triple A manager in 1958 and a big league manager in 1960.]*

— *Cal McLish*

Leo Durocher was way ahead of everything. He knew what was going on in the sixth and seventh inning when it was only the third or fourth. And you could talk to him. If a certain hitter was up and you felt you should play him a certain way, you'd tell him and he would do it.

Shotton was a good manager, too. He had meetings before every game and we'd go over the hitters, and he'd always tell stories to kind of loosen you up a little bit.

I played for Charlie Dressen out in the Coast League, and I thought he was the best manager I ever played for. He was sharp, like Leo, and then he always explained his moves after the game. He'd tell why he did this and why he did that. He was a great "I" man. He'd say, "I knew he was going to do this. I knew he could do that." We used to laugh about that.

— *Spider Jorgensen*

The thing I remember most about playing at the Polo Grounds was that Leo Durocher was always throwing a knockdown pitch at you.

— *Del Ennis*

I thought Lou Boudreau was an excellent manager. He was trying to get people to chart pitches and things which nobody did much back in those days. Because I played shortstop and he played shortstop, he helped me a lot. We were bringing in a lot of young guys to play, and some of the older guys who were shunned aside or being made to ride the bench awhile didn't particularly like him. But the younger guys did because he gave us a chance to play.

Mike Higgins was kind of a set guy. Once you made the lineup, you were there. He didn't change it very much.

— *Milt Bolling*

Boudreau was a good manager. Even though I was battling to take his place someday, he was really good to me. As a player-manager he probably missed out on a little camaraderie being with the boys, so to speak. But as a manager you're with your coaches all the time, and not so much running around with the gang.

— *Ray Boone*

Bobby Bragan had some interesting theories. Dale Long got in a hot streak, and he moved him up to leadoff batter. He said, "Okay, in the first inning they can't pitch around him because he's the leadoff batter. That'll at least give him one time they'll have to pitch to him."

He had a very good baseball mind. He would get in trouble public relations-wise, with the owners. In his knowledge of baseball and a creative mind, he was a very good manager.

— *Dick Hall*

Jimmy Dykes was a smart manager. But he was the only manager I ever talked back to. I had a sore arm, even stayed home from a road trip to recuperate. Then one of our pitchers broke a finger and they called me up and asked me if I could pitch. In those days everybody just said, "Yeah." So I flew out to Cleveland and pitched. I got by four innings or so and then I couldn't feel anything in my arm. We came back to Philadelphia and the first night there he put me in the bullpen. I came in to relieve. I got them out but I didn't throw well. Then he said to me, "What's the matter? You got a sore arm?"

That's what a manager said to me after I'd stayed home from a road trip with a sore arm. I won't repeat what I told him, but I went straight to the clubhouse. At the time I didn't care what happened.

— *Carl Scheib*

I used to laugh at Stanky a lot. I thought he was a little psycho or something, He'd go so crazy.

When I came down from the Giants *[in 1956]* — I had broken my finger and sprained the other one — I came down to Minneapolis. He was the manager, and he talked to me when I was out warming up, and I had my finger wrapped. It was on my throwing hand.

He said, "Oh, we got a putty ballplayer again here."

So I got mad and went after him and I told him, "I'll take you and any of these other guys and I'll show you who's a putty ballplayer."

And then he starts laughing and puts his arm around me, "That's what I like to hear."

He was really something else, Stanky was.

— *Bob Lennon*

Eddie Stanky was a good baseball man, but he was a little tough on the young players. He'd get a little too excited. He'd get the young pitchers shook up if they walked a guy. They could see him stomping up and down in the dugout sometimes. Throwing things, if they walked a guy in critical situations. But Stanky knew all the tricks, little things that could maybe win a ballgame for you. He had you work on things like, if the guy was stealing, try to block the catcher's vision with the bat, kind of wave it in front of him like you were going to bunt, then just pull it away. Maybe disrupt his throwing. He'd try to take advantage of the other team's mistakes, or try to do something to disrupt them a little bit.

— *Pete Castiglione*

When I was in the dugout I always watched the hitters hit. That's something Leo Durocher taught me when I first joined the Dodgers. He called me into the dugout one day and I sat right on the steps in front of him. He'd say, "Why is the guy standing up in the box? Why does he stand away? Why's he stand close to the plate?" I learned those things kind of at a young age because of Durocher.

It helped me later on when I realized that I needed to know a hitter's strengths and weaknesses, because I certainly realized that I wasn't going to be a Bob Feller or Bob Gibson, that I had to learn how to put a little sink on the ball, spin it at different speeds, and stuff like that or I would never have made it.

— *Cal McLish*

My favorite manager was Eddie Dyer. He was a pitcher himself *[15–15 in six big league seasons]*, and it seemed like he knew when a pitcher was ready to pitch. He'd always come to you and tell you when you're going to pitch, or ask if you were all right.

— *Max Lanier*

There's not much to tell about when I managed the Browns, except we lost every day. Other than that, it was a pretty miserable year. *[Marion's record after taking over the club in 1952 was 42–61. In 1953 it was 54–100. In two full seasons as White Sox manager in 1955 and 1956, he led them to two third place finishes, going 91–63 and 85–69.]* But unfortunately, if you don't have talent, you can't win. Hornsby was fired because he wasn't winning. If they were winning, Hornsby would still be here. Marion would still be here if they were winning. It's the easiest thing in the world to fire the manager because of fan's assumptions. You can't fire all the players.

I loved managing. I tried to out-figure everybody, I tried to outsmart everybody, all that kind of stuff. But one thing I did not like about managing: you cannot control the destiny of what the other people do. The successful managers are people who have talent on their ballclub. Give me the players, I'll be a great manager.

— *Marty Marion*

I broke in with Lou Boudreau for three years *[1952–1954]*, then I had Higgins for the next five and a half, then I played with Dykes at Detroit. Higgins and Dykes were, I don't say old school, I'm not questioning that they didn't know the game, don't misunderstand, but it was a different style. Lou was a little more upbeat, a little more "with it," if I can just say that, with the young guys coming alone. And he had a little more foresight, knowing that the club was going to evolve to have some of the younger players on the ball club. He had that personality to go with it. In retrospect, I think he might have given me a disservice in one respect. Every year in spring training he had me switch positions. In three different years I started at three different positions at opening day. So it could have been my salvation, the reason why I was able to play over ten years, by being versatile, but maybe I'd have been better off just to focus on one position.

— *Ted Lepcio*

My favorite manager to play for was Joe Gordon when he took over the *[1958]* club in Cleveland. I pitched the last night that Bobby Bragan was the manager, and I got beat 2–1 in the ninth inning on a home run by Ted Williams. Joe Gordon saw the game, and he said, "Well, I don't know, but that guy's pitching for me." And for some reason I responded to him. He left me alone, and we got along great.

— *Cal McLish*

I didn't care much for Durocher. After the Giants won the pennant in 1954, the next spring we played Cleveland in spring training. One night at a big dinner, Durocher was introducing the ballplayers. Of course Bob Lemon was with Cleveland, you know. And

Durocher introduced me as Bob Lemon. That was his little joke. Then he said, "'I'm sorry. I wish he *was* Bob Lemon."

I guess he did. Hell, he was a twenty game winner, right? *[Hall of Famer Lemon was 23–7 in 1954, one of his seven 20-win seasons.]*

— ***Bob Lennon***

I enjoyed Durocher. He was tough, and he got on you. If you made a mistake he let you know about it, but he didn't harp on it. The next day you were in his good graces, he put his arm around you and he'd forget about it. But he wanted to tell you when you made a mistake, that you threw to the wrong base or you didn't cover first base on a ground ball to the first baseman, or you made a bad pitch, or you weren't backing up this. He told you in a loud, rough way. He wanted it to stick.

But as I say, he didn't harp on it anymore. He said his piece and it was all over with. I enjoyed him. He got a lot out of a ballplayer.

His style was completely different from Charlie Grimm's. Charlie Grimm was easy-going, wouldn't raise his voice. Charlie talked to you about mistakes, also. Sometimes attempting bunts, you'd try to beat it out — you tried to drag instead of bunting the man over, sacrificing. You'd try to get a base hit out of it, and Charlie would say something to you about it, but in a nice, easy way. Leo would raise his voice and scream a little bit. He didn't want a base hit, he wanted a sacrifice.

They were completely different in personality, but I liked both of them as managers.

— ***Don Liddle***

My first manager was Charlie Dressen *[in 1956]*. He had been with Brooklyn *[1951–1953]* and got let out there, so I think it was kind of a disappointment for him when he had to come down to Washington, but nevertheless he was full of baseball. Breathed and lived baseball. He was just a real fine fellow and I enjoyed playing for him.

To be truthful, I don't think he ever left Brooklyn. If he was talking to his players in Washington, it was always, "The way we done it in Brooklyn." And his style of baseball, he still believed in the speed and that type of ball, but with Washington we didn't have a whole lot of speed, compared to what the Dodgers had. Just listening to him and some of the stories he'd tell was very interesting.

— ***Herb Plews***

I was pitching a ballgame against Washington *[in 1950 or 1951]*. It was one of these days the conditions were perfect, the weather was great, I felt great. I'm pitching and I can't get anybody out. So the first thing you know I see our coach Eddie Mayo came out to take me out of the ballgame. I told him, "Get the hell out of here, Eddie. I started this game, I'm going to finish it." So he goes back to the dugout and tells Steve O'Neill, "He won't come out of the game."

So first thing you know I see Mayo on the way back to the mound. He says, "Skipper says you don't come out it's going to cost you five hundred dollars." So I threw the ball up in the air and I said, "For five hundred dollars you can have it, I'm leaving."

— ***Mel Parnell***

When I was with the White Sox *[in 1956]*, Paul Richards wanted money from both ends, he wanted to be the field manager, and he wanted to be the general manager, which he was.

Unfortunately, the Chicago White Sox purchased me from the Baltimore Orioles and he called me up into the office, and said, "We bought you because we know that you're a great outfielder, and we want to put you in center field. We know you've played left and right most of the time. But we also know you're a great fielder, so can you play center?"

I said, "I used to play center many, many times. I love center field. I love to run." So we were very happy. And two weeks after that, he called me in the office again and said, "Cal, we just purchased Larry Doby from Cleveland. Now we can only keep one of you two. If you were the owner, Cal, who would you keep?"

I said, "Well, I'll be very frank, very honest." And in all modesty, I say, "I would keep the leadoff man. A leadoff man has a hell of a job. His job is to get on first base. Bunting, walking, getting hit with the ball. Whatever. He's got to be speedy. He's got to be alive, and energetic."

And he agreed with me. He said, "You're absolutely right, one hundred percent. However, the fans would rather see a home run." So he sent me down to the Miami Marlins.
— *Cal Abrams*

Paul Richards was a very intelligent manager. He knew little things that maybe some other manager hadn't stressed, like how to pick up a bunted ball with your bare hands with the ball near your foot rather than use your glove on a close play, just little things like that. That was one thing he taught in spring training, and I thought, "Gee, no one's ever said that." He was a good pitcher's manager 'cause he had a couple of different pitches that he tried to teach you. He knew the game very well.
— *Ernie Johnson*

I beat Boston up in Boston 2–1 and Paul Richards made me go out after the game and run for half an hour; he thought was getting tired. I beat them 2–1. In fact, I don't think Williams got a hit off me that day. Yet I had to go out and run after winning a ballgame. I don't think anybody heard of that before.
— *Bob Keegan*

When I was with Chicago, I was on first base. There was a hit to right. I took off and at third base the coach was hollering, "Come on!" and I went, and they threw me out pretty good. Paul Richards got on me bad.

I said, "Well, Coach hollered 'Come.'"

He said, "Don't pay them damn coaches no attention. They don't know what they're doin' half the time anyhow."
— *Tom Wright*

When I broke in in 1951 for Charlotte, I played for Cal Ermer, who managed the Twins later. He did more for me than anybody. Then in '52 he went to Chattanooga as the Double A manager, and I had the chance to play or him there, and we won the pennant. He did more for me to get to the big leagues than anybody. The communication with him was always great.
— *Bob Oldis*

With the Cubs they had coaches coming and going. It didn't work out too good. One day Glen Hobbie was pitching. They had just changed coaches that day. I went out there to try to settle Glen down. One of the coaches come out and said, "Is anything wrong?"

I said, "Well, he hurt his shoulder."

He said, "Why didn't you tell me?"

I said, "We got so many coaches, I didn't know who to ask."

He laughed and said, "Well, you got a point there."

— Sammy Taylor

I played for Steve O'Neill at Philadelphia *[in 1953]*. He was a saint. He was like a father to me 'cause he was probably old at that time, like in his fifties, an old guy to a 19-year-old kid. And he really liked me, and he kind of took me under his wing, and I will always be grateful to him. I used to have a penchant for using bad language at times. And I remember one night at Pittsburgh him taking me to the side of the dugout and—I used a particularly offensive word yelling at Frank Dascoli, the umpire at first base—and Steve said, "Geez, Ted, call him anything, but don't call him that."

— Ted Kazanski

You couldn't help but like the Ralph Houk. His leadership and everything, you just wanted to do so well for him. He treated everybody the same, and he was just good with everybody. He made you feel like you were part of the team, and just seemed to bring out the best in you. That's what a good manager will do. I was just fortunate to play for him, and I know when he went up to the Yankees all those players felt the same way about him.

— Herb Plews

It's nice when a manager has confidence in you. With the Cubs, Charlie Grimm was one of their "roving managers." I remember Opening Day in Los Angeles. I struck out four times against Don Drysdale, and he came over to my locker and said, "You're in there tomorrow."

And the next day against Newcombe I hit two home runs to win the ballgame for the Cubs.

— Frank Thomas

Rocky Marciano and I were good friends. We went out for lunch one day. It was time for me to get to the ballpark, and Rocky said, "Do you think they'd let me catch batting practice?" and I said, "Sure, Rocky, I think they'd be happy to have you."

So we get to the ballpark—Steve O'Neill was our manager at the time—and I take him into see Steve. I introduced Steve to Rocky. He was all excited to meet Rocky, and then I asked Steve, "Steve, do you mind if he catches batting practice?"

Steve just looked at me and said, "Not a chance in hell, pal."

I said, "What do you mean? He's capable. He can handle himself well enough."

Steve said, "No. Do you realize if he gets a broken hand or broken finger or something? You and I would be run right out of town."

He had a point, I didn't even think of that.

— Mel Parnell

Walter Alston was my manager my entire time with the Dodgers. When you're younger you look for a little pat on the back. And you didn't get it from him. He's not a Lasorda who runs around and hugs everybody. Alston would say things in the paper like, "He's doing a good job" or "He's my outstanding pitcher" or "He's my hitter," but he wouldn't say it in person. It didn't seem like he gave me enough accolades. But he actually treated you like professionals. You know, you're getting paid to do the job. I think that originated from the Brooklyn club he managed. All those guys knew their role, and they went out and did it.

— *Larry Sherry*

When I was growing up, the Cardinals were my favorite team and Marty Marion was my idol. And then *[in 1953]* he was my first major league manager. I told him that and said, "Marty, I'd appreciate anything that you can tell me about playing shortstop."

He said, "Bill, you play shortstop altogether differently than I played it. But I have no qualms about the way you play it. You play it more like Pee Wee Reese than Marty Marion."

— *Billy Hunter*

Aside from Marion and Stengel, other managers I had were Bobby Bragan, Jimmy Dykes, Lou Boudreau, Harry Craft, and Joe Gordon. So I had some pretty talented people trying to teach us the game.

— *Billy Hunter*

Chapter Six

Joe and Mickey, Ted and Stan

Joe and Mickey, Ted and Stan. No last names needed. Almost all who played with them or against them speak of those men in terms that seem almost to border on hyperbole. Those of us who were not there to share their playing fields can take delight that their magnificence has been captured by those who were. Taking the field once again are four of the era's brightest lights: Joe and Mickey, Ted and Stan.

What wonderful memories I have of the '50s — Mantle's speed and power, Williams' awesomeness at the plate, DiMaggio's grace and professionalism. I feel fortunate to have played "when it was a game.'"

— *Jim Dyck*

Joe DiMaggio could play that field with such grace and smoothness. He made plays look so easy that other guys were diving for the ball and stumbling over, and here comes DiMaggio gliding under that ball like he was poetry. One of our managers in the minors said that he thought DiMaggio might have gone to ballet school or something because he was so smooth.

— *Jim Greengrass*

Just playing against Joe DiMaggio was something. He had that bad heel one year. He was playing center field, and I know he wasn't full speed. I got a base hit right through the box toward him, and when I rounded first base, I saw he wasn't getting to the ball like he usually did, so I just kept on going. He looked up and he saw me, and I just made it to second base. He almost got me.

So when the inning was over, as I was going to right field and he was coming across toward his dugout, he said, "You'll never do that again, you little Dago." And he laughed. We're both Italian, you know.

But that stands out, because Joe was a real quiet person.

— *Al Zarilla*

DiMaggio was the catalyst for that whole Yankee ballclub. He was a living example; he didn't have to tell you anything. We were playing a doubleheader in Washington in 1950, and it was always hot there. Joe D was ailing; he had a bad ankle. He played the first game in center field, and Casey decided to play him at first base in the second game so he wouldn't have to do too much, and I came in to relieve late in the game. Somebody hit a swinging bunt down the first-base line. I was kind of indecisive about it. I fielded it and threw the ball into the runner just as Joe got to the bag. He could have got killed.

I thought to myself, "Boy, if I put Joe out of action, they'll send me out to Podunk."

But he survived. After the game, he told Stengel, "That's the last time I'm playing first base." He went back to the outfield. *[In his 13-year career, he played 1,721 games in the outfield, one game at first base.]*

Joe was a great model. He did everything to perfection. He exerted himself. When he left home plate on a base hit in the gap, he knew just what base he was going to end up at. Even with his bone spur on his heel, he forced himself to get to that point. He led by example, and he just had to give some of the guys a look once in awhile, that were dragging the wagon. They got the message.

— Tom Ferrick

My first trip to Yankee Stadium with Cleveland, I was playing catch with Hank Majeski before the game and I'm kind of in awe of the stadium. The Yankees were taking batting practice, and all of a sudden this roar goes up. Of course I look around, wondering what happened. Hank walked over to me and said, "Joe D just came out of the dugout."

Then he proceeded to tell me that Joe DiMaggio always stayed in the dugout when the regulars started hitting, and if he was third that day, as soon as the second man went in to hit, well, the crowd knew that Joe D would come out of the dugout, and as soon as they saw that Yankee hat, this roar went up.

I thought, "Man, that's pretty good."

He had that kind of charisma about him.

— Ray Boone

My first time against Mantle was in Shibe Park, and he rattled the seats up in there in left field.

All we heard was how he was supposed to take DiMaggio's place, and he was terrible out there. He could hardly catch a fly ball. He swung real hard at a ball, and when he hit it, he hit it a long ways, but he didn't hit too many at that time.

Of course, he sure developed into a good one. He learned how to play the outfield. *[Mantle had played shortstop in his two minor league seasons. In his first two years in the major leagues, 1951 and '52, his fielding averages as an outfielder were .959 and. 963; his lifetime fielding average was .985.]*

— Carl Scheib

Mickey Mantle was a tremendous talent; he made me lots of money. He was hurting all the time, bandaged. When he first came up he was very naive, as we all were, coming from a small town and having to deal with the pressures of coming in and trying to replace Joe DiMaggio, and then having all the pressure of his leg problems.

He was absolutely awesome, left-handed, right-handed. I would put him against anybody.

— Andy Carey

I hit a triple over Mantle's head and I tell people he was playing right behind second base on me. He was beautiful to watch, left-handed, right-handed. With two strikes on him you couldn't play him. You played him deep so he don't kill you, then he'd bunt the ball on you.

— *Bobby Malkmus*

In 1956, when Mantle had his great Triple Crown year, he actually made our ballpark in Detroit look like a Little League park. I think he hit eleven home runs in Detroit, and each one further than the one before. When somebody would join your ballclub in July, you'd say, "You see that row? Mantle hit one off of Foytack. And you see up there in deep right center? Count the rows, two from the top and three over from there. He hit one off of Bunning up there."

He actually hit a ball into dead center field — and this is hard to believe, but ask Bob Miller about it — Mantle hit a line drive off Miller, a left-hander. Miller thinks it ticked an ear. The ball went in the upper deck in Detroit. Four hundred and forty feet to the base of the fence. We're talking 440 plus the height. Miller walked to the back of the mound, threw up, and walked off the field, met the manager halfway who was coming to get him anyway. But the manager didn't need to bother coming out 'cause Miller was gone. He wasn't pitching any more that day.

The man was just the strongest, for his size, the fastest, who ever played. He'd strike out three or four times in a row, but then he'd beat out a bunt and the next time up would hit one downtown. You know, that's a baseball expression, meaning a home run. Well, when Mantle hit one downtown, it went downtown.

— *J.W. Porter*

I just wish people would have seen Mantle healthy. People do not realize how unhealthy he was with that osteomyelitis in one of his legs. I know he was hurting. I used to see him be wrapped up from ankle to thigh, all the way up his leg. And to steal thirty bases without trying. He was just tremendous. It's just a shame. I would loved to have seen what he could have done all healthy.

— *Jim Landis*

Mickey Mantle hit his first home run off me. I think it was in May, 1951. I didn't know this until after I was done playing. Somebody told me this and I said, "Well, I wasn't aware of that. I mean, I've had so many hit off me that one more didn't make much difference." I can still see it, though, as if it was yesterday, that ball he hit. I didn't know who he was, and I threw him a screwball and I got it up a little and he hit it into the center field visiting bullpen in Comiskey Park. I think if they hadn't torn it down it would still be rattling around in there.

— *Randy Gumpert*

It was amazing to see Mantle come up one time and hit a home run left handed and then maybe later on in the game hit one out from the right-handed side. And then he could lay down a bunt and beat it out. You just couldn't get over the stuff he could do.

— *Herb Plews*

Dick Tettebach, who saw brief duty with the Yankees and Senators (and who was a teammate of former President George Bush at Yale), gives this tongue-in-cheek account of his duel with Mickey Mantle for the American League home run title:

I was brought up too soon, unfortunately. I came up with the Yankees at the end of the '55 season and had five official at-bats with no hits. I say "unfortunately" because over the winter I was traded to Washington — then the following occurred:

Baseball's Opening Day, 1956 — with Eisenhower and Nixon in attendance, I started in left field for the Senators. In the first, Mantle hit one of his moon rockets to dead center (about 550 feet) over everything. In the bottom of the first, after Eddie Yost made out, I hoisted one over the left field fence off Don Larsen to tie the game 1–1 in my first at-bat for the Senators. Imagine the thrill if I hadn't had those five at-bats in 1955. But the biggest thrill was that until Mickey hit another homer in the 5th inning I was tied for the major league lead in homers, RBI, and runs scored — with the great Mantle — in his Triple crown year, yet! Mickey out-homered me that year 52–1, but there was a moment — one brief glorious moment — when a share of that Triple crown was mine.

— *Dick Tettelbach*

I played against Mantle and some of the Yankee greats. I played against Bobby Richardson and Kubek and fellows like that. And Ted Williams. I was able to throw Ted Williams out a couple of times from deep short right field. I tell people that for every time I'd throw him out he'd hit three or four balls go whizzing by me for hits. So we didn't have really any advantage playing the shift on him, except that we didn't get killed. Playing a regular second base we would have got killed.

— *Bobby Malkmus*

The best hitter I ever saw was Ted Williams. Bar none. I wasn't in the National League when Musial was there, but I pitched against Ted for two or three years before he retired, and he was just the ultimate, the ultimate.

— *Milt Pappas*

Fenway Park was unusual. It wasn't easy playing left field there. That wall was right on top of you. You could run into it with two steps, and the foul line was right against the wall, and cripes, you could go crazy out there chasing balls.

It wasn't easy, that's why I admired Ted Williams in that park. He never got credit for playing left field, and he played the hell out of it. He was the best.

— *Gene Woodling*

Ted Williams was a very underrated outfielder. He was a big, tall gangly looking type guy and didn't look graceful. But Ted moved around very well, and he could play that left-field wall better than anybody around.

— *Mel Parnell*

Ted gave a lot of advice on hitting. He obviously thought we should be better hitters than we ended up. Many times he'd get really p.o.'ed at me because I was fairly strong and I should be doing a lot more, be more patient. He was always reminding us about being patient. You know, let the pitcher work more than we were letting the opposing pitcher do. We were a little too anxious up there. He was always a constant reminder of that stuff. But he was great to be with, really and truly.

— *Ted Lepcio*

In one game Ted Williams hit three home runs against me and we wound up losing 4–0. I know at the time all the sportswriters were wondering why Lopez didn't take me out. Well, they weren't hitting me. Hey, they only got only four runs off me. I think Williams drove in all four runs.

And I was stubborn enough to where I wasn't going to walk him. I didn't pitch too smart to him. I thought I could throw fastballs and sliders, I guess, and get him out. I had done that before. He hadn't hit me too good before. So he hit one to left field, one to center, and one to right. Actually I pitched a pretty good ballgame.

— *Bob Keegan*

One day Williams popped up, came back in and took the water cooler off the wall and threw it on the floor. About a week later Piersall strikes out or pops up. He comes in and grabs the same water cooler. He can't budge it. Williams says, "You want me to get it off the wall for you, son?" He grabs it and throws it on the floor. That shows you how strong he was.

— *Don Buddin*

They say Ted Williams was very controversial, couldn't get along with the press. To tell you the truth, sometimes the press is unfair. All the things I heard about Ted Williams when I played was great. He talked hitting with players. The first time I saw him, I was with Washington. We were in Fenway Park and we were loosening up our arms. All of a sudden Ted Williams steps in the batting cage and starts swinging, and everybody stops and watches him for the five minutes or eight minutes he swung there. He was awesome to watch.

— *Bobby Malkmus*

Pedro Ramos struck out Ted Williams, so he threw the ball over to his dugout and told them to save the ball for him. After the game he comes strutting into our clubhouse and he goes over to Williams and asks if he'd sign the ball. So Williams naturally didn't want to sign a ball he struck out on. He's giving Pedro a rough time, and you can see tears coming out of Pedro's eyes. He wanted that ball signed by all means.

After awhile Williams felt bad for him, so he said, "I'll sign it." So he signed it. Pedro goes out smiling from ear to ear. Happy as a lark, he got what he wanted. So the next time he pitches against Ted, Ted hits one halfway up the bleachers in right field and he hollers to Pedro, "You find that son-of-a-bitch, I'll sign it too."

— *Mel Parnell*

I remember in spring training we always used to come North with the Red Sox. You'd leave Clearwater, and they'd leave Sarasota on the train, and we'd stop at these different places and get off and play an exhibition game, all the way up North. All the places we stopped, all the places would be packed. Everybody's there to see Ted Williams. And naturally, when he took batting practice, he would take up most of the batting time, and everybody would just watch him And the people would go crazy.

There we were, playing in some jerkwater towns, and snowing in some places, and people coming out, still cold, and there's Ted Williams, you know, hitting balls all over the place.

— *Ted Kazanski*

I was at Jacksonville. That was the Sally League then. On their way north the Red Sox would stop and play us a game. And I was playing center field. They were beating us about 6–2 or something like that, and Ted Williams came up toward the end of the game and I said to myself, "Gee, I'd like to see him hit one," and boy, he hit one way out.

I was happy to see him hit it. It didn't matter to us, but that's what everybody came to see.

— *Bob Lennon*

When I played with Ted Williams, if they called me to pinch hit he'd run over there and get his best bat and he'd hand that thing to me and he'd try to tell me what that pitcher throws, he helped me that way, a guy I'd never seen before.

He'd say, "Now he'll bring his slider, you got to pick up on it. He throws a fastball you'll hit to left field hard." Just things like that, just to give you a hint what you're going to see when you get up there. 'Cause when you don't play pretty regular in the major leagues you never get to see the same guy many times, so you're just like hitting at a brand new pitcher every time you go up there.

— *Tom Wright*

The greatest hitter I ever faced is Ted Williams, without question. I remember when I first came up and Boston came into town, I sat there in the dugout when everyone went up and watched him hit batting practice. He hit a line drive to left, a line drive to center, a line drive to right, then he hit about ten out of twelve for home runs. That was batting practice. He loved to hit in Detroit. The trouble was that he wasn't going to swing at a bad ball. So you've really got a problem. If you put it over, he can really hurt you badly. And yet he's not going to be enticed to swing at a bad pitch. I mean, he was just the toughest, or the best all-around hitter that I've ever seen.

— *Bob Shaw*

Ted was something to watch, I tell you. He was a master. What the players respected so much were his work habits. My gosh, the guy was out here hitting and trying to be better all the time. And that's the reason for his greatness. He worked at it so, and he was always willing to help other guys.

— *Boo Ferriss*

Ted thought that playing in Fenway Park he saw very little left-handed pitching because everybody coming in would throw right-handers against us, so he would ask Maury McDermott and me to throw batting practice to him, and we would. We'd throw to him under game conditions. By that we wouldn't tell him what we were going to throw.

I thought that worked to my advantage as well as his. I'm trying to figure him out and he's trying to figure me out, so it was good work for both of us.

Everybody says Ted had god-given ability. Probably he did, but he worked at it to master it. He was always doing something. He had hand grippers all the time that he was strengthening his wrists with. He had a bone in the clubhouse by the bat rack that he used to bone-rub his bat to make his bat harder. He worked at it.

Ted was the most perfect man I've ever seen. Anything he encountered he stuck with it to perfection. Such as fishing. You could go to a fishing supply store and buy all the lures you want. He wouldn't do that, he made his own. He could make them better than what he could buy. He was just a master of anything he encountered. And the stories of him in the Marines while flying with John Glenn are just unbelievable.

— *Mel Parnell*

Ted was great to play with. I loved it. I had my locker right next to his in spring training. That was a thrill for me. If you asked him for help, he'd give it to you. He didn't volunteer help, but if you asked him he'd sit down and talk to you.

— *Don Buddin*

My first [full] year up [1956], I'd just struck out 13 [against Cleveland] and [shut out] the Yankees. Then we go into Boston and I'm the starting pitcher in Fenway. Ted Williams was running to left field, and he made a comment to me. He said, "You're the kid with the good curveball, I hear, huh?"

And that was it. Ted Williams spoke to me. I was with the Orioles at the time. Our second baseman, Billy Gardner, was playing short right field. I threw Ted a curveball, and he stood there motionless. Strike one. Second one, I threw a curveball over the plate. Motionless again. So I said to myself, "Man, I can get this guy." Well, the third one I threw, he hit so hard that the force of the ball knocked Billy Gardner over in short right field. Billy caught a snow cone. As Ted rounded first base, he spat into the air and said, "Kid, you can take your curveball and shove it."

It was a very humbling experience. And the thing that impressed me about him was the fact that when he swung at a ball, he hit it. And when he took a ball, there was no lunging, no movement at all. It was awesome. And the umpires would never call him out on a third strike. They'd only call a third strike on Ted Williams if he dropped the bat and walked away.

— *Don Ferrarese*

The greatest hitter is Ted Williams, there's no doubt about that. Period. When Ted used to talk on hitting, he would mesmerize me. He would put me in a trance just to watch him hit.

When we put in the shift against him, I'd come over from third base and play almost behind second. The shortstop would play second, and the second baseman would go play short right field. There were several balls that the short right fielder or the shortstop or the second baseman would pick up and throw Ted out at first. He reacted like he always did, just nonchalant about it, just go about his business. Of course, I've always said it would be nice to not worry about that base hit because you know you're going to get one next time up.

— *Ray Boone*

We had a doubleheader scheduled in Boston. We had to be in uniform and ready to go on the field at eleven o'clock. In the meantime Boston is taking batting practice from ten to eleven. I would say seventy-five percent of us would be in uniform, dressed, on the field watching Williams take batting practice by ten o'clock. We would go an hour early just to watch his swing. It was something else to watch that guy hit. He just had that fluid, powerful motion. It just seemed like every ounce of his body got into the swing. It was just so rhythmic and flowing, kind of like watching Joe DiMaggio play outfield.

— *Jim Dyck*

Ted beat me in a ball game one night in Philadelphia in the 10th inning. Piersall was on first with two outs and I had three-and-two on him and he hit one on the fists, and you know they played him to right field — and he hit the ball and it hit the dirt at third base. One of them dying quails, I call them. It spun out back of third base. It hit the dirt, it didn't go nowhere, but everybody played him to pull and he ended up on second. Piersall scored.

Of course, I was mad. I walked out toward second base and he told me that I threw the ball by him.

I said, "If I can throw the ball by you I'll turn around and walk off, I ain't got no more to say."

— *Sonny Dixon*

Ted and I would ride together on the train some and a lot of times the train would stop for thirty or forty minutes. He knew where all the ice cream shops were right close to the train station, and he'd invite me to go get an ice cream cone with him. On one occasion we stopped like that and he told me before we got in there, "Kid, some young sports writer wants to interview me up here when we stop over. I'll stop and talk to him."

I followed. The first thing that kid said to him was, "Ted, give me something sensational."

Ted said, "Sensational, my ass," and turned and walked back to the train. He wouldn't talk to him.

He said, "What'd he expect me to tell him, I was going to hit two or three home runs today?"

The kid just approached him wrong. Ted was sort of uptight a lot anyhow.

— *Tom Wright*

Ted Williams' hand-eye coordination was just unbelievable. He'd hit balls so hard. And he could hit to left field when he wanted to. Once in a while he'd just say, "Look, I'm going to hit one out there to show them I can do it."

And then he'd say, "Ah, the hell with it. That's what they want me to do. I'll just hit it through 'em, or over 'em." And he would.

— *Milt Bolling*

I think all around, Ted Williams was the best overall hitter during my era. I enjoyed pitching to him. I think I had pretty good success with him, but I was awfully wild. My last three or four years I threw him a lot of junk, and then I could show him the fastball, but I wanted to make him hit the breaking stuff if I could. But actually, I just tried to worry the hell out of him. I wouldn't throw it when he wanted me to throw it. I'd talk to him. I'd let him wait, and he'd get the red-ass. But anything to disrupt his thinking was my plan of attack. The guy was really a clever hitter, and he was well honed in on that ball. I just felt like if I could aggravate him a little bit and let him see the ball but not too close to where he wanted it, or where he could hurt me the most.

— *Tommy Byrne*

I'll never forget a sportswriter telling me: "You know, Ted Williams hadn't spoken to me in about five years and it's the last game of the season. So I'm down in the dugout before the game, and Ted's the only player in the dugout — the rest of them are in the clubhouse —

and Ted looked at me and said, 'Well, another season's about to end.' I couldn't believe he'd spoken to me, you know. And I said, 'Yeah, I guess it is.' Ted said, 'I hope you have a good winter. I hope you freeze your ass off.'"

That's just the kind of man he was, you know. But Lord, I used to go out to the ballpark there at Fenway Park early, just to watch him hit. He'd hit for an hour. And the thing he'd do — we'd always pull that shift on him, we'd have the whole infield on the right side. He didn't care. He'd try to hit right through that shift. And he would.

— *Gail Harris*

Naturally, Ted Williams was tough for everybody because he hit .370 every year. We used a shift on him and he still hit his .370. I got Williams out as good as anybody, but still it wasn't good enough. I always tried to keep the ball away from him, but that was kind of dangerous because if he'd come back through the middle of the box he'd take your head off. I'd change speeds on him, but he'd always get his hits. There was only one guy like him. He had the good eyes, the good reflexes, but that didn't come by accident, he worked at it. Even as great as he was, he used to come out to the batting circle and he never took his eye off that pitcher and he'd be at the ballpark three hours before anybody else taking batting practice even when he was hitting .350. He was the greatest hitter I ever saw.

— *Bob Kuzava*

When they used to hit fly balls to Ted Williams and me in practice, Ted and I would throw and try to hit the rubber on the top of the mound. We'd play for Cokes. If I beat him I'd go mark up Cokes on the board.

He came to me one day and said, "Kid, you marking up Cokes on me."

I said, "You bet I am. I beat you, didn't I?"

He said, "Yeah, but I don't mark them up when I beat you."

I said, "That's your problem."

— *Tom Wright*

Ted Williams was more a student of hitting than DiMaggio. But he didn't run well, he just had a mediocre arm. His fielding was acceptable, but nothing great. His bat was the thing that was outstanding. When I pitched to him, I just hoped to keep the ball in the ballpark. I remember one day with the White Sox, I was pitching in Fenway. We had a little outfielder by the name of Herbie Adams playing right field. Williams got hold of one of my pitches, and he always hit that real high, lofted fly ball, and Herbie Adams was playing where he always played for Williams, which was about fifteen feet in front of the fence. He started to back up and the ball kept going and kept going and kept going, and Herbie backed into the fence. They had to carry him off the field, and the ball that Williams hit went over the bullpen and into the bleachers. When Williams elevated the ball that way, he could really, really hit it.

— *Randy Gumpert*

Ted Williams' swing and his eye and temperament to hit the ball was just outstanding, and believe it or not, I remember one time in the White Sox ballpark, a couple of them I thought I had a shot at catching the ball at first and that spin on the ball, how he'd hit it and the spin would just all of a sudden make the balls take off and be home runs.

— *Jim Landis*

Williams was incessantly talking. He was a constant talker, always within the game frame, though. He was always talking about the pitcher that we were facing, or how guys are playing defense against us, and it was all part of the game.

— *Ted Lepcio*

You would try to neutralize Williams in Yankee Stadium, because they had right-handed hitters, so you would pitch around him. When you came to Yankee Stadium the right-handed hitters were neutralized; they just couldn't perform. If they were pull hitters or straight-away hitters, they had problems. Our pitchers knew how to pitch there and we knew how to defense them.

— *Charlie Silvera*

If Ted Williams was looking for a pitch and he got it, he'd rip it hard someplace. And he couldn't understand how anybody else that got a pitch they're looking for would foul it off or miss it.

He couldn't understand it. He'd say, "How could you do that'?"

And you'd say, "Ted, I wasn't trying to foul it off. I was really trying to hit it."

You know, he couldn't understand it. He'd cuss at you. He'd say, "How could you — that was your pitch. Were you looking for a fastball'?"

"Yeah."

"But you fouled it off."

"Yeah, I know."

If he'd been looking for the same pitch, he'd of tattooed it hard someplace. He was blessed, and he didn't realize it.

— *Milt Bolling*

I always had pretty good luck with Ted Williams. The three years I played against him I think he only got three hits off me. One was a home run. Then he hit one back through the box on me at Boston, like a shot, and I told him I didn't care how many or how far but for Gods' sake, don't hit it back through the box.

— *Sonny Dixon*

"Get a bat, Carroll, you are the hitter." That's what Mike Higgins, manager Boston Red Sox said to me during a game in late August, 1960. I promptly got a bat and went to the plate against Skinny Brown of the Baltimore Orioles as a pinch hitter for Ted Williams. I hit into a double play to end the inning, then grabbed my glove and went to left field.

Ted had fouled a pitch and it hit his instep so hard he had to leave the game. Nobody thought much about it at the time, but that turned out to be the only time anyone ever pinch hit for Ted Williams. Thus the answer to a baseball trivia question: "Who's the only man to ever pinch hit for Ted Williams?" is "Carroll Hardy."

— *Carroll Hardy*

I probably saw as much of Musial as I did Williams, although I was in awe of Williams, maybe a little more so than Musial or even Mays, really, with the bat, because the players used to come out during batting practice and stand in the dugout just to watch Williams take batting practice. I thought, "What's going on here?"

And then I said, "Jesus, I can see why. They're probably looking at the greatest hitter ever."

— *Wayne Terwilliger*

[Musial hit 475 home runs without ever leading the league in home runs. He led the league in triples five times, doubles eight times, hits six times, slugging average six times, batting average seven times, runs scored five times, RBI two times, walks once. His career batting average was .331 and he had 3630 hits.]

The best player I ever played with was Stan Musial. He showed up every game and played it like a professional. He hit like a professional. Whoever named him Stan the Man, they said it right. He was just a great person.

— *Wally Westlake*

The first time I faced Musial *[May 2, 1956]*, I was brought in from the bullpen with two on and two out. An error loaded the bases for Musial. The catcher came out and said, "Well, what do you want to do?" I said, "He's never seen me pitch before. I'm going to throw him a slider and try to get ahead of him. Then I'll try to do something from there." I threw him a slider about chest high and he picked up that leg, like he always did, and hit it clear out of Missouri. But it was a thrill to get to pitch against Musial, and I did pitch against him several times after that and had as good luck I guess with him as everybody else did — the guy hits off of everybody.

— *Jack McMahan*

Musial took what you gave him. I saw him hit five home runs in a doubleheader in Sportsman's Park one Sunday, all off left-handed pitching. He hit three off of Antonelli, and two off of John McCall, and — my Lord a mercy, he was just something else, but you know, if you shifted on Musial he'd pop a ball to left for a double. He was just a good, good hitter.

— *Gail Harris*

The Cardinals had just finished batting practice, so they had time to take a couple more swings. They said, "All right, two swings everybody." Musial stayed in the cage for a couple extra swings, so this rookie they had said, "Hey, Stan, you've already had your two swings."

Slaughter picked this rookie up and put him up against the back of the cage and said, "Just shut your mouth. That could be the World Series right there hitting."

— *Gail Harris*

I faced Stan Musial so many times and had good success at times and not so good success other times. One time I struck him out with the bases loaded in St. Louis. Another time I pitched 13 innings and he beat me with a 2-run homer. He's always going to get his hits. You just try to keep him from beating you in a ballgame, and he did that, and that's why he was such a great hitter. He could wait so long on the ball. And he was a smart hitter. If he'd crank up for the home run, he could get it. Or he'd just hit the ball on the ground and hit it in the hole or through the middle.

— *Bob Friend*

Musial gave me the greatest compliment I could ever had. When I was traded to the Cardinals, I lockered right next to Musial. He came over that first day and said, "Now I don't have to face that curveball of yours." Probably the greatest compliment I was ever given, for a hitter that good to tell me that my curveball worried him a little bit. I won't say worried him, but it gave him a little trouble or he wouldn't have said anything. That really made me feel good.

— *Don Liddle*

I had a no-hitter six and two-third innings, I was ahead 3–0 in Chicago one Saturday. A man got on right before Musial. I went 3 and 0 on Musial. He hit it on Waveland Avenue. The next day he walks up to me and says, "Lefthander, that was an awful thing I did to you yesterday, wasn't it? That's the reason they pay me fifty thousand dollars a year."

So help me, God, that's what he told me. And you know, if he was playing now, what he and Augie Busch and he would call each other? Partner. That's how good he was. And I played against him when he was getting up in age.

— *Taylor Phillips*

Preacher Roe has been known to throw a spitball once in awhile, and everybody on the club knew how he got it, but the umpire didn't know how he got it. So it was fun watching him work. I enjoyed watching him pitch against Stan Musial. He'd always throw three straight balls, more or less intentionally. He liked to work three balls and no strikes on Musial because — I don't know, Musial was always looking for something else when he was that far ahead. Preacher would always get him three two and then he'd throw him that wet one. Musial would know it was coming but he'd pop it up or something.

— *Bobby Morgan*

What a terrific player Musial was. Stan was a very nice guy, too. Very humble. Really down to earth. I mean, he never tried to act like the big shot, or anything. A tremendous hitter, one of the best hitters I've ever seen, really. He very seldom got fooled. He had an uncanny eye. Very hard to strike out. Even his outs were usually hit right on the nose. A very unorthodox looking hitter, he would lunge and hit off his front foot a lot, but still, he done the job, and that's what they always said, "Form don't mean nothing if you can do the job." That's what counts. That's what they pay off on.

They played Musial straightaway, because he'd hit all over. He'd hit balls down the left field line. Just as apt to pull one over the first baseman's head, that's the type of hitter he was. He went with the ball, mostly a line drive hitter, although he had power too. *[Musial hit over 30 home runs six times. He struck out once in roughly every eighteen plate appearances.]*

— *Pete Castiglione*

Mr. Musial competed with me as if I were Cy Young. I could get two quick strikes on Stan Musial. I could throw the ball where I wanted to, and I did, and it became evident that he wasn't going to go fishing on my next two pitches. And I was sitting there two and two on him, after I started out with two strikes. I'd think, "I'm not going any further with you, Stan, you're going to have to hit the ball in the hole somewhere to get a base hit."

And he did, about fifteen straight times. I tell people I could get Stan Musial out. He got fifteen straight hits off me, and I got him out the sixteenth time. And he had fun hitting against me, because he commented to me about it later. He said, "Red, why don't you come back in the National League? I need somebody I can get some hits off of."

I said, "Yep, if I was there, you'd still have to fight me to three and two before you got a hit off me."

That's the kind of camaraderie that I enjoyed.

— *Red Murff*

We was playing St. Louis one time. We *[the Cubs]* had them 2–1 going into the top of the ninth. We had *[Stan Musial]* 3–2; Moe Drabowski was pitching. He threw a curveball on the outside corner and Stan Musial hit it down the third base line for a double. Two runs scored and they went ahead 3 to 2. I was all disgusted and everything, and everybody was running out there getting the ball and trying to give him the ball, and I told him — didn't know history was being made, see — and I told him, "You need to get this game back in control. We need to get started playing ball."

He says, "Man, you know what's happening?"

I said, "I sure don't, and I could care less."

He said, "Stan Musial just got his three thousandth base hit."

I said, "Oh, my gosh."

I think I was catching when Musial got his four hundredth home run, too. I told him once, "If you don't make the Hall of Fame, it ain't my fault." *[Musial's 3,000th hit came on May 13, 1958, his 400th home run on May 7, 1959; Taylor caught both games for the Cubs.]*

— *Sammy Taylor*

CHAPTER SEVEN

The First Time

The first day in the big leagues. The first at bat. The first shutout. The first home run. No matter how long one plays and no matter how much success one has, those first moments tend to be etched more clearly in a player's memory. "Hey, this is me! I'm here! I made it!" No matter how high the plateau the player might reach, few things can ever match the thrill of the fulfillment of that lifelong dream. And every first that's achieved after that fulfills one more dream.

The day I broke into the Majors — late June of 1953 — Wrigley Field in Chicago, nineteen years old — just up from Baltimore — and scared to death.

I was lead-off man in the lineup. Pitching for the Cubs was Howie Pollet and catching, Joe Garagiola. Kiner and Sauer in the outfield — guys I had only read about, and now we were playing on the same field.

It was a beautiful, sunny June day, and I can still see the beautiful ivy on the outfield walls and smell the cigar smoke, and hear the sounds that make a ballpark special.

Pat Piper was the P.A. announcer — a little guy in a Panama hat, who sat on a stool right on the field against the backstop. As he announced, "Number seven for the Phillies," I walked into the batter's box on legs of Jell-o. Here it was the culmination of a life-long dream — "I'm in the Majors" — and proceeded to strike out on three pitches! Welcome to the Majors! The rest of the day, however, was great. We won the game and I did manage to help by getting three hits.

I used to love to go to the ballpark. We'd go out four or five hours before the game, strip down to our shorts, get a chew of tobacco, light up a nice cigar and have a great time just talking and fooling around like a bunch of kids, which I guess we were.
— *Ted Kazanski*

The first time I knew I wanted to be a ballplayer was the first time I saw a ball bounce.
— *Taylor Phillips*

I recall many moments working my way up in the minors, pushing aside failures and mistakes with this one burning desire to one day be pitching in the big show. It took me seven years (two out for the military) of hard work and dedication and love for the game, and the day I put on that Boston Red Sox uniform I felt joy too hard to explain.

I especially wanted to do well that first game. I wanted to say thank you to so many people who had helped me to get there. I wanted to make my family proud. I wished my parents would have been around, but they had passed away prior to me getting there.

Nevertheless, I made my first big league start in 1959 against the Washington Senators and had the day kids dream about. I beat them 7–3, struck out 8, and hit a 3-run home run. Wow!

— Jerry Casale

I won my first big league ballgame on my twenty-first birthday *[August 29, 1951]*. I beat the Chicago Cubs 3–1. Chuck Connors, the Rifleman, hit a triple off me in the top of the ninth inning and ruined my shutout. *[It was Connors' only big league triple.]*

— Dave Cole

The first time I ever pitched in the major leagues was with the Red Sox in 1951. We were at Yankee Stadium. I walked in from the bullpen. They had Johnny Mize on first base. DiMaggio in the outfield. Mantle's there. Yogi Berra's catching. Rizzuto's out at shortstop. Man, I was about halfway nervous, and I shut them out for three straight innings. I felt good about that.

— Ben Flowers

I was with the Dodgers at the start of the 1958 season. I stuck around for a month, pitched about four innings and couldn't get anybody out, so they sent me down. I got a second chance in July of 1959. They brought me up because they had doubleheaders back-to-back, on the 4th and 5th of July, and Podres had hurt his back and they needed a starting pitcher.

I remember picking up the paper with my wife and going over the Chicago Cub lineup — Ernie Banks, Alvin Dark, Moose Moryn — and trying to see how to pitch to these guys. That was my first stab back at it in Chicago. I lost the game 2–1 on two unearned runs. Someone missed a fly ball and someone made an error that let in two runs. That was my first game back. But I pitched well. I thought, here's the second chance at the brass ring, so to speak. I was determined not to go back to the minor leagues.

— Larry Sherry

I played in the big leagues for eleven years, hit some home runs and drove in runs, yet the at-bat I remember most was my very first one, back in 1952.

Teams were allowed to carry 28 ballplayers during the first month of the season. I was one of those extra three, sent down but brought back up when Dropo was traded to Detroit. I pinch hit in Washington against one of their Latin American pitchers. They had several back then — Marrero, Consuegra, Moreno and a couple of others.

It's nothing dramatic, there's no movie script here: I hit the ball hard, but was out. All minor leaguers have aspirations of playing in the big leagues, and that was an important moment, exciting for me to finally come to bat in a big league game and hit the ball with authority. It made me feel like I belonged.

— Dick Gernert

Ted Williams was the first batter I ever faced in the big leagues. I was with the White Sox at the end of the '49 season. We were getting beat pretty bad in Boston, and they brought me in to relieve. And with Williams not knowing me, I had the count three and two on him and I threw a curveball. He stood there and took it and the umpire called him out. Well, that was probably the last time I struck him out.

— *Bob Cain*

Sure, I remember my first game in the big leagues. I dream about that every night. About my second day with the team *[June 8, 1956]* I was sittin' on the bench and one of the coaches come down and says, "You go on over to the bullpen." He says, "Spahnie, you go with him." Warren Spahn. He says, "They want you to throw some down there. Get ready for your start." Talking to Spahn, of course.

I guess I was scared to death, anyhow. I had one of the greatest thrills of my life, running across that field with Warren Spahn. We was playing the Giants. They wanted me to get up and throw. I thought, "What the heck, what do they want me to throw for? I'm not going into that ballgame." Very naive. Well, they called me in to pitch.

That was the longest walk I have ever taken in my life. Our bullpen was in center field. It was a horseshoe shaped stadium, and I saw all those people. Comin' from Douglasville, where they had about fifteen hundred people, that's not a lot of people. I went in and Whitey Lockman was the first hitter, and I never will forget, Del Crandall was catching, and the first pitch I threw — warm up pitch — was up on the screen. He motioned, "Get it down a little."

The next one was still on the screen. He come out there and said, "Hold on to it just a little longer." The next one was in the dirt. Finally I found the strike zone. I guess Whitey was scared to death, afraid I was going to hit him. Anyhow, I struck him out on three pitches. Next inning Willie Mays led off and I struck him out. I do remember that they said, "Don't throw him anything off speed or he'll kill you," so I throwed him a couple of fastballs, a curveball — I was going to throw him a real good curveball and I don't know if it slipped out of my hand, but it seemed like it took five minutes to get there. And he swung and missed — and you remember how his hat used to fly off? Well, his hat flew off and I struck him out. The first two hitters I faced in the big leagues I struck out. I pitched 2⅓ innings and had 3 strike outs, didn't give up any runs. I think I give up one hit, walked one person.

Three or four days later *[actually August 9]* I started against the Cardinals and I pitched a complete game, give up 3 hits — Musial, Blasingame, and Wally Moon — all of them left-handed hitters. Beat them 3–1. And I beat Cincinnati once, and I lost to the Giants. That's something you dream about, and you still dream about it. I was fortunate, you know, with a little ability and a little talent if you get in the right spot at the right time what you can do.

Three or four years later, I threw Mays that same change-up curveball. He hit it ten miles. That was his 180th home run. He hit his 200th home run off me, too. *[Mays hit home runs 150 (September 17, 1956) and 197 (May 16, 1958) off of Phillips.]*

— *Taylor Phillips*

The first time I stepped onto a big league field as a player was as a pinch runner at second base at Yankee Stadium. It was special because New York is where I was born and raised. My family, later on in life, told me they hoped I didn't get picked off.

— *Frank Malzone*

The first game I played in the big leagues, the first time I got up I walked. I was nervous, naturally. I got to first base. And Jake Pitler was the coach at first base. And he came over to the bag, and he patted me on the backside, and he said, "Nice going, Abie. But don't forget, but next week, stay home for three days."

I said, "I just came up from the minor leagues, I am now a major league ballplayer with the Brooklyn Dodgers. My dreams — I'm on cloud nine, and you're telling me to stay home?" He said, "Idiot. That's the Jewish holidays. You play, and I'll look like an idiot." That's the way it went in those days. *[Abrams' first game was April 19, 1949, against the Giants.]*
— *Cal Abrams*

I remember my one home run. You don't forget those things. I hit it off Lou Kretlow in Chicago. It was hit over the right-center field wall, which was really the deepest part of the ballpark. It went right over the bullpen, about five rows up. Of course, when I hit it the boys on the bench said, "Give him the silent treatment when he comes back." So I'm coming back expecting to get congratulated. After awhile they broke out in laughter because they're watching my reaction.

Kretlow probably threw the hardest of anybody in the league at that time, including Bob Feller. *[Parnell's home run was hit on September 15, 1952.]*
— *Mel Parnell*

The first major league game I ever saw, I pitched a 3-hitter against Cincinnati at Ebbets Field July 15, 1955. I started the last game the Brooklyn Dodgers played and the first game the New York Mets played. *[Craig went 10–24 and 5–22 his first two years with the Mets; he was 59–53 in his other big league seasons.]*
— *Roger Craig*

My first day in the big leagues I hit two home runs. A doubleheader in Chicago. Claude Passeau in the first game and Hi Bithorn in the second game. *[The game, on May 5, 1946, was in fact Ennis' eighth.]*
— *Del Ennis*

I think, the very first time playing in Yankee Stadium, how large it was compared to the little town of Alameda, where I came from, where the tallest building was two stories. It was awesome to me, the history of the stadium and all the magnificent players that had played before, and to actually be there, not having ever seen a major league game in my life. I think I made an error, possibly two, because of the sun, my first game, and when they sent me down in '52, that's one thing I practiced a lot, using sunglasses.
— *Andy Carey*

I broke in at Waterloo, in the Three-I League, in 1951. And the Indians signed a pitcher named Billy Joe Davidson, a big lefthander that struck out everybody he ever faced up until then. He went to Cedar Rapids. *[Davidson reportedly signed a record high contract, topping that of Porter's and then Paul Pettit's.]*

Well, the first game ever between Billy Joe Davidson and J.W. Porter, *Time* and *Life* magazines were there, along with somebody from every major newspaper from the Eastern United States. They had cameramen up and down from home to first and from home to third, taking a picture of Billy Joe every time he cocked his arm or of me every time I swung a bat.

[Davidson was out of baseball in 1956 at age 23 after six minor league seasons without ever playing in the majors. His best season was a 16–8 mark in Class B in 1952.]
— *J.W. Porter*

In my first game of pro ball, I pitched three innings in relief and I struck out five out of nine. They didn't hit a ball out of the infield, and of course all the guys and the manager were patting me on the back. Then I went out the next five or six times I got in a ball game and I couldn't get anybody out. Either I couldn't get the ball over the plate or when I did they hit it. That's when I was sent to a Class D team in Lima, Ohio.

But that first day I said, "Boy, there's nothing to this pro ball." *[He went 4–2 in 13 games that year, 1944, and went on to pitch 18 years in the big leagues.]*
— *Johnny Klippstein*

I remember the first game I won in the big leagues. I hit a home run and pitched against I think Bob Chipman, who was with the Boston Braves.

Of course, I didn't hit that many home runs, only five. I hit one off Forrest Main, that's a name that will live in infamy. Forrest, I don't think he was there but a couple years with Pittsburgh.

I hit one off Johnny Lindell. That was the old Yankee who converted back to pitching, had a knuckleball. And Murry Dickson, and Don McMahon.

Those were the five, and every one I hit was off a breaking ball. I guess when I first came up I thought I was going to be a pretty good hitter. I hit .333 my first year, I was 11 for 33. After that, it was downhill. I started hitting off guys like Blackwell and Curt Simmons and those guys and I said, "Oh-oh, things are different up here." *[The home run and win against Chipman came on July 17, 1950.]*
— *Johnny Klippstein*

I was nervous my first big league game *[August 11, 1957]*. I was with Detroit, and my first big league game I went in against Chicago. I remember when I went to tie my shoelaces my legs were jumping so I had a hard time tying my shoelaces. That's a fairly normal thing when you've worked so hard so long and then you finally get there that the adrenalin is really pumping.

I got my first hitter; it was either a pop out or ground ball, then I came in the next inning and walked a guy and Walt Dropo hit one in the upper deck. *[Shaw went three innings in the no-decision.]*
— *Bob Shaw*

I remember my first *[start]* in the big leagues very well. We were playing against Bob Feller, and the first time up I got a double to right center.

I went three for five that night, but I made an error that was rather costly. We were playing in on the infield and Luke Easter hit one that I barely saw. I'll have to say that I stepped aside a little bit. It was a one-hopper, like a limousine coming at me, and I tried to backhand it, and it was a costly error I made.

But God, it was hit hard, and we were playing in on that infield, and if you remember Luke Easter, he hit 'em like a bullet. *[Kell started at second base, in his fifth major league game, on April 29, 1952.]*
— *Skeeter Kell*

I'll always remember was the first Gold Glove I won because that was a Major League Gold Glove Award; it wasn't the American League, it was for both leagues. There are only nine players who have that glove, and I'm one of them, so that was probably one of the biggest achievements in my career. That one means a lot to me. *[The first year they gave the Gold Gloves was 1957. There was just one Major League winner at each position. Beginning in 1958 they awarded the Gold Gloves by league. In 1958 and 1959 Malzone was the American League winner at third base. In 1960, Brooks Robinson, in his fifth year in the league, began his streak of sixteen straight Gold Gloves.]*

Every time I see Brooks, I say, "Well, there's one you're not going to win."

— *Frank Malzone*

I played my first big league game against Philadelphia Athletics in 1948 and got three hits. My first hit was off Dick Fowler. I got three for five, and the next day I got three for four and thought, "This is easy." *[He went 8 for 14 in 4 games, then hit .315 in 58 games in 1949. In 10 years as Berra's back-up, he hit .282.]*

— *Charlie Silvera*

I hit a home run in my first game in the big leagues against the Bud Podbielan of the Dodgers, and won the game.

You remember your grand slams. You remember a few of the games you won in the last inning. You remember your five-for-five games. *[The home run came in Jackson's fifth game, not his first, in which he had two hits against the Phillies.]*

— *Randy Jackson*

The first game I played in the big leagues was against Baltimore *[on April 17, 1956]*. The pitcher was Bill Wight, a left-handed pitcher. I got a base hit my first time up. I got a hit off Skinny Brown my second time up. I went three for five that day. I thought it was going to be easy, but it wasn't.

— *Don Buddin*

My first day in the big leagues *[September 9, 1952]* I got to Boston in the middle of the first game of a doubleheader. When I got dressed and went out to the bench, Hornsby saw me and said, "Are you ready to play?"

I said, "Hell, yes. That's what I came here for." I don't know 'til this day why I said that. But anyway, he brightened up and he said, "Well, you're going to pinch-hit in this ballgame and you're going to play in the next one."

Sure enough, I pinch-hit in the first game. Del Rice was the catcher. Jocko Conlin was the umpire, little old Jocko, the Irishman. Spahn was on the mound. I got up there, and the weirdest thing, I got in the batter's box and got ready and all of a sudden my right leg started to thump. Jumping up and down, like a rabbit. I called time and backed out. I thought, this has never happened to me before. I didn't feel nervous, but I must have been. I got back in the batter's box again. He got his sign, and my leg started jumping again. I backed out. I did this about four times.

Jocko stepped around Rice and bent over and brushed off the plate. It didn't need to be brushed off. He just said, "For Christ sake, kid. Let him throw the ball or we'll be here all night."

I got back in there and I just dug in. I just grabbed that ground with my feet. He threw that first pitch. It was a high fastball out of the strike zone. But when that ball went by me, all that nervousness left. I was all right from then on. He struck me out on a called third strike, which was a slider, but it was inside. But he got the call. Of course, being a great pitcher, he probably should have got it. I should have hit the ball probably, but I didn't. It wasn't a strike, anyway.

Hornsby said, "Don't worry about that, son. You go up there to the plate, you're going up there to swing it. When you've got two strikes on you, if you can reach it, hit it."

The next game I played, Max Surkont was pitching. Great big Max. I got three hits and drove in the only three runs we got and we beat them. That was the start of my career.

My first big league home run was against Johnny Rutherford of the Dodgers. They walked Kluszewski to load the bases and get to me. I hit that sucker into the upper deck in left field, a grand slam home run, and we beat them 4 to 0. *[Greengrass hit 69 big league home runs and 130 in the minors.]*

— *Jim Greengrass*

My third time up in the big leagues *[April 30, 1958]* I hit a two-run homer to win a ballgame at Wrigley Field. Off the Braves, who traded me. I hit it off Bob Buhl.

— *Sammy Taylor*

Opening Day in '55 was my most memorable day in the big leagues. I was in old Crosley Field in Cincinnati. The wind was blowing. We had an overflow crowd. At Crosley Field you have a bank right before the fence in the outfield. Fans were standing on the bank, inside the playing field. The wind was blowing out. Bob Rush was pitching against Johnny Klippstein. We had them 1–0 going into the seventh. Thurman came up to pinch hit. He hit a ball in center field nine country miles high into short center. I kept easing in, slowly, because I know the wind has to bring the ball out. The cockeyed ball was coming down, so I move in a little quicker on it. I certainly couldn't let it drop in front of me. When that ball got about thirty feet above my head a gust of wind caught it. I stepped back a step and then fell back. The ball was in the webbing of the glove. And when I hit the ground on my back it went out. The guy winds up with a triple. That's how high the ball was in the air.

They gave me an error. Had the ball stayed in the glove, I might have stayed in the big leagues awhile. But it shattered my confidence. Gus Bell came up and doubled off the top of the wall. I made one hell of a try for that one. I went through people and up against the wall and came within a hair of getting that one. Bob Rush got beat 2 to 1.

— *Gale Wade*

I popped up in my first big league at-bat. It was against the Philadelphia Athletics. It was the first night I was in uniform. I hit a pop fly and the catcher caught it. The first game I started I hit a home run off Howie Pollet. *[Jackson's first game was June 15, 1952; his first start, July 5.]*

— *Ron Jackson*

In my first big league start *[May 10, 1953]* I pitched a two-hit [one-run game] against the Chicago Cubs. The starting line-up had Spahn and Crandall, and they had me in the bullpen. Spahnie's side was hurting him so Charlie Grimm sent word out to me to come, he wanted to talk to me. He said I'd be starting. He changed the catcher and put Walker Cooper in because Walker was an old-time catcher, and me being a rookie pitcher Grimm thought maybe Walker could do a better job of handling me. I made a little bit of an enemy with Del Crandall. I think that Del felt all along that I asked for Walker, but I didn't. Later on I pitched to Crandall. He was a very good catcher. Walker Cooper was a great catcher. I really, really loved the catcher at New York, Wes Westrum.

— *Don Liddle*

Maurie McDermott got me my starter position with the Red Sox. We were at Washington in 1954 and he hit Parnell with a pitch and broke a bone in his arm, so I took Mel's position in the rotation. They had been roommates all those years in Boston and they were really great friends, so it was accidental. I got the call three or four days later and beat the Yankees 3–1 or something like that. Anyway, I won the first game in Yankee Stadium I ever pitched.

— *Frank Sullivan*

In my first game in the big leagues we scored a couple runs in the first inning and got beat something like 7–2. *[The score was in fact 14–4.]* I got a base hit the first time up. I beat out an infield ball behind second base. I got two hits, and Ken Boyer — it was his first game in the big leagues, too — he got a couple hits. I think he hit a home run and a single. Musial was on the club and drove in the two first inning runs. *[Virdon's first game was April 12, 1955.]*

— *Bill Virdon*

In my first major league at-bat I got a base hit against Billy Pierce of the White Sox. I was scared, it was my first time at bat. I just kept thinking, "Oh, what am I going to do? What am I going to do, for goodness sakes." *[Upton's first at-bat did produce a hit, but it came against Bob Kuzava, not Pierce, on April 19, 1950.]*

— *Tom Upton*

I remember my first big league game. We went into Chicago and got there just before the game. They put me up to pinch-hit. We were about three runs behind and they put me up with nobody on in about the seventh inning. I was nervous. I didn't even look at the coach.

I just looked at that pitcher. That first pitch, I hit up against the right center field fence. It was a triple. I came around to score. Joe McCarthy — I think it was about the only words he said to me when I was with him — "Kid, you don't take much, do you?" *[Wright batted twice that year, 1948, with one triple. He had 11 triples in his 341 big league games.]*

— *Tom Wright*

Chapter Eight

I Remember Him!

Baseball is great theater—both high drama and comedy. The performance is carried out with a cast consisting of big-name stars and also those who fill the all-important supporting roles, the bit players. Through the years the scenes are played out again and again, continually thrilling both repeat audiences and those of a new generation, who are seeing the classic moments in baseball's classic theater for the first time.

Hank Aaron was probably the greatest hitter I ever played with. And I played with some great hitters: Ernie Banks, Frank Robinson with the Reds, Roberto Clemente with the Pirates. But I never saw him fooled on a pitch.
— *Frank Thomas*

Harry Agganis was a super athlete. He was the Golden Greek. He was all muscle. I saw him play football in Mobile in the Senior Bowl. He was an outstanding football player out of Boston University also *[an All-American quarterback]*. He was a good first baseman. He was a good hitter, and he probably would have been a real star in the major leagues if he hadn't gotten sick and died. *[Agganis died of leukemia in 1955, his second season in the major leagues, at the age of 26.]*

Ted Williams and Harry and I were on the disabled list and we all stayed back when the club was on the road, and worked out at Fenway. Harry looked weak, but he worked out harder than anybody. We kept telling him to take it easy, get his strength back. *[In his rookie year, at the age of 24, Agganis played 132 games, batting .251 with 11 home runs and a .990 fielding average. In 1955 he hit .313 in 25 games.]*
— *Milt Bolling*

I was the guy who brought Luis Aparicio in from Memphis to become one of the greatest shortstops of all time. I was responsible for him, for which I'm so happy, because little Louie, he was one of the best kids I've ever seen, a Hall of Famer.
— *Marty Marion*

Aparicio was very good. Some players will get one shot at making it. They might have had good credentials from the minors but they get one shot and then they shuffle them along, or they sit them on the bench or what have you, and they kind of break their spirit, whereas with Louie I know several other players on the team thought he shouldn't have been playing. But they kept playing him and after a good length of time he started to produce. In other situations, you'd never have heard of Aparicio. So it's good to have a good star to be born under at times. And he certainly proved to be one of the best of all time.

— *Ron Jackson*

Richie Ashburn was a tough guy for me to get out. He could really control home plate. He was a guy who fouled off all the pitches and then got one he liked. He always found a way to get on base.

— *Bob Friend*

Richie Ashburn was a very notorious bunter. If he caught you playing back a little bit, he'd try to bunt on you. I'd play in close on him because he was a left-handed hitter. But he laid down some beautiful bunts. It's just like the ball comes dead almost, just pop it up about five or six or seven feet down the line, and it just kind of hits and almost completely comes to a stop. Almost every team had pretty good bunters. Pee Wee Reese. Red Schoendienst. I could bunt good, but I didn't have the great speed of some of those guys, so I didn't bunt that much for hits, only to sacrifice.

— *Pete Castiglione*

I'm glad to see Richie Ashburn got in the Hall of Fame. But there's one thing I didn't like about him in the outfield. Del Ennis was in left, I was in right. There'd be thirty, forty thousand people there. And when the ball was hit to the outfield Richie would holler, "I got it!" Well, when the guy hits the ball the crowd lets out a big yell, and Del Ennis could never hear him. Richie would just put his head down and start going — he could run like the wind — and he'd get there. Del would be standing there waiting for the ball to come down, and Richie would run into him. Richie would come in and say, "Well, I called for it." But he'd call for it as soon as it was hit instead of waiting 'til it came down.

But Richie deserves to be in the Hall of the Fame. He was probably the number one leadoff hitter of all time. He could hit a ball back to the pitcher, and if it would take four bounces to get to the pitcher you'd never get him out. He could beat the throw. When he hit the ball he was already two steps toward first base. I've seen him leave the bat hanging in the air on a bunt and be out of the batter's box going to first when the ball made contact with the bat. They never had a prayer of getting him out. He was a great outfielder. The only complaint I had with him playing beside him was that he called for the ball too soon.

— *Jim Greengrass*

Ernie came in '53 and we played side by side two or three years. You knew right away that he was going to be great. He could just flip those wrists and the ball would just shoot.

So you knew he had it. It was just a matter of getting settled down for a year or so and getting in the groove. And a nice guy. About as nice a guy as you'll find.

— *Randy Jackson*

Hank Bauer, when I was in the Yankee organization, kind of went out of his way to be nice to me. I think Musial was that way, and Schoendienst was that way when I broke in with the Cardinals. They were kind to me, and they helped me relax and get my feet on the ground. So I think that's important.

— *Bill Virdon*

When I got up to the Yankees I had the normal amount of teaching, tutoring, coaching. People like Hank Bauer helped me a little bit. Gene Woodling was the kind of a guy at spring training that said, "Hey, this is my position."

I said, "That's fine, Gene. I appreciate that. But I want to tell you one thing, I'm right behind you. So, don't stutter, 'cause I'm right behind you."

— *Bill Renna*

Everybody had trouble with Yogi Berra because he had no strike zone. He could hit a ball out of the ballpark on a ball over his head or down on the ground. It finally got to the point where I'd pitch him belt high down the plate and let him hit a long fly ball to center field.

— *Bob Cain*

Yogi got to be a terrific receiver. And he got to where he could get rid of the ball without taking two or three steps. Dickey worked with him a lot on his catching. He called a good game and he was a hard worker. He didn't get lackadaisical back there and let balls get by him. Yogi could catch the ball and control the mitt to the point that if it was close the umpire had to give it that extra look. He wouldn't turn it over and let that ball knock the glove down to where they'd say "ball." And he was short, so you could throw down to him. He wasn't real, real tall like Dickey, who got bad knees toward the end of his career, and consequently he couldn't bend down as far.

I always told everybody that I was the guy that had Yogi reaching up and goin' down and in and out and everything; I kept him in shape for guys like Lopat and Reynolds and Raschi, you know. Believe it or not, he'd lose two or three extra pounds if I was pitching.

— *Tommy Byrne*

Yogi talked to everybody behind the plate. In fact, I was always accusing him later, "That guy hit that ball pretty good. Are you telling him what's coming?"

He says, "Heck, no, I ain't telling him what's coming." He says, "You're only throwing two pitches. You've got to guess good once."

But Yogi, he'd talk to them about anything. It was like he hadn't seen them in six years. They're coming up to home plate the first time in a game, and he'd take his mask off and he'd kick his heels against his shin guards and even meet them.

I said, "When you going to shake hands with them?"

But he's really trying to do his thing and get them thinking about something else. Which is pretty good. He had a way with folks. He's a good boy.

— *Tommy Byrne*

Berra was the best hitter that I saw in my major league career that in the last at bat in the ballgame. He would be just unbelievable. You couldn't get him out in that last time up. If it's a close game and you've got to get him out, somehow or other he'd get a base hit.

He was a hell of a hitter, and he could hit bad balls. It made it really tough.

— *Bob Shaw*

Yogi Berra had such a short stride. He could hit a ball anyplace — high, low, outside, up over his head. He had such good balance in his feet and never got out of position when a ball was being pitched, and consequently he could hit it in any position, any place. His swing would be a good one to copy. He just had a short swing and a compact swing, and I think he was the kind of guy that said, "Throw it and I'll hit it."
— *Carl Scheib*

Joe Black had a great relief year in '53, and the next spring Charlie Dressen told him, "You need a curveball. We're going to make a starting pitcher out of you."

Black started working on a curveball, and he hurt his arm and never could get that good slider working again. He never had another great year after that.
— *Jim Greengrass*

Bobby Brown, who later became the American League president, played third base for us. He didn't get to play much because McDougald played, but Stengel would use him to pinch hit. He was a tough a guy as anybody with a man on third and one out or less. He'd pick up that runner most of the time.
— *Bob Kuzava*

One of the toughest pitchers for me to hit was Jim Bunning. He hit me between the eyes with a fastball in 1960. Never figured out why he hit me, I never hit him. That was pretty serious, I missed a month. You really never get over it. You want to stay in that batter's box. Your heart's there but your fanny's not.
— *Don Buddin*

I'm lucky to have caught Jim Bunning a lot. He won over a hundred games in both leagues and pitched no-hitters in both leagues, and at the time of his retirement was fifth all time in strikeouts. He had good stuff, he had the long, lanky body. And he threw a little bit from the side. But he was like Drysdale in the fact that they thought they were better than you. They came at you, never gave you an inch.
— *J.W. Porter*

Burdette would go through all these motions out there to make you think he was throwing a spitter. He said he didn't throw that many, only when he was really in trouble and needed the strikeout.
— *Jim Greengrass*

When I pitched to Smoky Burgess the first time, somehow, immediately, he sensed exactly how I pitched, and it was like he'd been catching me for ten years, it was amazing. I had a kind of riding fastball and a little bitty slider, but there weren't any balls in the dirt, or wild pitches or anything, so I was an easy pitcher to catch, and people weren't stealing bases that game, so it turned out he's a fine catcher as long as he wasn't pressed to throw. 'Cause he was a much better hitter than he was a defensive catcher.
— *Dick Hall*

Carrasquel was a great shortstop and a good hitter. Did everything well. I thought he was better than Aparicio. Aparicio was faster, but when I saw Carrasquel in '53, I thought

he was a great shortstop. Good arm, good bat. *[Carrasquel, a four-time All-Star, had problems controlling his weight, and his 10-year big league career ended in 1959 at the age of 33.]*
— *Bob Keegan*

Jerry Coleman was just uncanny making the double play. You couldn't see the ball go through his glove. He was just a magician with the glove. And a better ballplayer than Billy Martin. But Jerry had to go into the Marine Corps for that second hitch, like Ted Williams did. That's the only way Billy got to play. Billy did play and had a great Series in '52. That's what brought him to the spotlight.
— *Bob Kuzava*

Joe Collins knew how to play first base with anybody. He got no credit because he played behind Mize, and then later Skowron, but he was a brilliant first baseman. And that's why he was on the team, he had power and he could play first base, and every time Mize would get in the seventh inning in came Collins, who was the best defensive first baseman in baseball. Only Ferris Fain would be as good. Fain had a better arm than Collins.
— *Jerry Coleman*

Clint Courtney was just a battler. He just wanted to win and he'd do anything to win, really. You know, it's amazing, though. Clint never played baseball until he got in the service. He never played as a youngster or anything and still was able to make the big leagues. He just battled you all the time.
— *Herb Plews*

Frank Crosetti was our guru. Of course, he'd been a great Yankee infielder himself. But his approach to the game was exactly what you needed — no nonsense.

We used to take infield about a half hour before the game. Every now and then Scooter and I'd get out there, and — I always enjoyed playing with Phil, he was so brilliant — but we'd say, "Let's get fancy." We'd start one-handing the ball and Crosetti would say, "Oh, wise guys, wise guys, huh'?" and he'd throw the bat down and walk off right in front of sixty thousand people. He'd just leave us out there.
— *Jerry Coleman*

Alvin Dark was the shortstop when I was with the Giants *[in 1955 and 1956]*. He really made my job easy at second base, especially on double plays. He had the lightest, quickest throw. It was easiest to handle of anybody I'd ever played with.

And I talked with him about positioning and stuff like that. I learned a lot from him.
— *Wayne Terwilliger*

Dom DiMaggio should be in the Hall of Fame. He was probably the best center fielder in the American League at that time. Not only that, he was a great leadoff hitter. Dom could get on base either by a base on balls or a base hit. For a leadoff man he had a lot of RBI's. We did have a pretty good hitting pitching staff. We'd get on base and Dom could move us around.

The one thing that hurt Dom most of all was the fact that everybody knew him as Joe's little brother and not as Dominic, the great ballplayer. I think with Dom and Johnny Pesky as our one-two hitters, they were probably the best one-two punch in baseball at that time. If Dominic would get on base, Pesky could handle the bat very well. He could find the holes.

— Mel Parnell

Joe Dobson was a good curveball pitcher. I can remember in '52 when I was with the White Sox. Coming up from the South in spring training, like they did years ago, you'd play a club in all these little towns going North. We were in Nashville, Tennessee. In the old Nashville park right field was a real problem. It was like a goatwalk up there. You had to go up a mound and then they had a little ledge up there where the right fielder would stand.

I always stayed in good shape. I'd run all the time. Dobson was on the club, so Paul Richards, our manager, said, "Randy, take Joe with you and run up and down that bank for about twenty minutes." Joe was mumbling and grumbling. We finally got over to the bank and we started to run up and he pulled a Charley Horse on his leg. Every time I saw him in later years, he'd say, "You're the fella that caused me to miss a couple weeks of pitching with a Charley Horse."

— Randy Gumpert

We had Dick Donovan on our Washington club. He was quite a pitcher, spent most of his time with the White Sox. He had a routine. The day he pitched, he'd come out of the dugout carrying his jacket, his towel, his glove, and he'd hang his towel on a hook there, his jacket, and put his glove down there. And then every inning when he pitched, why he'd come right to that spot, and if someone was sitting at that spot he'd just pick them up and throw them out of the way. He wanted that same spot all the time. And on days he didn't pitch, he was the biggest umpire–baiter you ever saw.

— Sid Hudson

Del Ennis was real easy-going. A big guy. Kind of like Kluszewski. Hit 20 home runs every year, drove in a hundred runs. Would never say a word. When he got up to bat and didn't hit a home run, the people in Philadelphia would boo him. They had a "boo Del Ennis club."

— Jim Greengrass

Del Ennis was a great guy. I felt sorry for him because he was a hometown guy, and he was a great player. Yet he took so much abuse from the fans in Philly, it was unbelievable. But he was such a good, easy-going guy, a different type of personality wouldn't have been able to handle it. He was fantastic. He was a great hitter.

They used to just boo him, you know. But then, by the same token, he'd hit one out and they'd go crazy. I think I remember one day he dropped a fly ball with the bases loaded, and I think everybody scored, and it was unbelievable, but then he came up the next time and hit one out and they forgave him and everything was fantastic.

— Ted Kazanski

I'll tell you one guy who was a great ballplayer, Bob Elliott. He played with Pittsburgh, then he came over to Boston, and he was my roommate. I swear, he was one of the best ballplayers. If you needed a base hit, you got it. If you needed a good catch, you got it. If you needed a good slide or something you got it from him. Mr. Baseball. Mr. Team, I should say, he was so good for us.

— Danny Litwhiler

Ferris Fain liked to fight. In fact, we had to hide some of the guys out when we'd leave town or go on a train or something like that so he couldn't get at 'em. But he was a nice guy. He fought hard. He played hard. He charged those batters: he'd go right down their throat at them. He'd keep you on the ball, he was a go-go guy. He wanted to win, there's no doubt about that. That man would sit on the top step of the dugout, and if you had a fight on the field, he was the first one there. He didn't back off from anything.

He won the batting championship one year. You know, ballplayers have a favorite bat. Well, he broke his bat. And we were walking in the hotel in Washington one day, and he found one that a kid had left out in the lawn, and he used that the rest of the year and he kept getting hits with it.

— *Carl Scheib*

The one thing that I remember about Ferris Fain is that nobody could bunt down the first base line on him. In bunting situations where everybody in the ballpark knew where a hitter was going to bunt, Ferris Fain would almost take it off the bat. So to me he was just a hard-nosed guy that played the game as hard as you could play it. A good defensive ballplayer. Also a good offensive ballplayer. He was a good hitter. He did everything right, as far as I was concerned. Except sometimes his attitude toward his own teammates. He'd get a little upset about things.

— *Virgil Trucks*

There's not a better competitor in baseball than Bob Feller. Right from the time he went to the bullpen to warm up to the time he'd take the mound until the game was over. He was tough.

I made an eighth inning error in a Bob Feller no-hitter. When the next batter came up I said, "Dear Lord, don't let this guy get a base hit." Then Feller got him out, so I was off the hook, so to speak. I didn't want to make an error on an out and spoil his no-hitter. That was his third, and last.

— *Ray Boone*

Boo Ferriss was a great hitting pitcher. He was ambidextrous; he could throw left handed and right handed. Of course, he was a right-handed pitcher. He had two great years, then he hurt his arm He would have been a great, great pitcher if he hadn't hurt his arm And a real class guy, real fine.

— *Billy Hitchcock*

Nellie Fox was a competitor. He was a good second baseman, and he was one of those guys you couldn't strike out either. He used that big old bottle bat which he was famous for, choked up on it. You just couldn't strike him out. He'd hit the ball someplace. Consequently, he'd hit for a high average almost every year. *[From 1951 to 1960, Fox played an average of 153 games a year—in a 154 game season—never hitting below .285. For his 19-year career he struck out an average of once in every 46 at-bats.]*

— *Carl Scheib*

[Before Nellie Fox was elected to Baseball's Hall of Fame in 1997 by the Veteran's Committee, Bob Keegan speculated on why Fox was not in the Hall of Fame.]

He didn't play in a big media center, and he wasn't one to cater to the press. He didn't have a lot of natural ability. He didn't have a good arm. Didn't run that well. But a good hitter, always got a piece of the ball. Good fielder. And always hustled. Hated to come out of a ballgame. He had the real good attitude. He was quick and always got to the ball in a hurry. And usually he got everything that was hit at him. Other guys had more natural ability than he had, but for hustle and everything — the guy should be in the Hall of Fame. But, you know, if you played in New York and some of the great media centers, why, you've got publicity.

And I think he played in, what was it, 12 straight All-Star games? *[Fox was an All-Star from 1951 to 1961 and in '63. He hit .288 lifetime and fielded .984 at second base.]*

— **Bob Keegan**

I played with Nellie that year we won the pennant *[1959]*; he was the Most Valuable Player in the American League. It certainly goes to show that Nellie Fox just got the total maximum out of his ability. He was a great competitor, I mean he was almost impossible to strike out. A great clutch player.

He was just a great all-around ballplayer, and the reason why I would think that he would be considered for the Hall of Fame is that he did it year after year.

We'd be in a tough situation and Nellie Fox might come in and tell me — he knew I was single — he'd say, "Boy, did you see that good-looking redhead up there in about the fifth row?" Just to relieve the tension.

— **Bob Shaw**

The batter that gave me the most trouble was Nellie Fox of Chicago. I couldn't get him out. Of course, he was one of these "bunt, hit to all fields." The only way to pitch to him I would say is just throw the ball as hard as I could right down the middle and don't give him a chance to control the bat.

— **Sonny Dixon**

They told Nellie Fox to teach me how to bunt and Nellie said, "I can't teach you how to bunt. I don't know the fundamentals of bunting; it just comes natural to me."

— **Jim Landis**

I was there when Bill Veeck introduced the midget to baseball. Gaedel's playing was a complete surprise, I think only the manager Zack Taylor knew about it. Being one of his player coaches, I asked Bill after the game, "My God Bill, what would have happened if that guy went up there and started swinging."

He said, "I had told him if he dares to swing I was going to blow him away because I had a shotgun up in the press box."

— **Johnny Berardino**

The midget's name was Gaedel, and the fella pitching against him was a boy named Sugar Cain. Bob Cain. He was a left hander. Bob Swift was the catcher, and he was laying almost flat on the ground, down as low as he could get. Everybody knew he wasn't going to swing, but he still walked him.

— **Tommy Byrne**

Garver was just a standout pitcher. The guy had unbelievable stamina. He was like having an extra hitter in the lineup. Good fielder. He was no out when he went to the plate, that's for sure. We hardly ever replaced him with a reliever because he was the best we had. And he'd take the ball anytime you'd give it to him.

— *Jim Dyck*

I was rooming with Harvey Haddix when he pitched his twelve perfect innings. The only problem, I was down in the bullpen so I couldn't see the game that well.

After the game it wasn't as wild as you might have thought, probably because we lost the game. But Harvey and I didn't get any sleep that night. The phone was ringing all night. People were coming to see Harvey. Being with him, I got to bask a little in that glory. *[Haddix's famous game, which ended in a loss, was May 26, 1959.]*

— *Bob Smith*

"Hurricane" Hazel, Bob Hazel, was doing very well in the minors and then they took him up to the big leagues, and he hit exceptionally well and was one of the big reasons Milwaukee won the pennant in 1957, and then you never heard of him again. *[Hazel hit .403 in 41 games for Milwaukee in 1957, then hit .211 for Milwaukee and Detroit in 63 games the next year, his last in the big leagues. His lifetime average was .310 in 110 big league games. He finished in 1960, hitting .291 in Double A after hitting .266 in Triple A in 1959.]*

— *Ron Jackson*

One of the best catchers I ever pitched to — now I'm not talking about his bat, I'm talking about his arm and knowing how to receive the ball — was Jim Hegan. Another catcher I thought did a good job with pitchers was Birdie Tebbetts. Yogi was a good catcher.

— *Bob Kuzava*

Tommy Henrich was great. He used to hit me probably a hundred ground balls a day. Tommy was a left-handed hitter, and he loved to hit that ball down through that first base as hard as he could and watch it ricochet off my knees. That made him happy. But it also helped me to catch ground balls.

— *Gail Harris*

Tommy Holmes wasn't what you'd call the greatest outfielder, but he was a good outfielder. He didn't have a great arm, and he didn't have great speed, but he knew the field and he knew how to play. But he was a great hitter. He understood hitting about as good as anybody I've ever been around. If he saw you play, he'd be looking at you a little bit and you'd say, "Tommy, what am I doing wrong?" He'd just give you a little tip, and bang, you'd be back again. He was good at that.

— *Danny Litwhiler*

Both Ralph Houk and Charlie Silvera could receive the ball pretty well, and they both had good attitudes, and I really believe they were where they wanted to be, backing up Yogi and looking forward to that World Series check. They gave one hundred percent whenever they were called on, but they didn't get called on very much. Little Charlie, he could receive the ball well, and he'd hold it there, not trying to show up an umpire or anything, but if you had a close pitch, he'd get right in there with it. Houk was just a bulldog back there. He'd be grabbing his chest protector and all, trying to get you worked up, making sure you had your mind on what you were doing.

— *Tommy Byrne*

The hitter that I was more cautious of than anyone else was Frank Howard. I played him back.

— Andy Carey

Billy Hunter came to the Browns, and anything that could move he could catch. I remember one time we were playing an exhibition game and he was chasing a ball and he kept climbing up the screen. He was kind of a showboat. He was a good ballplayer. He would have been better on a better ball club.

— Marty Marion

Jackie Jensen was probably the best all-around player we had on the Red Sox. He could do a lot of things. He was a good outfielder, a good hitter, and had power. He could steal a base. He hit into a lot of double plays because he just didn't get out of the box good, but he had good speed once he got going.

It's tough to get a lot of publicity when you're playing with a Ted Williams, but the people that played with him really respected his ability. *[In his first six seasons with the Red Sox, Jensen drove in over 100 runs five times and hit more than 20 home runs all six years. He also led the league in triples one year and in stolen bases one year.]*

— Milt Bolling

Puddinhead Jones, the third baseman for the Philadelphia Phillies, gave me a lot of trouble. For some reason he could hit the ball on the handle and it would go over the shortstop's head; he could hit on the end of the bat and it would roll down the first base line and stay fair.

He used to holler at me, "Hey, Liddle, when you going to pitch? My batting average is going down."

He hit the ball good off me a lot times, but he could get those fluky hits too. I ought of got him out, but I didn't.

— Don Liddle

You see some other great ballplayers are a little more flashy than Al Kaline, but he did everything real smooth. I think he was one of the best ballplayers I ever played against and with. He threw well, ran well, and caught the ball real good. He was a good outfielder, good hitter, really and truly, he's one of those really smooth, solid players.

— Ted Lepcio

Standout opposing players? Number one, Al Kaline, with Detroit. Coming in and leading the league in batting at 20 years old? Give me a break. *[Kaline played for the Tigers in 1953 and '54 at the age of 18 and 19, with no previous professional experience. He won the batting title in 1955 with a .340 average at the age of 20, the youngest player to win the title. He had 3,007 lifetime hits.]*

— Andy Carey

Al Kaline was just a super all-around player. He did everything there was to help you win. His defense was outstanding. In 1954 the Indians were only shutout once; I shut them out one night in Detroit. *[Garver pitched three shutouts that year; he pitched 18 in his career].* We had that house packed. Dale Mitchell hit a ball that Kaline tried to catch and then he had to hold up. He put the brakes on and he slid out there on his rear end. The ball hit the ground and it was going to skip by him, and he reached out with his bare hand and grabbed that ball. Mitchell tried to go to second, and Kaline threw to second from a sitting position and threw him out. I mean, believe you me, that was a super play.

We had another guy, Bill Tuttle, the center fielder. Now if you get a good jump on the ball, you've got a chance to catch it. But if you get a slow start, you might miss it by two feet. I mean, Geez Louise, it's amazing, they hit that ball and your head would snap around and Tuttle would already be in high gear. He was just a mighty fine center fielder.

— *Ned Garver*

George Kell was a tough out for me because he just used the whole field. He'd get two strikes and he'd just try to put the bat on the ball and go the other way.

— *Bob Kuzava*

The man that stands out in my mind as the toughest I ever pitched against — I pitched against a few of them — was George Kell of the Detroit Tigers. He was one of those slap hitters. And a slap hitter was one that I didn't like to face. I preferred to pitch against sluggers. You could try to outguess them, while a slap hitter outguessed you most of the time.

— *Joe Ostrowski*

Ralph Kiner was one of the nicest pros that I've ever run into. If I were to come out and pitch him batting practice at Chicago early in the morning, he would turn around and pitch me just as many as I would throw him I mean, he was that type of person, he wouldn't walk off the field since I was a rookie and he was an established star. I mean, if I threw him ten minutes, by gosh he got on the mound and he threw to me ten minutes. That impresses you if you're a rookie.

— *Elvin Tappe*

I pitched a one-hitter in Pittsburgh. I got a no-hitter going in the seventh inning and I'm throwing little bitty b-b's, and, you know, throwing right where I want to be. And I said I want a strike, so I just slopped up a damn baseball to Ralph Kiner — Ralph was a good hitter. I honestly believe that Ralph Kiner could have hit .400 if he had gone for base hits, but they wanted home runs in Pittsburgh. Anyway, Ralph golfed at it two times and then hit it. Dick Sisler jumped for the ball in the short Greenberg Gardens. If it had been in real Pittsburgh, he'd have caught the ball. But who else better to do the no-hitter than Ralph Kiner? *[Kiner's home run came with two outs in the bottom of the seventh, August 5, 1951.]*

— *Bubba Church*

Ted Kluszewski was a good fielder. Anything he got his paws on, or got to, you could bet he was going to catch. He maybe didn't cover as much ground as some of the fellows who were of a lighter stature, but he was a good first baseman. He was pretty good on balls in the dirt.

— *Johnny Klippstein*

Kluszewski would scare you to death. He hit a home run off me one night in Cincinnati. They had that moon deck in right. It was a sun deck in the day and a moon deck at night. He hit one about half way up the stands off me one night. He had a big old roundhouse

swing. That bat looked like a wagon tongue. He wore them cutoff sleeves and them arms looked like legs. He'd scare you to death.
— *Taylor Phillips*

I always thought Ted Kluszewski was underrated. He was a great hitter. He was big and strong, and he was good, he had great hands around first base. I think people looked more or less at him as a football player, he was so big, but he had a lot of talent.
— *Bob Friend*

Klu would get fooled by a pitch and he'd turn loose of the bat with his left hand and he'd hit it out of the ballpark with his right hand. He could hit a ball one-handed farther than most guys could hit it with two.
— *Jim Greengrass*

When I faced Frank Lary I might as well have gone to the plate without a bat. I'm swinging at a ball that's not there. His slider looks like a fastball that's going to be right down the middle of the plate. At the last minute it breaks about a foot and it's outside the plate, and my eyes and my bat seem to think it's going to be right down the middle.

Many other guys, like Early Wynn, threw a slider, but Wynn's was flatter and it was slower and I could pick that up, but I could not pick up Frank Lary's slider. I was helpless. Believe me, I say that sincerely. If I got a hit off Frank Lary, it was an accident. I heard Ted Williams make the comment that when the slider became a pitch that a lot of people were using, nobody will hit four hundred again.
— *Billy Hunter*

Bob Lemon was in the Cleveland organization prewar as a third baseman, outfielder. He could hit and he could run. He had a great arm. He didn't start pitching until he got in the service over in Hawaii. It took a little while for them to find out he could pitch on the Cleveland club, and they finally put him on the mound. And from there he took off to the Hall of Fame. *[Lemon played 16 big league games at third base and the outfield at the start of his career.]*
— *Tom Ferrick*

Johnny Lindell came over to Pittsburgh as a pitcher. He was a knuckleballer. He played with the Yankees originally. He got sent down and worked on his pitching and came back in the big leagues and had a few years and wasn't a bad pitcher. Nice fellow. Jovial guy. He liked his good times. He'd be the first to admit it if he was still around.
— *Pete Castiglione*

Ted Lepcio was a good ballplayer. The old Seton Hall guy. He just didn't have a chance to play regular as much as he should have. But he had a great arm, good hands, and he had some power. I would say that 90% of us that played in the major leagues were just the ordinary or average ballplayers that had an opportunity to play and took advantage of it maybe, or got a break and were able to stay there, while the guys exceptional players were only maybe five or ten percent. There were just as many guys in the high minor leagues that were just as good as we were but just didn't have the opportunity that we did. Or we got there and took advantage of the opportunity, one of the two.
— *Milt Bolling*

One of the best throwing outfielders was Dale Long in the Coast League. He threw me out one day; I was going from first to third. I could run then. The guy threw me out, and I could not believe it. The ball was hit right down the line. And he went over and he threw a strike. He didn't bounce the ball. The third baseman decoyed the hell out of me, too.

I slid, but it didn't make no difference. But it had to be perfect. And he was standing there like nothing was going on and boy, then the ball was in his glove and he reached down and tagged me. I couldn't believe it. *[Long, a big league first baseman, played some outfield for San Francisco and Hollywood in the Coast League.]*

— *Pete Milne*

I know Preacher Roe didn't throw very hard, but Lopat threw a lot softer. I remember, the first time I faced Lopat I got three hits off him, and somebody said, "Geez, how do you hit that guy?" And I started thinking about him throwing off speed stuff, and he got me out the rest of my career, I think, by throwing fastballs by me. I started looking for stuff I shouldn't have.

— *Wayne Terwilliger*

Sal Maglie, a man of determination and good character, took no nonsense from anyone and kept you anxious at the plate.

— *Danny Gardella*

The Chicago White Sox had great speed. They had Rivera and Fox and Torgeson and Minoso, and they watered down the whole left side of the diamond, so you couldn't field the bunt in the quagmire. The whole Chicago team could bunt, but I didn't worry too much about them. You see, I had Malzone at third base most of my career, and Malzie could handle all that kind of stuff. One day at Washington I looked at Malzone and he came walking over to me and he said, "Okay, that's enough." If he'd caught another one, or two more, he'd have had the record for assists for a nine inning game, or something like that. I mean, he was like a vacuum cleaner down there.

— *Frank Sullivan*

Marty Marion was the best shortstop I ever saw. You didn't realize how good he was until you played in the outfield behind him. With any other shortstop, the ball would be hit and you know it's your ball, you just come in and pick it up. But when I was with the Cardinals, I'd see the ball hit toward me and I'd come in to get it and the old glove would go out and boom, he's got it. He was great. The toughest ball for him was a slow hit ball that he had to come in on. Marty Marion got credit for fielding, an outstanding fielder. But on the Cardinal team, while I was with them, he was the type of hitter, that if you needed a base hit, I would want him up in place of Musial. He was so tough. He'd just hang up there and throw that bat at the ball and get a base hit. When it came down to the time that you really needed a hit, he could give it to you.

— *Danny Litwhiler*

Billy Martin was a back-up infielder in '50 and '51. In 1952, in spring training with the Yankees, he broke his ankle making a spaghetti commercial. He was sliding — one those action scenes — and he broke his ankle.

Poor Billy groaned all night long, and I didn't know whether to choke him or shoot him, but you know, Billy was an accident looking for an accident.
— *Jerry Coleman*

The thing that would really burn Higgins up *[Pinky Higgins, the Red Sox manager]*— Billy Martin used to come over the first game that we'd play them the year after they won the pennant ask Higgins if he wanted to order some World Series tickets for the coming year. That would be Martin's first rip. I thought that was pretty good.
— *Frank Sullivan*

Willie Mays could do it all. Probably the greatest all-around ballplayer I ever saw. Every phase of the game he was good at. Boy, he could wear you out. In Cincinnati here's how we'd keep him from hurting us. He didn't like getting knocked down. The first time at bat every time he came to Cincinnati — hat, bat, went every which way.
— *Jim Greengrass*

I was with the Giants in 1951 when Mays came up. He had a struggle at first. He went 0 for 21, you know. Some of those pitchers said he'll never hit in the big leagues. The hell he won't. I was there the day he hit his first home run. I think it was off Spahn. He cranked one into the upper deck in left field, and from then on he really took off. *[Mays finished the season with 20 home runs and a .274 batting average.]*
— *Spider Jorgensen*

Mays was a hell of a base runner. He never did use a coach. He could look over his shoulder on the big, long strides of his, and make up his mind what he was going to do. He knew when he had a chance to go, or when he shouldn't take a chance. He didn't look like he was running fast, but he had those long strides, and he covered a lot of ground.
— *Wayne Terwilliger*

Mays was always loosey-goosey, he was always talking and fooling around and pinching you and talking a lot.
— *Wayne Terwilliger*

We played an exhibition game in Williamsport back in the middle fifties, and they were talking about Mazerowski. "Oh, you ought to see this hotshot shortstop we've got at Williamsport." He was a shortstop then, and he was already famous for his fielding, and he was a pretty good hitter.

The good ones, you could spot early on, and he was one of them. *[Mazerowski played two and a half years in the minors, his first as a shortstop and his next one and a half as a second baseman.]*
— *Dick Hall*

Mazerowski was probably the best second baseman ever to play the game. I played third base and left field and first base with him, and you get a different perspective at all three places. When I played first base I never thought the ball touched his glove. I thought it was just into his bare hand, barely touching his glove and over to first base — the quickest hands as far as second basemen are concerned, soft hands — really a great second baseman.
— *Frank Thomas*

I think Mazerowski is underrated. He belongs in the Hall of Fame. He just made everything look routine, and he did it for twenty years with the Pirates. He was so consistent at second base. He had the quickest release getting rid of the ball at second on the double play.
— *Bob Friend*

Mazerowski probably had the quickest release on the double play of anybody I've ever seen. The ball hit his glove and it was on its way to first base.
— *Bob Smith*

Maury McDermott was a great talent. He had great baseball ability and probably could have been one of the better in baseball had he wanted to be and took it serious. But he lived a fast life and Maury never did settle down. He continued to be a kid all through his career, instead of taking it real serious and concentrating on his baseball ability. He impressed everybody. He could run, he could hit, he could throw, he could do it all. He could also imitate a lot of entertainers. He could give you a little bit of everybody.

He used to sing in a nightclub in Boston they called The Cave, or The Cove. He'd sound a little bit like Dean Martin, a little bit like Sinatra. He was such a great imitator that he could pick up voice sounds and everything and give you a good show.
— *Mel Parnell*

Gil McDougald played three different positions on World Championship teams, and nobody even gives him credit for it. He was a marvelous, marvelous player. *[McDougald was the Yankees regular third baseman, shortstop, and second baseman on World Champions during the 1950s.]*
— *Jerry Coleman*

Gil McDougald was one of those fellows if you were a batting instructor and you saw him, you might try to change him, but they had enough sense in the Yankee organization to leave him alone. He kind of laid the bat perpendicular to the ground and had his elbows in, but he hit the ball well.

I recall the first game we played in spring training one year. A ground ball hit to me, there was a guy on first, I come up with it and threw the ball right across the bag, and Gil was already gone. He's about six feet on the inside of the bag, already off of it. Of course, the ball went on into right field.

He said, "Bill, I want that ball six feet inside the bag."

I said, "Well, that's where it'll be from now on." And it was.

That's probably the best thing that could have happened that particular day, because it made a big hit in my mind. It never happened again. Better it happened in a spring training game than in the World Series.
— *Billy Hunter*

The best defensive shortstop, the guy I used to really like to watch, was Roy McMillan with Cincinnati. He had such great quickness in his feet, a good quick arm, good lateral movement.
— *Bobby Morgan*

The guy that I thought really kept our Cincinnati club together was Roy McMillan. Roy was just a gung-ho guy. Whether he was hitting .230 or .265, he gave you that hundred and twenty percent all the time. He's probably one of the better competitors I ever played with. He's the best defensive shortstop I ever played with. I always thought he and Aparicio with the White Sox were as good as I saw. Reese didn't have the range that the other two had. But he was pretty baseball-wise and played the hitters probably better than a lot of guys ever did. At Cincinnati in '56 we had three of the best defensive shortstops probably in the league. We had McMillan, Alex Grammas, and Rocky Bridges. We could pinch hit in the fifth and the seventh and never really hurt our ball club that much at short.

— *Johnny Klippstein*

Roy McMillan really stood out as a great shortstop. You really don't really realize how great a shortstop he was until you played behind him. When I played left field and watched some of the plays he made, it was just unbelievable. *[When* The Sporting News *started awarding Gold Gloves for fielding excellence in 1957, McMillan's seventh big league season, he won the award at shortstop the first three years.]*

— *Frank Thomas*

Stu Miller had the strangest delivery in the world. He looked like he was throwing the ball and his arm was still back behind him. He had everybody just step back on their feet just waiting for the ball to get there.

— *Ben Flowers*

We were in St. Louis and Stu Miller was pitching. He couldn't break that window from right here. He had that side-armed curveball that defied gravity. You could stand there and count ten before the ball got to you. Unbelievable. The guys are telling me, "Just wait. You gotta wait, Jim." I'm waiting up there and I hit a home run off the scoreboard.

— *Jim Greengrass*

The best defensive player I ever played with was Willie Miranda. He couldn't hit a lick. But he could field. Defensively, he had the ability to go behind third base better than anybody I ever saw. He'd throw the guy out from the grass. Luis Aparicio had a good arm, but not as strong as Willie.

I saw Willie get pinch hit for against the Yankees in the first inning. That's devastating.

— *Don Ferrarese*

Hal Newhouser should have gotten in the Hall of Fame long before he did. But he didn't get in because they said, "Well, the guy pitched during the second war." Well, that wasn't his fault. I went in the service because there was a war going on and I was drafted. If they'd said I couldn't go in the service, I'd have played ball too.

And Newhouser proved in '46 and '47 and '48 and '49 that he was a great pitcher. Him and Feller would hook up every time those two clubs met, and they would fill the ballpark. What they do on the field is what you're voting on. *[Newhouser was voted into the Hall of Fame in 1992. His major league record was 207–150. His win totals from 1944 to 1950 were 29, 25, 26, 17, 21, 19, 15.]*

— *Bob Kuzava*

One catcher that I thought was the greatest defensive catcher — Bob Oldis. You didn't have to worry about throwing the ball in the dirt, he would block the ball regardless of where it was at. He was just a heck of a guy to pitch to, you had nothing to worry about. I've always said I thought he was the best defensive catcher there was.

— *Sonny Dixon*

Satchel Paige was in the league when I was with the Browns. He was with Cleveland, but then he came to St. Louis after I left. He was pretty effective; he was a pretty good-looking pitcher. Of course, he didn't have the speed that he once had.

He could change speeds. He could throw the ball by you. He knew how to pitch. I had seen him earlier, right after the war. Of course, at that time they didn't have any radar guns, but he threw well into the 90s. He had a live arm and he had good control. He could put the ball on a tomato can.

— *Tom Ferrick*

When I pitched with Paige *[with the Browns in 1952]*, he was a terrific pitcher and a terrific fellow to be around.

He had his own way of getting in shape and everything. He knew how to do it, even in exhibition games, especially out in California with the cool and the dampness. Just before he was ready to pitch in a ballgame he'd go in and pour hot water over his wrist, let water run on his wrist for awhile. He'd put some oil on it, what he called his snake oil. He said that's all he needed to warm up. He'd throw maybe one or two pitches and he'd be ready to pitch in the ballgame.

Down there in St. Louis, especially in '53, Bill Veeck told him he didn't have to be at the ballgame until around the fifth inning. Satch liked the idea of going fishing, and this one particular night we were playing a ball game and Satch came in late. After the ballgame we went in to take our shower and the whole shower was filled with fish. Satch had been fishing all day and brought his fish right out to the ballpark and put them in the shower. He was forever pulling stunts such as that.

— *Bob Cain*

I was with the Browns *[in 1953]* when Satchel Paige was there. Veeck, the showman that he was, had one of those La-Z-Boy chairs in the bullpen, and Satch strolled down there about the fourth or fifth inning. He didn't go down to the bullpen for the whole game. He would sit there in his easy chair. He was some specimen. I don't mean he could throw consistently like a Nolan Ryan or somebody like that, but on a given pitch he could. He certainly would have been something special had he been able to pitch in the major leagues during his prime.

— *Billy Hunter*

Satchel? Oh, he was beautiful. He was nice. I enjoyed him. He would always go down there and sit in the bullpen to get away from that fan they had. It was so hot there in St. Louis, they had a big fan blowing down a little runway there, and you'd take cold sitting around that thing.

So I'd go down there and talk to him. We'd visit and talk about his early days, my early days, and all that stuff. He was a real delight and very bright. All that good background in baseball, it was really fun visiting with him.

— *Tommy Byrne*

Satchel Paige, what a character he was. When I came up in 1952, I was the youngest player in either league. In fact, I'm the youngest player ever to have played with the Browns.

I was six foot two, one-eighty, strong, healthy — well, here we've got the youngest player in the league, in either league, and the oldest player in the history of either league on the same team.

Our trainer was a fellow by the name of Bob Bowman. Bowman, back then, was considered the best, the most knowledgeable, the one closest to a college-trained type of trainer. So somebody got this brilliant idea. They waited until Satchel and I were coming out of the shower, and they said, "Hey, you two, come over and sit over here on the bench, next to each other." They blindfolded Bowman. He was to touch these two guys, their leg muscles and whatever, and pick the younger of the two. He picked Satchel. That didn't really make me feel so bad at all because Satchel was a giant. *[Paige was 6'3½" and 180 pounds.]* You just wonder what have might have been, had he been able to play in the majors his whole career.

— J.W. Porter

Satchel Paige was unbelievable with his control. We brought Satch in relief to pitch to one hitter, like with the bases loaded with two outs, and we had to get the hitter out or they were either going to tie or win the game. The guy hit a one-hopper right back to Satch. He fielded the ball, and he never even glanced toward first. He threw it under his left arm and he threw a perfect strike to the first baseman.

When he threw the ball, he turned and started walking to the dugout, never looked to see where it went, and of course he threw it right, a perfect throw, without looking.

I followed him from third base into the dugout. Hornsby was on the top step and he said, "That just cost you five hundred dollars. You ever do that again and I'll see that you never play for me again."

And Satch never even slowed down. He just walked on by, and I walked up the runway behind him, and I could hear Satch saying, "That crazy old man, what'd he think, they's going to move first base? It's been there ever since I've played."

— Jim Dyck

I think Satchel Paige was absolutely the epitome, the end of the line. I don't think this life will ever see another one of him. In '56 the Phillies sent me to their Miami club. Satchel was with the Miami club. The first day I get there, here comes the eighth, ninth inning, and Satchel comes out there pitching. Most pitchers find their spot on the rubber real early. They find it while they're warming up, and they pitch out of that one spot. Satchel walked out there and he pitched off one spot. He threw a couple pitches from there. He moved over a little bit, and then he was on the other end of the rubber. Then he was standing on top of the rubber, which is a no-no. After the game I said to him, "Satch, I saw you moving around on the rubber. The way I learned this thing was find your spot on the rubber and then stay there. But you went from one end of the rubber to the other. You even went on top of the rubber."

He said, "That's the way I gets my triangle."

I said, "Satch, I understand up and down in the strike zone, inside, up in the strike zone, outside — down in the strike zone, inside, and down in the strike zone, outside."

And he said, "No, I's a getting my triangle."

I said, "You telling me that you got a triangle up, down, in, and out?"

He said, "You got it. You're the first white man that ever caught it."

That's how fine that guy could throw the baseball. He had more patience than anybody

I've ever seen in my life. When he walked out there on that mound it was his. I saw him take nine minutes to throw three pitches to Luke Easter and pop him up. That man knew gamesmanship. He was the greatest pitcher I have ever seen in my life. All he could do was throw strikes, and he could throw it in a thimble. And I think he was fifty-three then.
— *Bubba Church*

Parnell never threw a ball above the knees so the hitter couldn't get it off the ground. Great sinker and a great slider. Mel was a great pitcher, great to play behind. You knew where the guy was going to hit the ball before he hit it.
— *Don Buddin*

We were playing Cleveland, and Satchel Paige relieved. Eddie Joost, I think it was, hit a home run in the ninth inning, and the game was over. Everybody was off the field and old Satch was still standing out on the mound, just dumbfounded. The next day the same thing happened. They called me in for a pinch hitter and put him in for relief. There were two out, I think, at the time. He threw me a fastball and I swung and missed. He threw me another fastball and I swung at it and missed. He threw me a third fastball and I hit a double out in right center field against the wall, and that won the game. Everybody was off the field, and he was still standing there. But that man could throw. *[Paige was in his 40s before coming to the big leagues, where his lifetime record was 28–31 with 32 saves. Box scores confirming Scheib's account were not found, but Paige was with Cleveland in 1948 and 1949.]*
— *Carl Scheib*

When Satchel Paige came down there to St. Louis *[in 1951]*, in the fall of the year we barnstormed. That was pretty big stuff in those days. We barnstormed a pretty good-sized trip. We'd go up through Colorado, Nebraska, Iowa. We played a pretty good schedule. When I think about that now, Satchel Paige started every cussed game, can you imagine that? In other words, he was the big attraction. We had guys like Bob Turley, Walker Cooper, Roy Sievers, we had a lot of good guys, but Satchel Paige was still a big star. We had about five pitchers with our team, so we would play one day and then pitch a little maybe the next and then be off a day and then pitch again, but not Satch. He started every cussed game. In cold weather, too. Isn't that amazing?
— *Ned Garver*

Jimmy Piersall was a high-strung fella, but he was an outstanding ballplayer. He was one of the greatest defensive ballplayers I ever saw. He wasn't a bad hitter either. He was a real excellent ballplayer, wasn't any doubt about that. He could go get that ball. I saw him make some unbelievable catches.
— *Boo Ferriss*

I roomed with Piersall when I came up in '52, and that's the year he had his mental breakdown. I came up at the end of the year, and I'd played with him at Birmingham. They thought, for some reason, that I would be a steadying influence for him if I roomed with him.

It was really a tough chore for me. He had to be the center of attraction, and if he wasn't, he did something to be the center of attraction. Like if we were in an elevator and nobody would recognize him, he'd do something to make sure they recognized him before we got off the elevator, or if we were in a restaurant and nobody recognized him, he would make some sort of scene before we left so they would know that Jimmy Piersall was there.

Even on the field, playing with a guy like Ted Williams, who was getting the publicity, I think that's why I think he did so many things — to try to get the limelight put on him. In center field, Piersall would sometimes try to distract the hitter, like Stanky had done one time in the forties, get behind second base and wave his arms to distract the hitter. I guess the hitter complained and they made him stop doing it.

I can remember him one time between doubleheaders in New Orleans in the minor leagues, Piersall went out to get a hot dog in his jock strap under the stands.

But he was a very good defensive outfielder. He was a centerfielder. In '53 they put him in right field, because we had a guy came up named Tommy Umphlett who was a good centerfielder. They put Piersall in right, which was good in Fenway because right field was a larger area, and he could play that one too.

He hurt his arm in a throwing contest with Willie Mays, in either '53 or '54, I think. We played an exhibition game against the Giants. We had these contests where you throw for distance and accuracy, a home run hitting contest, these different things. They threw from the outfield, and Mays had a great arm and Piersall tried to stay up with him, and he hurt his arm. He never did throw that well afterwards, but he played a shallow outfield, and he could go get the ball. He was a good hustler. He'd battle you and he'd hit his .280. *[In his 17 big league seasons, Piersall hit .272 and fielded .990.]*
— **Milt Bolling**

One day in Nashville Jim Piersall took a water pistol out and shot the umpire right in the face for calling him out on strikes.
— *Bob Lennon*

Piersall was always full of surprises. Lou Boudreau tried to make a shortstop out of him, and that didn't work. I recall a game I was pitching against Satchel Paige in Boston. It was reported that twenty thousand were turned away at the gate. It was the night game of a day-night doubleheader. I was trying to get into the ballpark and I couldn't get through the crowd coming from behind the left-field fence to come around to get into the parking lot. Luckily, a policeman on horseback saw me trying to get me through the crowd so he came along on horseback and opened up the crowd so I could get into the ballpark. Had he had not done that, I probably would have been late for the start of the game.

Anyway, the game gets into the ninth inning. We were tied 2–2. Jimmy Piersall was in the on-deck circle. Vern Stephens was the hitter. Piersall was jumping up and down and acting like a monkey in the on-deck circle while Satchel Paige was pitching. He distracted Satchel and Stephens hit one out of the ballpark and we won the ballgame. Satchel Paige said what a stupid fool he was to let a real monkey, meaning Piersall, break his concentration.

Most of Piersall's antics were done down in the minor leagues, from what I've heard. They kind of straightened him out some when he got to the big leagues. There's the so-called fight between him and Billy Martin. But that never did happen. I was there. They got into a heated discussion around the batting cage, and some of the guys called them two little banty roosters and said, "Why don't you two little banty roosters go down to the tunnel of the dugout and fight it out?" So they did, they went down to the tunnel of the dugout. Ellis Kinder came along and butted their two heads together and that was the end of it.

Another time Piersall was accused of kicking Vern Stephens' kid in the rear. I was in the clubhouse when it supposedly happened, and it never did happen. He wasn't within five yards of Vern Stephens' kid when he went through a kicking motion. He couldn't have reached him with a ten foot leg. It made a good story anyway.

— *Mel Parnell*

One time I said to Pee Wee Reese, "Jesus, there were times in my career so far where I've hoped that the ball wouldn't be hit to me. Have you ever felt like that?"

I didn't expect him to say yes, I guess. But he told me, "Yes, I have, are you kidding?"

That really made me feel good. Up until then I was thinking, "Am I the only guy in this game that gets at times when you say, "Gee, I hope the ball doesn't come my way?" And he said the same thing. I think it helped me the rest of my career. So I didn't worry about it.

— *Wayne Terwilliger*

One day in Ebbets Field Pee Wee Reese was making a double play and he stepped over me while I was trying to take him out to keep him from making that double play. He tripped and fell down. He got up and I got up and was brushing my pants off and he came by me and tapped me on the head and said, "Nice slide, Jim."

Now, there's a guy. He knew his job and knew what my job was and thought I did a pretty good job of getting him out of there. He played hard. He could really play that shortstop. He wasn't a little guy, he got his nickname from shootin' marbles.

— *Jim Greengrass*

Any time we went in to New York I knew it was going to be a challenge because most of the time I got Allie Reynolds. And if not him then it was Vic Raschi. So it was Kinder and I and Reynolds and Raschi. I knew I had a better shot against Raschi. But any time I caught Reynolds I knew I had one hell of a battle. As a matter of fact, he did pitch a no-hitter against me. Reynolds was a hell of a pitcher. Any time you battled him you were in for a tough one. He should be in the Hall of Fame without a doubt.

— *Mel Parnell*

Allie Reynolds was the toughest pitcher I've ever faced. He was a hard thrower, but say you got a base hit off him the first time up. The second time up you might hit a ball hard, and next time up you hit a base hit, and you're feeling pretty good. But if you come up there in the ninth inning with the ballgame on the line, you're not going to see the same guy. He could just pace himself so well.

He was a tough competitor. I'm sure if he had not left the starting ranks and went to being a reliever, he might have tacked on another thirty or forty wins or more. He was a money ballplayer.

— *Ray Boone*

Wally Westlake is a very close friend of mine, and a terrific teammate, and we sort of palled around together. And he got traded. Here's what happened: we were taken to a luncheon at the Duquesne Club in Pittsburgh. The Duquesne Club in Pittsburgh was the most exclusive club in Pittsburgh, and it was made up of all the people that had all the affluence and what have you. Very restricted. So at this luncheon Branch Rickey was the featured speaker, and he had Westlake and I there as representatives of the Pittsburgh Pirates.

Rickey got up and made this pompous speech about what he was going to do for Pittsburgh — in the early days, when he first came there, in 1951, I guess it was. And he made this speech, and of course he was charming; he was a great speaker, and extremely intelligent.

He said, "And on this team there are two people that will never be traded from this ballclub, and they're both sitting right here. Wally Westlake and Ralph Kiner." That afternoon Westlake was traded away from our club to St. Louis.

I was traded away the next year. But that's the way he was.

— *Ralph Kiner*

I had a lot of dealings with Branch Rickey when he joined the Pittsburgh club, because he took over as general manager. He changed the organization around quite a bit. He was a very innovative guy. He brought a lot of things into baseball. He was a very shrewd guy, but he was also awful tight, I'll put it that way. He was a tough man to deal with, as far as your salary. He didn't want to give you anything.

He was a great believer in the farm system. He did a great job at St. Louis, and also, even with the Dodgers. He built the Dodger team up even before he came to Pittsburgh. He was partly responsible for those good players they had, and good teams they had in the last forties and really early fifties before he left the Brooklyn club.

— *Pete Castiglione*

One year Preacher Roe went 21–2. Rickey gave Preacher a blank contract and told him to fill in the amount. He did. Rickey looked at it and said, "I'd have given you more, but since you signed this one, that's what you get."

Another time I hadn't signed and went to spring training. I wanted a $500 cost of living raise. Rickey met me there and I gave him the unsigned contract. I told him I wanted the raise.

He asked, "Have you unpacked yet?" I told him I hadn't.

He said, "Don't bother. Go back to Brooklyn."

I told my wife and she said, "We don't have train fare back to Brooklyn." So we had no choice but to sign. There was no raise.

— *Cal Abrams*

Branch Rickey and I got along real well. I respected him and I guess he respected me as far as judging young kids or pitchers. He was just great to me. He tried to make me a manager, but I was not for it. I don't like paperwork, for one thing. That wasn't my cup of soup.

— *Mike Sandlock*

Branch Rickey was the first one to have his players use batting helmets. Before then we had those little inside liners that we had in our caps, but we didn't have helmets. You didn't think about getting hit. That's a negative way to approach the game. You might expect to get knocked down if the fellow ahead of you just hit one, but that was just part of the game.

— *Billy Hitchcock*

Branch Rickey treated the ballplayers good. He was probably the first one that started having a bus pick the players up at the hotel and take us to the ballpark. We'd had to take cabs out there. On the road we'd get three or four and take a cab. Of course, we'd have to pay for it. And he was one of the ones that let us sign checks in the hotel rather than give us meal money. I remember when Mike McCormick came to us from the Braves, he said, "Geez, I heard that this guy was tight and all that. But they're treating us better than anybody I know in the big leagues."

— *Spider Jorgensen*

Branch Rickey was the greatest personality I've ever known. I used to do impersonations of him. I could impersonate him well. Branch Jr. was a great guy. Branch Sr. was in the dining room in Fort Myers getting his ankles taped. He had a big sheet over him, lying on his back, and he had a big belly — Branch Jr. said, "Go in and do an impersonation of him."

I said, "Oh, man, I don't want to do that. I don't want to embarrass myself."

He said, "Go ahead, he'd enjoy that."

I went in there. I started in, "There's nobody I'd rather see up with the bases loaded and the score tied the bottom of the ninth inning but Dick Cole, but not for my team."

He started to laugh a little bit.

"Bob Friend, they used to say he's got more native stuff than anybody on the staff, but, of course, he got most of it when he trained in Cuba."

He laughed, his belly started shaking. He said, "Oh, Judas Priest" — was his favorite expression — he said, "That's good, where did you learn to do that?"

I said, "Well, I've been in the organization for about nine years now. Of course, I haven't taken any money out of it."

And he said, "No, and you won't."

— *Nellie King*

My character's mellow. Jim Rivera and guys like that, they were the humor guys. I just kind of rode along and laughed at their situations. I can remember Dick Donovan, when he was pitching. He'd fold his towel every inning. I mean, it was really a superstition. Every time he'd move away from the towel Rivera would just throw it on the ground and stuff like that, and Donovan would get mad. But knowing it was Rivera, it was just a loosey-goosey situation.

— *Jim Landis*

Rizzuto was a great one. He was Most Valuable Player in the American League one year *[in 1950]*, and he was what, two foot tall. He played on five straight World Championship teams, and probably played on ten World Championship teams altogether *[Rizzuto played on nine pennant winners and seven World Champions]*, and the guy's two feet tall, so you know he's a hell of an athlete, playing every day.

— *Bob Kuzava*

Phil Rizzuto was a great bunter. He could start going to first base and pull that bat in there real good. In fact a lot of guys could bunt pretty good, even pitchers, 'cause they had to practice that quite a bit. That's mostly what they were called on half the time. If they called for a sacrifice, most of the time they could do it.

— *Carl Scheib*

Robin Roberts was a fine human being, and a great guy to be on the ball club. I remember one time we were playing against St. Louis. The bottom of the ninth, we were behind 3–2 I think. Robin was the pitcher and he went into the clubhouse and started to get dressed. I hit a home run off Howie Pollet and tied the score. Robin had to get dressed and come back out and finish the ballgame. I think we won it in the tenth or eleventh, and Robin came up to me and said, "I owe you one." Chalked that up to a loss, and he got a W.

— *Bobby Morgan*

Robbie was a guy that you loved to hit against. He had great control. But you could hit him. He didn't bother you any. He was the kind of guy you'd say, "Roberts is pitching today. You'll go up and get a comfortable oh for four."

He paid me a great compliment one day. I got three base hits in a game in 1954, and it cost him a ballgame. I came up to bat the next time I faced him and Seminick said, "Robbie's really ticked off at you, you'd better be loose."

I said, "I'm not worried. It won't hurt any." And he threw one under my chin, knocked me down. I got up and said, "That's the greatest compliment that guy could pay me."

When I was traded to Philly, Robbie asked me, "How'd you hit that ball that beat me? I threw a slider outside and you jerk it out to left-center for a double."

I said, "I'll tell you, Robbie. I was watching my son play in the yard, and I threw him a ball, and he reached out and hit a ball like that and I thought, by golly, that's a pretty good idea."

He just turned around and said, "Oh, you're so full of crap."

When I was Phillies, Andy Seminick said you could catch Roberts in a rocking chair.

Benny Bengough was our bullpen coach. Benny cut the legs down on a stool and he'd take Robbie to the bullpen and he'd sit on the outside corner of the plate on that stool holding the glove right there. Robbie would throw that slider right there and hit it time after time after time. He would hit ninety times out of a hundred with Benny never moving his glove.

— *Jim Greengrass*

I learned a lot about playing infield from just watching and talking to Brooks Robinson up at Vancouver when he was there. This was late in my career, too late for me to go back up. *[After Dyck's 1956 big league season, he finished his career with five years in the Pacific Coast League.]* The secret — the same thing Marty Marion had told me when I was at St. Louis — the secret was getting your eyes at a low level, so you're looking up at some of these bad hops instead of down on top of them. The lower you were looking up at the ball, the quicker you reacted. I could always hear Marty over at short with his glove up to his mouth, and he'd say, "Get your tail down, get your tail town."

— *Jim Dyck*

In my teens the Oakland American Legion team I played on in '49 and '50 were national champions both years. Never done before. In those two years, we only lost one game. The only other future major leaguer to play on those teams was Frank Robinson. He was good enough in the ninth grade to play on the team when I was a senior. And you could tell, even then, that he was something special.

— *J.W. Porter*

Back then we had a competitor who we played against twenty-two times a year named Jackie Robinson. He was the greatest competitor I ever saw in my life.

— *Bubba Church*

Jackie Robinson was a tough hitter for me when I first came up. A good line drive hitter. In fact, he stole home two times on me in the early fifties, and he did that when I was taking my stretch.

— *Bob Friend*

I don't think there is any question but what Robinson was one of the best base runners. He really wasn't that fast, little short choppy steps, you know. Pigeon-toed, and he didn't look like he was running that fast, but he was quick, he'd get off quick, and he didn't waste any motion.

He was a great slider. He slid hard right straight toward the bag. I think he had them buffaloed too. He was such an intimidating base runner. He'd get off and be jumping around, and they'd try to pick him off.

I remember one time when I was with the Cubs, we had a play. Robinson was on first base and I had a pickoff play with the catcher. He was going to pitch out and was going to circle around — it was a bunt situation — the first baseman faked, went in, and I went in behind Robinson. The catcher threw down there and I had him out. He stepped on my foot. He stepped so hard, it hurt me. I pulled my foot out of the way. I was more concerned with pulling my foot out of the way than I was getting him out. I tagged him, but the umpire said he was on the bag. I said, "Hell, he was on my foot."

But he was exciting to watch. Yeah, he was. He was the greatest guy — it's been written a hundred times about when you get him in a rundown. He could stay in that rundown and get out of it better than anybody I ever saw.

— *Wayne Terwilliger*

Preacher Roe couldn't hurt you with a pitch if he hit you in the middle of the forehead. But his control was perfect. He could spot the ball anywhere. If he did throw two or three balls, Campy would go to the mound.

Other catchers might rant and yell for him to get the ball over. Not Campy. He'd talk to Roe about his chicken farm or whatever, just to take Roe's mind off things to help him get his control back.

— *Cal Abrams*

Preacher Roe would get out there and he'd have a big conversation with nobody in particular. All the time he pitched he'd be talking. I turned and asked, "Campy, what's he talking about?" Campy said, "Don't nobody know, he's just talking."

— *Jim Greengrass*

Pete Runnels was a great hitter. He won two batting titles. He used that left field wall at Fenway about as good as anybody, even though he was a left-handed hitter.

— *Frank Malzone*

I remember Hank Sauer and his 40-ounce bat. He was by no means a natural hitter. He worked hard and kept a little black book on every pitcher in the league.

— *Paul Schramka*

I met a sports writer in Atlanta one day when I was down there for an old-timer's game, and a sports writer came up and asked me, "Jim, I need a story. Do you know any of these ballplayers? I'd like to get a good story from some of the oldtimers."

I said, "Well, there's a Hall of Famer right there. Enos Slaughter."

He said, "What did Enos Slaughter do?"

I said, "I'm sorry, but I don't think I can help you, friend." That tore me up. The guy didn't know who Enos Slaughter was.

— *Jim Greengrass*

I saw Enos Slaughter pop a ball up, I mean high, one of those major league popups, and he takes off— he always did. See, that's the difference between the ballplayers today and the ballplayers when I played. If you popped up and didn't run that ball out to first base, you were fined.

Well, he put his head down and took off. That ball was played as a fair ball. It was kind of misplayed in the infield because it was high or the sun or some reason. It kind of rolled away a little bit and Enos slid into third base. He got a three base error on a pop fly in the infield.

— *Danny Litwhiler*

I couldn't get a base hit off Gerry Staley. He was always out there smiling, or looked like he was smiling. I must have been distracted or something, I might have hit two foul balls off him all the times I batted against him. He'd just throw his glove out there and he had me.

He was a good pitcher, don't make any mistake about that. He threw overhand and he threw side-armed and he threw knuckleballs. He threw all kinds of stuff. He was the toughest pitcher for me to hit against.

— *Jim Greengrass*

I preferred hitting against left-handed pitchers, in a general sense, I guess most right-handers would have to say that. But there were right-handers I liked to hit against. Certain ones I wouldn't want to ever hit against. A guy like Mel Stottlemyre wore my thumbs out.

First of all, I just think Stottlemyre threw harder than you realized. He had a little bit of a sneaky motion, threw harder than you realized, and the ball really bore in on your fists. It was hard to get the bat out on front on him Many times my hands said "ouch" with him.

— *Jim Landis*

One of the toughest competitors was Vern Stephens. I think Ted was a team leader, in his own way, because of the great hitter he was. He set an example for the rest of us. He preached and talked hitting to us all the time. Billy Goodman and Pete Runnels and Pesky and Dom — all those people had a leader quality. Billy Klaus could keep you loose. He led off for us. If a pitcher got him out he used to come back and say, "Hey, we'll get this guy, he doesn't have anything today," you know, that kind of stuff. He'd build confidence in you and keep you loose.

— *Dick Gernert*

One fellow that got in my hair all the time was Vern Stephens. I could be going along pitching a fine ballgame and the first thing you know it would be the eighth or ninth inning and Stephens would come up and invariably he'd hurt me. I tried everything I could to get him out, but he always seemed to come up with that important base hit. So I'd say he was my nemesis. I never had much luck with him. Of course, a lot of them I didn't have too much luck with, but he stands out as one of the toughest guys for me to get out.

— *Randy Gumpert*

Clyde Sukeforth, the bullpen coach, claimed to the papers that with Cal Abrams and Carl Furillo in the outfield, Duke Snider wouldn't even be necessary, even though he was a great ballplayer. That meant that we could cover the whole outfield. I really appreciated that. It made me feel like I was a decent ballplayer in those days.

— *Cal Abrams*

Frank Sullivan was a very humorous, good guy. He's six-seven and really an upbeat, jovial guy, a breath of fresh air. We were in a tight ballgame, 1–1 with Detroit. I got put in the game in the eighth inning as a pinch hitter and got a base hit. I either knocked in a run or kept the inning alive where we scored the second run. Now we go into the last of the ninth. He walks two guys, a base hit, he's got the bases loaded, one out. He called time out and called me and Malzone and our shortstop — it was either Buddin or Bolling — to the mound and said, "I don't know what you three guys are going to do, but I'm going to throw this son of a bitch the best sinker and he's going to hit a ground ball, and you better get me out of this goddamn game." And sure enough, one or two pitches later the batter hits a shot to Frank at third and he throws it to me and bang-bang. We walk off the field and Frank's laughing. He was good to play behind.

— *Ted Lepcio*

George Susce stressed running the pitchers to keep our legs in shape. He was responsible for keeping us in good shape by using that fungo bat to hit fly balls to us. We had a left-hander on our ballclub who wasn't with us long. He didn't like chasing fungos. So he got to the ballpark early one day and went over to Susce's locker and got his fungo bat and had it cut in half. He stood back in the locker room, and Susce grabbed by the handle and the thing parted. Susce was quite mad. He was trying to find out who did it, but I don't think he ever did.

— *Mel Parnell*

Wayne Terwilliger was a hell of a utility man. There's a story that when he was in the service, he got a piece of shrapnel in his derriere, and it made him very nervous and edgy when there was a storm threatening over the ballfield while the players were on the field. He used to run for the dugout. I don't know if that's true or not.

— *Cal Abrams*

When I was with the Giants at the start of the '51 season, Bobby Thomson was in a terrible slump. He was playing left field because they had brought Mays up. At that time I was playing a little right field because Mueller was hurt, and pinch hitting. Then when he came back I more or less got expendable.

But Bobby was in a bad slump then, and eventually, after I left, they brought him in to play third base, and he started hitting the ball. I think it was Lockman, or somebody, who was talking to him and he kind of closed his stance a little bit, and he started really

ripping the ball good, which he continued for the rest of his career. But at that time he was all spread out, and he wasn't hitting worth a damn. *[Thomson's pennant-winning home run capped a season in which he finished with 32 home runs, 101 RBI, and a .293 batting average.]*
— *Spider Jorgensen*

Joe Tipton was a catcher who liked to talk to batters. He was always getting on Ted Williams. Williams couldn't hardly bat when Joe caught. Joe would be telling him stuff and Ted would have to back out and laugh.
— *Carl Scheib*

You're not going to believe this, but the toughest hitter for me was Earl Torgeson of the Braves. God knows, I'd make the best pitches on him. He'd hit it on the end of the bat and bloop it. He'd hit it off his hands and bloop it. I don't know what his batting average was, but I told him in later years, "You bastard, you must have hit seven hundred and fifty off of me." He just laughed. *[Torgeson played 15 years and had a lifetime average of .265.]*
— *Bubba Church*

We went to Boston for two years and never won a game up there. And finally, you'd of thought I won the World Series. I went up there in 1952 and had to pitch eleven innings, but we finally beat them, and I'm telling you, the press was all over me like I won the last game of the World Series. It was the first game we won up there in two years.

Old Diz Trout started the game against me. He went maybe seven or eight innings, then they brought in big Al Benton, and he went the rest of the way and I finally beat him. That winter I went hunting up in Maine with Dizzy and he mentioned that game.

He said, "You young son of a gun, you so and so. If I hadn't been so damn old I'd of outlasted you." *[Trout was 37; Scheib, the Athletics' pitcher, was 25.]* He was kind of a character, and a good guy.
— *Carl Scheib*

Jim Turner, the pitching coach when I was with the Yankees *[from 1948 to 1956]*, helped me the most of anybody. He was my Portland manager in Triple A *[in 1947]*. Then he came to the Yankees as pitching coach. He taught me more about catching and pitching than anybody. *[Turner was the Yankees pitching coach from 1949 to 1959 and from 1966 to 1973.]*
— *Charlie Silvera*

Elmer Valo was a real hustler. Every ballpark he ever played in he'd always run through a fence. *[Valo played 20 years, hit .282.]* He was a good hitter, and just a great hustler, a great guy. When he ran the bases he'd put his head down and run and somebody would always have to stop him some way.
— *Bill Renna*

Bobo Holloman pitched a no-hitter his first start *[May 6, 1953]*. It was against the Philadelphia Athletics. One play, Joe Astroth — he was strictly a pull hitter — hit a ground ball up the middle. I went over and dove and caught the ball and threw to first off my knees. Astroth was like Sherm Lollar or most catchers in that he didn't run very fast, so that saved the no-hitter.

Veeck used to wear those open-necked white shirts all the time, so he bought me a dozen shirts because of that play. He was a player's owner. He had his apartment right in the ballpark. He used to come into the clubhouse, and many times he'd come in prior to the game, and take off his wooden leg and throw it in the corner and we'd sit there and play cards on the training table until the team was supposed to report.

— *Billy Hunter*

Sammy White was a guy that added a little laughter around the clubhouse, kept everything loose. He was a good receiver. He could handle the low ball very good. He'd tell you, "Go ahead and throw it. If I can't catch it, I can block it." So that gave you a lot of confidence, throwing to Sammy.

— *Mel Parnell*

Complete opposites, Sam White and I had more fun before, during, and after the game than anyone should have. A great catcher, sometimes he caught me without signs.

— *Frank Sullivan*

We were playing the Giants. Hornsby was telling me how to hit Wilhelm's knuckleball. He said, "This knuckleball, just try to play pepper with him. You hit it by him you've got a base hit. He's only sixty feet six inches from you. Just try to hit a line drive. A nice easy short swing, right back him."

So I get up there. Wilhelm throws that dancer at me. I swung straight down at that damn ball. If I hadn't hit the ground with my bat I'd of hit my leg and broke it. Wes Westrum was catching. He just rolled over laughing. The umpire was laughing. Forty thousand people were laughing.

— *Jim Greengrass*

Gene Woodling was one hitter who gave me a fit. He stood over the plate, and there was no place to pitch him. He just hit the ball every time; he was hard to strike out. *[In his seven year career, Woodling struck out just once in roughly every 14 at-bats.]*

— *Carl Scheib*

Whitlow Wyatt was my pitching coach at Atlanta. And early in the 1951 season Whitlow come to me and said, "Don, you're too careful. You got too good a stuff to get behind hitters like you do. You're picking at the corners, and you're getting behind. Challenge them a little more. You've got a good fastball and you've got a good curveball. Bring it to them. Make them hit that ball.

And it give me a little different attitude. I think it made me a much better pitcher. I tried to throw the fastball not too much on the corner but just concentrate on just keeping it down. And if he hit the first pitch, fine, but I wanted to work harder on getting that first pitch over. I got ahead of hitters and then would make a shot at a corner. I become a good pitcher from there, 'cause in the next year I went to Milwaukee and I really had a great year in Triple A ball. *[In 1952 Liddle led the American Association in winning percentage. 810 with a 17–4 record, in strikeouts, 159, and with 2.70 ERA.]*

— *Don Liddle*

Early Wynn was kind of nasty on the mound. He'd just soon on a 3–0 pitch knock you down. He'll remind you that he knows what he's doing. You had to be very careful with a guy like him around.

— *Ted Lepcio*

Rudy York was at our spring training camp one time when I was with the Athletics, and he said, "Remember, when you're up at the plate, the pitcher's going to make one mistake, invariably will make one mistake, they can't throw the ball where they want all the time. So you've got to be ready to hit that mistake."

— *Bill Renna*

Eddie Yost had a reputation for walking. A lot of us could take the same third strike, and it would be a strike instead of a ball. Maybe his average could have been a little better if he'd have gone up there swinging more. It seemed like he was always hitting with two strikes on him, 'cause he'd always take two strikes.

He was leading off, and that was his game, was just try to work the pitcher for a walk, and he sure did. But he could hit home runs, he had good power. *[Yost led the AL in walks six times and hit 139 home runs.]*

— *Herb Plews*

At Philadelphia, they used to boo the hell out of Gus Zernial, poor guy. I thought he did a good job. The guy was always trying real hard and he could hit the ball well. He hit a lot of home runs, he drove in a lot of runs, but the fans were really on him in Philadelphia, because he wasn't the most agile person because he was so big. It looked like he wasn't really trying, but he had a desire and he was trying.

Gus personally was a real nice guy. In fact, we used to kind of run together after the games. He and Joe DeMaestri and Don Bollweg and I. They were rooming together and Don and I were rooming together. Don Bollweg and I were the two guys that were traded off the Yankee roster in '53 to the A's, and we were roommates on the A's. We used to sit on the bench and shake our heads sometimes at the way some of the guys weren't paying attention. We tried to get guys to go and get up for the game and get a little spirit on the bench and everything, but it was like throwing gas on a fire I guess.

— *Bill Renna*

I remember a lot of defensive standouts. Like Hoot Evers and George Kell, and Bob Swift, who was a great defensive catcher. Not very well known, but I loved to pitch to him. With the White Sox, we had guys like Sherman Lollar and Jim Rivera, who to me was one of the most outstanding ballplayers. I feel the same way that Rogers Hornsby did when he said when he managed him in St. Louis, "Rivera and Clint Courtney were the only two players he'd ever pay to go see play." Now that's making a big statement about a guy coming from Hornsby's mouth.

— *Virgil Trucks*

You never saw anybody catch a ball one-handed. The type of gloves we used were a lot smaller, and they had the big heel on them with the felt.

And we wore those stupid old flannel woolen jobs. They were big and baggy. If you perspired a lot and hit the dirt with those woolen jobs it was just like you had two more tons you were carrying around with you.

— *Sibbi Sisti*

Chapter Nine

Swinging the Lumber

Baseball's popularity stems from its delicate balance between the batter's success and the pitcher's success. Baseball is built around tension, expectation. The duel between pitcher and batter is usually won by the pitcher. Even the very best batters hit safely just slightly more than 30 times in each 100 times at bat. The beauty of the game depends on a typical pitcher, over the course of a season, successfully retiring a typical batter about three-fourths of the time—and then the surprises. One can never know which one-fourth of the time the pitcher or batter will be successful or which pitcher or batter will not be typical.

Not since 1941, when Ted Williams hit .406, has a major league hitter had as many as 40 hits per each 100 at-bats for a full season. Only four players during the entire twentieth century (Ted Williams, Mickey Mantle, Rogers Hornsby, and Babe Ruth) reached base safely (by hits or walks) more times in a single season than they were retired.

Each batter has a different approach to hitting, a personal philosophy of how to best match his skills against a particular pitcher. Pitchers themselves reveal what it is like to be able to demonstrate their hitting skills. And, of course, all batters recall clearly special moments when they won that pitcher-batter duel.

Sure, I was nervous. Nervous is good with the game on the line, when you need to make the big play, get the key hit. It helps you keep that fine edge, maintain concentration. There's a difference between being nervous and being scared. Crucial situations never scared me; I enjoyed the challenge each and every time. I'm just glad I had a chance to come up so often in crucial situations, to do battle with the pitcher. Before every game if you're not a little nervous you should retire.
— *Jerry Lynch*

They asked Ted Williams one time who's the toughest hitter to get out late in the ballgame, and he named me. That's a hell of a compliment from a guy like him.
— *Gene Woodling*

If I got thrown at, it was by mistake.
— *Bobby Malkmus*

If you can't hit the fastball, you're not going to be in the big leagues, period. That's the name of the game. I was a first-ball hitter, and the pitchers knew it. If they threw a fastball close, I'm swinging. Because that's my strength, and because I had a hard time hitting the changes, which most everybody does — changes and curveballs.

— *Al Zarilla*

I was a switch-hitter all except one year. I think I just stayed left-handed one year. But I did switch from then on. I was better left-handed. I wasn't a long ball hitter. I was like Dixie Walker, and I'd flop them into left field or pull them through the box or something like that. Timing. I used to try to hit the ball wherever it was pitched.

— *Mike Sandlock*

Pitchers throwing inside didn't bother me personally. I got hit my share. I guess one reason why they didn't throw at us more than they did, it made a better hitter out of us. When they threw at me, they were letting me know they respected me. I took that as an act of desperation on their part. I was a spray hitter, I hit the ball where it was pitched. My theory on hitting was that I was going to comb that pitcher off the mound. I hit line drives, flat, hard line drives, not these little old squibs. I didn't strike out very many times, I usually hit the ball when I swung at it.

— *Pete Milne*

As a pinch hitter, I went up swinging. I'm not looking for a certain pitch and stand up there and take two. Then the pitcher's way out ahead, then you've got to hit in self-defense.

— *Pete Milne*

I had my game bat and I had bats that I used in batting practice. If I got one that was real good for a game bat, I'd set it aside. In 1953 when I was playing with Oakland in the Pacific Coast League, I played in 174 games and had 210 hits, and I used the same bat the whole year. I used a 36 ounce, 34 inch bat.

— *Pete Milne*

Shortstop was a lot easier for me than catching. I could concentrate on my hitting better. Every year I played shortstop I hit around three hundred, and when I got to be catching, I think the bat got heavy a little bit, or I slowed up or something.

— *Mike Sandlock*

I didn't like the guys who threw curveballs and all the other garbage. I was a fastball hitter and I wanted to see fastballs come up. I remember hitting two home runs in one game against Pedro Ramos. I beat him 2–0 that day. He reminds me of that every time I see him.

— *Milt Pappas*

Most of the time I was just trying to drive the ball. I knew if I hit the ball just right I was strong enough to hit it out of the ballpark. So I was just trying to make good contact and let the home runs come. There's occasions where you go for a home run because a home run was necessary, but on most of those occasions I either popped up or struck out. I think you have to approach pitchers differently. There were some left-handers like Score and Pierce and Parnell and those kind of guys that could keep the ball away from you enough that you couldn't actually pull the ball unless they made a mistake. Of course, pitchers do make mistakes and hitters gotta capitalize on them. I was always trying to drive the ball hard, and not necessarily pulling it. I did hit some balls over the center field fence, but never to right field. I think three balls I hit to right field went for home runs. [*Zernial hit 237 home runs in the big leagues.*]

— *Gus Zernial*

When I first started to play professional baseball *[1948]*, I hit everything to right field, right-center, and dead center. I couldn't pull the ball. Then Rip Sewell said, "Move closer to the plate." I moved on top of the plate and I developed my forearms and wrists, and started to pull everything, and then I couldn't hit anything on the other side of the diamond. Stan Musial stated that Frank Robinson and I were probably the two best pull hitters he's ever seen play the game, and that's a pretty good compliment coming from a man like him.

— *Frank Thomas*

I fashioned my hitting after Lloyd Waner, making contact, driving the ball the other way, toward third. If a fellow gave me trouble, I might bunt. I'd make him throw strikes. I tried to outfox the pitcher. I was never afraid of any pitcher.

When I first faced Mike "The Bear" Garcia I hit four line drives that almost hit him. Then he struck me out twice. So I made adjustments. Hitting is a matter of making adjustments.

— *Cal Abrams*

I bunted a lot, but I wish I had bunted more. I had good power and if I had gone with the bunting and not worried about the power I think I would have had better averages overall and maybe played longer. But I didn't, and that's history. [*Coan had a .254 lifetime average. His major league high in home runs was nine in 1951, when he hit .303. In the minors, he led both the Appalachian League and Southern Association in home runs.*]

— *Gil Coan*

There were so many players, like in the Coast League, that would have 130 RBIs and 45 home runs, and maybe at the end of the season they'd go up to the major league club and sit on the bench for about a week, and then they'd let him pinch hit, and he'd strike out on a curveball or get a fastball blown by him, and they'd sit him down for another three or four days and then give him another at bat, and they'd get him out. Then they'd send him back and say, "This guy can't hit the curve," and this guy would go back, and maybe for ten consecutive years would have a hundred RBIs or more in the Coast League or the American Association or maybe the International League.

And if you were the Yankees or the Cardinals or the Dodgers or whoever, if you took him up there and stuck him in his position and left him for a season, he'd give you a hundred RBIs and .30 to 40 home runs. They never got a chance. We had a player in Seattle late in my career by the name of Joe Durham [*Durham got 202 big league at-bats with the Orioles and Cardinals; he hit .188 with five home runs. Durham led the Piedmont league in stolen bases in 1953. In 1954 he led the Texas League in triples and drove in 108 runs. In 1957 he hit .391 in 50 games with San Antonio. After the '57 season, Durham had only five more big league at-bats.*]

I hit behind him for two or three years. I know how he could hit. Gosh, the guy was phenomenal. And they'd always send him back. He went up three or four times. He didn't get to play. They'd send him back, and say, "He can't hit the curveball." Well, I'd sit in the on-deck circle and watched him hit a lot of curveballs — and hit them a long ways. There were a lot of guys like that. You just had to be in the right place at the right time.

— *Jim Dyck*

The toughest pitcher I ever faced was Herb Score. I was a left-handed hitter and he threw that thing a hundred miles an hour. You just hoped he didn't hit you. I liked a guy named Connie Johnson, who used to pitch with the Orioles. I think I had four or five home runs off him one year. I just looked for the fastball. I don't think you can look for the curveball and hit the fastball. The main difference was, in '58 with the Tigers, 2–0 and 3–1, they gave me fastballs to hit, and I hit 20 home runs and drove in 83 runs, so the next year instead of giving me fastballs 2–0 and 3–1, they'd throw that flop curve up there, and I'd kill every worm in the infield. Ground balls. But they'd get a book on you.

— *Gail Harris*

In the big leagues I hit .305 one year and .288 another year. I could hit the ball, but the farther you went — you see, pitchers never get much batting practice, so it became tougher and tougher, I thought, to retain your hitting skills.

— *Ned Garver*

I loved to hit, and I wasn't a bad hitter. I was a right-handed hitter, but I could hit pretty good left-handed. We were in Augusta, Georgia, and the pitchers all used to come out early to get their hitting in. They'd get some infielder or somebody to pitch to us. I had hit one off the fence right-handed. Then the pitchers started hitting the opposite way, if you hit right-handed, you had to hit left-handed. So a few minutes later, I was hitting again, and Appleton, the manager, came walking through the stands going to the clubhouse. And the pitcher threw the ball and I hit that one off the right field wall left-handed. So that night during the ballgame the pitcher was due to hit and we had a man on third base. Appleton was coaching third and he's motioning for a left-handed hitter. Well, there's no left-handed hitter on the bench. So he motions for me to hit. I hit a fly ball to drive in the run. So from then on I started switch-hitting. Kept on switch-hitting from then on.

— *Sonny Dixon*

One reason you always pitched to Mantle was that he had Yogi batting behind him. But if you missed on Mantle, he'd crucify you. The first game I caught in '56, I think only two balls had ever been hit out of Griffith Stadium, and Mantle hit the two the same day off Pascual. He tried to pitch him high and tight, and he got it out over the plate a little bit. He hit one over dead center, 434, into a tree without leaves, and later in the game hit it over the tree. You could take a chance with Mantle, but you generally didn't make out too well. But if you walked him, you had Yogi right behind him. Yogi didn't have a weakness. He would hit any pitch pretty damn good. Why walk Mantle with an open base to get to Yogi?

— *Lou Berberet*

I was a pretty good hitter in college. I think my last year I hit something like .593. There's many a game in the majors I stayed in the 7th, 8th, or 9th — in fact, I was hitting for people in the 9th inning, ahead of some guys, the last few years I was playing.

I wondered whether I should have played first base or the outfield anyway. The last year I played I hit three home runs and only went to bat 37 times. I think the year before that I hit three and only went 50 some times. I was primarily relief pitching the last couple of years. I hit one about every 14, 15 times at bat those last two years. So I could swing the bat pretty good, but I just waited too late to get serious about it.

— *Tommy Byrne*

Sometimes it was the better pitchers I had pretty good luck against. Guys like Robin Roberts, who was one of the better pitchers in those years. Also against Newcombe, him and Carl Erskine. Sal Maglie, fair against him. But then there was guys like Bob Rush of the Cubs, Vern Bickford with the old Braves, and Lew Burdette, that I could hardly buy hits off of. I just couldn't seem to do the job against some of them. It's hard to explain why that happens that way. Sometimes you just have more confidence against certain teams and against certain pitchers than you do against certain others.

— *Pete Castiglione*

I loved to hit lefties. If I'd been a platoon player, just hitting lefthanders, I'd have been phenomenal. I hit Score. I hit Lopat. I hit two home runs off Lopat in a game. And I hit Whitey Ford, and I hit Bobby Shantz. They had a Jim Dyck day in St. Louis, it was a doubleheader. I was a little concerned about who was going to pitch because I wanted to do well in front of my hometown fans, and when I heard Shantz was pitching I was delighted. I only got one hit off him, but I hit a couple others in the hole that they made great plays on. But I liked those lefthanders.

— *Jim Dyck*

It's a shame that they tried to change Mazerowski's hitting, because when he first came up he hit 19 home runs, and he never hit that many after that in one year. *[Mazerowski hit eight in his first full season and 19 in his second full season. He played for 17 years, averaging eight home runs a year.]* But they said, "You've got to hit to different fields."

Sisler tried to do the same thing with me and I told him, "George, I'm not the same type of hitter as you." *[Sisler, a Hall of Famer, had a career average of .340 but was not a home run hitter.]*

— *Frank Thomas*

It was just automatic in the old days, you go up and the count's 2 and 0 and you look down and you've got a take sign, then pretty soon the count's 3 and 1, you look down, you've got a take sign, especially if you're behind. getting men on base and winning the game.

— *Jim Dyck*

The biggest thing I learned coming up from the minor leagues, there was a difference in pitching as I got higher up. In the lower minors they threw just as hard, they all had pretty good stuff, but they didn't have the control they had later on. When I moved up higher, in Triple A especially, they started working me different. They started using the outer half of the plate more. Pinky Higgins was my manager at Louisville at the time, and I went to him and said, "Geez, I'm having trouble with that ball away from me."

He asked me, "A slider or fastball?"

I said, "It's a slider, mostly."

He said, "Well, why don't you just move up on the plate a little bit, get better plate coverage?"

I did, and it really helped me. You know, I realized which was a strike and which wasn't.

There were certain pitchers in the league that you had to change for. There were guys that would always throw the ball just about knee high or lower. You had to move up on the plate or else you'd be swinging at too many bad balls off him. And you move around in the batter's box a lot to adjust to certain pitchers. But most of the time I had the same approach — you know, look for a ball that I liked in the area that I liked until got two strikes, and then give in to the pitcher a little bit and get better plate coverage and try to hit the ball to straightaway. And if he made a mistake I could still pull it.

— *Frank Malzone*

One game when I was with Detroit the Yankees had 2 guys on in the 12th inning, and Mantle beat out a swinging bunt down the third base line. And I thought, "Well, I'll get Yogi out." I threw one up about neck high and he hit it out of the park and I was a loser again.

— *Bob Smith*

The reason for my two straight three hundred seasons *[Coan hit .303 in 1950 and 1951]* was that I learned a little more about hitting, how to look for a pitch, and when you get a pitch, to hit it. That's the difference in a good hitter and a poor hitter. The good hitter looks for a pitch, and when he gets it he hits it. But the poor hitter, he may get the pitch he's looking for, but he doesn't hit it. Of course, I was so green those first two or three years that those pitchers could make me look bad.

— *Gil Coan*

My career shows I hit better against right-handed pitchers. I can't understand that because I loved to hit against left-handed pitchers. I suppose my claim to fame was being a leather man, more defense than offense. I got my fame for my defense. But got my share of RBIs at the right time.

Of course, when we'd go to Cincinnati, and they'd say, "Hey, Ewell Blackwell's going to pitch tonight," I didn't like that. He was tough on me.

— *Marty Marion*

Al Rosen, a right-handed hitter for Cleveland, always gave me trouble, no matter what kind of stuff I had. I'd have good stuff or mediocre stuff and every time I went out there he'd give me a hard time. I'd throw him fastballs at different spots and he might hit the ball hard and get a base hit and then the next time up he might just bloop one and get a base hit. He just had my number.

— *Bob Kuzava*

In Fenway those of us who had pretty good strength and the ball bounced off our bat, we probably pulled the ball a little too much. I was probably too much a pull hitter against top notch pitchers like Bunning or Frank Lary and those guys, you know, sliders away from you were pretty tough. I didn't acclimate enough to really do it, but Fenway maybe forces you to try to pull the ball too much.

— *Ted Lepcio*

I wasn't a spring hitter, and that hurt me probably as much as anything. If you hit better in the spring early, you get more chances. Some of the good spring hitters faded when the hot months came, July and August. Now, Nellie Fox, he could play a game in the heat and come back the next day and play the same way, just as good. A guy like Walt Dropo, for instance, a very strong man, he didn't have the same recuperative powers that Nellie had. You could just sort of watch him as the weather got hot. He'd get a little behind, a little bit off the ball, and he would try to make up for it by trying to swing a little sooner or a little harder, and he'd go into slumps. A guy like Ted Williams, whenever he went to the plate, he was pretty much Ted Williams every time he went to the plate, regardless of the weather.

— *Ron Jackson*

I wasn't that good a hitter. Good curveball pitchers, I didn't have much of a chance against. Robin Roberts. The good pitchers would curve me, most of them. But I did the same to them. Pitchers don't hit the curveball very good, most of them. That was kind of a law, don't let him hit a fastball off of you.

— *Don Liddle*

I hit two home runs in one game at Brooklyn, but we hit five that day, so nobody paid much attention. I don't recall who I hit them off of, but he must have got sent down so far nobody ever heard from him again. *[Diering's home runs came on July 27, 1950, against Chris Van Cuyk and Joe Landrum.]*

— *Chuck Diering*

I ended up being a pull hitter. At first I hit the ball to all fields and was fairly sound as far as striking the ball goes. But I hit two doubles one day in Kansas City, to right center field, and Lopez gave me hell for it both times, for hitting the ball away from left field. It was kind of confusing to me.

— *Ron Jackson*

I enjoyed pinch hitting. When you're pinch hitting you look for a certain pitch until you get two strikes on you. Then you protect yourself. I always looked for that fastball right down the middle, first pitch. They figure your just coming off the bench, you ain't played, you're not loosened up good or cold or something like that.

— *Sammy Taylor*

Most of the major league pitchers you had played against in the minor leagues, and I felt like I could have hit them if I'd had a chance. I just felt that I never got a chance to get my feet wet to play. I mean, I'd sit on the bench and pinch hit. You play a few games, you sit down. I never really got a chance to play.

I always felt if I did play, I could have hit — I don't know what kind of an average I would have hit, I knew I would have hit a lot of home runs. Like in '55 when I separated my shoulder, it took Rocky Colavito and Roger Maris and Marv Throneberry a month to catch me in home runs. *[In the American Association in 1955, Lennon hit 31 home runs in 114 games, Throneberry hit 36 in 156 games, Colavito hit 30 in 150 games, and Maris hit 20 in 138 games.]*

— *Bob Lennon*

We worked on bunting a lot during spring training. The regular players and the pitchers both. I'm sure a lot of pitchers would just as soon not hit. Because if you're capable of getting some base hits once in awhile, why that means you've got to run the bases. And on a real hot day if somebody fouls off two or three on a three-two count and you're running, things like that, it'll take a little away from you at times.

I had good base running instincts. I knew where the outfielders were playing. I knew how fast I could run. I knew if I could take a chance in taking another base or whatever, trying to score, and all that.

— *Sid Hudson*

I'm one for one as a pinch hitter. Billy Pierce was pitching the ballgame and I went in to pinch hit. Paul Richards had used, I don't know, thirty-some pinch hitters and nobody got a base hit, something like that, so he sent me up and I got a base hit, a line drive to left field.

I hit it off Alex Kellner, a left-handed pitcher for the Athletics. He threw me a curveball and I took it, and I said, "I bet that son of a gun's going to throw me another one. He thinks I can't hit the curveball." And I got a curveball, and I whacked it. So that was a big thrill. *[Keegan had 32 career hits for a .163 average.]*

— *Bob Keegan*

That's the dessert of baseball, getting up there with that bat. That's the biggest challenge you've got. Red Ruffing for the Yankees was a good hitter *[Ruffing hit .269 with 36 home runs in his 22 year career — was 273–225 as pitcher]*. Schoolboy Rowe, who used to pitch for Detroit and later pitched for the Phillies *[Rowe hit .263 with 18 home runs in his 15 year career — was 158–101 as pitcher]*, he was a good hitter. Those guys could hit the ball out of the ballpark for you. You always have a few pitchers in the league that can rap that ball pretty good.

— *Jimmy Bloodworth*

We had some pitchers on our ballclub who could hit. I can remember three left-handed pitchers who could hit real good — Mel Parnell, Maury McDermott, and Willard Nixon. In fact, they used to pinch hit for some of us once in awhile, you know, late in the game and the right-hander was still in there. *[McDermott was used as a pinch hitter 127 times in his career; Nixon had a .242 lifetime average; Parnell hit .198 lifetime.]* Tommy Brewer, a right-hander. He was a good athlete, he was a good hitter. *[Brewer hit .207 with 114 hits in 8 seasons.]* Up until pro football and pro basketball came into its own, baseball got most of the best athletes. Bob Lemon comes to mind, too. He was a good hitting pitcher. *[Lemon hit .232 with 37 career home runs.]*

— *Milt Bolling*

I was always a pretty good hitting pitcher, along with a lot of the guys who came through the Dodger organization. Newcombe was, Drysdale was, there were some guys who could swing the bat pretty good in the organization. And I played other positions in school. I originally signed as a pitcher-outfielder. I didn't run very well.

Yeah, I loved to swing the bat. Then, when we played, the complete pitcher was a guy who could bunt, and hit, and field his position — was a pretty good athlete. *[Sherry was .169 with three home runs in his 11 year career. He went two-for-four in the 1959 World Series.]*

— *Larry Sherry*

When a guy in front of you hit a home run you always expect to get brushed back. That was more or less expected, and we had a few donnybrooks in our day. It was more or less expected that if you got a count of no balls and two strikes you could figure they're coming in tight on you. It was just general practice, the same thing as sliding into second base trying to break up the double play.

If I was playing second, I was hoping I could get rid of the ball before they hit me, and if I was on first I'm going into second base to see if I could break up the double play situation. The thing that used to burn us up, get the infielders mad, was when an outfielder would come and slide into you because you had no way to retaliate on him unless you came down on him or something, because he wasn't an infielder. So you couldn't slide into him to get even.

— *Sibbi Sisti*

The biggest thing about the brushback when I was playing, the guys who did it knew what they were doing. They weren't headhunters. They knew they had a purpose, and you knew pretty much when they were going to use it. There were two or three guys in the league you could always pick the time they were going to say, "Well, this is the time now to loosen you up. Maybe you've had too many good swings." They just wanted to let you know that they're on the mound, that they're in the ballgame, that they didn't forget what's taking place.

— *Frank Malzone*

When I was in the minors I was a pretty good hitter, but as you go up the line you have to have a lot of practice with it. When you're at home, the pitchers hit early. They get forty-five minutes of hitting with the coaches lobbing the ball. Now when the regulars come out and hit, the pitching is a little more presentable. But they can't spend too much time on 10 or 11 pitchers. Batting practice was allotted to the regular players.

When you went on the road, pitchers didn't get to hit because they needed that batting time that was allotted to them for the regular players. So when you went on the road for two weeks you didn't practice hitting. The only thing they tried to stress was bunting the ball, moving the man over, which I think is more important.

[Ferrick batted .184 for his nine year career.]

— *Tom Ferrick*

[In Hall's first three seasons he played as a position player. In his next two seasons he was both a pitcher and position player. In his last 14 seasons as a pitcher only, he went 44–231, a .190 average.]

In 1955 I played every day at Lincoln. Then in '56 I pinch hit for Pittsburgh. I was up 16 times as a pinch hitter, and I had four walks and six hits in 16 plate appearances. But then, after '57 and '58 I stopped playing winter ball. Little by little, as you get away from hitting, you can't hit as well, because you just don't see the pitching.

I had various theories that I tried. I would go up and swing at the first pitch. If it was a fastball I'd jump on it, and if it was a curveball I'd miss it by ten feet. And then two strikes, I know they're going to throw me a curveball. So sure enough, here comes a curveball, and it was a little bit slower, and bing!, I'd get a little base hit. Some years I'd only get up four or five times a year. I would just kind of guess up there.

— *Dick Hall*

My hitting helped me a lot. *[Scheib hit .250 with 5 home runs in his 11 year career and was used 57 times as a pinch hitter.]* It'll help any pitcher, I think. It gets close, they're apt to pull a poor hitter out quicker than if a man could hit pretty good. I think it kept me in games quite a bit.

— *Carl Scheib*

That was part of the fun, being able to get a bat in your hand and hit. Well, I don't say I was a good hitter, but I could make contact, I could put the ball in play. *[Hudson hit .220 with 164 hits in his 12 year career.]* Anyway, I pinch hit for one of our pitchers one day in Washington. We were playing Detroit. It was the year they were fighting the Yankees for the pennant, 1950, I think. *[In 1950 the Tigers finished second, 3 games behind the Yankees.]*

We had a couple of men on, second and third, two outs, in the last of the 8th inning. I got a base hit and it put us ahead. I know when I got to first base the first baseman said, "What are you trying to do, knock us out of the pennant?" I had just beaten them the day before pitching, and boy, I was really going to get a write-up that day, you know, driving in two runs with my bat.

Well, they scored two runs off Dick Weik in the ninth inning and won the game.

— *Sid Hudson*

There's two reasons why pitchers, as a group, can't hit. Half of them can't hit anyway, no matter how much they play. And the ones that might be halfway decent athletes still have to see a lot of good pitching to stay sharp as a hitter. I got some hits as a pitcher, but part of that was due to the fact that I played three years of pro ball as a hitter, and then went to pitching. There's one good thing about pitching relief and not having to bat much: I hit three hundred five times — I was one-for-three one year, two-for-five another year. *[Hall also went 10–29, .345; 13–28, .464; 5–15, .333].*

— *Dick Hall*

[Sibbi Sisti, a good all-around player, played until 1954. He tells a story from earlier in his career, playing for Stengel at Boston, where he displayed his bunting skill.] I bunted quite a bit. Stengel was managing us at the time, and I had beaten out three bunts in one game against the Cardinals. An old friend of his, Jesse Burkett, was at the game. He came down to the dugout and he mentioned the fact that if I beat out another bunt would tie his record of four bunt singles in one game. So Casey told me to go ahead and do it.

Well, when I went up there, they drilled me right between the shoulder blades on the first pitch. They weren't going to let me beat out another one.

— *Sibbi Sisti*

I didn't hit against anyone guy enough to figure that I had him figured out. Bob Kuzava, a left-handed pitcher, used to throw me a change-up curve. Not very many people would throw a change-up to a pitcher. He'd flop up that blamed change curve, and I'd think, gosh, if I was to play every day, I believe I'd have to learn how to hit that thing.
— *Ned Garver*

I always thought I could hit. I had a lot of confidence in hitting. There's one thing now that I'm in my older days that I wish would have been changed. I wish I could have become an outfielder. Playing the outfield, to me, was a cinch. I could do it. I always shagged fly balls. They were easy to catch, and I could throw pretty good. And they *[the Athletics]* talked many a time about making me an outfielder, and as young as I was I could have done the job and I could have prolonged my career another five, ten years, I think. But every time they talked about it, they were out of pitchers. *[Scheib played his 11th, and last, big league season at the age of 27.]*

But I had a lot of confidence in hitting, and I did pretty well in pinch hitting. I think I came in second in both leagues as leading pinch hitter one year. I think Paul Lehner beat me out. *[In 1948 Scheib went 7 for 16—.438; Lehner, an outfielder with the Browns, went 6 For 13—.462.]* I won a couple games in the ninth inning for our club, you know, two or three, which is a lot for a pitcher to win with the last out in the 9th inning.
— *Carl Scheib*

I was set up to pull the ball all the time. I would have hit for well over a three hundred average, but they used a so-called reverse Ted Williams shift and put the second baseman on the shortstop side, and that cost me a lot of singles, because I couldn't hit the ball through the infield on the ground.

But with our ballclub, there was no sense in trying to go the other way; because we didn't score enough runs, and the shift was devised to keep me from hitting home runs. They wanted me to try to hit singles to right field, and I wasn't about to go for that. The only disadvantage was it cost some base hits.

But I was a pull hitter. In my career I'd say I didn't hit ten home runs to right field. That's a guess. I don't know. I didn't hit many, that's the crux of it all.
— *Ralph Kiner*

Well, I was told in the minors, and I thought it was always true, "One thing you remember, if you hit the fastball you'll play in the bigs. If you don't hit the fastball, you'll never play in the big leagues." And I always felt that even after getting there—if you can hit the fastball, you'll stay around. 'Cause you do start adapting more and more to breaking balls and such the more you see of it.

But if somebody keeps throwing it by you, it doesn't matter about anything else anyway.
— *Jim Landis*

I was on the first train going up North in 1956. Spring training's over, and here we are, eight major league ballclubs on one train, going up the East Coast, and Spahn and Burdette came by and said, "Come on, Murff, let's go and get something cold to drink." So we went to the first club car and ordered a drink and the porter said, "I'm sorry, but those other fellows got all the drinks."

We said, "What other fellows?"

He said, "Those other fellows."

And we went through another club car, and he told us the same thing, and we finally found the other fellows. It was all of the front line hitters that the train had on the eight teams on it. All of them were sitting in a club car. There were about forty-five hitters out of eight teams, about five or six for each ballclub, and all the top hitters were in that car. Musial, Adcock, Aaron, Mays, Mathews, Ted Williams all the hitters that would compete with you down the line and wanted to get to be better hitters.

And they were talking hitting like chemists talk about chemistry. The skills of mixing this and that in a hitting sequence — they were describing it. And I was sitting back there open-mouthed. No wonder they can beat us, they study more. And they were dissecting each pitch that all pitchers threw at that time. And when one of them got through, he would just kind of lean over and say, "Ted, is that the way —" you know, just look at him in the eye, and say, "Is that the way you would do it?" or "What else do you have to add to this?"

Ted Williams was the best hitter in that car on that day. There's no doubt in anybody's mind that attended that meeting, that Ted Williams was the hitter. And Ted Williams made a statement that day that's stuck with me ever since. He said, "That new pitch, the slider, man, you might just as well forget about it. You can't tell it's coming because it looks like a fastball until it starts moving, And with that pitch getting better and better, there will never be another four hundred hitter in baseball as long as the pitchers can throw that pitch."

That came from him when he could still hit as good as anybody in baseball.

— *Red Murff*

Pinch hitting is the toughest job in the world. Every time they asked Snider to do it, his face got red and his hands trembled. Jerry Lynch did the same thing at Cincinnati, and I did too. It's nothing to be ashamed of. When they call on you to pinch hit, you know there's a load on your shoulders and if you have the pride I had, you want to be absolutely certain you do your best. *[Walls was the most successful pinch hitter in the majors in 1962 with the Dodgers, going 13 for 27, a .481 average].*

— *Lee Walls*

I don't think I ever wore a batting helmet until I got to the majors. In those days they didn't have batting helmets, they had little liner inserts, and that's what I wore. In fact, when I was with Kansas City *[the Yankees Triple A team]* I led the league in getting hit. I think I was hit 21 or 22 times in, probably in '51. They told me I was nuts not to wear a helmet, so then I started wearing them.

— *Andy Carey*

We started wearing batting helmets the last couple years that I played. Before that, they had some fiberglass liners that you could wear in your cap. They weren't very much protection, because all they had in them was a little foam rubber lining around where it went around your head — nothing like they have today.

— *Gil Coan*

We *[the Pittsburgh Pirates]* were the first club to wear batting helmets. In fact, we even wore them in the field. Branch Rickey was the first to do that. I came up in 1951 and we were wearing them, so it was around that time that we started.

— *Frank Thomas*

Chapter Ten

The Hurlers

It's said that pitchers are a different breed. They approach the game a little differently than the other players. After all, everything is riding on them. It's only when they release the ball that the action can begin. If they release it in the proper spot at the proper speed with the proper movement, good things can happen for their team. If not, it's a quick walk to the showers. All pitchers have different styles; all hitters have to study each pitcher's style, and, all too often end up facing a long day when their nemesis takes the mound.

Among the biggest changes in baseball since the 1950s is in the handling of the pitching staffs. It was not unusual for a pitcher to throw more than 300 innings a season and have 25 or more complete games. Except in rare instances, closers were not a part of baseball. Starting pitchers were generally expected to keep throwing until they tired or got into trouble. The pitcher's task was, however, the same as now: Decide on the best way to get the batter out, and then execute the pitches.

As a starting pitcher, our goal was to pitch a complete game.
— *Bob Keegan*

In those days I used to move a guy off the plate by maybe throwing at his knees a little bit. That way you're not going to kill the guy and you've got him skipping a little bit of rope. You can't let guys lean over the plate and take your bread and butter.
— *Bob Kuzava*

When we pitched, it was just hurry up, get the ball over, you've got eight guys behind you, they're not going to beat you on home runs. If you've got any kind of stuff at all — a good live fastball, curve and change-up is about all they figured we needed.
— *Carl Scheib*

I just had a good career. I wish it could have been better, but I gave it a hundred percent. It was good enough to get my pension. The reason I got my pension was that I was left-handed, and I understand that. Left-handers were always in demand. I might have lasted two and a half or three years longer than if I'd been right-handed, but they kept taking a chance on a left-hander and I'm grateful.

— *Taylor Phillips*

When we played, you'd establish yourself as a short reliever, but you had one or two other guys in your bullpen that also handled that role, so you might have rotated with the three of you working, maybe two in one game and one guy the next day. The hot guy would close more than anybody else, but then you used all three — that way you could save the one guy.

Sometimes I'd come in the sixth inning and finish the game. And sometimes I'd come in only in the ninth inning

A lot of my relief appearances were for four or five innings, sometimes more. *[In 1962, Sherry started just three games but pitched 142 innings. He went 1–2 as a starter with one complete game. He relieved 54 times, with seven saves and a 13–8 record in relief.]*

— *Larry Sherry*

The pitching approach is totally different now. Back then, finishing a game was really macho. The hitters would say, "Look, it's a hot day, we'll make this guy work, we'll get him the third time around." Well, today that third time around there's somebody else coming out of the bullpen.

— *Jerry Coleman*

Pitchers went inside quite a bit. Drysdale had no qualms about hitting you. I mean, not coming inside, but hitting you. We had a little plastic liner that you could put in your cap if you wanted to. Pittsburgh was the first team that started wearing the helmets. Then it became a rule that you had to wear a helmet.

But when I first started, you didn't. You had never had any protection all your life, so it wasn't an issue. At that time, we probably were a little stupid. You just never even talked about it.

— *Ted Kazanski*

I consider talent the ability to pitch, not just throw the ball hard and overpower people. Bob Feller could throw harder and had the great curve and he had the best stuff of anybody I ever saw. But guys like Eddie Lopat and Early Wynn were top-notch pitchers. Wynn moved the ball around, and Lopat went out there with a bunch of junk, but he still changed speeds and he pitched to locations. I'd get goose bumps watching those guys pitch. That was a learning experience for me.

When I was a kid in 1948 out in San Bernardino, Tommy Bridges was with one of those Pacific Coast League teams, and he told me, "Hitting is timing, and pitching is breaking up that timing." That's what pitching is. Pitching wasn't going out there and throwing the ball past everybody. That wasn't pitching, that was throwing. But pitching, how Tommy described it, is what Lopat and Wynn did.

— *Ned Garver*

Back in those days most pitchers had the long wind-up, and I used to kick my foot up high. Patterned my style after Paul Derringer because I'd watched him pitch in several World Series back in Cincinnati.

I thought the more I could do before I released the ball, maybe the more I could confuse the hitter, but it didn't seem to work that way for some reason. *[Gumpert had a lifetime record of 51–58.]*

— *Randy Gumpert*

Boo Ferriss, who went 46–16 his first two seasons with the Red Sox (1945–46) before an arm injury, tells of the pitching style that helped him to that mark: I relied on a sinking fastball. I had to pitch low, around the knees, and relied on control, moving the ball in and out, and setting up the hitters. I had a pretty decent curve and changeup. But the fastball was my best pitch — a sinking fastball.

I couldn't pitch high. Of course, I'd come up high to show it to them. But if I'd get up high, I'd get hurt. I had to stay around the knees and move it in and out and mix my pitches up. Now, of course, they measure everything by that radar gun. I guess I was probably in the upper 80s. I don't think I was ever in the low 90s; I was never that fast. *[Ferriss had a lifetime record of 65–30.]*

— *Boo Ferriss*

I always used to make it a habit of watching the opponents take batting practice as it gave me confidence. In batting practice the hitters know what's coming and usually they're hitting a fastball. Even under those circumstances they rarely would get what you would call a good hit in more than or 3 out of 5 or 6 swings.

I knew that if I threw strikes and kept the ball low with movement, the percentages were in my favor. They were and are still today in the pitcher's favor.

— *Nellie King*

I think I had a major league fastball and I had a decent curveball, too. It needed a little more refinement, but it was still a pretty good curveball. I needed to learn to change speeds a little bit and learn to get better control so I could throw to spots better.

If I'd pitched a little bit longer, I think I would have come around a little bit. As age matures you, your control gets better.

— *Paul Pettit*

In our day the brushback was a pitch — it was part of a pitcher's arsenal. If he's getting paid, he's gonna try to shake somebody up.

They'd never knock Williams down. They never knocked Berra down or Mantle down or DiMaggio down because that would only infuriate them and make them better hitters.

But they knocked some hitters down. And the way hitters fought that is for the batter to drag the ball toward first base and say to the pitcher, "Now cover, and I'm going to run up your back." That was the way to retaliate. When you go to the mound to fight you don't do anything but endanger yourself and your own teammates.

— *Billy Hitchcock*

I was hit fourteen times one year. I feel that's part of baseball. I always looked at it this way: when a pitcher threw that close to me, he respected me and I respected him for doing that, for brushing me back, because he was trying to protect his part of the plate.

— *Frank Thomas*

Throwing at batters was part of the game. They either had to or they weren't part of the team. It was ordered by the manager. There were headhunters out there. Most of the top guys threw at you.

— *Ralph Kiner*

As a pitcher, everything revolves around you. You control the flow of the game and that is a big responsibility.

I can still to this day recall a pitching sequence I made to Frank Robinson in Cincinnati in June of 1956 when I came into a game to relieve Elroy Face with the tying run on third and the winning run on first. Jack Shepard, the catcher, came out and said, "We'll start him off with a low outside fastball" to which I replied, "First I'll get ahead of him then work him low and outside." I did and threw a fastball in on him for a strike, then went away with a curveball for a strike swinging, then wasted a curveball outside. Shepard wanted another curve outside. I shook him off and wanted a fastball which I threw right on the outside corner. Robinson knew everything I threw outside was a curve and he thought this was also and suddenly I could see the look in his eyes as he saw it was a fastball. He swung, too late, as the ball backed up and caught the outside corner for the game-ending strikeout. We went into first place that night. Concentration is so intense in pitching that things like this are forever etched in your mind.

— *Nellie King*

Johnny Sain was a great pitching coach, because he never was overbearing. He always planted a thought and kind of worked his way in slowly. He walked by and saw you throwing a pitch and said, "Hey, looks pretty good, you're doing a good job with that." And he'd keep on walking. He was planting the seed.

Or he'd say, "Well, why don't you just try it on the side a little bit?" Pretty soon he had you throwing it. He was pretty clever, rather than coming up, "Hey, you can't do this, you have to do this this way." He didn't approach it that way. So he worked very well with pitchers.

— *Johnny Klippstein*

We always tried to keep the ball away from the good hitters, especially the breaking stuff, and we'd come in them occasionally, but we wouldn't come in on the plate, we would come maybe six or eight inches inside the plate. And back when I played, we didn't wear helmets. You threw inside then, you sent a real message to that hitter. But we didn't fight. If they came inside it was kind of a sign of respect, you know. A guy that couldn't hit, hell, they never came inside on him, they never knocked him down. They were afraid they'd hit him.

— *Elvin Tappe*

I pitched the great hitters the same way I did everybody else. Guys like Williams and DiMaggio and Keller were already in the league when I came up. And me, being an inexperienced pitcher and knowing I could throw hard, I just threw power against power.

If I'm going to pitch against DiMaggio or Williams or any of those guys who are great hitters — in fact, I pitched against Jimmy Foxx, Joe Cronin — any of those guys, I just cranked up and threw the ball, and threw it as hard as I could and tried to throw strikes. That was the only way I knew how to pitch, and I loved to pitch that way. 'Til the last day

I pitched in the major leagues, I'd crank up and throw the ball as hard as I could throw it. If they could hit it, fine and good.

— *Virgil Trucks*

I thought that pitchers that worked kind of fast were easier to play behind because you didn't get back on your heels so much between pitches. Erskine was good to play behind. Don Newcombe was good to play behind. Most all the Dodger pitchers worked fairly fast. You didn't have anybody that got off the mound and fidgeted around and rubbed the ball — they all worked fairly fast, and that's what makes the whole ballclub behind a pitcher alert.

— *Bobby Morgan*

I pitched twelve years in the minors with eight different ballclubs before I came up with Washington, and always won more than I lost. I was a starter and a reliever. I started and in the next two days I was a stopper. In other words, I was the workhorse.

I guess I'd rather relieve. If you start, you go to work for three or four hours and it's all over with. But I figured in relief I was in every ballgame. I had an interest in every ball game because I was just watching what was going to happen next.

In other words, if you're starting and four days later or five days later you're starting again then in between you don't have really the interest in the game. *[Dixon pitched 102 big league games, 12 as a starter.]*

— *Sonny Dixon*

To throw a ball high and tight is the best set-up pitch you've got for a ball low and away. You need it. I mean, I think it's part of pitching. And we're not trying to hit the man, we're trying to stop him from moving that front foot in toward the plate. To make him go straight. Then you can pitch him on the outside corner. But if he strides in to go to the opposite field, it takes the effectiveness of the pitch away from you.

I still think you ought to be able to pitch a man inside without somebody coming out and warning you that you're throwing at him. I'm strongly against that. But I wasn't a hitter. They look at it different, I guess.

— *Don Liddle*

The techniques of the spitter? Prepare, pucker, and pop. Three p's. You have to prepare. You use a lozenge, put it under your tongue. Slippery elm lozenge. In those days you would take your glove off and I would spit it in the palm of my hand and then rub it in the ball where it says Reich. On one of the four sides where the wide part is, there's always an emblem on every ball. So you prepare that spot. You have to prepare the ball. Most people don't know what they're doing, that's why very few guys threw the spitter. Drysdale did, Ford did, Jack Hamilton, Burdette.

But there really were very, very few — because most of them didn't know what they were doing. You have to know. You put it on the ball where it's prepared, but you pucker your fingers, and then you've got to really pop your wrist. The thumb is dry and the fingers are wet, and it's coming off the leather so the ball slips out in reverse.

— *Bob Shaw*

The pitchers and the catchers tried to never let DiMaggio and Williams come up in a crucial part of the ballgame because you know that DiMaggio and Williams can beat you.

If somebody's going to beat you, you didn't want them to beat you, because you know they can. It's the .220 hitter, .230 hitter, .240 hitter — that's the guy you want up there in the jam, because you think you can get him out. So consequently, they were pitched around a lot.

In other words, you'd rather walk Williams then let him beat you. And DiMaggio was the same way. But they knew that, and they stood there, and they wouldn't swing at a bad ball. So consequently, when you had to come in there, that's when they beat you.

— *Joe Ginsberg*

Consistently, Feller and I were the only two at that time that threw almost every pitch a hundred miles an hour or better. In fact, I have a picture on my wall signed by Ted Williams that says, "If they say the ballplayers throw a hundred miles an hour today, you threw a hundred and ten." It's right there on the picture. And of course, he's always been one of my favorite people. He's always praised me one way or the other, but he should, he hit enough off me.

— *Virgil Trucks*

If you threw strikes, your infield were up on their toes, your outfield were up because they knew that you were going to throw strikes.

And your three hundred hitter is going to get three hits out of every ten times at bat. No matter what happens. He's going to get three hits. Your two hundred hitter is going to get two hits out of every ten times at bat. So you got him out eight times. You got your three hundred hitter out seven times. The trick of pitching is to get these people out when they can hurt you. I'm talking about knocking a run in, I'm talking about advancing the runner, but get them out. You don't go for strikeouts. You make them hit the ball.

With our ballclub in 1950 all we had to do was keep it in the ballpark. We had a little guy named Richie Ashburn — he wasn't little, hell, he's as big as I am. But he could fly, and he could catch it. Keep it in the ballpark, they'd run it down. Del Ennis was the most underrated outfielder in National League baseball. Dick Sisler was a good outfielder and a pretty good first baseman. But the name of the game is run, catch, hit, and throw it. Now they've got another category called hit for power. Get the guy that hits three hundred out — your home run hitter's going to get his home run, he's going to guess right with you, but — uh uh, what a game!

— *Bubba Church*

I felt that pitching was a very exciting event. Every time I was on the mound I was excited about my contest with that hitter. I'm going to have to face him three or four times and he's going to be resting, and I'm going to get tireder, so I've got to have something left for that last time at bat. It's hard to beat a guy four times in a row.

— *Red Murff*

I was a right-hander, I platooned a lot at that time and I happened to have to go against Koufax all the time. He and Score and those people had great arms. And both of them had great breaking balls. They talk about Feller, how hard he threw, but they forget about his breaking stuff. Once Koufax started to harness his stuff and be able to throw enough strikes he became a Hall of Famer. If Score wasn't as fast as Koufax, they were right next to each other.

— *Dick Gernert*

The easiest pitchers to catch are the pitches that have good control. Any pitcher that's around the plate a lot is fairly easy to catch. It's the guy that's a little wild, he's up and down and in the dirt, now those are the hard pitchers to catch. The knuckleball pitchers, like Hoyt Wilhelm, they're always hard to catch. Early Wynn had great control. He pitched from behind. He was always 2 and 0 and 3 and 1, but that's the way he wanted to pitch. When he had to have control, he always threw strikes, so he was fairly easy to catch. Early liked to knock hitters down, no doubt about it. He just thought that the plate was his, and if they crowded the plate, he would knock you down. In those years, the hitters just accepted that. They hit a home run, they expected to get knocked down the next time up. Pitchers threw hard and inside. They wanted to get you backed up a little bit, and they sent a message to you: "That plate, the inside part of the plate, is mine just as well as it is ours."

— *Joe Ginsberg*

When I was pitching semi-pro ball, I didn't have great control, but I remember going to a tryout camp with this guy, Roy Dissinger. He told me, "Use your body. Let everything go in front of your belt buckle." Everybody finds a key, I guess. Like a golf swing, you have a key. And if you let everything go in front of your belt buckle, you're following through, and you're not aiming the ball. You just have a rhythmic throw to it. Robin Roberts pitched that way. It looked like it was effortless, 'cause he could really buzz it.

I didn't have a great fastball, but I developed a sinker because of an older guy, a second baseman, Cotton Bosarge, I was playing with in Geneva, Alabama.

He said, "You've got pretty good control, you keep the ball down low, but your fastball doesn't move at all. How do you hold your fastball?"

I said, "I hold it across the seams."

He said, "Why do you do that?"

I said, "Well, I read in a book that's the way Bob Feller holds his fastball."

He said, "Shoot, you can't throw as fast as Bob Feller. Why don't you hold it the other way, with the seams. That way, it'll start moving a little bit. You need movement on your fastball."

So I changed. I got a hell of a sinker. The next year I won twenty games at New Iberia where I got released the year before. Then I won 16 in the Interstate League. Had a so-so year with Charleston in '50, went in the Army for two years, came out and led the Western League in pitching [*in 1953 King went 15–3 for Denver with a 2.00 ERA*], then led the Southern Association in pitching [*in 1954 King went 16–5 for New Orleans and led the league with a 2.25 ERA*]. Just because of one guy giving me the advantage of his knowledge. Cotton Bosarge.

— *Nellie King*

I pitched several one-hitters in the major leagues and pitched one no-hitter in the minor leagues, at Wichita Falls, Texas. I came close to no-hitters twice in Chicago. Once Frankie Baumholtz beat out a swinging bunt in the eighth inning. The closest I came was two outs in the 8th. But I wasn't what you'd call a strikeout pitcher. I had a good hard sinker and good control. You aren't going to throw a lot of no-hitters throwing sinkers. That was my best pitch.

— *Bob Friend*

Mel Parnell, Ellis Kinder were good to play behind. McDermott was tough to play behind because of being behind in the count so much. Dizzy Trout was good to play behind, and Bill Wight, with a great move to first base. It's probably tougher to play behind the guys that don't pitch ahead as much.

— Dick Gernert

Nobody's supposed to walk the pitcher, and the things you are supposed to do are the hardest things to do sometimes. Particularly with the pitcher like that, when he's not going to swing until you throw strikes. He'll take two strikes if he has to. You understand that, but it's not quite that easy to throw a ball from sixty feet six inches over a plate that's 17 inches wide, and then you've got to throw it between the knees and the belt. It's a pretty good art form.

— Nellie King

I figured if I could be in better shape than others, and finish ballgames, and stay in the ballgames through nine innings I had a better chance to win. If I could field my position better than somebody else, I had a better chance to win. If I could hit better than somebody else, I had a better chance to win. I worked on those things. I think I led the league in complete games in 1952. The year before, the last 19 games I started, I didn't get knocked out of the box. So you take 19 there, and then 24 out of 30 the next year, and the start of the next year, 1952, with shutouts the first two starts, there was only about 7 times out of probably fifty-some that I didn't finish games.

— Ned Garver

I remember Mickey Vernon, a great left handed hitter with Washington. I pitched against him in spring training in 1954. I threw him a sinker low and outside. He hit a two hopper to second base. And I never saw him again until the next year. I threw him the same pitch and he hit a double to left center field because he knows the pitch. Those guys have a memory, a recall of that stuff. You don't pitch them the same way.

— Nellie King

We had a pitch that we called the knockdown pitch. And it came from the bench. The manager would say, "Well, this guy's got two for two, and he's standing in there, he's digging in too much, we want him knocked down."

Well, we had a sign for that. If we gave him the sign sometimes the hitter would turn around to me and say, "I know you gave him that sign." They would look at me rather than the pitcher.

— Joe Ginsberg

Spahn's theory of winning twenty ballgames was: "You're going to get thirty-five starts, and five of them will not be decisions. So you're got thirty decisions. If you're 15–15, you're a good pitcher. You can make it 16–14 if you're a good hitter. You can make it 17–13 if you're a good fielder. You can make it 18–12 if you're a good runner. And you can scramble like hell to get those other two." And that was his theory. *[Spahn started between 32 and 39 games for 17 straight seasons.]* Those other two you can get if you will just pull a little bit harder.

So I thought his theory was excellent, you're a five hundred pitcher if you throw strikes with major league equipment. But he had it figured out, and it's easy to see that he was successful. He played a lot of years and set a lot of records. I enjoyed my association with those big people like Spahn. He probably would have chosen to be an outfielder today, with the DH, because he was that kind of hitter. If he's taking batting practice and getting acquainted with pitchers every day, he could have been a three hundred hitter in the major leagues, I'm sure, and he would have hit a lot of home runs.

— *Red Murff*

I can honestly say that I could get any right-hander out that they had. There wasn't a right-hander in the league that I thought I couldn't get out. But I had a lot of problems with lefthanders. That's why I was real successful in Boston. In Fenway. The only guy that really ate me alive was Vic Wertz. Finally we traded for him. And he was a wonderful fellow too, by the way.

But my style was strictly — I threw breaking balls for control, and really, I actually closed my eyes and threw my fastball as hard as I could throw the damn thing, and as I slowed down, as I got tired, the ball moved more. So when I lacked the speed in the later innings, I never got hurt much with my fastball to a right-handed hitter because it kept breaking in on him so bad, and then I kept throwing strikes with my sliders and stuff. So I kind of thought it was a little unique to the era, where if I got behind I went to breaking balls and had all kinds of change of paces and change-ups and so forth, that I really felt that I had good control — although the year I won the most games I think I walked the most people. *[In 1955 Sullivan went 18–13 and had a career high 100 walks in 260 innings, an average of just under 3½ walks per nine innings.]*

— *Frank Sullivan*

Starting was just an expected thing back then. When I came out of the service in '53, I went to Denver, and I think more relief pitching started to come in. It's a different mental attitude. Everything's on the line there. It's a mental game.

The hardest outs in baseball are the last three. The game's up for grabs there. You've gotta close it out. It's like playing golf, you have to play eighteen holes. They don't give a damn what you did on the first seventeen, but if the match is in the eighteenth, you gotta finish it. There's no clock to run out in baseball. I used to say I'd like to be able to stand on the mound with the count three and two on a guy like Musial with the bases loaded and let the clock run out.

That's one of the fascinations of the game. You get them out one, two, three, and it might take you thirty minutes to get the last out. But relief pitching is something I did well because I could throw strikes and I had a good sinker, and the guy in Denver who made me a relief pitcher, Andy Cohen, had a lot of faith in me. I wasn't sure I would be a good relief pitcher, because I never thought of myself as being a very confident or macho sort of a pitcher. But that relieving made me appreciate that part of pitching and gave me an awful lot of confidence.

— *Nellie King*

That staff they had over at Cleveland — boy, that was fun for the right-handers. Be on a road trip and go in there for four games against those guys. Lemon, Wynn, Garcia, Feller, Newhouser. My God. It was funny, too, because it seemed like I got to play almost every game in Cleveland. There'd be one of the right-handed hitters who'd say, "Oh, I don't think I can make it today, my arm's hurting."

And I'd be in the lineup.

— *Jim Dyck*

I had decent luck against the Cleveland pitching staff when I went over to Detroit *[in 1953]*, maybe because I watched them pitch so much, and I wasn't in awe of them as much as maybe somebody else was. But when I was still with Cleveland *[1948 to June 15, 1953]* I'll never forget one time, I was on second base. We were making a pitching change, and a guy on the other team said to me, "You don't know how lucky you are."

I said, "How's that?"

He said, "You don't have to hit off these guys."

Well, I went home and I figured out: "Let's see, if I was playing with somebody else and we played this many games and I came to bat forty or fifty times against them during the season and didn't do too well..." and then I'd take it off my average to see what I'd hit.

There can make a big difference, when you're playing on a ballclub with great pitchers. Like if you're playing on the Dodgers when they had Koufax and Drysdale. At least you don't have to face those guys.

— *Ray Boone*

Bob Feller had real raw talent. He'd rear back and throw that ball 95, 96 miles an hour all the time, and he had a pretty good curveball. I don't know if he was as mean as Lemon or Wynn, but he didn't have to be.

— *Bob Kuzava*

I don't think any ballplayer in his right mind would enjoy hitting against Bob Feller when he was playing for the Cleveland Indians.

He had a great curveball, a mean one. Lots of good hitters, the better hitters in the league, thought he was wild inside, and they'd duck out of there and hit the ground against that curveball, and the ball would be over for a perfect strike. Yeah, he had a terrific curveball.

— *Jimmy Bloodworth*

The best lefthander was Whitey Ford. He just knew how to pitch, and was sneaky fast. He'd throw you a lot of curveballs and off-speed stuff and then he'd throw a fastball right by you when he wanted to.

Of course, the '54 pitching staff that Cleveland had was outstanding, with Lemon, Wynn, and Garcia. Of course, Feller was still pitching, although he didn't throw hard then, but he still had a great curveball. And Art Houtteman. Then you had Narleski and Mossi in the bullpen. Gee, if you did get one of the starters out of there and you were facing those two guys out of the pen — they really had a great pitching staff that year.

The toughest pitcher I ever hit at, ever, was Bob Lemon.

He just couldn't throw a ball straight. His fastball moved real good in on you. He did not have the best fastball or the best slider or the best curve I ever hit at, but he had a good one of each with control. And he had that bulldog attitude that he was going to get you out. He was a minor league third baseman.

He became a pitcher because the first baseman kept complaining to the manager, "Play somebody else over there. I can't catch the ball that he's throwing across to me."

"Why not?"

He said, "He can't throw one straight."

Then won 20 games forever. He was just born to be a pitcher. *[In 1942, before going into the service for three years, Lemon hit .268 with 21 home runs in Double A. He made his debut as a pitcher in 1946 with Cleveland, going 4–5. In 1947 he went 11–5. Beginning in 1948 he won at least 17 games in each of the next nine seasons, winning 20 or more seven times. He batted .232 lifetime.]*

— *J.W. Porter*

No one could ever figure out why Herb Score didn't pitch as well after he got hurt. *[After two great seasons to start his career, Score was hit in the eye by a Gil McDougald line drive in 1956.]* The first thing you would look for would be a recoil — you know, after you throw the ball you recoil and not finish the pitch in fear that the ball might be hit back at you. But there was no recoil, nobody could see that recoil.

His stuff, his velocity and the whole bit, looked just as good as before.

— *Cal McLish*

Ewell Blackwell of Cincinnati was a great pitcher. He was tough on lefthanders as well as right-handers because he had good control. He had two types of fastball. He'd throw a sink, sink, sink, sink, sink, and all of a sudden he'd hit the outside corner in a more or less straight, three-quarter fastball. Instead of sinking, it'd just shoot across the outside corner. He was tough in that respect.

— *Spider Jorgensen*

If you went into Cleveland with the pitching rotation that they had — Herb Score, Mike Garcia, Mossi, you know, guys of that caliber — if you got one or two hits during the whole series, you felt lucky. They had tremendous, awesome pitching.

— *Andy Carey*

Williams was pretty rough all the time and I always seemed to have trouble with Luke Easter, when he was with Cleveland. Even though I was a left-handed pitcher, it seemed like I was always having as much trouble with left-handers, maybe a little more trouble with left-handers, than with right-handers. I have no idea why, unless I was trying to pitch too many of them on the inside, or trying to pitch them away and got it over the plate. I never could figure that out.

— *Bob Cain*

We had a pretty good right-hander named Robin Roberts, who wouldn't throw at anybody. He'd just get out there and reach back and get a little bit more and a little bit more and a little bit more. You got any idea how many baseball games that guy pitched the last two weeks of 1950? You need to look it up. The last two innings in Brooklyn when we won the pennant, we were beaten in the ninth inning, but we were champions in the tenth. The last three outs of that ballgame was a thing of art. Vintage Roberts. He pitched right out of it. He popped up Gil Hodges. He popped up Carl Furillo. He was great.

Preacher Roe was a second Satchel Paige as far as I was concerned. He knew more about pitching. He was just a master. Harry Brecheen was a master. Don Newcombe was a strong-armed pitcher, a good pitcher. He just threw little bitty baseballs. I enjoyed watching Larry Jansen pitch. Carl Erskine had the good curveball. Great competitor, and a wonderful person.

— *Bubba Church*

Pitchers would knock you down, that was part of the game. I had the dirtiest uniform in the National League. I was hitting behind Gus Bell and Kluszewski, and they'd hit home runs ahead of me. Down I'd go. I expected it. I'd get up. It didn't bother me any and I hit a few myself.

— *Jim Greengrass*

In the fifties if you were pitching well they just left you in the ballgame. If I came in the second or third inning and the starter got knocked out, and I could get them out and I was ahead I pitched the rest of the game. And if you were a starting pitcher and you were winning the game going into the 8th or 9th inning you just stayed in the game. Once in awhile they would take you out, but the relief pitcher was just that. If you were in trouble here he comes. But very seldom did the relief pitcher come on in the last inning with the starting pitcher pitching well enough.

— *Ernie Johnson*

Pitching inside was part of the game. For example, years ago, Williams hits a home run in front of me — they're going to tell me, "Don't dig in." They're either going to brush me back or do something. Two strikes and no balls, they're going to be close a lot of times.

Once in awhile if you take one on the arm or take one on the thigh or something like that, it's telling the guy, "Hey, I have to make a living too. You do your thing, I'll do mine, but don't think you're just going to dive into the ball all the time and take me downtown, and all that kind of stuff."

Pitchers have to make their livelihood, the same as hitters, and they have to leave a message for you. Hey, you just go to first base and let's go.

— *Dick Gernert*

My main strengths in pitching were my fastball and control. I did not have a good curve at all. I had what they called a nickel curve. My fastball was my out pitch. I tried to keep the curveball out of the strike zone, you know, just enough to let them see it, to think I had one maybe.

— *Sonny Dixon*

Cal McLish came up with a straight change of pace that made him into an eighteen, nineteen game winner in the big leagues. I was with him with Cleveland, and then with the Phillies. He pitched right-handed, but he could throw with either hand. Cal got a lot of mileage by throwing a straight change. He tried to teach it to me and I couldn't learn the damn thing.

— *Don Ferrarese*

If I had to win one game in the big leagues, Robin Roberts would be my pitcher. He had perfect control.

— *Del Ennis*

I threw three-quarters — a right-handed pitcher — I threw three-quarter, I could throw side-armed. I had a flexible delivery. Right-handed hitters didn't like side-armed pitching, and I found out quickly who they were and I could be more effective against them by throwing them side-arm. They'd give ground. I had to use control because I wasn't a power pitcher.

— *Tom Ferrick*

I won 22 games in 1958, and I had tried nine times to win that 20th game. Dick Stuart, who was a great hitter with the Pirates, a long ball hitter, had mentioned before that game against the Giants that this was the night he was going to hit the home run to win it — and he *did* hit the home run off Marv Grissom in the 10th inning — so I won my 20th game.

— *Bob Friend*

Eddie Lopat pitched one of the first games *[May 18, 1952]* I played in the big leagues. The guys in the dugout told me all the pitches he used, the slow curves, the fast curves, slider, fastball, change of pace. Nobody said a word about knuckleball. I went up to hit, and I'll be damned if he didn't throw me a knuckleball. I checked my swing and hit the ball and popped it up over shortstop for a base hit. The guys were laughing at me for getting such a cheap hit, and when I went into the dugout I said, "Well, you guys told me about fifteen different pitches he threw, you never said nothin' about a knuckleball."

Whitey Ford was almost a Lopat clone, although Whitey actually had better stuff. But you never knew what Lopat was going to throw: he was really a smart pitcher. He was another one of those guys that had pinpoint control. He knew how to pitch and he could execute. He was a great pitcher.

— *Jim Dyck*

In the summer of 1961 I was playing for the Phillies against the Milwaukee Braves in County Stadium in Milwaukee. Warren Spahn was on the mound. He was the type of pitcher you would like to hit off but would come away with a comfortable 0–4 at the plate. This one time, though, he had me one ball and two strikes. The next fastball was up and in on the plate and I hit the pitch down the left field line. It cleared the fence for a home run. As I started to run from home I could hear Spahnie say, "You'll never see that pitch again."

— *Bobby Malkmus*

Now Raschi and Reynolds were guys that could get up on their toes, and if you're not ready up there it'd be in the glove. Plus, Vic had a good motion with his curve. It was a big curve, but it was slow and he had relatively good control of it. And when he'd get ahead of them with the fastball, he'd throw that breaking ball and it'd be hard for them to lay off of it, because he was always right around there with it. Fellas like Williams or Mantle or DiMaggio, they liked to hit at a consistency of speed. When you change speeds, it upsets the timing a little bit.

Reynolds threw a hard curve and a hard fastball. He could pump that ball for nine innings just like Vic, and he'd take the bat out of your hands if you weren't careful.

I told Raschi and Reynolds one time, "Look, you guys could walk Williams and put him on first. Then with Dropo and Stephens hitting behind him, you could make them hit those grounders. He won't steal second, you'll get the double play." But they'd just get after Williams if they could, and every now and then he'd crank one on them. But you know, you've gotta have fun. If you don't have fun, it's a lot of hard work.

— *Tommy Byrne*

They all said I was a great knuckleball catcher, but somebody else has to judge that, I just went out and did my job. I didn't use the big glove because a big glove with a knuckleball — you know how it flutters — if you've got the big glove somewhere near your eyes, reaching for the ball, you could lose it. The little glove is much easier, it's like a first baseman's glove, you could snap at it and it didn't blind your view of the ball, because sometimes the ball broke just at the last minute. And many of them I caught bare-handed when they broke a little bit more than I expected.

I caught some good knuckleballers. Lindell was an outfielder for the New York Yankees, and was a great low-ball hitter, and he had that great knuckleball — at Hollywood he won 20 games I guess *[He led the Pacific Coast League with 24 wins in 1952, and strikeouts with 190]*, and that's what brought him up again. Him and Ramsdell. *[Willie Ramsdell had a big league record of 24–39.]* I must have had about half a dozen of those knuckleball pitchers. LaPalme, Ramsdell, Lindell. The first knuckleball I ran into was Kirby Higbe's, in 1946 with the Dodgers. Higbe's knuckleball got near home plate and would break right down into the dirt, and I ate a lot of dirt that day in four or five innings.

— *Mike Sandlock*

I enjoyed playing behind Whitey Ford and Vic Raschi. They pitched fast, they didn't take a lot of time. The worst pitcher to play behind was Bob Turley. He'd drive me nuts because he'd take so much time between pitches. I wish the pitchers would realize that pitching quickly lets the fielder get into a groove, whereas if you're waiting around all the time, you just sort of get out of it. Tommy Byrne used to drive me nuts, 'cause he'd be very slow. A helluva pitcher, though, and a good hitter, too.

— *Andy Carey*

I'd rather take a glass of iodine than face a good left-handed pitcher. Parnell and Ford were two of the toughest. Of course, a lot of the right-handers were tough for me, too. Bob Feller wasn't a piece of cake.

— *Ferris Fain*

One day I was out there pitching pretty good and getting them out rather easily, and we'd gone five or six innings and we had about a five run lead. Well, between about twenty pitches and ten foul balls, I walked the bases loaded. With one out Casey *[Stengel]* sent Jim Turner *[the Yankee pitching coach]* out to talk to me. Yogi and I are out there at the mound as Turner comes out, and he's taking his time, we can hear them gloves poppin' down in the bullpen. I said, "Well, it looks like Turner wants to kill a little time." And Yogi said, "Yeah, it sounds like it, doesn't it."

Turner walked up out on the mound and said, "How do you feel?"

And I said, "Well, pretty good. I've got good stuff, I'm still all right."

He said, "Let me ask you something. Are you throwing to spots?"

Well, with a five run lead you generally don't normally go to that much trouble to pitch to spots. I looked at Yogi and I looked at Turner, and I said, "Well, I don't know, but I think I've hit every spot up there." He got real red in the face, and he turned around and walked back to the dugout and Yogi started back to the plate. I watched him all the way in the dugout, and he sat down next to Casey and I watched Casey say something to him and Turner wouldn't answer him Casey probably wanted to know, "What'd he say?"

A couple pitches later somebody hit into a double play. They didn't score any runs and I walked off like we really knew what we were doing. I went in the dugout and got a drink of water and sat down next to Turner. He got up and walked away from me because he was afraid I was going to ask him something, with Casey hearing it. Casey was a real comedian, but he got real serious too, when the game was going on. I was always serious, but it's kind of hard to stay serious a hundred percent of the time. You have to be a little wacky even to go through that kind of ordeal.

— *Tommy Byrne*

Bob Feller and I pitched a double one-hitter on April 23, 1952. That set a record for the fewest total hits in an American League game. *[In Sandy Koufax' perfect game in 1965, the Dodgers got only one hit, off the Cubs' Bob Hendley.]* Our very first hitter, Bobby Young, hit a fly ball to left field off Feller. Jim Fridley was the left fielder for the Indians. He started toward center field. Young was a left-handed hitter, and the ball curled back over Fridley's head. If he hadn't moved toward center, he'd probably caught the ball. But it went as a triple. *[Young had nine triples that year, two behind Avila's league-leading 11.]* An out or two later Marty Marion hit a ground ball and he scored. That was the only run we got and the only hit we got off Feller.

In the fifth inning, Luke Easter, who had been to bat nineteen times without a hit, singled off me. As a matter of fact, Easter's first time at bat he hit a long fly ball to right center field. Jim Rivera, our center fielder, made a terrific catch out in right center field up against the fence or that would have been a double or even a triple. I ended up with just seven strikeouts in that particular game, and I can always remember it because I think I had the first three, one in the fifth inning and the last three in the ballgame.

The one hit situation didn't even come into my mind at that time. I was still looking at that one run. I was just happy that we ended up winning the ballgame. I think that was Feller's twelfth one-hitter, and it was the only one he ever lost. *[Cain finished the season at 12–10; Feller, 9–13.]*

— *Bob Cain*

When you're a relief pitcher, you have good days and bad days. When I was with the Browns I lost two games in one day. That's not very comfortable. But then later on that same year I won two ballgames in one day. So you have the highs and the lows. *[Ferrick actually won both ends of an August 4, 1946, doubleheader for St. Louis; he lost both ends of one on August 20, 1947, while with Washington.]*

— *Tom Ferrick*

Don Larsen's perfect game was absolutely unreal. The guy was in complete control. A lot of us were in the bullpen, and Charlie Silvera was like a cat on a hot tin roof. I mean, he was really excited. He was running up and down that runway there, you know, and I said, "Sit down there, Charley. Relax. Things are going to work out all right."

Don was a great athlete. He could hit. He could field his position for a big man, he could run like hell, but he wouldn't run enough to stay in shape for nine innings.

Not many people remember that the guy pitching against him was a guy named Sal Maglie. He struck out the side in the eighth inning, and he was no spring chicken then. Of course he didn't have to pitch the ninth inning because we were playing in Yankee Stadium *[Maglie was 39 years old. In 1956 he went 13–6 with a 2.89 ERA and 3 shutouts.]*

— *Tommy Byrne*

The first game I ever started in the big leagues with the A's was against the Browns *[on August 21, 1941]*. I pitched a shutout. But there was a need to put somebody in the bullpen.

And I had some success relieving. I was able to make them hit the ball, I had good control, and this became my strength, being a reliever. You know, I needed a job. I was willing to accept any role. You have to be ready to pitch every day. I accepted that. I loved baseball. I wanted to do something.

— *Tom Ferrick*

I was on the Yankees roster in the 1947 World Series against the Dodgers, but I didn't get to pitch.

Then I was named to the 1951 All-Star game. *[Five other White Sox players were named to the All-Star game that year: Nellie Fox, Jim Busby, Minnie Minoso, Eddie Robinson, Chico Carrasquel.]* I had won seven and lost none at that time, so they picked me as one of the pitchers. But I didn't get in that game either.

They were telling me something, I think. *[The AL used five pitchers in an 8–3 loss: Ned Garver, Eddie Lopat, Fred Hutchinson, Mel Parnell, Bob Lemon.]*

— *Randy Gumpert*

I remember a lot about my 20th win. *[In 1951 Garver went 20–12 for the 52–102 last place Browns and batted .305. He completed 24 of 30 starts and went 2–1 in three relief appearances.]*

I remember that before the game started, the Globetrotters played basketball there on a court that they set up behind third base. It was Goose Tatum and Marcus Haynes and those guys. I wanted to play because I'd played a lot of basketball. But I couldn't do that because I was pitching.

Then the game started. I got hit pretty good, but the game was tied in about the fifth inning and I hit a ball over the left-field fence in the stands and it put us ahead and it kept us there. I hit it off Randy Gumpert, a Chicago White Sox pitcher. I hit that son of a biscuit over the Sealy Mattress sign in left-center field. Boy!

Yep, I won't forget that. I mean, I'll have Alzheimer's pretty bad before I forget that.

— *Ned Garver*

1952 was a strange year. I was 5–19, but it could have been the other way around just as easily. We didn't score many runs. *[Detroit finished last at 50–104. Trucks' ERA was 3.97, but Detroit was last in runs scored, averaging just 3.6 runs a game.]* I pitched two no-hitters, a one-hitter, and a two-hitter. Three of my five wins were 1–0.

I almost had three no-hitters that year. A month after my no-hitter against Washington, they came back to Detroit, and the first pitch I threw, Eddie Yost hits a clean single between George Kell and the shortstop. I retired the next 27 batters and won another 1–0 ball game. I knew Eddie Yost was a first-ball hitter. If he didn't swing at the first pitch, generally he walked. That was the way pitchers knew him. I got a little lax, I guess, and didn't put as much as I should on the ball, and he hit it. It was a clean base hit; there was no doubt about that.

— *Virgil Trucks*

Drysdale was the toughest for me, without a doubt. I probably struck out more against him than any other pitcher in the National League. He threw kind of sidearm, three-quarters, and his ball really bore in on a right-handed hitter. He was tall and lanky and he was halfway to the plate practically before he delivered the ball. Then when you looked for the pitch on the inside he'd give you that sweeping curveball and you're looking at the motion instead of the ball and you're swinging at a lot of bad pitches.

— *Frank Thomas*

Clem Labine had a big curveball. I couldn't figure out how anybody could hit that thing.
— *Wayne Terwilliger*

We had a fella that came up in the Yankee organization, Al Cicotte, and Al could throw as hard as anybody. But his reputation was that he was a little wild. So when he came up to the big leagues, he'd never get a break. When it was three and two, it seemed like even when it was over the plate, it'd be ball four. Where some pitchers have the reputation of having good control. They could be four inches outside or inside, and it would always be strike three. It seemed like that's the way Eddie Yost was, he had a reputation for walking, and maybe a lot of us could take the same third strike, and it would be a strike instead of a ball.

— *Herb Plews*

Parnell was fun to play behind because he was around the plate all the time and they hit a lot of ground balls. Kinder, he threw strikes. Frank was always around the strike zone. Maurie McDermott had great stuff, but he was three-two on most of the hitters. Nixon was a little much like three-two on a lot of hitters. Tommy Brewer was three-two on all hitters for God's sake. When you get three-two on a lot of hitters you get back on your heels.

— *Ted Lepcio*

The pitcher that really scared me was Sal Maglie. He was tough. First of all, he never shaved, and he looked really menacing. And he had great stuff. Geez, he had two or three different breaking pitches and he would always let you know that he was in control out there, because he would deck you. I mean, he had no qualms about hitting you.

— *Ted Kazanski*

Sal Maglie didn't like for you to even come up to the plate. That's why they used to call him "The Barber." He'd throw you a curveball outside. You were kind of looking outside and he'd throw you a ball right around your chest inside. You kind of had to be loose up there with him. I think probably of all of them that I faced, he was probably the one where I ended up with the most dirty uniforms.

— *Randy Jackson*

You knew that Robin Roberts was going to get the ball over the plate. If he missed it by an inch the umpire still called it a strike. The umpires were very lenient with Robin. You knew he would never throw at you, never hit you. So usually the ball was going to be around the plate and therefore you were a little more comfortable. Some of those guys were around the plate, but if you got too close to the plate they'd get your attention by knocking you down. But you never had to worry about that with Roberts.

— *Randy Jackson*

Whitey Ford was tough on me. For some reason or other Marty Marion always played me when he pitched. I think I had about three hits off him, maybe four, and they were all off his fastball. I had trouble with his curveball. I went down to the minors, to Vancouver. When I came back, the first night I'm there I got in about five o'clock and went to the ballpark. We were playing the Yankees and I go up to pinch-hit, and he strikes me out, Whitey Ford does. I come back to the bench and Marion says, "You didn't learn a damn thing while you were gone." So, yeah, Ford was my nemesis for sure.

— *Ron Jackson*

Billy Pierce was a good pitcher. He should be in the Hall of Fame, but he'll never make it. Pierce had better stuff than Whitey Ford, but he played with the White Sox. If he'd played with the Yankees he'd have won twenty-some ball games every year. *[A 211 game winner, Pierce was 195–143 from 1950 to 1962.]*

— *Bob Keegan*

My pitching style changed quite a bit after I started relieving. I was mainly a fastball pitcher for years when I was starting. I mean, I threw probably seventy percent fastballs, and probably twenty percent breaking balls, and probably ten percent change. And then when I became a reliever I started throwing a lot more sliders, and a lot more change of speeds, and I started having better luck and better control, really. I don't know if it was a combination of working with more pitches or if it was the fact that I was getting out there more often and felt more comfortable. When you're throwing strikes and you're throwing the ball where you want to, naturally your confidence goes up a notch. You're not afraid 3-1 or 2-0 to be throwing curveballs or sliders, because you feel you can throw them for strikes.

— *Johnny Klippstein*

Allie Reynolds was probably the guy you'd want to win one ballgame. He had a great fastball and a great overhand curve. Bob Feller had real raw talent. He'd rear back and throw that ball all the time 95–96 miles an hour, and he had a pretty good curveball. I don't know if Bob was as mean as Reynolds, but he didn't have to be.

I was a fastball pitcher. I had a fastball that was alive, and I had a pretty good curveball. Being a relief pitcher later on, I could throw strikes. The secret of pitching is getting ahead of your hitters. You come down there and you get strike one. Now you're the boss. Because if you've got three or four pitches, he don't know what you're going to throw now.

— *Bob Kuzava*

The guys who gave me the most trouble as pitchers were the guys who could move the ball around and had a decent breaking ball. I didn't worry about guys who had a good fastball. I used to think I could handle anybody's fastball. I had good success against Ryne Duren. He gave you that eyeglass bit, but I never had any problems with him because he never had much of a breaking ball. And if he did throw a breaking ball, he did you a favor. As a matter of fact, I hit a home run off him to beat him in extra innings at Fenway, and that always sticks out because it was the Yankees. Any time you beat the Yankees it was always great.

— *Frank Malzone*

I pitched a couple one-hitters in the minor leagues. Once the first batter up beat out a ball to first base and they never got another hit.

— *Don Liddle*

Vernon Law was by far the easiest pitcher to catch. You could put your glove on the outside part of the plate and you could turn around almost and talk to the umpire and the ball would hit your glove. He had great control. Harvey Haddix had great control. Those guys with great control, they're beautiful, they're easy to catch. A guy with a tough curveball, like Bob Friend, he was tough. Elroy Face's fork ball would do unbelievable things.

— *Bob Oldis*

The one that gave me the biggest help was in the minors, an ex-big league ballplayer, Herb Pennock. He was the one that taught me and instructed me about pitching curveballs. From then on I made good progress because of his help. With the Yankees I sat in the bullpen and got to watch the big three — Vic Raschi, Allie Reynolds, and Eddie Lopat. They were just outstanding to watch. Reynolds and Raschi were fastball pitchers. Lopat had a great screwball. He was confident, he was cocky, and he had excellent control. He knew what he was doing with every pitch.

— *Joe Ostrowski*

I never changed my style of pitching because of the hitter. I knew that for me to be successful I had to keep the ball down low, and when I started coming up with the baseballs when I started getting into trouble. If the guy was strictly a low ball hitter, then obviously I'd have to change a little bit to bring the ball up, which is something I never wanted to do. I always challenged them with my fastball and slider. If I was going to get beat, I was going to get beat with my best stuff.

— *Milt Pappas*

The guy that surprised me most in the '51 World Series was Allie Reynolds. He was just a powerful pitcher, and then the guy I didn't mind hitting against was Eddie Lopat, and I never got a hit off Lopat. Figure it out. Eddie was a junk ball pitcher, and this guy Reynolds, he was so much more powerful.

— *Bobby Thomson*

Chapter Eleven

A Little Bit of Money

Are today's players more greedy than those of the '40s and '50s? Do they love the game less? Or have they merely been brought into the game with a different set of salary expectations? Many players from that earlier era admit that if they were part of today's game, they would not refuse the millions of dollars offered. However, their era had no free agency. They had no control of their destiny, be it choice of team once they signed their initial contract, or in the amount of raise they might receive in their annual — not long-term — contract. So, all they could do was play the game for as long as they could, as hard as they could, and hope for a bit of generosity on the part of the owners

---

I can remember the minimum in '53 was five thousand, and finally jumped to six thousand and got to seventy-five hundred I think in 1960 when I was with the Pirates and we won the World Series.

— *Bob Oldis*

[Taylor Phillips came up to the big leagues in 1956, pitched until 1960, then came back for nine games in 1963.] In 1969 I was throwing batting practice for the Braves and working night shift at the post office. Paul Richard was the general manager with Milwaukee. He put me on the active list the last three weeks of the season so I could get updated on my pension. They gave me a quarter share when they won the pennant *[the Western Division Championship — they lost to the Mets]*. I got a quarter share for pitching batting practice, twenty-five hundred dollars, and I got raises on my pension up through 1981. So I owe everything to Paul Richards.

— *Taylor Phillips*

Either take this or stay home. We've got a farm system, you ain't that good. You know, I believed them. I went to the big leagues, the minimum salary was sixty-five hundred. I looked down at the contract and it says six thousand. I asked Mr. Quinn, "I thought the minimum was sixty-five hundred." He says, "You want to play here or go back to Wichita?" I like to broke his arm taking that pen away from him. When I was with the Cubs Mr. Wrigley — and this is going to blow our mind — he says, "If you are a starter on my ball team, you are going to make a minimum of fifteen thousand dollars a year." I was a starting pitcher, and I got paid at the rate of fifteen thousand dollars a year. I had signed a contract for eighty-five hundred. I missed a start and my pay went back to eighty-five hundred. I made a couple more starts and it went back up. But they were fair over there.

— *Taylor Phillips*

What happened an awful lot in my career, I'd have a good year and then I'd kind of hold out. I'd get there late and I'd get off to a slow start that year, and they'd trade me.

And I wasn't a superstar type of guy. I was kind of an average pitcher, but if I thought I deserved what I wanted I didn't go. I was kind of stubborn about it. It helped me and hurt me. I got more money, then I wouldn't do so well then they'd trade me, and I'd get off to a little slow start and not do as well. It doesn't help your reputation if you get traded a lot.

— *Bob Shaw*

You always had problems with negotiations. They were kind of like dictators. They told you what to do and if the general manager said jump, you said the proverbial "How high?" You just didn't have much say-so back in those days.

I think the biggest raise I ever got was probably twenty-five hundred dollars. And that was after playing in the All-Star game and hitting twenty-one home runs and knocking in seventy-some odd runs.

— *Randy Jackson*

In 1946 we were in spring training and they wouldn't let me work out until I signed a contract. I'd won 17 games and one in the World Series before I went in the service and they wanted to give me a five hundred dollar raise. *[In 1944 Lanier was 17–12 with a 2.65 ERA and 5 shutouts.]*

Eddie Dyer was the Manager, and he told Me, "Max, I'm going to get on the phone and you get on the other phone. I'm going to call St. Louis and talk to Sam Breadon to see if I can't get you a raise."

Breadon said, "I'm going to give him five hundred, and he can take it or go home."

So I took it, but I wasn't satisfied. So that's one reason I went to Mexico. I came back to the Major Leagues in the middle of 1949. I just played one year in Mexico. They wanted to cut our salary. We played in Cuba in the winter time a couple years. I played up in Drummondville, Canada, in '49, and I was pitching for a semi-pro club and making more than the Cardinals were paying me.

— *Max Lanier*

You did what the owners told you. Curt Flood was the first one to question baseball and he got blackballed. If you refused to sign a contract they wouldn't let you come to spring training.

They'd say, "Well, stay home. Get a job in a factory."

Sometimes I wanted two thousand dollars more and I couldn't get it, and what were you going to do? It's like me saying to you, "Hey, give me ten dollars, and you say, 'no.'" Well, what am I going to do?

The only guys that didn't have to get jobs during the winter were your superstars.

— *Bob Kuzava*

Connie Mack and Clark Griffith were individual owners; they didn't have great wealth. And a lot of times the American League had to bail them out. The league sent them money so they could finish the year. The same way with the Browns. They were always borrowing money, and the league had to support them in a lot of ways.

— *Tom Ferrick*

I signed my first contract for the Washington Senators for two hundred dollars a month *[in 1940]*. Then I got a raise, and got another little raise. I ended up making three thousand dollars the first year. Clark Griffith was a nice guy, and he'd treat you nice, but he'd try to get you just as cheap as he could. He always managed to seem to give you a tiny little raise each year to keep you happy.

In 1950 I won 14 and lost 14 for Washington *[the only Senator pitcher to win more than eight that year]*. A week before the season ended, Clark Griffith called me into his office and said, "Sid, you played great this year, I think you deserve a bonus. How much do you think you deserve?"

Well, I didn't know what to say, so I finally said, "Well, I think I ought to have a thousand dollars."

He said, "I think you ought to have two."

So he gave me two thousand. But that was the raise for next year.

— *Sid Hudson*

Playing baseball was always something that I wanted to do since I was a kid. So the money was important, but not that important, just so long as I could play in the big leagues.

Playing in the fifties was great. Everybody was dedicated to the game and of course everybody wanted more money, but you know they didn't hold out that long, you didn't have agents or anything, so you wound up playing.

The year I won sixteen, I had to negotiate for that. You'd think I was asking for millions of dollars, and I got about a three thousand dollar raise, after winning sixteen and losing nine.

— *Bob Keegan*

I loved Branch Rickey, but he was tight with his money. One year in Pittsburgh I hit .286 with 15 home runs and went in to Rickey asking for a raise. Rickey said, "You're a leadoff man. If I'd wanted you to hit home runs, I'd have batted you third or fourth."

I didn't get my raise. Back then they didn't give money out like they do now. I started in the majors at $5,000 a year. Eight years later I was making $21,000. But I didn't mind. I always played my heart out. And I'd do it all over again. I'd ride the buses. We played back then because we loved the game.

— *Cal Abrams*

We just tried to get out there and hustle and try to increase our salary a little bit. We knew we were going to have to go to work after our careers were over and we just tried to do the best we could and make whatever money we could at that time. Whatever money we were making was more than you could make if you went to work someplace, so you stayed in it as long as you could, at the major league level anyway. In fact, a lot of guys in the minor leagues played a long time because they could make more money in the spring and summer playing baseball and getting a job in the offseason than they could finding a full-time job, back in those days. The attitude was good; people thought they were doing okay.

— *Milt Bolling*

I got paid well for what I did in my day, and you gotta remember, our money bought something. The same car we paid $1800 for costs 35–38 thousand today. That is one heck of a difference.

— *Gene Woodling*

Back then we got paid very well for being major league baseball players, compared to the average working man in the street. But I thought we had a relationship with the fans who were the average working person. We got paid one year salaries at a time, and we got paid based on our previous year's performance.

— *Bobby Thomson*

I think the low minors probably was pretty tough, and the income that they made wasn't too good. I always made good income, a lot more than I could have made working in a factory or teaching school or something like that.

— *Ron Jackson*

The money wasn't much. DiMaggio was our icon, he was the guy, the leader. He made a hundred thousand. The rest of us if we got to thirty or forty, we thought that was great. Most were in the twenties and below. But the money was never a major factor.

— *Jerry Coleman*

Meal money was six dollars a day. That covered your tips and meals, and if you had to go anyplace in a taxi. You couldn't go very far. If you went in a good restaurant and had a good meal, it was about four and a half. And if you'd eat in the hotel for breakfast that was another two dollars, or two and a half. You know, hotels were a little expensive. So that shot your meal money, you know. Didn't have any left for beer.

— *Carl Scheib*

Getting money out of the Yankees was like squeezing blood out of a turnip. They had this huge reputation, and they'd tell you, "You're wearing the Yankee pinstripes, that's worth something." Well, I never did figure out what the hell that was worth. But that's what they used to tell us.

My first year in the Brownie organization. I made more money than I ever made with the Yankees. I was doubling my salary every year by playing winter ball. Just like that, boom. Then when I became a major leaguer, I became ineligible for winter ball. So actually my first year in the big leagues I made less money than I did the year before.

I made the *Sporting News* Rookie Team, and had a very respectable year, and the second year I thought I was worth more money. I went down to St. Louis and talked contract with Veeck, and he said, "You're right, you're entitled to it." And he gave it to me. In those days, once you established a figure for salary, and if you moved or you were even shipped from the major leagues to the Coast League, that gave you a good basis to maintain a respectable wage.

— *Jim Dyck*

My first big league contract was for six thousand dollars. I came out of the service *[in 1958]* and Mr. Cronin asked me how much I wanted and I said, "I don't know."

He said, "How about twelve thousand?"

I thought, "Boy, I'm doubling my salary. That's great." I thought I was a rich man.

I never made any money. Most of us didn't make much money. We played for the love of the game.

— *Don Buddin*

The players didn't have much say-so when it came to money. It wasn't the tail wagging the dog in those days, buddy. I was playing for San Antonio in the Texas League and a semi-pro team in Fort Wayne offered me more money to play than San Antonio was offering me. I told San Antonio that, and they said, "Well, maybe your future is there in Fort Wayne."

They didn't care. I mean, you didn't scare anybody. If you didn't want to play for what they told you, you could just stay home.

— *Ned Garver*

My first contract was for three hundred dollars a month. Some were signing for seventy-five. But then I had a room in a boarding house with three meals and a bed, a dollar a day.

— *Tom Wright*

My first year in the big leagues I was a starting pitcher with the White Sox, in 1949, with Billy Pierce and Howie Judson, Max Surkont, and Randy Gumpert. My salary was fifty-five hundred dollars. I think in my best year I made nineteen thousand dollars. But there's nothing you could do. In spring training you got nothing. You got your room and board period.

— *Bob Kuzava*

I went down to Caracas, Venezuela in the winter of '55. They had some major leaguers down that way. I don't know what happened, but I pitched thirty-one innings down there before I gave up an earned run. I got paid one thousand dollars a month and expenses and all. I saved thirty-five hundred dollars to put on my house. Then at Boston I was paid eighty-five hundred. I saved some good money that year.

— *Ben Flowers*

When I was in the Coast League, Portland wanted to cut my salary. I said, "There ain't no way." They said, "Jim, that's a major league salary." I said, "If you cut my salary, I'm gone. I'll go home." Ralph Kiner was the general manager at San Diego. He apparently got wind of it and said, "We'll take his salary."

He called me and I said, "Sure." So I moved my family and we went down to San Diego. That *[1960]* was my last year. *[Greengrass actually played part of the 1961 season as well, but not in the Pacific Coast League.]*

— *Jim Greengrass*

In 1957 with Washington I went in for the raise I was promised September 1st from Cal Griffith, Dressen had been fired and I was hitting .305 *[finished the season at .261]* and I hadn't made an error all year, and all he said was, "Dressen's been let go, you have no witness." But the funny thing was, the end of the season, I was working in a liquor warehouse and the boss, the general manager, came in, and he said, "Oh, congratulations! I see you didn't make an error all year." And the warehouse foreman said, "Yeah, but he sure made one here. He tipped over a box and broke six quarts of liquor."

— *Lou Berberet*

Not many guys held out unless you had real good years. You might write back and ask for a five hundred or thousand dollar raise. They didn't offer more than that. It was tough to get big raises unless you had outstanding years. I think it was '57 that Roy Sievers had a great year and had to hold out for a fifteen hundred dollar raise the next year. I think he hit almost 30 home runs in that Washington ballpark which was unbelievable, because it was a mammoth ballpark for right-handed hitters. *[Sievers hit 29 home runs in 1956 and a league-leading 42 in 1957.]* But you couldn't hold out too long, because you were easily replaceable.

— *Milt Bolling*

I got fifteen hundred dollars to sign in 1950 and was signed to a Class B contract. But I had to beat out twelve first basemen to make a Class D ball club. I mean, they had minor league teams in every town in the United States. I think the Giants must have had twelve or fourteen minor league teams then. Maybe more. But one thing it did, it gave a person a chance to develop.

— *Gail Harris*

I really think the ballplayers in those days just played ball because they really enjoyed getting out there and playing. In other words, showing off, you could say. You know, getting in front of the crowd. All the great big stars made money, but just the mediocre players, they didn't make any money. I've seen many of them come broke and go home broke at the end of the season, making just enough to get by.

— *Carl Scheib*

Chapter Twelve

Now That Was a Moment!

Much of baseball's beauty and joy is as a retrospective. Over the long winter months when most fans do not have the pleasures of current baseball games, they can reflect on moments from the past, moments that tend to stay in the memory as clearly as if they had happened only the day before. Most players, too, have moments that stay with them, even after thirty years, or forty, or fifty. And sometimes, like the pleasure of a classic film, the joy captured in the mind's recording of that moment increases though age.

Some moments take place on a special stage frequented by the very best the league can offer — in the All-Star game. Every summer since 1933 (except for 1945, when the All-Star game was canceled due to severe wartime travel restrictions), fans have had the pleasure of debating who is the "best of the best." Which of their heroes will be named to the All-Star squad? There always seem to be deserving players cheated from a spot on the team by fans who other fans claim are "voting for their favorites" rather than for the best, or by managers who don't have enough roster spots to let them select every player with All-Star credentials. For those who are chosen for their league's squad, the selection becomes something to look back on with pride. The game itself is often one they can look back on with joy.

Some other moments take place on an even larger stage on which the best teams in each league perform. You play a whole season, 154 games, for the right to represent your league in the World Series. And often, after six months and all those games, the pennant winner is determined by a single pitch delivered in the right or wrong spot, one swing of the bat, a fielder stretching toward the saving catch. The loser goes home to remember forever what could have been, the possible World Series ring so close, so close. The winner goes on to what all players yearn for, the right to play in that Fall Classic, where each clutch hit, each well-pitched game, and all exceptional catches are forever remembered, magnified, immortalized.

The best day I ever had in the major leagues was in a doubleheader in New York, the 4th of July — that was the year that I hit .303 and was leading the league part of the year *[1951]* and I thought I might possibly get named to the All-Star team. Just before we got to New York, Casey Stengel named the extra players, and I wasn't included. I was probably hitting about three-thirty, three-forty at the time. They had a good cast of outfielders, but

I thought I might make it on the outside. *[AL outfielders who played in the 1951 All-Star game were Dom DiMaggio, Ted Williams, Jim Busby, Vic Wertz, Minnie Minoso, and Larry Doby.]*

In the first game of the doubleheader, I hit two home runs and knocked in six runs and we won the ballgame. I hit two 3-run home runs, one off Vic Raschi and one off a left-hander — I can't remember his name. Then in the second game, the ballgame was tied in the 8th inning, and they brought Joe Page in as a reliever to pitch to me with the winning run on second base, and I got a base hit to left-center field to knock in the winning run. The next night was a night game, and I hit a home run off Bob Kuzava, a lefthander, my first time at bat, and got a couple other base hits.

I don't know if it was the desire or what, but the doubleheader on that July 4th was the best day I ever had in the major leagues.

— ***Gil Coan***

During my time, the National League won most of the All-Star games. I played in three All-Star games, won two and lost one. I remember the game I started in Kansas City [in 1960]. I shut them out for three innings. *[Friend was the winning pitcher in a 5–3 game. He won the 1956 game 7–3 with three scoreless innings. He gave up two runs in the 1958 game and lost 4–3.]*

You have to be lucky to win an All-Star game because you've got to be there when we're scoring runs. I remember it was very hot; it must have been a hundred degrees in Kansas City, and a hundred and fifteen degrees on that mound. *[Official temperature: 101 degrees. TV cameras had to be wrapped in ice to keep them from overheating. There was a full capacity crowd of 30,619.]*

— ***Bob Friend***

Being voted to start in the 1954 All-Star game and especially going back and being a starter in Cleveland and then hitting the home run off Robin Roberts is something I've never forgotten, especially because Al Rosen, who had been my roomie at Cleveland and in the minors, homered. Then I followed him with a home run. That was the first ever back-to-back homers in the All-Star game, so I was kind of proud about that.

— ***Ray Boone***

There always is a strong competitive feeling, even when you have a meeting before the ballgame with the manager and the coaches and the President of the National League — they all want to win. I played in three All-Star games. In '58 I was voted as a starter by my peers, and that's what makes that one so much important as far as I am concerned. You're playing with the greatest players in that era, and to be rubbing shoulders and to play with them on the same club with them is quite a thrill. I remember when Musial hit the home run in Milwaukee in the twelfth inning off Frank Sullivan *[to win the 1955 game 6–5]*. It's just a great thing to be part of it.

— ***Frank Thomas***

Nothing beats the roar of the crowd. I heard it throughout the 1960 All-Star game, saw the fans in the packed ballpark in Kansas City cheering as I watched the game from the center field bullpen. Then, in the ninth inning I was called on to pitch.

I stepped through the bullpen gate onto the field. My home crowd rose as one in a standing ovation for me. Few things can match the feeling of a bullpen gate opening to let you be swallowed by the roar of the crowd.

— *Bud Daley*

Playing in the All-Star game was one of my greatest moments. As a kid I'm sitting on the bus going out to the ballpark to play the game and I'm sitting next to one of my greatest idols, Stan Musial.

Ted Williams is on the bus, another idol. And here I am just sitting on the bus going to the ballpark with people like that. That was a beautiful feeling. You're floating all along through the whole thing, that's all I can tell you. It's just something you never forget.

— *Jim Landis*

I started the All-Star Game in '49 in Brooklyn. I also pitched in an All-Star game in 1951 in Detroit. In 1953 I should have been selected to the All-Star Game because I had the most wins of anybody in the major leagues, but Casey Stengel didn't take me or Bob Porterfield, I guess because we were beating the Yankees consistently. *[Porterfield led the league in wins in '53, 22–10; and Parnell was 21–8. Stengel picked his own Reynolds, 13–7; and Sain, 14–7.]* It was disappointing, but getting three day's rest from not going to the All-Star game enabled me to get an extra start. And that's the reason I won 21 games, so that turned out to be a plus for me.

— *Mel Parnell*

In the 1955 All-Star Game, I got beat in the 12th inning. I went in in the eighth and replaced Ford. An error tied the game, and then I went on to pitch the rest.

I got them out in the ninth, and I pitched the 9th, 10th, and 11th, because if you pitched in relief could you pitch more than three innings. And it was the first pitch of the 12th inning — and the thing is, every time they show it on TV, they say, "Sullivan's first pitch —"

They forget I'd already pitched more than three scoreless innings. Everybody thinks I went in for one throw and that was it.

I remember coming in afterwards — I wasn't too upset, but hey, I'm not the only guy in the world Musial's hit a ball off of. I threw him an eye-high fastball. He jumped up out of that crouch and tomahawked it out of there. I remember Berra saying later, "Geez, I forgot to tell you, he's a high fastball hitter."

— *Frank Sullivan*

On April 27, 1949, we played Brooklyn. We led 6–0, then the Dodgers came back to take an 8–6 lead. In the seventh, we filled the bases with a couple of walks and an infield single, and Leo Durocher said to me, "Grab a bat and go up and hit for Hansen."

My heart began pumping. I can still see the first pitch coming in. It was a fastball, just below waist high over the outside part of the plate. I lashed at it and hit it good. I got every bit of it. The Polo Grounds is a football field, so it was almost 500 feet to centerfield. I hit a shot of a line drive and Duke Snider went after it but couldn't get to it. He chased it to the wall and by the time the ball got back to the infield I had rounded the bases.

The *New York Daily News* had a huge picture of me sliding and Roy Campanella still waiting for the throw. The headline read: "Milne's 4-run homer beats Bums." When I left the stadium people were everywhere. Of course, I didn't mind it. It was the first time they'd paid attention to me. I got telegrams from all over the country from everybody I knew.

The next day I was sitting on the bench again, waiting for another chance to pinch hit. It was my only major league home run, and a writer from *Baseball Digest* has researched the hit and believes it is the only pinch hit, inside-the-park grand slam in history.

— *Pete Milne*

It was disappointing to lose both the 1948 and 1949 pennants, after coming so close. In 1948 I was pitching against the Yankees on the last day of the season. If we beat the Yankees and Detroit beat the Indians, Cleveland and us would tie for the pennant. I got in trouble in the sixth inning, I believe. The Yankees loaded the bases with Hank Bauer and DiMaggio coming up. I got Bauer on a sacrifice fly to Ted in left field and got DiMaggio out and we went on to win the game. I think it was 10–5, and of course Fenway was going wild because the scoreboard showed Detroit was beating Cleveland. We did end in a tie and that brought about the first playoff game in American League history the next day, and sad to say we lost that. Gene Bearden beat us 8–3 there in Fenway. But it was a memorable moment for me, going into that game that had so much riding on it at the time.

I wasn't around in '49 — I was inactive due to arm trouble — and we lost the pennant the last day of the season to the Yankees in Yankee Stadium. We went in on Saturday with a one game lead and lost both games and lost the pennant again by one game.

— *Boo Ferriss*

The biggest pennant race that I recall was the '49 pennant race; we were one behind with two to go. Of course, we had a lot of tough ones, we were behind in a lot of races. But we'd get ourselves together and have a meeting and say, "Well, let's go, they're trying to take it from us." I didn't play much, but I was there. We would talk to the rookies and say, "Hey, this is the way it is. Just don't get caught in a bar, and let's do the job we have to do."

— *Charlie Silvera*

You know the Ancient Mariner who had that Albatross hung around his neck? That was the last day of the 1949 season between the Red Sox and the Yankees. It was a very emotional day and as it turned out, we won that ballgame 5–3, but the thing that to me superseded anything that ever happened to me in baseball before or since — because that was the first championship. I don't think I've ever been as high as I was on that particular day. Going into it you felt like you were walking out the final thirteen steps to the gallows because there were seventy thousand people in the stands. It was just one of those emotional moments in your life that can never be recreated again.

My hit in the seventh inning *[a three run double]* didn't seem like much at the time because it just expanded the lead from 2–0 to 5–0. Then all of a sudden Raschi was tiring and DiMaggio left the field, which was another incredible thing. I think Doerr hit a ball over his head that he should have caught. He just left, he said he couldn't make it. You know, he had the flu or whatever, a case of some kind of virus. Then the Red Sox had the tying run at the plate when, I'm not sure who it was, popped up to Tommy Henrich in foul territory at first base and that was the highlight of my career. It happened my first year and it never was passed after that.

— *Jerry Coleman*

I remember that last day of the 1950 season, when Sisler hit the home run into the left field stands. That put us three runs ahead. Then we got them out. The last man popped it up, and Eddie Waitkus trotted over there and caught it, and it was all ours then.

We won the close ballgames that year.

Granny Hamner was one of the best shortstops I've seen in my life in 1950. That son of a gun made great plays, and on top of that he hit good in the clutch. Old Puddinhead Jones, the third baseman, played great ball. Andy Seminick was just as good a catcher as I'd ever seen. It was just a great ballclub. Del Ennis was just a wonderful outfielder. It was just a pleasure to be around those guys.

In the last of the ninth they had a chance to win but the centerfielder, Richie Ashburn, threw the man out at home. He came in and got the ball and threw it home, and he had the runner by 10–12 feet. It was just a perfect throw. It just got over the pitcher's mound between the pitcher's mound and home plate, a perfect bounce. Stan Lopata had gone in to catch — he weighed about 220 pounds, and there's no way that Cal Abrams could get into home plate. He was just beat too far.

— *Jimmy Bloodworth*

The Phillies beat the Dodgers the last day in 1950 to avoid a playoff when Dick Sisler hit a home run. Our pitching staff was in great shape and theirs was really depleted. I think Robin Roberts pitched about sixteen, seventeen innings the last two days. I think we would really have had a great chance to beat them in a playoff.

— *Bobby Morgan*

It was in August, 1951. The pennant race was close. We were in Cleveland for a crucial series and our starting rotation was not totally ready. Casey summoned the bullpen and informed us that one of the relievers would start the game. The selection would be made at the Cleveland park. Stubby Overmire was chosen. He was to oppose Early Wynn, one of the mainstays of a strong Indian's pitching corp. Both starters pitched brilliantly, allowing no score. Overmire got into trouble in the 6th or 7th inning with men on third and first and one out. I got the call to relieve Stubby and put out the threat — a foul out to the third baseman and one to left field.

In the top of the next inning I was the first scheduled hitter and with my anemic batting average I expected a pinch-hitter to bat for me. *[Ostrowski batted. 161—19 for 118 — for his career.]* Instead, Casey permitted me to go to the plate and I responded with a base hit to right field. With two out, Gene Woodling homered and the Yanks won 2–0, giving them the needed surge toward the pennant and the World Series win. This was in the string of five pennants and five World Series wins in succession. I was in three of them, during my four and a half years in the American League.

— *Joe Ostrowski*

The thing I treasure most is getting a World Series ring. And number two was being able to put up a World Series win on the board. Those are two important things that happened to me in baseball. *[Ferrick won Game Three of the 1950 Series against the Phillies 3–2 with a scoreless ninth inning in relief. The Yankees swept the Phillies in four straight.]*

— *Tom Ferrick*

There was a moment in the 6th game of the '51 World Series — pinch-hitting in the top of the 9th at Yankee Stadium with the Yankees up 3 games to 2 — the tying run on 2nd, 2 out, my first time at bat in the Series.

I lined hard to right. Bauer came in fast and made a nice catch to end the game, and the Series. I have good thoughts about that moment, to be put in that spot and almost doing the job.

— *Sal Yvars*

I got to pinch hit in both the '52 and '53 World Series against the Yankees. Both balls I hit were hit hard, a line drive to left and a line drive to right, but both were caught. That's the only thing you can do, if they don't fall in, they don't fall in. I thought Yankee Stadium was awesome. The manager says you're going to pinch hit the next inning and you say, "Oh, my God, millions of people out there. The old adrenalin really gets going. In Yankee Stadium I hit against Whitey Ford, and Bob Kuzava in Ebbets Field.

— *Bobby Morgan*

I can remember the very first World Series game that I attended, against the Dodgers in '53. I wasn't eligible to play in '52. I was up and down *[between the minors and Yankees]* two times, but not eligible to play in the Series.

Then in '53, I remember going to the World Series in Brooklyn, and having the police escort, and then when we got into Brooklyn having people throwing eggs and tomatoes, you know, just rabid fans. Our bus looked like a fruit, or salad.

— *Andy Carey*

In August of 1953 the White Sox came into town one game out of first. They had a hell of a ballclub that year. They had Fox and Rivera and Minoso. They had Lollar and Mele and Pierce. We were in first place. Friday night Raschi shut them out. Saturday Ford beat them in the first game 1 0. I beat them in the second game 3–0. The next day Reynolds beat them. So now they're five out. They leave us and go to Washington and they lose four in a row in Washington. So the pennant race was over. I think they went back home to Chicago eight games out, and that happened within like eight days. So that's how fast a pennant race can turn around. *[Cleveland finished second, 7 games out; the White Sox finished third, 9 games out.]* That's telling you how great a percentage pitching is in the game of baseball. I think we shut them out three of the four games, and every pitcher went nine innings.

— *Bob Kuzava*

I opened the 1953 World Series in Yankee stadium — coming off a 20–6 record. However, I had a shaky first inning and didn't last long. *[The Yankees won the opener, 9–5, and then won Game Two 4–2 to take a two game lead.]* Charlie Dressen asked me to start the third game with just one day's rest. I was so pleased to get a chance to redeem myself that I told my roommate Duke Snider that I was going to pitch each inning like my life depended on it.

Campy homered off Vic Raschi in the eighth to give me a 3–2 lead. In the ninth I faced Don Bollweg, a left-handed pinch hitter — then Johnny Mize. I struck them both out. Collins hit an easy hopper back to me for the final out. In the clubhouse Preacher Roe told me I had set a new World Series strikeout record of 14 in one game. I struck out Mantle and Collins four times each.

It was my best day.

— *Carl Erskine*

When I played third base, they always told me, "Just knock the ball down and throw them out." I had a great arm from the outfield, and at third base I would hold the ball until the man was about five feet from the bag and then I'd throw it over there and make it a bang-bang play at first base.

But that kind of stopped when I threw one in Milwaukee with Dale Long playing first base, and it ended up in the second row of the stands. The manager said, "Hey, that's enough of that. As soon as you get the ball throw it over there."

— *Frank Thomas*

It was a thrill for me to start and win the fourth game of the 1954 World Series, clinching the championship in four straight games over the winningest team in the history of major league baseball. *[The Cleveland Indians won a record 111 games while losing only 43 before being swept by the Giants in the World Series in four straight games.]*

— *Don Liddle*

That year with Cleveland *[1954]*, the World Series against the Giants was a disaster. You know we got wiped out in four games. That was a real disaster, it should never have happened, but it did. Everybody was positive there was no way we could lose.

The real reason we lost, I think, was that we won the pennant too early. We were having a good time and partying for two weeks. If we'd won the first game in New York, which we could have won as easily as we lost, I think it would have been a dandy Series.

— *Wally Westlake*

Pitching in a World Series is something I guess every kid dreams about. In '49 I got my first chance to pitch in a World Series, against the Dodgers at Brooklyn. I think I walked Reese and then he tried to go to second on a pop fly. Yogi caught the pop fly going back toward the screen and he doubled him up. I think I got the next seven guys out and then the first thing you know I got a man or two on and walked the bases loaded. Casey came and got me. But Page relieved early in that game and he went on to win it, 4–3. *[This was Game Three. Byrne left with the game tied 1–1 in the fourth. There was no more scoring until the ninth when the Yankees scored 3 runs in the top half and the Dodgers scored 2 in the last of the ninth on two solo home runs. The Yankees won Game One, 1–0, behind Reynolds. Preacher Roe won Game Two for Brooklyn 1–0. Page beat Branca in Game Three. Lopat beat Newcombe 6–4 in Game Five, and Raschi beat Rex Barney 10–6 in Game Five.]*

But I did win a game in '55. I was probably 35 or 36 years old then, and I had to change my way of pitching or otherwise I would have gone by the wayside. I had to learn some more pitches and let them see the ball a little bit better. Winning that second game of the World Series was one of the highlights of my career. I got a base hit and knocked in a couple of runs, and we beat them 4–2. And I think that was the only game a lefthander had completed and won against Brooklyn in about a year and a half. They had a good right-handed hitting ballclub. Great, as a matter of fact—Campanella, Hodges, Furillo, Robinson—they had a real good team. *[Byrne's complete game victory was the only one by a lefthander against the Dodgers in 1955. He also started Game Seven, won by Podres and the Dodgers 2–0 when Amoros made his game-saving catch against Berra.]*

— *Tommy Byrne*

I'll never forget jumping over the bullpen fence to enter my first World Series game in 1957. "I made a World Series game." So few players do. *[Johnson pitched seven innings in three games, striking out eight, walking one, and giving up only two hits and one run. He was the losing pitcher, though, in Game Six when Bauer hit a seventh-inning home run off him. The Braves won the Series in seven games.]*

And I had a pretty good Series. I pitched in three games, but I made a mistake to Hank Bauer in game number six. I'd been getting him out with side-armed curves, and I hung a curveball. He hit a line drive, and it hit the foul pole in left field for a game-winning home run. It put them ahead by a run. I pitched pretty well. I think in seven innings or so I only allowed that one run, but that beat us that particular day. But fortunately, in Game Seven Burdette came out and shut them out. Burdette had such a super World Series, he won three games. They didn't hit him hard at all. *[Burdette gave up just two runs in 27 innings. He shut out the Yankees for the last 24 innings.]*

Burdette was not overpowering, but he had a good screwball. He kept the ball low, he had a good sinker. A great competitor. So the fact that he pitched so well didn't surprise me at all. It probably shouldn't have surprised the Yankees either. *[Burdette was 17–9. For his career he was 203–144 with 33 shutouts. From 1953 to 1961 he averaged 17 wins a season.]*

— *Ernie Johnson*

In my last season, 1957, we lost the World Series to the Braves in seven games. I'd liked to have finished on a win, but it didn't work out. Lew Burdette beat us three times. The first game he pitched against us he had tremendous stuff. The second game was just decent. The third game he had nothing and we still couldn't beat him. It was one of those things, if we hit the ball hard it would be right into someone's glove. We just never got going against him. Turley won the sixth game for us 3–2 back in New York. We lost the seventh game 5–0, but we had the bases loaded when the game ended. Skowron hit a one-hop shot to Mathews. He made a spectacular back-handed grab, touched third and the game was over. And we thought he couldn't field.

— *Jerry Coleman*

I was very fortunate to have actually participated in five World Series. I was eligible for five but only played in four. I was eligible in '53 when we played the Dodgers, but I didn't even get to bat even though I hit .321 that year. Casey just let the old timers play, the guys that had been there before. To me, it was just like a training period.

We played the Braves in '57 and they beat us. In '58 they had us down 3 games to 1 and we came back and beat them. I think at that time they're only been one other team in World Series history that had been down 3–1 and came back to win the Series. *[In 1925 the Pirates had come back from a 3–1 deficit to beat the Senators 4 games to 3.]*

— *Andy Carey*

1959 was my favorite year. Of course, that was the year the White Sox won the pennant. I think we went into Cleveland tied for first, and I believe I pitched the first game on a Friday night. If I'm not mistaken Minoso, who was with Cleveland then, was actually under the ball, it looked like it was a routine catch, and it flipped out of his glove and went over the fence for a home run, and we won the game. Then Wynn won for us the next day, and Donovan and Pierce won on Sunday, and we left four games in front. But the accident of the ball jumping out of Minnie Minoso's glove was just kind of a break for us, got us rolling.

— *Bob Shaw*

In 1959 our Cleveland club was leading the league up until we had a four game series with the White Sox, and they won all four of them and that knocked us out of it. That was probably the closest that any of the teams I really contributed to came to winning a pennant. I was on that '46 Dodger team when they tied and played St. Louis in the best two out of three playoff, but I wasn't contributing anything, because I'd just come out of the service. I had arm trouble, but the Dodgers had to keep me on the roster.

Then I was with Philadelphia, in '64. I'd hurt my arm at the end of the '63 season, rotator cuff, and we had some simulated games, and Gene Mauch was trying to get my arm in shape where I could help them, wait for the hot weather, but it just wouldn't respond, so about June 1 is when they cut me loose. So I wasn't with the team when the Cards came back and won it, when the Phillies had that six and a half game lead with twelve to play. *[The Phillies lost ten straight before winning their last two, and the Cardinals won the pennant by one game.]*

— *Cal McLish*

The moment I recall most in my career is the day I relieved in Cleveland with the bases loaded and one out. I made one pitch for a double play. That clinched the American League Pennant in 1959 and sent us to the World Series.

— *Gerry Staley*

There were about fifty thousand people at a doubleheader in New York. Berra caught the first game, and he sat out the second game. So they sent him up to pinch-hit late in the game. He was such a free swinger, my theory with him was to throw the first pitch low and away and hope he hit to somebody. Because I couldn't throw hard enough to get it past him, so the more pitches I threw to him, the more it seemed he zeroed in on it. I kept throwing him basically low and away, and he fouled off pitch after pitch. I must have thrown him ten pitches. I said, "I'll going to bust him inside." So I threw it right on the inside corner and he hit it up in the seats for a home run. It was like his two thousandth hit or something, so it was a big, big thing. I can remember that upsetting me. I went wandering around New York afterwards. I stopped at a book store and bought a book.

I never did go to sleep that night, one of the few times in my career. Normally — you're going to give up home runs and stuff, but I guess there was enough commotion with fifty thousand people there, and Berra getting his landmark hit, it put a little more adrenalin in me than I realized. *[The Berra home run appears to have come on June 9, 1962, the day before the Yankees and Orioles played their doubleheader.]*

— *Dick Hall*

There had never been a more enjoyable time in baseball than the nine days I spent taking part in the 1960 World Series *[as a Pirate outfielder]*. It's a dream of all professional players. It's without a doubt like walking on air for the whole time.

— *Bill Virdon*

I was with the Pirates when they won the World Series in 1960. When I got back from a barnstorming tour with Satchel Paige I sent a letter in July to the Pirates' manager Danny Murtaugh, who I'd known for a long time. I said, "I can still throw good, and you're working our way into a pennant. If you can use me I'd like to come over and just throw batting practice for you." He gave it to Joe Brown, and Joe called me the next day and said, "Yeah, come on over." He paid my way to Pittsburgh, and I traveled with the club and threw batting practice. That's how I got with the Pirates, and they went on to win the pennant and the Series.

— *Virgil Trucks*

One day we were in Brooklyn and Dick Young was the official scorekeeper. There was a play at third base, and Furillo tried to throw a guy out. He had a great arm, but the ball was tough to handle. It would hit the ground and really skip and shoot. It was a close play and the ball got by me and went over and hit the stands. Joe Hatten, the pitcher, didn't back up third base, so the run scored. Dick Young gave Hatten an error on the play.

The next day we go West to Cincinnati. Those reporters on that train argued all the way there — Dick Young against the rest of them — about that error he gave Joe Hatten. I'm telling you, there were some heated arguments.

Dick would say, "He should have been backing up third base. He gets the error." The others said I was the one who should have got the error; it had nothing to do with Joe. But Dick Young stuck with it, and that's the way it went. It was humorous to listen to, all those arguments back and forth, back and forth, all the way to Cincinnati.

— *Spider Jorgensen*

I was mostly used in relief at Detroit after being discharged *[in January 1946]* from the Navy. When I wasn't starting, I followed my usual pregame routine, along with the other pitchers. After our pregame hitting, we pitchers got in our running during batting practice and worked up a pretty good sweat. Then we went into our clubhouse and put on clean shirt and socks. This one day, while I was changing, one of the players came in from our dugout and said manager Rolfe wanted to see me. So — this was about 25 minutes before game time — I dressed and went to the dugout. Rolfe told me I was starting as Virgil Trucks' arm wasn't right when he started to warm up. So I pitched nine innings against the White Sox and won 10–3 after the White Sox scored 3 runs in the first inning.

It's all in how you prepare for a game.

— *Hal White*

My first major league start was against Cleveland *[on May 5, 1956]*. I struck out thirteen and lost 2–1. Four days *[actually seven, May 12]* later I'm in Yankee Stadium, warming up, and Casey Stengel, the manager of the Yankees, came by and patted me on the butt, because he's the guy that signed me, in '48. I start the ninth inning with a no-hitter. We were leading 1–0. I drove the only run in off Turley. The first hitter up is Andy Carey, who went to college with me at St. Mary's College in Maragua. I had him two strikes and I threw him a good curveball, and it hit the rubber on the plate, bounced in fair territory so high that by the time I caught the ball, looking into the sun, he crossed first base with the first hit.

Billy Martin came up, and he said, "Hey, Casey, hell, I hit Ferrarese in high school, I can hit that guy." I struck his butt out. We had to laugh about that later, because I became his roommate in Cleveland.

Don Larsen, who played with me in Hawaii and hit a couple home runs off me in Hawaii said, "Case, let me hit that guy, I can hit him" And he popped up.

Then Hank Bauer came up. And he got a single over third base. He broke his bat. So here I am, first and second. I had just lost the game before 2–1. And here comes Mickey Mantle. I said, "Oh, my God."

Anyhow, I got him out, a fly ball, and won the game 1–0. It was quite a thrill. That was my first major league win. Another thing to that story. Carl Erskine of the Dodgers was pitching a no-hitter against the Giants in the Polo Grounds, and we were simultaneously on national television. People were going back and forth, watching these double no-hitters. In the ninth inning, Hank Thompson, the third baseman for the Giants, hit a home run that at the last second went foul, just by the skin of his hair, and Carl got the no-hitter. We would have made a bundle of money. In fact, they'd still be talking about it, trivia, being the double no-hitters. That would have been the first time that two no-hitters would have been pitched in the same town. *[On June 29, 1990, Dave Stewart of Oakland pitched a 5–0 no-hitter against Toronto. Later that same day, Fernando Valenzuela of the Dodgers no-hit the Cardinals 6–0.]*

— *Don Ferrarese*

Every player likes to be appreciated for a good play. I remember a game at Brooklyn. I was brought in to play right field for defense. With two out in the last of the ninth and the winning run at second, Furillo lined a hit to right. I threw a one-hop strike to home to end the inning. Whitey Kurowski hit a home run in the tenth to win the game for us. He got all the accolades in the clubhouse.

But it meant a lot to me when one of the other players said to me, "It was your throw that saved the game for us."

— *Chuck Diering*

Outfield was a lot easier, and if moving back and forth from one position to the other hurt at all, it hurt only because every game I played in the outfield was lost experience as far as third base goes.

I actually turned into a pretty respectable third baseman after I learned how to play the position. And I played alongside some good ballplayers. Marty Marion, for instance, at shortstop when I was at St. Louis, really helped me.

I liked the outfield, but I liked to be more involved than that in the game. And third base was pretty involved.

— *Jim Dyck*

I recall the day our first born, Barry, was born in New York City, at Lennox Hill Hospital, August 26, 1953. I was a rookie on the New York Yankees team, and we were playing Detroit in Detroit. My wife was without family 3,000 miles from home, and having our baby prematurely (at seven months). Bill Dickey's wife Vi — John Sain's wife and Don Bollweg's wife were with her. Ted Gray, a left hander, was pitching for Detroit that day and Casey Stengel, our manager, had me in the line-up instead of left handed hitting Gene Woodling. My first time up I hit a home run. I was really thrilled. I also hit a home run one year later, on Barry's first birthday. *[Renna hit two home runs in 1953 and thirteen in 1954.]*

— *Bill Renna*

The no-hitter was within reach. All I had to do in the ninth was retire Peanuts Lowry, Red Schoendienst, Stan (the Man) Musial. Lowry grounded out. Schoendienst popped to short. Musial took a ball and a strike, then grounded out to second base.

Why isn't it in the record books? Did I only dream it, wish it were so?

No, it happened, but in spring training, 1951, Browns vs. Cardinals, in Houston. Ned Garver pitched eight innings, left for a pinch hitter, Johnny Bero. He drove in the game's only run and rookie Lou Sleater came in to pitch.

Lowry, Schoendienst, Musial. What a trio. I can't help but wonder—was there ever another time in his career that Stan the Man was the final out in a no-hitter?

— *Lou Sleater*

I signed a bonus contract with the Orioles in 1955. I was a rookie awed by the Major League players. Not long after I joined the team we played the Chicago white Sox. It was in the 12th inning and our manager Paul Richards had used all his pinch hitters but this young player, Jim Pyburn, that the white Sox pitcher" Jack Harshman had probably never heard of.

Harshman got behind in the count and threw a fastball down the middle. I was ready. It was my first home run, a game-winner in extra innings. Dreams do come true sometimes.

— *Jim Pyburn*

The most memorable game for me is the third game of the 1951 Giants-Brooklyn Dodgers playoff. Of course, the "shot heard around the world" home run by Bobby Thomson will live on for ages.

— *Al Corwin*

I got a pinch hit double off Rip Coleman to drive in the winning run in I think the 12th inning to break a 13-game losing streak. The picture on my wall shows me being met by the manager and my teammates as I got back to the dugout.

— *J.W. Porter*

My only big league win came in 1953 against the Reds. We were fortunate enough to get ahead and Rogers Hornsby was managing the other team, and he was always the type of manager who would have the batter take the first strike when they were behind. I was able to get the first strike over there and was able to get the hitters out by getting ahead of them. The final score was 7–3 or something like that. I was taken out in the eighth inning when I started to tire a little bit, but I pitched real good that night. I had hurt my arm in 1950 and this was '53.

I was able to throw decent but I was never able to throw with the same speed and same stuff after I hurt my arm.

I was adequate. I was still trying to make it in the big leagues as a pitcher. In 1952 I won 15 games in the Coast League as a 20 year old. The following year in '53 I was one of five guys taken off the Pacific Coast League pennant-winning team to go to the Pirates. I would probably have stayed with the Pirates but they made a big ten-player trade with the Cubs. It was the trade that sent Kiner to the Cubs.

One of the players the Pirates got was a left-handed pitcher named Bob Schultz. He more or less took my place on the roster. Fred Haney said that if he was trying to get into the first division, he would have kept me. But since I was young, I wasn't going to pitch very often and he wanted to send me out. After I went out, I kind of reinjured my arm again. After having injury after injury after injury, I gave up pitching and decided to try to make it back to the big leagues with the bat, but I never got any higher than Triple A.

— *Paul Pettit*

One day I had to finish Yogi's at-bat when he got kicked out of a game. Yogi had moaned on a 2–0 strike in Boston and it went 2–1. And then he moaned on a 3–1 strike and Bill Grieve threw him out of the game. I had to come in with two strikes on me and I took a called third strike. He was going to throw me out of the game too, but I couldn't get myself thrown out. The next day I went to Sammy White, who was the catcher, and asked him, "Where was the pitch I got called out on?"

He said, "Inside."

— *Charlie Silvera*

Umpires are not my favorite people. I felt that every time they blew a call they were giving me a chance to lose a ballgame. But one time they did help me. I was pitching against the White Sox on a Sunday afternoon in Baltimore. It was the top of the eighth inning and it was about ninety-five degrees. We were winning the game 3 to 1. The White Sox had two men on base and Ted Kluszewski came up to pinch hit. He hit a monstrous home run off me and it made the score 4–3, except that Ed Hurley saw some of the White Sox guys in the bullpen who were supposedly not warming up where they were supposed to be and he called time before I threw the ball. So he called the home run back. Then I came back and I threw Kluszewski just about the same pitch and this time he popped it up and I won the ballgame 3–1.

— *Milt Pappas*

[In 1953 Bobo Holloman no-hit the Athletics 6–0. The game was Holloman's first big league start after four relief appearances. He walked five and struck out three. He had two hits and three runs batted in. He started nine more games, but did not complete any. His record in that, his only big league season, was 3–7. In 7 previous minor league seasons he was 110–69.]

Bobo could throw. He couldn't throw exactly where he was looking every time, but he could throw hard. I don't know where he got the name Bobo, but he was well-named. He was kind of a goofy guy, really. I remember that he just bugged the hell out of the manager at the time for a start. He wanted at least a chance to show that he could start the game. And finally they handed him the ball and said, "Go on out there now and let's see if your arm can talk as big as your mouth."

And he did.

It was funny because he didn't have his exceptional good stuff that particular night, and there were several balls that were hit, that were really smashed, and hit right at somebody. The one I remember, where I saved him, was in the seventh inning or so. If I remember right, it was the big first baseman, Eddie Robinson, although I wouldn't swear to it. *[Robinson had been traded to the Athletics from the White Sox at the start of the season for Ferris Fain.]* He hit one in the hole between left and center, and I just took off and put my head down and went, and I timed my jump and got my utmost out of my body and just did snag it in the web of the glove. It would have been a double or triple otherwise. It was probably the best catch I ever made in the big leagues.

It just went that way for Bobo that night. There were several other good catches, too. That was his only complete game. He had problems getting the ball over the plate, and you get in trouble when you can't get the ball over the plate. He had three good pitches he could use but he'd usually dig his own hole. *[In 65⅓ big league innings, Holloman struck out 25 and walked 50.]*

— *Jim Dyck*

We were playing the White Sox in Yankee Stadium August 8, 1953, and I was pitching against Virgil Trucks. I had a no-hitter with one out in the ninth inning. Bob Boyd, a little left-handed hitter with the White Sox, hit a line drive over Billy Martin's head, a clean hit, for a double, and I got the next two guys out. I threw the pitch where I wanted it to Boyd, down and in, a strike on the inside part of the plate. And he hit the ball good. I'm glad he did. I'm glad he didn't bloop it or something. You take your hat off to him. To get a no-hitter you've got to earn it. He got a base hit and he earned it.

I knew I had a no-hitter going. Anybody who's pitching a no-hitter — if they tell you they don't know it, they're kidding you. The dugout was pretty normal, but nobody talks to you very much when you're going with a no-hitter — they kind of leave you alone. They believe it's bad luck to mention it. Everybody in the park knows you've got a no-hitter going, plus you. They're all pulling for you, naturally. It was Ladies' Day, I can remember that, and there were about 70,000 people there. I won the ball game three to nothing, I think. I got a one-hitter, but it cost me some money. Because that was a Saturday, and the next night I could probably have been on "The Ed Sullivan Show" if I'd pitched a no-hitter. If you pitched a no-hitter in those days, you usually picked up a few bucks by going on Ed Sullivan's show.

— *Bob Kuzava*

[*Red Murff's first pro season was in a Class C league at age 29. As a pitcher he went 17-4. He played left field when he wasn't pitching and batted .334 with 78 RBI in less than a hundred games and was Rookie of the Year. He faced a career decision: pursue a career as a pitcher or as a position player?*]

We had an exhibition game after the season was over, and our team, as a group, played a group of what they called barnstorming major leaguers. And I was a pretty good hitter in that league because we had Class C pitching, but the night we played that major league barnstorming team, a young pitcher for the Philadelphia Phillies named Bubba Church showed me the best fastball I'd ever seen in my life, and I said, "Hey, that's the pitch I've got to hit if I stay a hitter, or that's the pitch I've got to throw if I get to the big leagues."

I couldn't throw as hard as Bubba Church, but I had better control and better command of pitches than he ever did. But Bubba Church showed me my first introduction to a real major league fastball, and I marveled at the difference between his fastball and those I saw in C ball. That impressed me more than anything else my first year of baseball, Bubba Church's fastball.

The next year I went to Double A spring training. I was asked by the manager what position I wanted to play. "You want to be a pitcher? Or do you want to be a hitter in Double A baseball?"

I said, "If you'll give me four or five days I can make an easier decision on that." And I went right in and I took batting practice against a major league pitcher named Bobo Holloman. He had pitched his ballclub to the Caribbean World Series, and he was throwing batting practice and it was tougher than anything I had faced the year before in the full season. So after he knocked my fingernails off with a hard sinker a few times on cold days in Florida, I trotted out to the manager — his name was Don Osborn — and said, "Hey, we've got it settled. I'm going to be a pitcher from now on."

— *Red Murff*

Baltimore's a very humid city. I was maybe thirty-nine years old, and we played a miserably hot Sunday doubleheader. Geez, everybody was bushed. I mean, you're going to lose fifteen, sixteen pounds on a day like that, and that saps your body.

The writers were in Paul Richards' room, and Richards said, "You know, you go down to the clubhouse and there's one guy who's not tired out there." And he named me.

Here I am, twenty years older than most of the guys in the room. The writers came out and they asked me if I was tired. I told them, "Hell no. Am I supposed to tell you I'm tired when I'm not?"

— *Gene Woodling*

In 1959 I got called up in July 4, so I'd spent two months that year in the minors. I was up for a short time in '58, when they'd first moved to Los Angeles. I was there only thirty days, so I still had rookie status. I got beat out in the Rookie of the Year balloting by Willie McCovey. McCovey had a great year, too. He came up around that time also — a little bit ahead of me — he came up in June. He hit .360 or something, had an outstanding half year. *[McCovey played 52 games and hit .354 with 13 home runs. Sherry pitched 23 games, went 7–2 with three saves, and had a 2.19 ERA. As a batter, Sherry went 7–32, a .219 average, with two home runs.]*

So I was probably in the running, but the season is what they counted rather than the Series. The Series is where I excelled quite a bit. In fact, after losing my first two games of the season, I won seven in a row and two in the series, so I won nine in a row as I finished the season. And the two starts that I lost, I could have very easily won those, so I could easily have pitched the whole season without losing a game.

— *Larry Sherry*

My biggest moment in the big leagues was just standing on the mound at Yankee Stadium with the national anthem playing for what seemed like two hours. I was scared to death standing there waiting for the game to start.

One day my home town sent their Boys' Club to Kansas City to see me pitch against the Yankees. I struck Mantle out with the bases loaded. So I was a big hero with those boys.

— *Jack McMahan*

I had two one-hitters, which were getting close to being no-hitters but I didn't get either one of them. I had two out in the eighth inning up in Milwaukee and Bob "Hurricane" Hazle got a base hit. I had one man out in the ninth against the Dodgers when I was with Cincinnati in '56, and Pee Wee Reese got a broken bat base hit.

— *Johnny Klippstein*

I hit four grand slams in 1953, which made me the tenth player in history to do that. When they put it in the Detroit paper, and to look and see those guys included in those ten, when you see your Gehrigs and your Babe Ruths and guys like that, then you see your name — I don't care who you are — you say, "What am I doing there?"

[The other nine players were Babe Ruth, Lou Gehrig, Rudy York, Tommy Henrich, Al Rosen, Wildfire Schulte, Vince DiMaggio, Ralph Kiner, and Sid Gordon. The record has since been tied and broken by several.]

— *Ray Boone*

I know the record book's not big enough for all the "could have beens" and "almosts." But in 1958, my last season with the Pirates, we played in San Francisco, the Giants' first year there, in Seals Stadium. It was my birthday, June 11. My teammates loaded the bases for me three times in one game.

The first time my long drive curved foul at the last second; my almost grand slam ended up as a walk, giving me a run batted in. The second time there was no doubt. Fair ball. Grand slam. Could have been my second. Five runs batted in so far. The third time — like the first, curving just foul at the last second; then I struck out, Missing three grand slams by mere feet.

I hit a second home run that day, that one with one runner on, giving me seven runs batted in for the game. Yet it was close to being fourteen in one game. *[Thomas faced Ruben Gomez, Mike McCormick, and Marv Grissom.]*

— *Frank Thomas*

In a ballgame in late August of 1951 we *[the Pirates]* trailed the Dodgers 9 to 3 going into the seventh inning. We scored eight runs in the seventh and ended up winning the game 12 to 11. I went three for four, scored three runs and hit two homers off Don Newcombe. It turned out to be a critical loss for the Dodgers, who lost the NL championship in a playoff when Bobby Thomson hit his famous homer off Ralph Branca to put the Giants in the World Series.

— *Pete Castiglione*

August 18, 1955. I pitched a perfect game in Columbus, Ohio, when playing for the AAA Montreal Royals.

Pitching in the 1952 World Series fulfilled a boyhood dream.

— *Ken Lehman*

I pitched against the Dodgers and Sandy Koufax in the Los Angeles Coliseum and shut them out in a ten-inning game. We *[the Cubs]* beat them 3–0. I was the only left-hander to shut them out in the Coliseum. Sometime later when I learned that they were constructing a new ballpark, the thought crossed my mind that I might have established an unbreakable record — shutting the Dodgers out in the Coliseum. *[The September 6, 1959, shutout against the Dodgers was one of three in Ceccarelli's five-year career.]*

— *Art Ceccarelli*

I was pitching against Virgil Trucks, who was another tough customer to pitch against. Trucks and I were into the eleventh inning 2 to 2. We had two men out and Al Zarilla was on second base. I got a base hit to left center off Trucks that drove in the winning run. That's one that lingers in my mind.

— *Mel Parnell*

You play with Willie Mays or guys of that caliber, definitely they stand out. I was playing right field in Ebbets Field one day and I went to make a catch in right center field and at the last minute he called me off and Geez, I had to dive and roll out of the way to keep from running into him. Don Mueller said when I came in, "Boy, if you ever ran into him they would have sent you out to Podunk."

— *Bob Lennon*

Two no-hit bids stand out — one by Virgil Trucks, one by Vic Raschi. I spoiled one, caught the other. I was behind the plate for the first of Trucks' two no-hitters in 1951, a 1–0 win against Washington. I was at the plate against Raschi in the 9th in his no-hit bid. He needed two more outs, me and Hoot Evers.

He never got them. Though we lost the game 11–1, my home run spoiled it.

— *Joe Ginsberg*

In July 1952 I was on the Washington Senators' pitching staff when the Detroit Tigers came to town. The Tigers' Walt Dropo had just got a bunch of consecutive hits in a doubleheader against the Yankees in New York the day before. We played them in a twilight doubleheader, and Dropo was still red hot. He continued his streak of consecutive hits into the second game. I came into the second game in relief of Bob Porterfield.

In the middle of the game Walt tied the consecutive hit record off me with his twelfth straight hit. The record had been set in 1938 by Mike "Pinky" Higgins of the Boston Red Sox. The next time at bat against me, going for the record thirteenth straight hit, he popped up a fastball to the catcher, Mickey Grasso.

— *Lou Sleater*

I almost had three no-hitters in 1952. I pitched a no-hitter against Washington, and a month later Washington comes back into Detroit, and the first pitch I threw, Eddie Yost hits a clean single between George Kell and the shortstop. They never got another hit the whole ballgame.

I knew Eddie Yost was a first ball hitter. If he didn't swing at the first pitch, generally he walked. That was a rule, and the way pitchers knew him, and the way pitchers functioned. I got a little lax, I guess, and didn't put as much as I should on the ball, and he hit it. It was a clean base hit, there was no doubt about that.

In '54 I don't remember exactly what inning it was in, but Kell with the Red Sox got a base hit in that one. Or maybe it was Sam Mele.

And I had one other close call. After the first no-hitter against Washington, I pitched six and two thirds innings against Philadelphia before they got a base hit, and it was the only base hit they got. Hank Majeski got that base hit.

So I had a lot of close calls where there could have been other no-hitters. But when you're playing you're not expecting to pitch no-hitters, you're just trying to win a ball game.

— *Virgil Trucks*

When Kluszewski would be leading off the inning, he'd be walking off the field and Temple would come by, jogging in. When Temple would get even with him Klu would throw him his glove. Johnny would bring his glove in to the dugout. Then Klu would go to home plate and wait for the batboy to bring his bat out, getting ready to hit.

One day Hornsby asked Temple, "You Kluszewski's caddy or something, he can't bring his own glove in? Don't do that anymore. Let him bring his own damn glove in here." Johnny said, "Okay, whatever you say." So Kluszewski is coming in and he tossed his glove to Johnny, and Johnny just let it drop. Klu kind of looked at him, kind of bewildered. Then he stood at home plate, waiting for the batboy to bring him his bat. The batboy started to take his bat up there, and Rogers said, "Don't take that bat up there, let him get his own bat."

The inning's ready to start, the pitcher's ready to go. Kluszewski's standing up there with no bat. He finally came over to the dugout and got his own bat and had that mean look on his face, you know, "What's going on here?" He put his glove down and got his bat and went back up there to home plate. Well, that broke his concentration so bad that day that he took a called third strike. He came back to the dugout just boiling, really mad after that. He threw that bat down and said, "That ball was two inches outside."

Hornsby jumped up off that bench right in his face and said, "Klu, if you don't want to swing that bat, don't take it up there!" And boy, he turned red as a beet, and there was kind of bad blood between Klu and Rogers after that.

— *Jim Greengrass*

My most gratifying moment in baseball wasn't in the big leagues; it came when I was playing in Mexico City in 1955. I made a Willie Mays type catch to win the pennant for us down there. I was playing right field for the Mexico City Tigers and we were playing the Reds on the next to last day of the season. We were leading by a run in the eighth inning. With one out the ball was hit into deep right center field. I just took off and started running straight back and kind of toward center field. The center fielder was moving over at the same time and he said "Look up!" and when I looked up I noticed that the ball was behind me so I stuck my mitt back behind my head and turned at an angle and the ball just stuck in the glove. I turned and threw the ball back toward first base.

The catch saved the game because they probably would have scored at least a couple runs off of that and gone ahead because it would have been at least a triple and maybe an inside the park home run. We were playing in a very large park in Mexico City — 350 down both lines — 420 to center. That game clinched the pennant for us.

— *Paul Pettit*

Twice in my career I won 19 games and had a chance to win 20. The first year, in '49, I could have won the twenty games, but there were errors made in my last start; I could have won that ballgame.

The other year was '54 with the White Sox. I was scheduled to pitch the last game of the year, but someone suggested I start a day earlier in order to face a rookie, Digger O'Dell. I agreed to it, and I got beat 2-1. The next night, when I was supposed to pitch, we won 11-1. So I just missed out on twenty wins both those years.

[*Billy "Digger" O'Dell, a bonus player with no minor league experience, started two games as a rookie in 1954, going 1–1. In his 13 year big league career, he went 105–100.*]

— *Virgil Trucks*

In '56 or '57 we had a make-up game against Cleveland. It wasn't advertised in the paper hardly, and there were only about four hundred or five hundred people in the stadium. It was about the seventh inning and it started to rain, and old Bill Summers said, "Tell Dressen that's it. We're not waiting for the rain. The game's gone."

Summers said, "Don't bother to wait around."

Neither team could do much about it. Lemon won his 20th that day, I think.

— *Lou Berberet*

It was a hot, Sunday afternoon in St. Louis in 1954. Eddie Stanky was the manager of the Cardinals, and he kept stalling. It must have been a hundred and some degrees. And then there was a thunderstorm, and it was hotter after that. We were playing a doubleheader, and in the first game we had a big brawl. At that time the manager could go out and talk to the pitcher as many times as he wanted. So Stanky kept going out there. It's a hundred and some degrees and the umpires are boiling. So Pinelli was behind the plate and I was at bat, and he said, "If that son of a bitch comes out again one more time, Ted, I'm going to forfeit this game." And here he comes out of the dugout and Pinelli turned around to the press box and said, "That's it."

They all had to go in front of the commissioner. It was funny because I think it was right after the All-Star break, and they had fired our manager, Steve O'Neill. Terry Moore took over, and he had been fired by Stanky when Terry was a coach at St. Louis. So there was no love there.

— *Ted Kazanski*

When I was with the Dodgers in '56, we had a key late season game against the Phillies. They were beating us 5–2 in the bottom of the ninth. Reese singled and then we got three straight home runs from Snider, me, and Gil Hodges. When you're behind like that in the bottom of the ninth, and every game counts when you're getting toward the end of the season, it's just an elation, it's like winning a pennant or World Series or something. The fans went wild. I don't know if it's a record or not, three straight home runs in the last of the ninth to win a game.

— *Randy Jackson*

My no-hitter in '57 was against Washington. They weren't too deep in pitching, but they had a pretty good hitting ball club. Jim Lemon. Roy Sievers. Eddie Yost. I think Pete Runnels was with them then. As I remember, there wasn't anything close to being a hit. They didn't hit more than one or two balls good. They didn't talk much in the dugout, and of course I knew I had a no-hitter going. Right from the first inning. The pitcher always knows. In the last inning I was determined. Walt Dropo caught a pop up in foul territory along first base for the final out.

— *Bob Keegan*

One of my first major league home runs was a grand slam home run off Sad Sam Jones *[on September 15, 1960]*. As I circled the bases I was really elated and I was thanking the Lord as I touched each base, and as I got to home plate I said to myself, "Did I touch first? Did I touch second? Did I touch third?" I couldn't wait for the next pitch to be thrown. I didn't want to lose that home run.

— *Bobby Malkmus*

In Parnell's no-hitter *[July 14, 1956]* we were playing the White Sox. Billy Goodman was playing second base. About the sixth inning with one out, somebody hit a ground ball to me and I threw it a little bit low to first base. The next guy was Aparicio and he could fly. He hit a ball over second base and Goodman back-handed it and made a force out at second base. They'd have never got him at first. So I told Mel I saved his no-hitter by making an error.

— *Don Buddin*

In 1959 we were playing the Yankees. It was on national TV back then. Once a week they had baseball. Dizzy Dean and whoever his other announcer was — anyway, the game went extra innings. We had the bases loaded, one out, Bob Turley was pitching for the Yankees and I hit a grand slam. That stands out pretty good. We beat the Yankees five days in a row that year, something that didn't happen too often.

— *Don Buddin*

In the early fifties I was with the Athletics, and the A's always played the Yankees good, and of course everybody wanted to beat the Yankees. When had Bobby Shantz and Alex Kellner and Harry Byrd and Laurin Martin, we could hold our own. We played them a five game series in Philadelphia. We won the first four games, a feat almost unheard of. We came to the ballpark on Monday night for the fifth game and Pete Suder gets to the plate. He and Yogi were big buddies. And Yogi always talked to guys when they came to the plate, especially Suder. This night Yogi doesn't say anything to him, and Pete turns around and looks at him "What's the Matter, Yogi? Can't you talk?"

Yogi wouldn't say a word, didn't even say a word to Suder. So later Yogi ends up on second base and Suder walked over to him and says, "Say, Yogi, what's the matter with you? Why won't you talk to me?"

And Yogi says, "Listen Suder, get away from me. Stengel told me if we talked to you fellas tonight he was going to fine us two hundred and fifty dollars. I can't talk to you." So I guess money talks.

— *Billy Hitchcock*

My 25-7 season in 1949 was one of those years when everything seemed to break right for me. It was a warm spring in Boston, which helped me a lot. It usually took me awhile to get acclimated to that cold weather. We were having a pretty good race with the Yankees, so beating them was a big thing. And I did have good success against the Yankees my whole career. I got the nickname "Yankee killer" because of that. In 1953 I pitched four shutouts against them in my other start. I had 27 complete games that year.

— *Mel Parnell*

Billy Pierce, when he had a perfect game with two outs in the ninth — it was sad. Ed Fitzgerald of the Senators hits the foul line — besides, the right field foul line — a blooper, you know, with two strikes.

I said, "Ohh." But the greatest thing: Billy walked off the mound like a man. He came in the clubhouse, well, as Billy Pierce, like nothing ever happened.

Two strikes on him — I mean, one more strike. Or a popup where it can be caught, and it hits right on the chalk. Right field. Opposite field besides, a blooper. He got a little bit jammed. You hit a ball like that, it usually means the pitcher made a pretty good pitch. So it was very sad.

It was quiet, very quiet during that no-hitter. I don't know why, it's a ritual. It's still pretty much that way today. That's the way it's going to be. *[Pierce's nearly perfect game was on June 27, 1958.]*

— *Jim Landis*

One year in Venezuela I was leading the league down there in home runs. It was unbelievable. I thought I was Babe Ruth. I never did hit like that afterwards. One night I was watching from the stands. I would be playing Chico Carrasquel's team the next night. From right behind home plate that's where your fans divide. One team's fans on the right field side, the other fans on the left. I could understand enough Spanish to overhear the owner of Chico's team tell another I was to go down every time I came to the plate.

The next day I went to our manager, Martin Dihigo. I told him what I overheard. I wanted him to talk to their manager. He said, "Oh, they won't do anything." I thought, okay. I was hitting third. When I came up — they had a big right-hander. Man, I'm telling you. Talk about putting me down. Just luckily, I spun and went down. I get back up and here comes another one. I spun and got hit in the shoulder.

I get up the second time, down I go again. I'm getting a little light footed now. And here it comes again. Right in the ribs. So I go down to first base. I'm not thinking about who's covering second. But the guy hitting is Norm Larker, a left-handed hitter. If I was breaking on the ball, why, Chico would be covering. I wasn't thinking of who'd be covering. And I could have stolen the base clean, but I wasn't meaning to steal it clean. I meant for somebody to pay the price at second base. I break, and I don't break real fast. I want to give whoever's covering at second a good chance to get at the bag.

Just as Chico is taking the throw at second I went into him with a rolling body block, and I took him about half way into left-center field, and he was knocked out.

The crowd went wild at his side of the field. But they have guards all around, so they couldn't get on the field. They finally take Chico off the field and take him back behind the dugout.

After awhile I'm sitting on the bench and somebody hits one down the right field line. I'm looking down there and all at once out of the corner of my left eye I see something. Chico had got dressed and came around to our dugout and he was going to blindside me. He took a swing, and I pulled back. Then I was all over him. I took him right down to the bottom of the dugout. His players came over from their dugout. There were guys beating my back. Finally somebody got their arms around me and was pulling me up. I thought, oh, my God, somebody is going to nail me for sure now. It was Norm Larker. And me and him stood back to back in that dugout.

Chico was not a factor. These guys from the dugout came over with bats in their hands, waving them like they were going to hit us. And old Norm Larker stood back to back with me. There were six Americans on that team and the rest of them become rabbits. To this day I'll always remember him for standing back to back with me looking them people in the face.

The guards came in then, after the game was over. We go in, and this crowd is out of side. I was getting dressed pretty slow. I was the last one getting dressed, and Norm said, "Gale, you want me to walk out with you?"

I said, "No."

He said, "There's a lot of people out there. There's a lot of noise."

I said, "I'll handle it." I got dressed and I had on a shirt that had a pocket on the left side. I grabbed me a fungo bat. I thought, if there's going to get me I'm going to take somebody with me. I walked out, and here was this hellacious crowd. Then right between them the crowd opened up just like someone took a knife and opened it up. It opened up about ten to twelve feet wide, a path from the outside fence gate coming right toward the clubhouse. And here come three guys, one on each side, and this one guy had enough brass on his shirt and cap and coat. I'd never seen anything like it. I knew it was a high official in the army. He came straight at me, and I said, "Oh heck." I was gone then, sure enough.

As he got closer he was smiling. I was standing still just outside the door. He walked up. He could speak perfect English. He said, "Are you having a little trouble?"

I said, "Yes sir. I'm having a lot of trouble."

All at once he stuck something in my shirt pocket. It was a gun. I reached there and said, "oh, no." I handed it back to him.

He just stood there and smiled. He was the Chief of Security of Venezuela. In our country he'd be like the vice president. His name was Colonel Benjamin Maldanoldo. He said, "Well, I think we probably need to take you." I said, "I'd really appreciate it."

As we walked out of there, there was not one sound from that crowd. And he gave me his card, and he said, "If you have any problems here in Caracas, you just show this card. That's all you have to do." It was a laminated card with his name on it.

— *Gale Wade*

We had altercations, sure. We had fights. The only thing that ever got to me is when they came in and never wanted to slide at the plate, when they wanted to bowl you over. They didn't try to hurt you, but they wanted to score so bad, they wanted to knock the ball out of your hand, and consequently they did really want to put a pretty good hurt on you. That's when you got into some fights.

— *Joe Ginsberg*

One of the biggest thrills I could have had — we didn't get it — but starting two triple plays in one ballgame. In Chicago I started a triple play on a ball that Andy Pafko hit. And then later in the ballgame Smalley hit a ground ball to me at third, and I started a round-the-horn play, and we just missed the play at first, which could have been called an out. The umpire gave the safe sign. I touched third and threw to second. Danny Murtaugh was playing second at that time for us. His throw I think actually had him. Most of the people thought we had it. The call could have gone our way just as easy. It would have been something, you know, two in one game.

— *Pete Castiglione*

One time we were playing the Phillies in an important late season game. I was due up with the winning run on second base, and normally they would have pinch hit for me, but I guess they wanted to keep me in for defense. I went up against Robin Roberts and got a base hit to right field. That was a big moment for me.

— *Chuck Diering*

Chuck Churn was pitching for Cincinnati, and he was throwing a spitter, you know, so we kept hollering at the umpire to check the ball, and he wouldn't do it, so Dusty Rhodes ran out of the dugout to the mound with a bucket of water and said, "Here it is, dip it."

— *Gail Harris*

[*All baseball is played on a stage, its unscripted theatrics often high drama, sometimes farce. The versatility of the casts results in no two performances ever being exactly the same. And on good days, they even remember their parts. Detroit Tiger catcher Red Wilson describes a moment in a game in Boston between the Red Sox and Tigers that we can only hope was a dress rehearsal.*]

SCENE I:

I drive the ball into center field. Piersall fields the ball and throws to the plate. Sammy White attempts to tag out Tuttle trying to score from second. On a close play the umpire calls "Safe" and White goes into hysterics.

While he is arguing I ease off first. I'm looking to sneak down to second base when White reels around and throws the ball to a vacated center field. No Piersall anywhere.

I head for second and look for a signal from the second base umpire. No reaction from him so I proceed to third. I get no reaction from the third base umpire either. From his left field position Ted Williams is loping after the ball.

I proceed to home. Frank Umont, the plate umpire is bent over the plate brushing it off with his rear facing the mound. I step around him, touch the plate, and proceed to the Tiger dugout.

SCENE II:

White has been ejected. Boston changes pitchers and catchers. A new pitcher finishes warming up. The game begins again. He takes his stretch to hold the runner (me) on first. I'm gone. Where am I, they wonder. Another rhubarb and Pinky Higgins is ousted.

No one had called time out. My run counts.

The curtain closes.

— *Red Wilson*

I was the last Giant to hit a home run before we left the Polo Grounds. That particular day *[September 21, 1957, at Forbes Field]* I had 7 RBIs with a couple home runs, a triple, a single, and that was probably my best day in the majors. Then the next day I went 0 for 3 and went back on the bench.

— *Gail Harris*

I was with Philadelphia in 1956. Dale Long had homered in six straight games to tie a record. The first time at bat I think Stu Miller was pitching. Long hit one about two or three feet from going out of the ballpark. I was in for relief the next time he came up. I threw swinging fastballs right by him. And of all things, the catcher called for a knuckleball, and I hadn't thrown one in a long time. That knuckleball didn't do anything, and Long hit the seventh one off of me. His next game he hit his eighth off Carl Erskine of the Dodgers. There was an article in the paper right after that. They asked him about the toughest pitchers he'd faced and he had my name in it.

— *Ben Flowers*

My friend and I would play pepper every day in the summertime. We'd field the ball and get rid of it quick. We had some pretty quick hands. That was because we played so much pepper. I started out as a third baseman. I developed some great reflexes. I played on the town team when I was eight years old.

In the big leagues they used to play pepper games in front of the stands, cause it's showtime. There's a little showboating in everybody. The fans liked to watch you play. It was interesting; you make some superb plays playing pepper. But then they started complaining that it was tearing up the grass. So they moved everybody in the outfield. Then they didn't want you playing pepper on the playing surface. Then the guys stopped playing pepper.

— *Jim Greengrass*

In my no-hitter in 1956 I had a good screwball going. I probably could have put it anyplace I wanted it. My slider was working really good, and I had a pretty good fastball, but I wasn't going to let the hitters hit the fastball except if there wasn't anybody on base. With runners on base I threw mostly the screwball or slider. In the seventh inning, Jackie

Jenson came up to me and said, "You're going for a no-hitter. Don't let them hit the ball to right field. I don't want to be the guy to mess it up for you."

I said, "Jackie, forget it. All I'm looking for is a win. If it happens, it happens." In the ninth inning, Walter Dropo was sent in to pinch hit. He hit a ground ball back toward the mound, to the first base side of the mound. I came off the mound, caught the ball and continued running to first base. Mickey Vernon, our first baseman, said, "What's the matter, fella, you afraid to throw the ball to me?"

I said, "I wasn't afraid of that. I was afraid I might throw it away."

I think that's the only no-hitter that the pitcher has made the unassisted last out. *[Parnell's no-hitter came on July 14, 1956.]*

— *Mel Parnell*

The biggest thing in my career was my no-hitter. It's something every pitcher dreams of. You never expect it to happen. Then, when it does happen you're living on cloud nine. I've heard many pitchers say that they didn't know they were going for a no-hitter. I can't believe they're being truthful when they say that. If a guy gets a base hit off you, you remember the pitch that he hit and you're probably going to pitch him a little different the next time up. I can't believe you don't know you're going for it.

In the clubhouse it was just jammed with reporters and guys trying to make tapes for radio broadcasts and TV cameras and stuff. Tommy Dorsey, who was a good friend, had the Saturday night program from New York and his sponsor was Buick. He called me in the clubhouse and said, "Mel, if you can get over to New York I can give the key to a brand new Buick on television." I couldn't make it, there was no way I could get out of there. There was too much commotion going on in the clubhouse.

After pitching my no-hitter, the first one to meet me at the clubhouse was Tom Yawkey, standing in the door waiting for me. He had a contract and a fountain pen in his hand. He said, "Mel, sign this."

I said, "Mr. Yawkey, you don't have to do this, you're paying to do these kind of things already."

He said, "Sign the contract," so I did.

— *Mel Parnell*

Just to prove the run does not set on the same dog all the time! On August 27, 1951, at Shibe Park I had three at-bats and took three swings. Three home runs.

Number one — ball away, slider dead center — upper deck.

Number 2 — just fair to left field upper deck.

Number 3 — slider high on the roof.

They were the only runs in the game. We beat Cincinnati 3–0.

[The first two home runs were off Ken Raffensberger. The third was off Frank Smith.]

— *Del Wilber*

One game when I was with Detroit the Yankees had 2 guys on in the 12th inning, and Mantle beat out a swinging bunt down the third base line. And I thought, "Well, I'll get Yogi out." I threw one up about neck high and he hit it out of the park and I was a loser again.

— *Bob Smith*

I guess it was my sixth game in the major leagues. We were playing the Dodgers, and I wasn't in the line-up. Drysdale is pitching and we're hitting him pretty good. Johnny Logan was kind of a pop offish guy, and he's popping off on the bench to Drysdale, and Drysdale looked over into the dugout, and knowing Johnny Logan, you could tell his voice anywhere.

So the next inning we were hitting and he gets his bat and goes up into the on deck circle and as he's on the way out of the dugout, he says, "Fellas, get ready."

When he got up to the plate, the first pitch was in his ribs. He started walking to first, and all of a sudden he ran for the pitcher's mound, and both teams then ran out onto the field. Del Crandall was my roomie, so I hung close to him we're walking back, and he's walking next to Campanella, along with me, and Campanella's got all his garb on, his mask, chest protector, shin guards and so forth.

Del says to him, "How come in the fight you keep your mask on?" He says, "Well, when I first came up to the big leagues, I was a rookie, I took my mask off and got a mouth full of knuckles." He says, "No more."

— *Bobby Malkmus*

Stan Musial was hitting one time and the umpire, Vic Delmore, we called him Deacon — the ball come high inside, and Stan fouled the ball, what he done. It tipped the bat, and old Deacon called ball four. I said, "Ball four?" I was arguing.

Alvin Dark was playing third base for us. Ernie was at short. Tony Taylor was on second and Dale Long on first. Bobby Anderson was pitching. I was arguing with the umpire and he handed me a ball. I don't know why he did it since he'd called it ball four. Anyway, I tossed it to Anderson. Somebody yelled, "Stan's going to second base!"

Alvin Dark had retrieved the ball behind me. About this time Musial's around first and somebody yelled, "Stan's going to second base!" Both Dark and Anderson threw a ball to second. Anderson's throw went into center field, so Musial started toward third. I guess he only saw the ball Anderson threw. Banks ended up with the ball Dark threw and tagged Musial out. So we had two balls in play.

The umpire yelled "You're out!" Which ball was in play was the one we got him out with.

Solly Hemus was managing the Cardinals. He come out and I told Deacon, "You done messed up now. Here comes old Solly. He's going to fuss at you awhile."

Deacon got over there and before Solly could open his mouth he said, "You're out of the ballgame."

— *Sammy Taylor*

We had a throwing contest one time with the Cardinals. Fred Hutchinson ordered Harvey Haddix to knock Kluszewski down. Harvey hit Klu right in the ribs. The ball bounced all the way back to Harvey. Klu was the nicest man you'd ever want to meet, just a super guy. He wouldn't swat a fly and kill it. But he was mad. Klu had that great big post he used for a bat. He hit the bat on the ground and busted it right in two. Harvey saw that and started moving toward left field. He didn't want to get too close to Klu.

Birdie Tebbetts, little Chirpie, was our manager. He said, "Wait 'til Musial comes up. Then throw at his legs." Musial came up and skipped the rope twice.

Hutchinson came out of the dugout yelling, "That's our franchise you're throwing at! You hurt him we're out of business."

Birdie said, "Well, Kluszewski and Bell and Greengrass are my franchise. If they go out we go out. If you're throwing at them, we're throwing at your guy." The umpire said, "No more of this." He got it straightened out.

— *Jim Greengrass*

With the Cubs Glen Hobbie and Dave Hillman always wanted me catching them. We were playing Milwaukee in County Stadium one time in the Game of the Week. Leo Durocher was our manager. We had them 2 to 1 in the bottom of the ninth. Hobbie walked the bases loaded and I went out there and said, "Man, what's going on here?"

He said, "What do you want!"

I said, "Well, I just got one thing to say. You got yourself in one heck of a mess." He had Eddie Matthews, Hank Aaron and Joe Adcock coming up.

On the way back I took my sponge out of my mitt, and he seen me. I was giving him a hint he wasn't throwing hard enough.

He struck out the side. He about tore my hand off. Leo Durocher bought him a gold watch after the ballgame for being the player of the day.

— *Sammy Taylor*

In the minors I led the league five years in stolen bases. I always remember Maury Wills passing along some good tips to him for base stealing. Maury was not fast, and you don't have to be exceptionally fast to steal bases. There's an art to base stealing.

I carried a notebook and I catalogued every single pitcher from the moment I sat on the bench. When anybody was on base I'm watching the pitcher's every move, just focusing on him. The thing you look for is the first part of his body — it could be any part from his knees to the top of his head — but there's one piece of his body that's going to move first when he's going to home plate. You've got to figure out what that is, but it's there. Every one of them does it. You don't worry about him coming to first, what you want to know is that first little move that takes him to the plate, because that's when you're going to break. Of course, sometimes you'd have a pitcher catalogued one year and you'd face him the next year and he's changed a couple things.

On second base, Johnny Sain was the toughest guy in the world to steal third on because Sain turned toward second when he was getting ready to deliver to the plate. And he could deliver to second base just as easy — there's no way you could figure him out.

— *Gale Wade*

At Brooklyn, Happy Felton had his pregame radio show. A player would play ball with three kids. The one who the player chose as the best player got to talk to a player in the dugout, and the player got 50 dollars. Snider and Hodges made about a thousand dollars a year from playing with the kids and talking to them in the dugout. I got asked one time to play with the kids. Fifty dollars. So I said to this one kid, "I'm going to choose you, no matter how you do. Now, when they ask you who you want to talk to, say, 'Cal Abrams.'" I figured I'd make an extra 50 dollars.

When we were done playing, they asked me which kid won. I lied and named this kid. But when they asked him who he wanted to talk to in the dugout, he told them, "Jackie Robinson."

The fans in Ebbets Field were great. The kids used to mill around Rotunda and get autographs on penny postcards. One kid came to me every day for three weeks, getting my autograph. Finally, I got a little curious and asked him, "Why do you want to keep getting my autograph?" He said, "I need 21 Cal Abrams to trade for a Jackie Robinson."

— *Cal Abrams*

In 1952, with Detroit, the year Virgil Trucks pitched his two no-hitters, I was pitching one myself against Cleveland. We had a 13–0 lead going into the ninth inning and I hadn't allowed any hits. With two outs I got two balls and one strike on a mediocre hitter, Suitcase Simpson. I shook the catcher off, and Simpson got a base hit. A little single. He was a left-handed hitter, and he hit a bouncing ball that the third baseman couldn't reach and the shortstop couldn't reach, and the ball stopped about 20 feet past the bag.

But the point is, this was the only pitch I shook Ginsberg off the whole game. He called for a curveball, and I wanted to throw a sinker. I just didn't want to throw the breaking ball he called for. What a time to make a decision, huh?

— *Art Houtteman*

Our normal third base coach when I was with the Reds was Dick Bartell. What a great mind he had. He had a sign for everybody on that ballclub. He had a separate set of signs for all twenty-five guys. That way they couldn't nobody steal the signs. And how he remembered them things was beyond me, but he never missed.

Hornsby usually stayed in the dugout, but for some reason he was coaching at third in a game against the Dodgers. We had a five run lead against Ralph Branca going into about the fifth inning. Temple was on first. I looked down toward third and Hornsby had the bunt sign on. I thought that was peculiar because he never wanted me to bunt, he wanted me to swing the bat. Ralph looked over at first base, and when he did I just squared around and put the bat out, getting ready to bunt. He turned back around and looked me in the eye and hit me dead center with his fastball. Right in the chest. Laid me flatter than a pancake. I had the imprint of that baseball on my chest for a couple weeks.

I finally got up and got my breath back and rubbed my chest went to first base. Branca got the ball and was walking around the mound, rubbing the ball up. He looked over at me and said, "That'll teach you to bunt with a five run lead."

I said, "Hey, look at this number. I'm number 23. Look at Hornsby over there. He's number 1. I just work here. I just do what I'm told."

After the game Rogers asked me, "Jim, how come you turned around to bunt that ball?"

I said, "Well, you gave me the bunt sign."

He said, "I didn't give you a bunt sign."

I said, "Yes, you did. I couldn't figure out why. I started to stop and ask you, and I thought, I'm not going to ask you. If you want me to bunt, I'll bunt."

He said, "I didn't know I gave it to you."

I had the imprint of that baseball on my chest for a couple weeks.

— *Jim Greengrass*

Toward the end of the season, we had a fight with the Giants. We were playing the Giants in Philadelphia, and they had a little guy named Eddie Stanky. He was a competitor. He couldn't run, he couldn't hit, couldn't catch and he couldn't throw. All he knew how to do was win. Don't misunderstand what I'm saying, he could do those things. He was just a great competitor. He was not the flashy guy. He was just a ballgamer.

We're in Philadelphia and Andy Seminick hit a home run to beat the Giants. The next day when Andy came to bat Stanky got in line with the pitcher. Visualize the second baseman jumping up and down, doing side-straddle hops, throwing his arms over his shoulders and all that sort of stuff. Andy got hit in the elbow. He got hit bad. Take your elbow and look just above the joint. That's where he got hit. He came in the clubhouse, and he got some stuff on it, and I mean before the ballgame was over that damn thing was swollen and it was blue, green, and black. But Andy came back out and played the next day. The commissioner said, "If Stanky does it again, he's out of the ballgame." So when Andy came to bat Stanky did it again. He's gone, the umpire had orders. The Giants replaced him with Bill Rigney. Andy gets on base. There's a routine double play ball hit, and Andy slid, short, and is forced at second. Rigney jumped right in the middle of him. Seminick weighed about 205 pounds. We used to call him "The Mad Russian." The first thing we saw was Rigney's body coming up about six inches. 'Cause Andy was sitting there, laying on his back, and just poppin' him, one side, one side, he never hit him in the face. Popped him in the stomach, popped him in the chest, anywhere he could get him. By that time we're all out there. It was a good donnybrook. I came from the bullpen, and the first one I saw was Durocher making his noise, and I never did like that fellow. I took Durocher and I threw him from shortstop about halfway out to center field. The fight lasted about ten minutes. Nobody got hurt. The next good fight was at Cincinnati, a little bit later. Willie Jones slid a little bit hard into Connie Ryan. Connie's from New Orleans, and he did what New Orleans people do, he jumped right into the middle of Willie's face, and here we go again.

— ***Bubba Church***

Ed Bailey denies this, but here's what happened in the Coast League. He was with San Diego in the Cincinnati chain, and I was in LA. He had a real good arm. We were taking batting practice and he came up to the batting cage. He was always needling me about my hitting. I said, "Ed, you think you've got a great arm, don't you."

He said, "I've got a pretty good arm."

I said, "You know what I think of your arm?"

He said, "What?"

I said, "I'll tell you what I'll do. If I get on tonight, I'll even tell you when I'm going to steal second. You can't throw me out." The guy pitching that night was slow going to the plate, he didn't have a good move. I knew I could steal on him. Even if Ed pitched out there was no way he could throw me out.

Ed said, "By God, that's a deal." I said, "I'll tell you what, if I get on tonight, when I get ready to steal I'll reach down and get my belt buckle with my right hand, okay?"

He said, "By God, I'll get you."

I did get on — and what happened is the god's truth, but Ed won't admit it. He and the pitcher both went to sleep. The count went to three-two. I reached down and got my belt, looking right at him. I broke on the three-two. I was breaking to steal, because he could have struck the guy out. But Ed was so tied up in this thing that he called for a pitchout, and the pitcher pitched it out. When I broke, and naturally when you break you're looking in toward home plate. Ed stepped out before the guy ever delivered the ball, and the ball was high and outside. I stopped running and started walking and laughing. And oh, my God, I came up to the plate next time and he says, "You SOB, you ever show me up again...." To this day he won't admit that.

— ***Gale Wade***

Chapter Thirteen

Trades

Once a player signed with a team, he had no control over whether he would stay with that team or be traded to another. Sometimes the trade was to greener pastures; at other teams a player might leave a first place club to a cellar-dweller. And sometimes the player being traded was one of the last ones to find out.

Getting traded in '61 to the Dodgers was a big break for me, what with a pennant and a World Series. I got to room with my lifelong buddy Don Drysdale. We named our third child after Don.

— *Lee Walls*

I hated to leave Milwaukee after the '57 season. That was the greatest city in the country. You had the best fans, you had a good ballpark, you had a new ballpark, you had a good ball team, you had a good front office, you had good management. But I wasn't upset going to Chicago. In Milwaukee you had a pitching staff like Spahn, Burdette, Conley, Buhl, you know you're not going to start. In Chicago you had Drott, Drabowsky, Jim Brosnan. I got to start. And I started the whole year. We had a pretty ball team for the first part of the year. I enjoyed Chicago. I didn't want to leave Milwaukee, but after I got to Chicago I was very happy.

— *Taylor Phillips*

In '51 I played third base and hit .379 with Muskegon and led the league, the old Class A Central League. I was hitting .392 with a week to go. My manager said, "You don't have to play if you don't want to. Keep your average up, it'll look good next year and help you get to Double A or Triple A ball."

I said, "No, I want to hit .400, I'm not satisfied with .390. I'll never know if I could do it or not if I don't play."

I hit some of the most vicious line drives for a week you ever saw but right at somebody. In the last game I could have gone four for four if I'd bunted, because the third baseman was playing me back on the grass. They told me, "Lay it down, Jim. It's a base hit." But I didn't want to bunt, I swung the bat. Four times at bat, three of the times he made sensational plays and threw me out at first.

The Yankees sent me to Beaumont in the Texas League the next year and made me an outfielder. Harry Craft was the manager. He was a great outfielder, and he taught me to play the outfield. They tell me he played the shallowest center field of anybody. He taught me how to get a jump on the ball. I got to where I really loved it out there. In 1952 I hit about .280 but I had a hundred RBI's. At that time the Yankees needed a pitcher to win them about four games at the end of the season. They were looking at Cincinnati's Ewell Blackwell. Rogers Hornsby, who managed Cincinnati, and Gabe Paul, the GM, were out scouting the Yankee minor league teams.

They saw me play. Hornsby told me, "I saw you play, I knew you could hit." *[Greengrass his 22 home runs and 16 triples that season.]* I hit two home runs that game. But what he liked about me, I got a base on balls and ran to first. He loved guys who hustled.

They called Harry Craft about the trade and told him they wanted me to report, and he told them, "He has 97 RBI's. I'd like him to get a hundred before he leaves. Looks better than ninety-seven." Harry called me to the office and said, "When you get that one hundredth RBI, you just come into the dugout and keep right on goin'." I packed all my stuff every day, three or four days, and then I hit a three run homer. When I got in the dugout, of course everybody was cheering and hollering and all, and I shook everybody's hand and I got to Harry and he said, "Good bye, Jimmy. Good luck to you, buddy. You can do it."

— *Jim Greengrass*

The Yankees didn't really want to trade me *[in '52 when Greengrass went to the Reds]* because they were planning to bring me up the next year. I found that later. In 1977, in an old-timers' game in Cincinnati, Stengel told me this himself. I walked into the clubhouse with my son. Casey was sitting in front of an empty locker putting on his uniform. He said, "Hey, Jim, come over here." I went over and he said, "Jim, I'm going to tell you why we traded you."

I was dumbfounded. I didn't even know he knew my name. I'd only met him two or three times. And this trade happened twenty-five years earlier. He said, "I needed a pitcher to win me some ballgames, and Ewell Blackwell was the guy I had on my mind." Blackwell was at the end of his career, but because of his unusual sidearm delivery that none of the American Leaguers had seen, I guess the Yankees thought he could get them out. Stengel said, "I knew he could do it, and I needed him to win me four ballgames, and Cincinnati wanted you." He said that because my power was straight away, I wouldn't be the best fit for Yankee Stadium. I think it was best for me. I would have had to change my hitting style, try to pull more. Besides, the Yankees already had some good outfielders at that time.

— *Jim Greengrass*

I got a telegram that said, "You've been traded to the Phillies. Good luck." And that was it. I was really upset. *[In December of 1960, Sullivan, at 6'7" the tallest pitcher in the American League, was traded to the Phillies for Gene Conley, who at 6'8" was the tallest pitcher in the National League.]* After a whole lot of years with the Red Sox I thought maybe I'd get a phone call or something, but I just got a telegram and that was the end of it. It was different in those days.

So when I went to the Phillies, boy, it was difficult. Because Boston, if nothing else, when Yawkey had the club at least, things were awful nice. It was a wonderful clubhouse. When I went to the Phillies, it was like going back to high school. The locker room was lousy. I didn't realize it, but I was just starting into what turned out to be Addison's Disease, which was a problem with adrenalin, so I had a real lousy year. So it was a very tough time in my life. *[Sullivan averaged 15 wins a year for Boston from 1954 to 1958. He went 6–16 for Boston in 1959 and 3–16 for the Phillies in 1961. The two bad seasons lowered his career percentage to under five hundred; he finished at 97–100.]*

We lost 107 games that year. But a lot of people don't realize, before we lost the 23 in a row we lost 11 in a row. And I'll tell you something else, the funny thing about it was, we had some good players on that team You know, Callison, and we had some good pitching. There was Mahaffey and Robin Roberts, and Jack Baldschun, who was a good pitcher, and Owens. It wasn't a team without talent. We were in almost every one of those games. It wasn't like we were getting our butts kicked all the time, we lost every possible way known to man.

— *Frank Sullivan*

When the Giants traded me to Milwaukee I could see the handwriting on the wall. Willie Mays was back to play center field. Well, he had been playing center field in 1951. But they had a chance to get a pitcher like Johnny Antonelli and that was it. You know, you hear things. I could feel it coming, but when I got traded to Milwaukee I felt good about going to a good ballclub. *[Thomson was traded to Milwaukee in February, 1954, with Sammy Calderone for Johnny Antonelli, Don Liddle, Billy Klaus, Ebba St. Claire, and cash.]* If I had my choice, I'd rather not get traded. But that's baseball. That's business. Johnny Antonelli just came and won the pennant for the Giants in 1954, winning 21 games. *[Antonelli was 21–7 and led the NL in ERA and shutouts.]* He made the difference.

The same thing happened in Milwaukee; they needed a good solid second baseman to pull that infield together. I kind of disappointed myself with my overall performance at Milwaukee. I didn't do what I would like to have done. Of course, I broke my ankle starting out there. But I felt like I was just starting to shape up and I felt like I was going to be doing some of the things that I should be doing, and they traded me back to the Giants. *[In June, 1957 Thomson was traded to the Giants with Danny O'Connell and Ray Crone for Red Schoendienst.]* I was sorry to leave Milwaukee.

— *Bobby Thomson*

The Detroit fans were the greatest fans that ever existed on this earth. To me, they were the greatest, just like, to the Dodgers who played with the Dodgers in the fifties, forties, the Dodger fans and the Detroit fans, I think, were the greatest baseball fans who ever existed. They appreciated the ballplayers, and the ballplayers appreciated them. It worked both ways.

I had spent twelve straight years with Detroit. All my life I wanted to stay there the rest of my life. I never wanted to leave Detroit, I wanted to play there my entire career. They traded me, but you know, it's a self-satisfaction when you can go out and beat a ballclub that traded you. My first game back against them with the Browns, I think I won something like 11–0. That was a great satisfaction.

— *Virgil Trucks*

Back in the winter of 1953 when Mr. Perini, the owner of the Milwaukee Braves called me and told me I'd been traded, I wasn't happy. I really thought we had a chance to win the pennant with the Milwaukee Braves. We'd finished second the year before, and I'd spent my whole career in the Boston organization. Then, to finally get up there for one year and get traded, I wasn't happy. I thought, "Boy, the Giants finished fifth, we finished second, I got traded downhill."

My Lord. You never know what's going to happen, but it was the greatest thing that ever happened to me. *[Liddle pitched for the World Champion New York Giants in 1954.]*
— *Don Liddle*

In most cases, I was pretty surprised about being traded. I guess the biggest break that I ever got and of course at the time I didn't know what kind of a break it was going to be — I was traded to the Dodgers in the middle of the '58 season. Steve Bilko and I were traded for Don Newcombe. Cincinnati had been trying to get Newcombe for two or three years, and of course Newcombe was getting toward the end of his career then, and he finally decided maybe he only had a couple of years left.

So I went over to the Dodgers. I had been a starter most of my career, and Alston put me in the bullpen, and I pitched I think 42 or 45 games — I can't remember which — from June 15 to the end of the year. I found out that I could pitch two or three days a week and it didn't bother me, arm-wise, and I became a relief pitcher. That added another eight years to my career. So that was a big break for me. The fact that he gave me the opportunity and the fact that I was able to find out that I could throw that often.
— *Johnny Klippstein*

We knew that you were like a slave, you were going to go somewhere. You just hoped it was someplace where the team was good. But it was tough leaving Pittsburgh, because that was basically my team. The only compensation for it was going to Chicago. I liked Chicago. Unfortunately, the Cubs were lousy.
— *Ralph Kiner*

One thing about switching leagues was that I'd be pitching against new people, and I thought that might get me by for a couple years. I didn't do that poorly with the Orioles when I look back at my record. I guess I was 4–1 or 3–1. I had some good games in relief.

They obviously didn't think so. I was released, and I went to Cleveland. Then my arm really acted up in spring training, so when I quit I knew my career was going to be over, I was going to be thirty-six years old.
— *Ernie Johnson*

I was only a spot player with the Giants. They had Bill White, would have been the first baseman in '57, but he went in the military. Then they had Cepeda coming on, and then of course right after Cepeda was McCovey, so there was no room over there for me with the Giants.

I went over to the Tigers. They had a guy named Jack Tighe who they later fired — they brought in a guy named Bill Norman, and he stuck me at first base. He said, "You're going to play first base the rest of the year, regardless of what you hit."

I had twenty home runs and drove in eighty-seven runs. And the next year we started off bad, they fired Norman and brought in Jimmy Dykes.

Jimmy was a good storyteller, but...

He'd light up his big cigar and tell you any story. Jimmy was a reporter's dream.
— *Gail Harris*

I got traded to St. Louis *[on June 14, 1953]*. I was kind of happy at the time 'cause Pittsburgh was going downhill, and I was probably about the oldest player left there then, when they traded me. I was kind of happy to go to the Cardinals, who were kind of a competitive team although they didn't win anything. They were a first division team. They had some great ballplayers, like Musial, Schoendienst, Slaughter, guys like that. A solid staff—Harvey Haddix and Gerry Staley and fellows like that pitching. So it was a good ballclub.

I enjoyed my time in St. Louis. Unfortunately, I didn't play too long there. They started bringing up younger players, too. That's how sports runs. Time comes along and then it ends just as quick sometimes.

— Pete Castiglione

Being traded was a shock. I didn't expect to get traded. I mean, no inkling was in the paper, you know how things leak out. I'd reached my peak of ability; the Cardinals knew I wasn't going to hit three hundred, and they weren't worried about the outfield situation, but they wanted to get somebody to hit home runs and hit for higher average, and they had some younger guys coming up that potentially could do that.

That's the way it was in our regime at that time. You always had players that were ready to take your place, and that's how your turnover took effect. But when I went to the Giants, I didn't know why the Giants even got me, but I think Mays was going to go in the service, so I think they were keeping me for insurance, but that for me was the worst period of time that I had in baseball. I don't even count that year, '52, at all. Nice guys, but I never got to play. Leo talked to just a few guys. You know, he had his certain guys. Mays was just the apple of his eye. I don't even remember him saying one word to me, and I was glad when I left the team. They sent me back to the minor leagues. I was happy.

— Chuck Diering

When I got traded from Detroit I was disappointed, it being my home and all. But I got traded to the Cleveland Indians in 1954 from Detroit, and that's the year that Cleveland won the pennant, so actually they did me a favor. They were in the World Series, and I got a pretty good check from the World Series money, so that wasn't a disappointment at all.

Getting traded around really wasn't too bad, because the game is the same actually on every team you play for. Especially being a catcher, all you have to do is, you have to know the pitching staff. So being traded as many times as I was, I was a pretty good veteran, a pretty good catcher, and I knew that I was a big league baseball player, so I was always glad that someone wanted me.

— Joe Ginsberg

The first time I was traded was when I was with the Cubs in 1951. I was sitting in the john in our apartment in Chicago and had the radio going, and I heard the trade announced. They said, "A big trade today, the Cubs and Dodgers." And they started naming them off. *[Terwilliger was traded to the Dodgers with Andy Pafko, Johnny Schmitz, and Rube Walker for Bruce Edwards, Joe Hatten, Eddie Miksis, and Gene Hermanski.]* I think I was the last one named off, and I couldn't believe it. That's the way I found out. The Dodgers were in town that day, so I went to the ballpark. There was no big deal or anything. I don't remember anybody saying anything to me.

I got my gear together and walked over to the Dodger locker room, put my stuff in there. And I didn't like it. Because I thought, "Holy smokes, here I am in the big leagues finally, and I know some guys on the club, and now I'm with a club where I know nobody."

Pee Wee Reese was great. When we got back to Brooklyn, I found a place to live. Reese said, "You tell me where you are and I'll come over and pick you up and take you to the park the first day. Get you straightened around." And he did that. He took me to the park the first day and showed me the way to go. I remember, he and Hodges were great, right off the bat. The bigger the star, the bigger the person was, I thought. They were a bunch of good guys, the Dodgers.

— *Wayne Terwilliger*

A sportswriter called me up and said, "You know you've been traded."
I said, "Really?"
He said, "Guess who you've been traded to." So I picked probably the team that was below us, Pittsburgh. Because the way the Cubs trade, they usually made a mistake about a hundred percent of the time.

He said no. I named a few more and he said, "No, you were traded to the Dodgers."

I said, "You have got to be teasing. This is a Christmas present." Because they had just won the World Series the year before, so this was really something. I could hardly wait to get to spring training, because I knew I was going to be on a winner, it was just an automatic thing.

You always want to go as high as you can go, play in the World Series, and this was probably my only chance. I certainly wouldn't have gotten it with the Cubs. So it was really a thrill for me, I just couldn't believe it. *[Jackson was traded to the Dodgers on December 9, 1955, along with Don Elston. The Cubs received Don Hoak, Russ Meyer, and Walt Moryn.]*

— *Randy Jackson*

I went to New York in the 17 player trade between the Yankees and the Orioles. *[Going to the Yankees: Don Larsen, Billy Hunter, Bob Turley, Harry Byrd, Mike Blyzka, Darrell Johnson, Jim Fridley, and Dick Kryhoski. To the Orioles: Jim McDonald, Willy Miranda, Hal Smith, Gus Triandos, Gene Woodling, Bill Miller, Kal Segrist, Don Leppart, and Ted Guercio.]* I thought I'd be taking over at shortstop for Rizzuto. Phil was at the end of his career, and the first year I was there *[1955]* I played 98 games. I was very pleased.

Then, in August, we just got back from a western road trip where I had hit 14 hits in 28 at-bats, and Casey took me out for a pinch hitter in the sixth inning. We were playing Cleveland and Herb Score was pitching. He took me straight back through the runway into the clubhouse and said, "I'm sending you to Denver."

I said, "No you're not."

He said, "Bill, we just got Enos Slaughter from the Cardinals so he'd be eligible for the World Series, and we only have two players on our team that have options. You and Elston Howard. There's no way I can send Elston Howard out."

And Elston wasn't even playing that much. I had played 98 eight games. I came home to Baltimore for four days. Houk was managing Denver. Ralph and I were good friends anyway, and he finally convinced me that I needed to come to Denver. I went out there and I broke my leg. Badly, too. In fact, I still have a screw in my ankle from that thing.

In '56 I was on the disabled list for the first part of the season and came off the disabled list and played most of the games near the end of the season. But probably the biggest disappointment I had as a member of the Yankees was that I did not play in any of the seven games in the '56 Series. *[Hunter played in 37 games in 1956 and batted .280.]*

I sat there on the bench the day that Larsen pitched his perfect game. But you know how we athletes are — sitting on the bench doesn't do it.

— *Billy Hunter*

I was traded a few times. I just looked at it this way: I always felt that the club that got me felt that I could help them, and baseball is played the same no matter where you go. People were saying, "Well, why were you traded so much? Were you a trouble-maker?"

No. You're not a trouble-maker when you're playing 150, 162 ballgames a year and you do the job for them. *[Thomas hit at least 20 home runs in 10 of his first 11 full-time seasons.]* But when you reach a certain age in baseball you become expendable because they want to protect their youngsters, and I can't blame them for that. Sometimes, though, it wasn't handled in the best way. I was promised by John McHale that I was going to be the Milwaukee Braves' left fielder come 1962, and that was in September, and I said to him, "If you have intentions of trading me please don't trade me, let me dicker with the club that I'm going with." And November I got a call when I was up hunting. My wife said to me, "Honey, you just got sold to the Mets." *[In 1962 Thomas led the Mets with 34 home runs; Marv Throneberry was 2nd with 16.]*

And then when I got sold to the Phillies, I got off the bus in Philadelphia — the same thing happened when I got traded from Chicago to Milwaukee and got off the bus in Milwaukee — they told me, "You're changing clubhouses."

— *Frank Thomas*

That trade from the Pirates to the Cardinals in 1951 really hurt me. I let it really bother me, which I shouldn't have done. I was going from a poor ballclub to a good club. It was just that it was unexpected in that I'd already changed positions *[from the outfield to third base]* and was having my best year — I was named to the All-Star team — and then all of a sudden I get the paper and I'm gone, you know.

I found out about the trade in the paper. Ralph Kiner and Bob Prince and I were talking about going into business back there in Pittsburgh and we were in a restaurant. One of the waitresses said, "Here, look at this." And here was the headline. I was gone. That's how I found it out. Mr. Branch Rickey was the general manager. I don't have any fond memories of him.

I was happy about the trade that sent me to Cleveland *[in 1952]*. I knew some people there and it was a hell of a ballclub. Those were the three best years in baseball that I had. You know, even though I was playing part-time, eighty, ninety ballgames, whatever, it was sure nice to win every day, or two days out of three.

— *Wally Westlake*

I was really down when I went to the Giants from the Dodgers *[in 1950]*. I kind of knew it was coming because I only played third, I wasn't a utility infielder. They wanted an all-around guy. Bobby Morgan was hitting well at Montreal, so I knew they were going to keep him, and I knew I was expendable. I hated leaving the Brooklyn club because I came up through the organization. But then I adjusted.

The difficult part about changing teams usually is that you have to move. You have to pack all your stuff up. Which I didn't have to do, joining the Giants.

In 1951 the Giants sold me to the Oakland club at the All-Star break. When they sold me to Oakland then I had to pack my stuff and make sure my wife and two-year-old daughter got settled. That was the tough part. With the Giants I was a utility man; it's hard to adjust to that. The thing I liked about going to the Coast League is that I was playing every day.

— *Spider Jorgensen*

I remember my feelings when I was traded to Detroit. I had a lot of good friends on the Dodgers. Podres and Drysdale, Koufax, Perranoski. Our families' wives were close, and I'd played about ten years, 1954 to '64, in the organization, counting my minor league time. That's where I learned all my baseball. And that was a big help to me after my playing days were over and I became an instructor and manager, because the Dodgers were great in teaching baseball. All phases, to all players, even if you were a pitcher.

You had a chance to learn every part of the game. Sliding, infield play. Outfield play, 'cause that's the way they did it. So I hated to have to go to Detroit. You're a professional, you move on, you go to another ballclub; but I have to admit I picked the paper up and looked to see how the Dodgers were doing.

— *Larry Sherry*

In 1952 we played two games in Cincinnati. I dressed for the third game and someone tapped me on the shoulder and said, "Go on over to the Reds' clubhouse. You've been traded." That's how they did it back then.

— *Cal Abrams*

I was traded to Detroit in 1958. It was a thrill to go to Detroit to play with my brother. *[Frank Bolling played for Detroit from 1954 to 1960; Milt in 1958.]* I never even thought anything about our playing together until a couple years ago, when I heard that there's only been four brother combinations in the history of baseball that played short and second, and we never even realized that when we did get a chance to do it. There was only fifteen months difference — I'm older — and we'd grown up together, and really never had played short and second.

In high school I was a third baseman and Frank was an outfielder most of the time. In Legion ball I was a shortstop and he was an outfielder. So except for barnstorming after a couple seasons we really had never played short and second together. The other brother combinations were the Ripkens, the Hamners, and the O'Brien twins. *[Garvin and Granny Hamner played together briefly in 1945, Garvin's only big league season. Granny started in 1944 and played 17 seasons.]*

In July of '58 the Phillies wanted to buy me to play second base over there, and I was just a utility infielder at Detroit with my brother, so that would probably have been a break if I could have gone over there and played second base. My skills were probably more adaptable to second base at that time because I lost a lot of my arm strength, and I might have been a little better hitter in that league because I could handle the low ball, but I had a difficult time with the high pitch.

— *Milt Bolling*

I was pinch-hitting for the White Sox the first part of June, 1953, in Yankee Stadium and hit a home run with the bases loaded to win the game against the Yankees, and I was traded that day, believe it or not.

We were on a train. It was a Sunday afternoon, and we were going to Washington to play the first of the week. We were in Philadelphia Station, sitting in the dining car, having a beer or two and just bragging, just carrying on, because we went into first place or were tied with the Yankees for first place at that time. And a fella named Short, a public relations man I think for the White Sox, came into the dining room and told me, "You've just been traded to Washington."

Well, it was ironic, because I was with the Yankees in '51, and I was traded to last place from the Yankees to the Browns, and now we're tied for first place and I feel pretty good about it, and I think maybe I'm going to help them before the year is out. I think I was 2 and 0 with them I think I pitched in 7 games and we won them all. And then I hit that home run I felt like, gee, maybe I'll get something going here, and hell, they traded me to last place again.

Then when I was sold from Washington, I lacked one day of being a ten year man, and Clark Griffith sold me to Charleston, and they paid my salary the rest of the year. Harridge, the league President, and the Commissioner got mad at him for doing that, lacking one day of being a ten year man and trading me like that, so they just paid my salary the rest of the year.

I went up to see Griffith and he said, "Tommy, you pitched pretty good for us," and I said, "Well I don't know that I did or not, but I know I didn't win any, but I haven't been here the whole year." *[Byrne pitched six games for Washington, going 0–5.]* But I struck out 12 I think the last game I played and got beat 3–2. But the point was, he said to me, "What happened to your hitting?" In other words, he traded for me to pitch and to hit, but evidently I didn't hit too well that short time I was there. Anyway, that's crazy, but that's what the old man said to me.

— *Tommy Byrne*

Getting traded from Detroit to Cleveland in 1953 was very surprising to me. Not that they were going to trade me, because you've got to move some people. When you've got a ballclub in bad shape you've got to be making some trades and doing some changeovers. It was very, very probable that I got traded, because I was a piece of merchandise.

The biggest surprise was, I did particularly well against New York, and my wife's from Jersey, that's where her home is, which would have been close, if I'd have been traded to the Yankees. Although I was born or raised in Detroit, if I had to go someplace, Yankee Stadium was built for my type of pitching. I had control enough to make you hit the ball to the long fields. Yogi hit probably twenty-five shots out there, four hundred feet, but they were to left-center, to right-center, to center field. There's some guy just waiting for them to come down. But that's the type of park it was, and I had done well against them, and when I got traded and they said Cleveland I couldn't believe it.

All that came to mind was Lemon, Wynn, Feller, Garcia — what the hell do they want with me? They had a bushel-basket full of pitching. That was probably the biggest surprise I ever had. Cleveland. It was an eight player trade, four on each team Gromek and Boone came here *[along with Al Aber and Dick Weik]*, and four of us from Detroit went to Cleveland *[Houtteman, Owen Friend, Joe Ginsberg, and Bill Wight]*.

We won 111 games at Cleveland in 1954, and that's only during in a 154 game year. I won 15 *[and lost seven]* and nobody knew I was on the ballclub. I was like a couple of other fellas. They would pitch Lemon, Garcia, and Wynn, and get a rainout or something and come back with those three guys again. So Feller and I didn't pitch much the first or last couple months or last couple weeks of the season. We pitched mostly in the hot part of the season when there were a lot of games. *[Games started in 1954: Wynn, 36; Garcia, 34; Lemon, 33; Houtteman, 25; Feller, 19].*

— *Art Houtteman*

The Yankees traded me and Whitey Herzog, Lou Berberet, Bob Wiesler, and Dick Tettelbach to Washington for Mickey McDermott and Bobby Kline. It gave me a chance to get to the big leagues. It was a change, coming from Denver to Washington. In '55 in Denver, in Triple A, the stadium held twenty thousand people, and we packed that every night. We outdrew the Washington Senators that year.

— *Herb Plews*

I was sold from Sanford, Florida in the Class D league to the Washington Senators. I was happy pitching for Washington. I was just happy being in the big leagues. The owner of the Sanford baseball club said, "I got a chance to send you to the big leagues. I have two teams that want to buy you, Washington and Cleveland. Whichever one you'd like to go to that's who I'll sell you to."

Of course at that time Cleveland had a pretty good-looking staff so I thought maybe I'd get a better chance if I went to Washington.

I enjoyed my stay in Washington. I met a lot of nice fellows. I'm still friends with some of them today. So I enjoyed every minute of it. I thought, though, I was going to the Yankees after the 1941 season. Phil Rizzuto told me I was going to be with them the next year. They tried to get a hold of me, but Griffith wanted too much for me, so that didn't develop.

I went to Boston in 1952 in a trade. I enjoyed Boston, too. First of all, it was a better club, and secondly, the weather was much better up there, it was cooler. Washington is very humid, and of course in those days we didn't have air conditioning.

— *Sid Hudson*

Chapter Fourteen

Injuries

Injuries have shortened the career of many a player. In the '50s injuries that could be easily treated today often meant the end of the line. Back then players dared not sit out with aches and pains, no matter how discomforting; hundreds of good players were toiling in the high minors, just waiting for a position to open in the big leagues. Today players go on the disabled list with aches that would not have kept players out of the line-up in the '50s. Were old-time players tougher? Or is it merely that modern players have long-term contracts — or perhaps the comfort of knowing they can sit out games without the fear that a minor leaguer might be called up to permanently take their spot. Thus, they need not risk aggravating an injury that might threaten their career. At any rate, one of the key questions virtually all players face at some time is, "Should I play hurt?" and if so, how hurt?

When I first came around to the major leagues, there were only eight clubs in the league. You had to really work hard and produce. The biggest thing, you never said you were hurt, because there were about half a dozen guys who would stomp all over you, ready to take your job.

Everybody played whether they were partially hurt or unless they were disabled, then they were out. But they played hard. I remember a lot of them had something wrong with them, but they kept on playing.

— *Mike Sandlock*

Some injuries hurt my chances to play much in the big leagues. To make the Hall of Fame or anything, you just got to stay healthy. When you get your chance in the majors, you've got to jump on it. If you're not healthy, you're gonna try it anyway, but it's better to be healthy.

— *Bob Lennon*

I had one serious injury. That's when I was a runner on second base. I tried to slide into third against the Washington Senators, and that was one aspect of baseball that I wasn't taught, how to slide. I tried to knock third base out of position, and I hurt my back and was out for about ten days or two weeks.

— *Joe Ostrowski*

In 1954 we were getting trounced in a game in Philadelphia. Back in those days, they used to water the fields by attaching hoses to spigots that they would have buried in the outfield. They'd put a rubber cover over them, but this particular day, I knew that that cover was off that sprinkler. You know, you're just aware of what's around.

But we were getting beat so bad — it was like 17–0 and we were in the top of the ninth inning, playing in Philadelphia — and the fans were all over us, you know, balls flying everywhere and I'd probably misjudged a couple of them. But I said, "I'll catch the next ball that's hit out here, no matter what happens."

Billy Consolo hit the ball into left-center, and I stepped in that hole where that water spigot was. It tripped me and I went down and landed on my left shoulder and broke it. Heck, I didn't even catch that ball. It hit me in the leg after I tripped.

— ***Gus Zernial***

When I was with the Yankees, we had one incident that was kind of major. We were in Philadelphia and we left the ballpark to go to the train station. We were all on this charter bus, and the overpass was too low and the bus driver hit it. He broke his arm, and we all flew around inside the bus, and some guys were shaken up pretty good. He must have been a new driver because he hit the steel beam and we all flew around the bus like you wouldn't believe. Finally, we all got on the train and went to New York to open up a series the next day. The insurance people were there at the ballpark wondering what happened and making cash settlements to the players that got hurt. *[This happened in 1954, Allie Reynolds' last season. He suffered a back injury which contributed to his retirement that year.]*

— ***Bob Kuzava***

Cleveland bought me in '53 out of the Dodger chain. That winter I went to Joplin, Missouri to meet my brother. There was a minor pitcher by the name of Red Crowder, who had drowned. Mickey Mantle, Cliff Mapes, the Boyer boys lived right there in the area — Don Gutteridge — they were getting up a benefit game for his widow there in the Joplin ballpark. They asked me if I wouldn't participate. I was glad to do it, naturally. Mickey was on the other team, and he decided he was going to pitch the ninth inning, the last inning. I led off and he threw a knuckleball that didn't knuckle. I hit it down in the right field corner, and I knew I was going for three due to where the outfielder was playing and where the ball was.

When I rounded second, the next step after I rounded second my right foot — the inside cleat on my right foot — hit a rock. It was down under the soil. It bruised it, bruised it bad. Over the winter it got to hurting so bad I couldn't hardly walk on it.

Greenberg wanted me to come to Cleveland and have it checked. I stopped in Asheville, North Carolina, and met with an orthopedic surgeon, who was a personal friend. He couldn't do anything because he wasn't permitted to because I needed to see the Indians' doctors. But he told me there was a bone spur forming. He said, "Simple, just remove it." No problem. But when I got to Cleveland, the doctors said no. They wanted to put shots in there. So they elected to go the shot route.

I went to spring training in '54 and that's the only time in my life that a job was given to me. Because Larry Doby was getting older and they were going to switch Doby to right field. Dale Mitchell was in left and he didn't have any kind of arm. So the center field job was given to me. But my right foot hurt so bad I actually couldn't run on it. I was limping. I was putting all the pressure on my left leg and then my left leg got sore, trying to carry the right one. I went with them north, then they optioned me down to Indianapolis in the American Association. The rest of my career I played with an extra sized shoe on my right foot with a piece of sponge under there. I had to tape it on every game for the rest of my career. Joplin, Missouri, was the turning point from an injury standpoint.

— *Gale Wade*

Paul Pettit was a bonus baby who got one hundred thousand dollars from Branch Rickey, but it was given to him in the period of ten years. The year that Branch Rickey started with those plastic helmets that you had to wear, Pettit was on first base. A ground ball was hit and he was running toward second. He wore glasses, and the second baseman threw the ball dead on. It smashed into the helmet. The ball went way up into the stands, the helmet flew one way. His glasses were crushed. He was on the ground, and everybody raced over to him. Luckily he got up. He was so lucky to be alive. If that had been a regular old cap, he would have been done for. So Mr. Rickey did something fine for baseball, starting with those things for safety's sake.

— *Cal Abrams*

I was never lucky enough to be on a contending team. After I had some fairly good years, my last year in the major leagues, '54, I went to spring training, and I pitched quite a few innings. This particular game I pitched five innings of shutout ball against the Brooklyn Dodgers in an exhibition game, and during the night calcium formed in my pitching wrist, and that really knocked me out of the major leagues right then and there. I never did get my fastball back or my curveball. I played in the minor leagues with different clubs hoping that I'd get another shot, which I did. I came back in '55 with the White Sox. Marty Marion was the manager, and I had thirteen and a third scoreless innings in spring training and I was sent out, and to this day I can't figure out why.

— *Bob Cain*

I tore my rotator cuff and I didn't know nothing about it. Before each game I'd let them numb it up and everything, which I done wrong, you know, but I was just trying to work to get my pension.

— *Sammy Taylor*

I was on first base in Pittsburgh *[late in the 1954 season]*, and Curt Roberts was playing second base. There was a ground ball to short. Curt took the throw, and I slid under him. He saw me coming on and he had me out anyway, so I just kind of slid straight in. He went up in the air to make his play and he knew I was under him, so instead of coming down with his cleats on my legs, he tucked his legs back and he hit me flush with his knee right on the side of my leg at the ankle. Well, it was just another bruise. I didn't think anything of it. But that developed into a three-inch blood clot in the inner vein. That caused the leg to swell later on in the week. And that developed into thrombophlebitis, because the doctor didn't know what he was doing anyway, and didn't treat it. So that stopped my career right there. I played after that but it got to where my legs swelled up so it looked like you put an air pump to them. It scared the daylights out of me. I was in the hospital for two weeks. When they released me, I got in a taxi, and when I got to *[general manager Gabe Paul's]* office, my leg had swollen my pants leg full. Gabe wanted me back in the hospital, but I told him the doctor didn't know what he was doing. I wanted to go back to Atlanta to see my own doctor.

The team arranged for me to fly down, arranging for wheelchairs do keep me off the leg. When I got to my own doctor he wasn't sure if he could save my leg. I was really scared. After a couple weeks of treatment in the hospital it finally got to where they'd let me walk. I had to learn to walk all over again. Get my balance and everything. I went back to the Reds the next spring. My leg was weak. I wasn't as strong as I was and I wasn't hitting that well, so *[in April 1955]* Tebbetts decided to trade me to the Phillies.

The Phillies sent me down to Johns Hopkins. He said it was unusual for a young man like me to have phlebitis. I spent about four weeks there, being studied by all the students at Johns Hopkins and by doctors from all over. I was in a big theater there, being looked by everybody and being asked a lot of questions. I finally got back to where I could play, but I couldn't play every day. And I lost a lot of power. I'd thanked Mr. Carpenter for getting me treated. He's the reason I'm walking around today. That finished my major league career. I went out to the Coast League *[in 1957]* and kept getting stronger and stronger. In those days if you'd been hurt, there was always that doubt. So I never got another shot.

— *Jim Greengrass*

I sprained my pinky one time diving, on my left hand, and I was leading off. And when I got up again, I kept my pinky off the bat. But I knew I couldn't swing hard, because it would hurt the pinky, so I would bunt or try to get a walk, that was my job anyway. I knew if I went into the trainer and said, "It's killing me," they would X-ray it, they would bandage it up, and Gene Hermanski would be playing the outfield, and that's the end of me.

— *Cal Abrams*

I hurt my arm in 1959. I assume it would have treatable today. They do a lot of things with this rotator cuff thing. I'd worked my way into the starting rotation, the first time I'd actually become a full-time starter.

I had ten starts in a row. I only had one bad inning in the ten starts. When I hurt it Frank Lane was the general manager — and I remember Piersall was in the locker next to me, and he said, "That guy's talking about you, saying you don't want to pitch."

And I said, "I can't even shave, let alone pitch."

We were fighting for the pennant. We were in first place almost all year, and the White Sox finally beat us out.

But I couldn't throw. Then I'd get a little better, and be able to throw in the bullpen a little bit, and they'd say, "Hell, he doesn't want to throw." But I couldn't — it was terrible. There was no treatment at all. They gave me a bunch of cortisone, and that was it. Nothing.

— *Don Ferrarese*

I missed the last part of the 1950 season after getting hit with a ball.

I missed with a fastball to Ted Kluszewski on September 15. I was going good. *[Church was 8–6 as a rookie with a 2.73 ERA.]* I pitched a shutout on July 4th or 5th, in the first game of a doubleheader. I won mine 7–0. They finally got me some damn runs. Robbie came back and pitched a 1–0 shutout, and we went in first place, and we never got out of first place from that day on.

But September 15 we're playing Cincinnati and there was a way we pitched Ted Kluszewski. He always took a strike. So I got my strike. And I started going in and up, in and up, in and up. Just go in and up. And then go away from him, and all that sort of stuff.

But I had my out pitch in my mind, where I wanted to go with it, but I missed the damn thing by a foot, and he got every stitch on it. Came right back up the middle, I saw it off the bat, tried to flag it down, didn't get it, and it came off my glove and hit me in the eye.

I saw Del Ennis field it on one hop in right field and then I went down and I might have been out for four or five seconds, something like that. which is no big deal. But I put my hands — I knew I was hurt — so I put my hands up to my face and all I found was blood. And by that time my people were there with me. So they carried me down to Jefferson Hospital in Philadelphia. Then three or four days after the swelling went down they did a little plastic surgery, and hell, I can see. It never bothered my eyes or anything like that, but I wanted to play.

But I missed by a foot with a fastball with Ted. If I'd a had that damn thing one more foot he'd of hit it right off his hands straight up to Eddie Waitkus.

Thank God for Mage McDonald, who was one of our coaches up there. I got out of the hospital and I said, "Mage, come on, let's go. Let's go down to the bullpen, let's go down to the left field fence and I'll feed you balls. I want to find out if I've got reflexes or if I'm afraid, or what have you. I want to know what the hell's going on. But I came back next year and won 15 games.

— *Bubba Church*

In 1950 I came up with a sore arm for the first time in my whole life. In those years we started and relieved, and I pitched opening day that year and got beat 1–0 by Satchel Paige in 11 innings, and I pitched the whole eleven innings. So two days later I'm back in the bullpen and I'm warming up to relieve, and I pulled a muscle in my arm, so I didn't play any more after that.

I blame that on Red Rolfe, I don't blame it on anybody else. I mean, after all, he had other guys he could use, but he wanted to win ballgames, and winning them in the first part of the year is naturally as important as winning them in the last part of the year. He wanted to win, and he figured I would be a stopper for him, and pitch one or two innings and maybe win the ballgame. But it didn't turn out that well for me. I wound up being on the disabled list the rest of the year. *[After going 19–11 in 1949, Trucks went 3–1 in 1950.]*

It was snowing at that time. You had snow and rain, or cold weather, and it had a factor in me possibly developing that sore arm

I was more than glad to do what I was doing. We all did. We all relieved and started in those years. There were no special bullpen relievers. Nowadays you've got three different bullpen men, you've got a long reliever, a short reliever, and s closer. We never had those sort of things. You closed, you started, or either you had somebody come in the last couple of innings maybe or one inning to save the ballgame for the club, not for the pitcher, just to save the ballgame.

But if I hadn't pitched and relieved in those innings, I probably would have never had a sore arm and maybe we would have gone on to win the pennant. It was the best chance we had since the '45 season.

— *Virgil Trucks*

I had my arm broke and got charged at a time at bat in a game against the Phillies in 1952. We had a couple men on base in the top of the ninth. They were one out away from winning and Andy Hansen fired a pitch high and inside to me and I tried to turn away from it. As I did, it hit me on the right elbow and sounded like the crack of the bat and the ball rolled down toward the pitcher's mound. He picked it up and threw to first and the ballgame was over.

I was standing at the plate holding my arm and jumping around there. The Phillies ran off the field. All the Pittsburgh club come out trying to argue with the umpire, but he said, "No, that hit the bat." That's how it was. Then they took me to the hospital a little bit after that, after everything settled down.

Tom Gorman was the umpire. I got charged for a time at bat and got a broken arm at the same time. I missed the rest of that season. That happened in July of that year, 1952.

It had a long-range effect. I understood later on that the Cleveland club was after me and I probably would have went then. Al Lopez was then managing Cleveland in those years. We weren't going no place and they were looking for another infielder. Chances are I would have got waived and probably would have joined Cleveland and played with a couple pretty good ballclubs over there, because they were a pretty contending team in the early fifties. They finished second in '52 and '53 I think, and they won the pennant in '54, although they got wiped out in the Series. They got another infielder from our club, George Strickland, because I couldn't play. It was a break for him and a bad break for me — in a couple ways, a bad break.

— *Pete Castiglione*

The Dodgers got me from the Cubs to take Jackie Robinson's place. This was his last year.

They started the [1956] season off with him, and Walter Alston told me he was going to do that, because Jackie had been there so long. I said, "That's certainly understandable." He didn't do too well and then they put me in and I started for about three months, two and a half months. I was batting clean-up and driving in runs in just about every game, and just really doing great, like they expected me to. And during All-Star break I was turning a shower off in my apartment in Brooklyn and the porcelain knob broke off in my hand, just ripped my thumb all to pieces, and that was pretty much the end of the season, so I just had to kind of coast from then on, and Jackie came back in and did a good job.

— *Randy Jackson*

I grew up in Brooklyn, and now I was with the Cubs in 1957, going back home. Back to Ebbets Field to play center field, to hit against Sal Maglie, one of the league's toughest pitchers, and I'd been out of action for six weeks with a bad arm, wondering if my career was over.

But that day in Ebbets Field, I doubled off Maglie, and homered, my first and only big league homer. And you know, hitting a pitcher like Maglie gave me as much pleasure as my big year at Nashville. *[In 1954 he hit 64 home runs for Nashville and batted .345.]* It gave me a sort of feeling that my arm would be okay.

It wasn't, though. But that's all right. I'm just happy I had the opportunity to play pro ball. I always loved baseball. I liked to find out who was going to be pitching that night, tried to figure out what pitches to look for.

Sometimes I was right, like against Maglie, back home in Brooklyn, in Ebbets Field, when I could sense my arm was getting better, and I could see a bunch of homers waiting to happen.

— *Bob Lennon*

In 1954 I was with the Phillies and I got my knee racked up in an exhibition game. The Phillies' trainer didn't treat it properly, and by Opening Day it was swollen and infected. I had been traded from Pittsburgh to Philadelphia, and Opening Day was at Pittsburgh. And I remember sitting on the bench and it started to snow, sleet and whatnot — it was one of those miserable Opening Days — and the club doctor for Pittsburgh sat down next to me and said, "What's wrong with you?"

I said, "I don't know. I've got some ligaments torn or something in my knee."

He said, "You want to go in the clubhouse and let me —?" and I said, "Gee, I don't know" — him being with the Pittsburgh club and me with Philadelphia, how would it look, me jumping from one trainer to another or something — but this guy was a doctor. So finally, he did find some way to get me into the clubhouse and he checked me out. The knee was so infected, he took me to the hospital and drained it. He said, "Look at this," and what squirted out — my God, it looked like old rotten custard. For a month or so, maybe longer, I had to have it drained every day. That was the end of my career major league career.

— *Mike Sandlock*

My injury happened my first year with the Pirates. It was a sudden thing. I was breaking off a curveball during a ballgame and the elbow snapped. You know, they told me to keep throwing, it would work out. My shoulder and elbow were both hurting after awhile because I was favoring my elbow. The elbow did come around, but the shoulder never did. It was always weak. In those days all they did was diathermy. Now, of course, they have cortisone shots and things like that.

If I'd had today's treatments, I think I would have come around okay. It would have come around faster and wouldn't have been so painful. By the time I ended my minor league career in 1960 I overcame a bone chip in my shoulder, and I'd been able to play a couple extra years by taking cortisone shots in my shoulder. So I know the difference between that type of treatment and what I was getting ten years earlier, in 1950.

— *Paul Pettit*

I pitched three years for Washington and then I went in the service and stayed thirty-eight months. I pitched a lot during the war. I pitched 250 innings the first year I was in the service. And I gave calisthenics to the cadets all the time I was in the service. I was in the Air Force.

I came out of there with a sore arm I went to see the doctor and he found a spur on my shoulder and he said it was excessive use of the shoulder. They sent me to Johns Hopkins Hospital. John Bennett was the doctor who took care of all the athletes in my time, and he said I was through unless I could learn to throw from the side-arm position to get away from that pain.

I could side-arm a hitter; I used to side-arm different hitters, but mostly threw from three-quarters. So I dropped down and tried to throw just nothing but side-arm all the way, so for the last seven or eight years I pitched, I threw every pitch side-armed. I was never quite the same as I was because they'd move those line-ups with those left-handed hitters against me, and me throwing side-armed it made it kind of tough.

[In his three seasons before the war Hudson won 40 games; in his first three seasons after the war he won 18.] But, anyway, somebody liked me along the way and I got to stay a long while.

— *Sid Hudson*

Sid Hudson could really throw hard, straight over handed, somewhere around 6'4", then he hurt his arm and shoulder in the military. Then when he came back to Washington he was strictly a side-armer. He had to go down as a submariner to be able to pitch. He had a bad arm But if he hadn't hurt his arm in the military, he'd have been a great pitcher.

— *Gil Coan*

The only time I had injuries is when I ran into a fence or something. I got bruised up a few times running into the fence in St. Louis, and popping my knees diving for balls in St. Louis. Just injuries trying to catch the ball. The fences were concrete or block walls. Even Yankee Stadium had that short wall, but it was a concrete wall. They had warning tracks, but they were short warning tracks. In St. Louis I played right field, they had a short right field. I never worried about the warning track because I played close to the wall anyway.

— *Al Zarilla*

[Malzone averaged over 152 games a season — at third base — for 8 straight years, in a 154 game season.] I never had any problems with injuries. I think I still hold the modern record for the Red Sox for consecutive games. The only injuries I had were slight bruises, things like that, no broken bones. My only serious injury was in the minor leagues my third year of baseball. I had a good year in C ball. I went to A ball and that's when I dislocated my ankle, and pulled all the ligaments. It really set me back. I was out a whole year. *[In 1949 he hit .329 with a league-leading 26 triples for Oneonta of the Canadian-American League; in 1950 he played only two games. He hit .283 in 1951, then spent 1952 and '53 in military service.]*

— *Frank Malzone*

I was doing real well my rookie year *[1953]*, and I slid into second base and busted up my ankle in August, and probably shouldn't have come back and played as soon as I did. *[Bolling played in 109 games at shortstop and hit .263 that year.]*

I'd torn all the ligaments in my ankle. Today they would cast it. Back then they didn't. They kept trying to get me to get back in the lineup, and forced me back into the lineup before I should have. And I started throwing awkwardly and really hurt my arm at that time, too, and I never did throw well after that because of it.

Then in '55 in spring training I was run over by Del Rice in an exhibition game in a freak play and dislocated my elbow and I was out just about the whole year, except I think I might have gotten in four or five games that year. *[Bolling had played 113 games in 1954, hitting .249. In 1955 he played in six games — only two in the field — hitting 1 for 5.]*

— *Milt Bolling*

When I went to spring training with the Yankees in 1948, I got to play every game during spring. I did well. I won a couple ballgames for them with late inning hits. It's possible I led the club in RBIs that spring. And they gave me the same story; back to Kansas City I went. Then, around Christmas time when I was thinking, gee, it wouldn't be long, early February, mid–February, we'd be in spring training. Well, I had hurt my right arm the last game of the season in 1941, during the time that the Yankees had tried to make a pitcher out of me, and the pain stayed with me all the rest of my career. This particular Christmas, 1948, it just was killing me. I called New York, and they arranged to have my arm operated on, and then they wouldn't let me come to spring training, because I was healing. I wanted to come down there and at least run, get my legs in shape and stuff. Instead they took Jerry Coleman, who I had played with quite a bit in my career.

Jerry was a good defensive infielder, but not much of a hitter. And by golly, Jerry went with them and he stayed. He had quite a career, too. So I missed the boat right there. *[Coleman played nine seasons with the Yankees, appeared in six World Series. He hit 16 career home runs and had a lifetime .263 batting average.]*

— *Jim Dyck*

Leo Durocher was a very colorful manager. He knew baseball. But he made a relief pitcher out of me and he pitched me too often. You didn't pitch one inning like you do now. Gosh, I pitched two and three innings in relief and it takes a lot out of you when you pitch every day. I was in the bullpen pitching four games in a row, and that's when I hurt my arm.

— *Max Lanier*

I pitched for two years needing a double hernia operation. I couldn't have the operation because I was afraid of losing my spot in the rotation. *[During this time McLish went 4–14 in 1960 with the Reds and 10–13 in 1961 with the White Sox.]* The White Sox, at the end of the '61 season, put me in the hospital and fixed it, but then that next spring they traded me to the Phillies. Then I came back and had two good years with the Phillies *[11–5 in 1962, 13–11 in 1963]* after I had the hernia repaired.

But I could remember those two years: I was logy, I didn't have any energy, but I pitched, because I didn't want to lose my spot. Whenever guys say, "You're going to pitch," you do it. You want to.

Because I was never secure enough to think that I had a spot in the rotation. Pitchers back then wouldn't tell anybody if they had anything wrong. If it wasn't something that they could see, you just didn't tell them. Somebody'd come along and take your spot.

— *Cal McLish*

I've seen guys in our time run into concrete fences. They had concrete fences then; now they've got foam fences out there. I've seen Elmer Valo run full speed into concrete walls and just shake it off and go back to playing. And not many people had pulled muscles in those days. If anything, it was broken bones or something like that from sliding or some kind of action.

— *Carl Scheib*

My only regret is maybe not taking care of my arm a little bit better. In 1962, I hurt my arm. We were in a pennant race and I kept pitching, and I think that hurt me a little bit. But we were in a pennant race and everybody was doing their part; you know, you did that.

I think the way I was used, making long relief appearances without much rest, might have hurt. It's hard to say if I should have backed off a little bit and said no, I couldn't pitch tonight. I might have had a little longer career, maybe another three or four years, because my arm would have held up a little better. That's about the only regret because I was very fortunate in most of my career. With every year of the five years with the Dodgers and the four years with Detroit I didn't finish any lower than third. Until I got traded to Houston I didn't know what it was to finish with a last place club. So I was very fortunate.

The second half of the season with Houston was like a whole season — that's how long it was. I mean, come to the park, guys' attitudes were poor. You weren't going anywhere. And all those other years, we always had a chance to win a pennant clear into the last month.
— *Larry Sherry*

When I played, I think you played with some injuries a little more than you should have. But back then it just seemed like you had the feeling that if you were out very long somebody else would be coming in and taking your place. They had a lot of good minor leaguers playing, so you always had the feeling that you'd better stay in there. I missed hardly any games.

I was lucky to not have any serious injuries during my career. I was prone to get kind of a tear in my muscle tissue in my left leg, so I might miss a week or ten days during a season because of that. *[Excluding the first and last seasons of his career, Doerr averaged 142 games a season.]*
— *Bobby Doerr*

The thing that ended my career basically was when I was with the Yankees in '59. I got mononucleosis. And after that I had no opportunity to keep my job because I couldn't do anything. In fact, they traded me to Kansas City, and I never took any batting practice or fielding practice, and I had a thousand cc of Vitamin B12 before each game, about an hour before, and that's how I got through the season.
— *Andy Carey*

When I was seven years old I accidentally rubbed some of the lime my dad was mixing with concrete into my right eye. I don't think I was expected to see again, but about six months later my sight started to come back, but it never came all the way back. When I was playing baseball I learned to recognize hitters by the way they walked and other mannerisms. I couldn't even see finger signals. I was fortunate to play.
— *Jack McMahan*

I had an injury that ended my career. I dislocated my shoulder in 1959 on July 4, and that was it. Because it became a chronic thing, and I had to have surgery on it to fix it, and when they fixed it, they had to restrict the movement of the arm to keep it from dislocating, and when they restrict the movement of your arm you can't reach up or reach out. That was an unbelievable day. We played two extra-inning games. The first game was 14 innings or something. The second game was the same, and I think I got hurt in the last inning of the second game. I hit a ball down the left field line, and I was trying to stretch it into a triple, and I dived into third and landed on my shoulder, and that was it.
— *Ted Kazanski*

I wish I hadn't of got hurt when I went to spring training with Boston. I had a good opportunity there after leading the American Association in '59 in home runs and RBI. But I slid into second base and upended a guy and he landed on my elbow. When I got let go, Ted Williams said to me, "I wish I would have had the opportunity to work with you." Perhaps it wouldn't have made any difference with my elbow the way it was. I'd come into the ballpark and my elbow would be bent way up, and they'd put ultrasound on it to let it down. And I was trying to play that way. The trainer said, "Don't tell anybody you got this, because your career would be over with. Nobody ever comes back from this kind of injury. You're damaged property right now. And you're not going to get any better." As a young man, that was kind of bad news.

— *Ron Jackson*

In '55 I went to winter ball and jammed my ankle in the playoffs sliding into third base. The owner of the club was the dictator there, and his brother-in-law owned our club, so he was giving money out, like five dollars for a single, ten dollars for a double, thirty for a triple, I think forty for a homer. I think ten dollars for a run batted in. Ten for a run scored. I hit one off the center field wall and was going for an extra ten dollars. The guy had me at third base by twenty feet. I was going to slide one way and then I tried to fake him out and my ankle went the other way and I twisted that and ripped all the ligaments. The next day they sent me to a voodoo doctor out in the boondocks and I couldn't even put my weight on it at all. The doctor gave me a lot of voodoo stuff. I started to laugh, but I had an interpreter with me. He said, "You have to believe in this." I said, "Okay." The guy was about eighty years old. So he wanted me to stamp my foot and I said, "I can't." Anyway, I went home and went to spring training with the Giants and I couldn't run on it.

— *Bob Lennon*

One relief pitcher, Duke Mass, hit me on my wrist *[in 1958]*. He fractured my wrist and I didn't play the rest of the year. Guys were throwing really tight back then.

— *Ted Lepcio*

My back was giving me trouble in 1953 and my doctor told Branch Rickey that I'd never play again, so Pittsburgh sold me to Hollywood. Treatments helped. For being a supposed "cripple" I played over 160 games every year in '53, '54, and '55, and averaged over .280. Bobby Bragan was my manager in '55 and brought me up to Pittsburgh when he managed them in 1956. I had a pretty good year there, hitting .274.

— *Lee Walls*

Chapter Fifteen

Outside the Lines

What fans see the most are those moments that the players spend between the foul lines in game situations. But most of the players' time is spent traveling between towns and the time spent away from the ballpark. Players today step into a jet, snap themselves into cushioned seats, listen to music or watch a film or take a nap, and in a flash are in the next city. That's a far cry from the bus and train trips that the players of the '50s and fans recall so well, the often long, noisy, sooty, uncomfortable travel from one town to another.

Yet in spite of the often uncomfortable nature of bus and train travel, many players recall fondly those train trips, those hours spent in dining cars or lounges with teammates, those hours when whole teams were thrown together, when there was time to get to know one another, to grab a beer, play cards, and most of all, to talk baseball.

Fans pick up the sports page and see the game unfold in the writer's eyes and through the box score's vivid portrait. What most fans do not see is how each player approaches the game — his preparation, his anxieties.

Some players remember well those times spent outside the lines.

I couldn't sleep on a train. You get on that berth and twist and turn and you get up, you get back in, all night long, and then, going out of Washington, going west, you always went up through Pittsburgh, through the mountains, and when the train was jerking and going around those curves up through there, I don't think anybody ever slept any.

— ***Gil Coan***

St. Louis was especially hot. And we didn't have what you'd call real clubhouses in those days. They were just a room.

I remember the one in St. Louis. It was boarded up. No air-conditioning, of course, in those days. That thing was so hot in there. All you had to do was sit and sweat would pour off you. Even out in the dugouts it was so hot. Chicago was the same way. Their clubhouse was real dark and hot.

Clubhouses were pretty rough in those days. They just had a bunch of old lockers in there. Uneven concrete floors. A couple of old showers, and that was about it. Boston was the only one that had fixed up, before I left the big leagues. They had finally got some tile

in there. Yankee Stadium wasn't too bad. They had a little carpet on their concrete floors. Pretty good showers and stuff. But most of them were pretty rough compared to today.
— *Carl Scheib*

I was named Most Valuable Player on the Oriole team in 1954; that's something they can't take away. I was considered the best, that one time at least.

When I went to Baltimore for the opening of their new stadium, someone came up to me with my old Baltimore Oriole shirt with my name on it. They offered to sell it to me for $1,200. I told them I didn't have that kind of money, and they said they'd give it to the Baltimore Oriole Hall of Fame.
— *Chuck Diering*

For players like me, who were not superstars, there was always pressure, worrying and wondering if you were going to be shipped down or traded.
— *Sibbi Sisti*

In '48 I played in the International League for the Giants. Our season ended up there around September 3rd. Paul Richards was managing Buffalo that year, and he got together an All-Star team and we were going to tour South America. I had my visa and I had my plane tickets, I had my bags packed and they were in the lobby. And there were people running all over the hotel, trying to find me. Because the Giants had called me up and wanted me to be in uniform that afternoon in the Polo Grounds. It was only a ten cent subway ride from Jersey City to the Polo Grounds. I had to call Paul Richards at the airport, and he said, "That's more important than what I'm going to be able to offer you. Go ahead." But it was that close. If they hadn't of found me before I left, I would have missed that chance.
— *Pete Milne*

Coming out of the minor leagues where you were crammed together, when you got to the major leagues we thought everything was first class. The clubhouses were bigger. You didn't see your uniform when you were on the road. You packed your uniform and you didn't see it again until you got to the ballpark; it was hanging up.

You traveled first class, usually by train. Sometimes we flew. Shoot, it was no problem at all. There were some clubhouses that weren't as good as others; Washington wasn't, I recall, but most of them were decent enough. The guys play their cards and autograph balls and sit around and talk after the game in the clubhouse. They were big enough. You know after coming up through the minor leagues, I'm not knocking the minor leagues, but some of the ballparks and some of the facilities that you dressed in weren't too good. Sometimes you even had to dress in hotels. Once you got to the major leagues, it really was first class compared to what we had been through. I'm sure the guys today might not be happy with those conditions, but we thought it was great.
— *Milt Bolling*

I was Howie Judson's roomie in spring training one year. Nobody had told me about his sleep-walking. One night I was reading a western and had the little lamp on. He's laying over there in his bed and all of a sudden he threw them covers up in the air, jumped out of that bed and ran, boom, right into the closet and stopped dead. I thought he was going right through the wall. Scared the daylights out of me.

I hollered, "Howie!" and when I did he said, "Ah, yeah, okay." And he turned around and went right back to bed.

I thought, that's kind of weird. The next day I asked him about it. I said, "You know, you jumped out of bed?"

He said, "Yeah, I do that sometimes. If I do that, just holler my name. Just call my name, I'll go right back to bed."

Well, about two nights later, he jumped out again. He woke me up this time. He ran around to the foot of my bed and he was hanging on to the end of my bed, staring at me. I reached over and got one of those heavy glass ashtrays. I was fixing to fire it at him. I hollered, "Howie! Wake up!"

He said, "Okay." He just relaxed and walked right back around and went right back to bed.

The next day I said, "Howie, I almost belted you with that heavy ashtray over there." So he took the ashtray out of the room. "Just holler my name. There's nothing to worry about."

So about two more days, I'm just laying there, I'm kind of edgy about going to sleep. I stay awake a little extra time until he goes to sleep. He does it again, he throws them covers straight up in the air and he's out of that bed like a flash and runs down the end of the bed and heads right for the window. I'm thinking he's going to dive right out the window.

I really screamed, and he stopped with his nose right up against that window. And I hollered his name, and he said, "Ah, oh, okay," and he just turned around and went back to bed.

I told the trainer and Tebbetts the next day, "You gotta get somebody else to room with Howie. He walks in his sleep and I thought he was going to go through the window last night. I ain't staying there. I'm gone."

So they changed rooms, and Howie roomed by himself after that. Or the trainer might have roomed with him. But I was out of there.

— *Jim Greengrass*

In Chicago if we lost a game I didn't speak to my wife. I took a loss very hard. If we won I wore the same clothes every day, and when we would lose I'd change the clothes, change the side of the street I walked on, etc. Whatever I did that day must be the reason we won, so I'd continue the ritual. That was when I was only twenty-two or twenty-three years old. As I got older my view changed a little.

— *Lee Walls*

My nickname, "Fire" Trucks, started my first year in pro ball. Andalusia, Alabama. Jack House, who was a sportswriter for the *Birmingham News* in Birmingham, Alabama, came down, and saw me throwing the ball over a hundred miles an hour, and with my last name, he put that nickname on me, and it's been there ever since.

— *Virgil Trucks*

Until about 1960, I guess, baseball got most of the good athletes, because it was the only sport where you could go to the Major League level and make some money. Then pro football and pro basketball started coming into their own. But back then if a guy could play baseball, he played it, because that was the most prestigious sport.

— *Milt Bolling*

Travel by train was good. It was a close-knit thing. You ate in the dining car with somebody all the time. There were usually quite a few players in there. And there were seats in the john, and you met in there and shot the breeze and talked baseball. You usually had a car of your own, and there was a lot of card playing, and a lot of players were together, so it was really close. It was fun.

I enjoyed the dining room, you could sit there after you'd eat and talk it over. I remember eating with Frank Frisch and listening to him talk about his career. It was interesting. It was entirely different than flying. Although you mingle on the plane, it's just not quite as close.

— *Wayne Terwilliger*

I seemed to always get the upper berth. A lot of times I would get shook up when they connected cars to a different train, and bang! It was pretty rough then. But hey, it still didn't bother me. I gotta work tomorrow, and that's it. I didn't care, I wanted to play ball. Put me in the line-up.

— *Mike Sandlock*

Before the game I was nervous. Did I prepare properly? Will the game be on TV for my friends to watch? I just hoped I wouldn't embarrass them. Will the slider and curve break sharply and will the fastball be alive? The game itself was filled with a wide range of feelings: pressure, joy, despair, elation, feelings of accomplishment. I always hoped I could pitch a complete game. (Today pitchers hope for six innings.)

After the game, if I won, food and beer always tasted great. Losing was always hard to take, even if I pitched well but lost.

— *Bob Keegan*

Before the game I had my own little ritual. I would drive around the country club and lake and refresh my mind and think about the lineup I would be facing that night. After the game I made it a point to never take the game home.

— *Bill Monbouquette*

I wore number 7, but after a bad season I threw away rabbits' feet, four-leaf clovers, lucky coins, etc., from my locker. I took number 13 for my last six years in the majors and into my managing career in the minors.

— *Sibbi Sisti*

I learned most from my dad. He was an amateur ballplayer here in Detroit. Baseball in Detroit was big, and I always spent my Sundays out at the ballpark.

My dad was about five foot ten, and he was outstanding. He was a real competitor. But during the real tough times, the Depression and whatnot, he got married and had a couple kids. Well, you know what that means, you've got to work and bring home the bread. I'm very fortunate that I didn't have that kind of pressure on me, and I had the opportunity. What I learned about pitching, ninety-nine percent was from him. He was quite a guy.

— *Art Houtteman*

I really enjoyed the train trips. It think it was a great thing for team togetherness. You were like a big family. There would be a certain group playing cards, another group standing back in the corner talking baseball. There would be a few guys that would read. I enjoyed it, and I think the guys back in those days did. Some long trips, Boston to St. Louis, were a little tough, but you had your berth where you could go lay down if you wanted to.

And it was interesting to sit and look at the countryside. It's like the difference of going on the freeway now or going back on the old country roads and seeing the country. Going by planes you don't see much, and by train you used to see quite a bit.

— *Bobby Doerr*

We traveled by train until the last couple years of my career. We all had our own compartments. We used to have card games in them. Time went fast on the train. You became like one big happy family, always together.

— *Del Ennis*

We traveled by train early on, and then we started taking charters in the middle fifties. Then when the Dodgers and Giants moved to the Coast, we had to fly. Our longest trip on the train was from Pittsburgh to Cincinnati, or Chicago. And if you were pitching the next day your legs were a little wobbly, but you got used to it.

— *Bob Friend*

We had special cars on the trains, a dining car and a sleeping car. You get a couple beers and get in those berths, and clickety-clack, clickety-clack, it'd just put you to sleep. I miss the train right now. I've often said I'd like to take a ride on a train again.

I learned a lot of baseball just on the trains. As a rookie I'd get in the smoking lounge, the bathroom, or whatever you want to call it. There's seats around there, and usually there's an old guy talking about years ago, and you learned the game pretty well that way.

— *Danny Litwhiler*

We'd just sit around on the train and play hearts or gin rummy and talk about that day's game. We always had our own dining car, so that made it nice, and if anything came up that you wanted to talk to anybody about, like with another pitcher about a certain hitter, we were always right there able to visit with one another. I think it probably made us a better team. At least it gave us the opportunity to be with each other and talk baseball.

— *Tommy Byrne*

Saul Rogavin had a sleeping problem. He used to go to sleep on the bench, on the bus. On the way back from a spring training game he was stretched out on the back seat of the bus, sound asleep. So we get back to Tampa and everybody piled off the bus. The bus driver didn't see him. He took that bus back to the bus barn. Locked it down. We're sitting in the lobby of the hotel about nine-thirty, that night. Saul's wife came in, and she said, "Saul hasn't come back. I'm getting worried." About eleven o'clock, here he come through the lobby in his uniform. Maaad. Muttering, "You left me on that bus ..."

— *Jim Greengrass*

You'd walk through the hotel lobby and guys would say, "Hey, want to go to the show and go have a beer?" I think it was great in the old days when we had a lot of togetherness.

I thought the travel was great, although I wasn't the greatest train sleeper. I thought it was great when you could travel on trains and the guys would talk baseball. I can remember being at Cincinnati when we were riding trains, and we'd have a lot of parties. You know, picnics for the kids and the wives and the whole family. We did a lot of that, and it was really great because you really got to know everybody real well. I think it made for a lot closer knit on the ballfield.

And then we started flying. For awhile it was fine. Then it became where guys started rooming alone and with very few exceptions, seldom even see each other off the ballfield a lot. I think that part is sad, I really do.

— *Johnny Klippstein*

We'd play a doubleheader on Sunday in Boston. After the game we'd run down and get dressed, and we'd run down and get on the train — we'd still be hot and sweaty from those old close clubhouses. They'd have to hold the train for us. We'd go from Boston to St. Louis. We'd have an off day for travel because it was twenty-six hours on the train. We'd all still be tired from the doubleheader in Boston and we'd eat on the train and sit around and try to go to sleep, which we never did, and get up in the morning and have to ride all day until 10–11 o'clock at night.

We'd have sleeping cars, and the fellows would make up the berths the next day and put a table in, and they'd play cards — Hearts — some would play Bridge. I read a lot. Sometimes it'd be hot as hell in there, though, I'll tell you that.

But not long after that, we got air-conditioning. It just kept getting better and better all the time. Later we'd make the same trip from Boston to St. Louis in the National League by plane. We'd take our time and get dressed and go out and get on our air-conditioned bus, and it'd take us to the airport. We'd get out of the air-conditioned bus and get into the air-conditioned plane, and when it took off you'd already ordered your meal ahead of time, and just as soon as you took off they'd start serving the meals. By the time you had your dinner, they'd say, "Put on your seatbelt, we're in St. Louis." It was so much different, it was really terrific.

— *Jimmy Bloodworth*

Traveling by train was a tough experience because a lot times you were on the train all night. A lot times trips were rough and you couldn't sleep. I tried to get on the train before it started moving and tried to go to sleep before it even started. A lot of coal dust would get in your system overnight, too. we just had to pull the drapes — we didn't have a regular drawing room or stuff like that.

— *Max Lanier*

If you played at night, you had your big meal after the night game, slept late the next day and went to the ballpark three or four o'clock, and if you wanted some extra practice you could get it. But as a daily routine, so many players, once the season started, did nothing as far as anything extra work of any kind, just showed up for the ballgame, took batting practice and played a ballgame.

If I had it to do over, I would be out there every day I could get somebody to be with me, working on fielding, the hitting, all these things. That's something that I did little of. I wasn't encouraged to do it. So few other people did. The only one I can think of offhand who worked at it so hard was Ted Williams. We went into Boston and he was out with all the batting practice pitchers and everybody hitting for an hour. But peons like me, you couldn't get anybody to throw to you.

— *Gil Coan*

Before the game it's all business, getting ready and concentrating. During the game itself you concentrate too hard in the field to even hear anything in the stands. After the game it can be anything from deathly quiet to an uproaring, noisy, funny house of joy.

— *Tom Upton*

During the pregame, you had to be at the clubhouse about two hours before the game. We'd talk about the game, about who's pitching against us and how we're going to play against them, all that sort of thing. And the pitchers would go down the lineup and tell you how they're going to pitch each player and how they wanted you to defense them.

— *Wally Westlake*

One time we went downtown in St. Louis to kill a couple hours before the train was leaving. Vic Wertz and I were roommates. We had the back seat and trunk of a car full of luggage. We parked on the street and went into a movie. When we came out the window had been busted and all our luggage was gone, and we had about ten minutes to catch the train. So we took off on a two week road trip with no luggage. We borrowed clothes and everything else to get through the trip. We had to buy some stuff.

— *Jim Dyck*

It seemed like I was always out in the field, taking ground balls. I always took a lot of pride in my fielding. I worked a lot on that. It was fun to do it. And of course batting practice was always fun. You always like to hit, and when you had a guy like Ted Williams on your ballclub, why, I think it made everybody just a little more conscious of their hitting.

We played a lot of day baseball, and after the game you'd go eat and then you'd go to a movie. I probably saw a movie every night. Ted liked that too. We'd go to movies. He liked westerns, and I liked westerns. Back in the early days you had your vaudeville, too.

— *Bobby Doerr*

At Washington we pitched every fourth day, and we'd throw batting practice in between. You had to be in pretty good shape to take that humidity in Washington and go nine innings. I did a lot of running, but other than that we didn't do anything special to keep in shape.

If I had it to do over again, I'd do it a little different in the off season. I'd throw about twice a week in the winter. But I never did throw any during the winter. I used to play a lot of golf before I'd go to spring training. I lived near a nine-hole golf course in Chattanooga, Tennessee. Before I'd go to spring training, I'd go out and play 45 holes a day by myself, just to try to get into shape.

— *Sid Hudson*

Spring training is important, especially for the players who came out of the northern section of the country. Using myself as an example — I'm here in Buffalo and the only place I had to work out was in the gym where I played handball or punched the bag or did calisthenics, whereas guys who lived in the southern climates, or California, would be doing things that could help them in spring training to get ready.

But coming out of the frozen north, it took me a little bit longer to get ready, timing-wise and exercise-wise and physical conditioning-wise, so the other guys from the Southern states and Western states would have an advantage over anybody coming out of the Northern states. It takes time to get your timing down and get in shape physically. You can't go down and start right in playing a ballgame right off the bat. You have to prepare yourself for it. Your arm, if you're a pitcher, especially.

— *Sibbi Sisti*

In the winters I swam a lot. I come from a family of swimmers. I had a brother who was national champion at Ohio State. The best conditioned athlete in the world is a swimmer. And the worst conditioned athlete is a baseball player. Swimming, you really have to train, and when you're in that pool ain't nobody helping you. I think that's what put that drive in me. I was never nervous. I had pressure since I was a little boy, from swimming. So pressure never bothered me.

Before the game I'd go out and run some in the outfield, and then we'd take our natural infield and outfield practice. That was it. I was always good and loose when the ballgame started. Oh, I was always ready to go. I think running is the basic thing for baseball. For pitchers and for everybody. Running will get your body in shape for anything.

The after-game routine was very normal. I'm not going to tell you I don't drink, but I drank in moderation. Anything you overdo is going to hurt you. I'll tell you one thing. You've gotta get your sleep. I managed to do that. I didn't abuse myself.

— *Gene Woodling*

You get in shape by running and throwing. That's about it. It's hard to realize why there are so many injuries now.

After a ballgame there were usually five or six of us who would go out for dinner. Together, you know. It was more of a group thing those days. We traveled by train; everybody was close by and it seemed like they helped each other. In those days if you got off the beaten path, they'd say, "Hey, you'd better shape yourself up or else."

And if the manager told you to do something, you'd better do it.

— *Al Zarilla*

Getting in shape for the season was a hard problem for me because I was from Pennsylvania, and of course in the wintertime it would get cold. They had no facilities whatsoever, outside of a YMCA. We had a county fairground that had a race track on it, and I'd run around it four or five times when the weather was permitting.

But really, I'd venture to say that three-quarters of the ballplayers, when they left the season, they had to go to work. They had a job they had to go to. That's one reason I think ballplayers today should be so far ahead of our time, since they have all these facilities, and they don't have to go to work. They have the money to keep in physical condition. And yet, look at how many of them get hurt.

I don't think a ballplayer should lift weights. I really don't. A ballplayer's got to have long, sinewy muscles. Not tight, tense muscles.

— *Carl Scheib*

The game itself was great fun, trying to out-maneuver great players, some you had pitched against 12–14 years. I was not overpowering, so location and change of speed were at a premium. I loved trying to deal with Williams, DiMaggio, etc.

Before the game I was not much fun to be around. I took the business so serious — probably too serious. I didn't want to talk much at all.

After the game was great getting with family or friends at a good eating place, knowing I had done my best against the world's best.

— *Ned Garver*

Most of the time in the big leagues we were playing night games, so it was kind of the same routine, get to bed at one or two in the morning, sleep 'til nine or ten, then we'd go to a movie or something like that in the afternoon and be at the ballpark at five. Jimmy Dykes was very liberal with us like that. He had his curfews and he expected everybody to be in.

Back then, everybody had to be in a coat and tie any time they were out of their hotel room. It wasn't like it is today. But you were pretty free to go and do what you wanted to do.

— *Skeeter Kell*

It was tough for me sitting on the bench, because I wanted to play, and I think most guys are the same way, but you also realize, "Well, there can only be nine guys playing." You'd like to be one of the nine but there's reasons why you're on the bench. And you'd rather be sitting on the bench with the opportunity to play in the big leagues than be at the Kansas City Blues or some place in the minor leagues playing every day, you know what I mean? You realize that the possibility is there for you to play. And sure, you want to be out there every day.

It's tough to sit on the bench, and it's tough to keep yourself ready, because you have to run before the game and then you have to take all the outfield practice you can to get the throw and all that. And you don't get as much batting practice, particularly when you're on the road. You only get five swings or so, then you go out and shag balls in your position, but it's tough to stay in shape, to stay ready. Particularly when you're a pinch hitter. I pinch hit quite a bit in my last couple years. It's a tough job, it really is. *[Renna's career average as a pinch hitter was .242 — 22–91; his overall career average was .239.]*

— *Bill Renna*

When you have a good year, you're getting some hits, you're doing some things, you're happier. My second year, I didn't have a good year. It's no fun going to the ballpark when you're in a slump. When you're having a fairly good year overall, you expect your good days.

That's the good thing about baseball, you've got a chance to get back and play the next day. Heck, I made some errors and booted a ballgame one night against the Cubs, and I felt terrible. I was the last one to leave the park. And I came back the next day and we won the ballgame. I got a couple a hits. You know, that's the good part about baseball.

— *Bobby Thomson*

Almost all the players back then were quality players. They knew the game, the fundamentals. They played hard. The players who were weak hitters, in the low .200s, were good glove men.

— *Cal Abrams*

In the majors you didn't have the camaraderie you had in the minors because you were in a big city and people lived all over town. You never went in groups, maybe two or three at the most. But you get in the plane or train and you're all in there together and get up card games or something. And you have your card games in the clubhouse, just passing time away.

— Randy Jackson

Chapter Sixteen

Team Play

Players recall not only specific moments in their careers but also their teammates and the teams that they were proud to have been a part of. They also recall some of the factors that caused some teams to separate themselves — for better or worse — in the standings. Some teams players were happy to be a part of; others, not so much.

We had an infield at Philadelphia — Hank Majeski, Eddie Joost, Pete Suder, and Ferris Fain. Every ball the infielders throw, if they have the time, should be overhanded, because if you throw it side-armed, the ball's going to sink or sail. I'll swear to goodness, every ball that those infielders threw to first were right in the face of our first baseman. Our club I believe still holds the record for double plays. In fact, I have the baseball right here. I pitched a game against Boston. I beat them — I think it was 2–0 or 4–0 — and I made the last play out of the game. It went from first to second and back to me at first. That broke the double play record at, I believe, 199. we wound the season up with 217. *[The Athletics set the record in 1949 — 217 double plays. It's still the Major League record, even with the 162-game season.]*
— **Carl Scheib**

When I played with the Red Sox, the good players had gone, like the Peskys and Doerrs, Vern Stephens and Dom DiMaggio and all those guys, and we were starting with a new group of people and weren't as good as the Yankees at that time. We had some outstanding players, like Piersall and Williams and Jensen and good pitchers like Mel Parnell and Ellis Kinder and those kind of people. Billy Goodman and George Kell were good hitters. But the Yankees overall were stronger than we were.
— **Milt Bolling**

The Yankees had tremendous balance; they had the superstars and then the lesser guys that sometimes when the superstars weren't doing as well, came through. There was no real decline, or no real losing streak. We had great pitching, we had great defense, and we had tremendous offense. And when you have all three of those, it's tough to lose. Wherever we went, in the fifties, we packed the stadiums. Everybody came to see us lose.
— **Andy Carey**

We didn't draw too well in the early fifties, and you couldn't expect it. We had a second division ballclub. But when we started coming on, like when Dale Long hit those home runs in eight consecutive games, people started coming in. I pitched the game against Carl Erskine when Dale hit the home run in his eighth consecutive game. He got a standing ovation. We had thirty-five thousand people in the house, and the stadium seated thirty-three. So as I said, from that day on, we started getting more fans in there.

— *Bob Friend*

The Browns had good individualists, but they didn't have enough depth. The fact is, everybody wanted their players, and the reason they wanted their players was, they could play and when they got to the other club they performed well. The other thing was, the Browns could survive with the money they got from the clubs they traded to.

One big difference between the Browns and the Yankees was the shortstop combination. I was a ground ball pitcher, a sinker baller, and if I threw a ball low, if they hit it on the ground Rizzuto and Coleman were tremendous double play people. Usually with the Browns, instead of getting a double play you'd only get one and then you'd have to pitch to an extra man.

— *Tom Ferrick*

I played seven different positions for the Braves, and I was even available in '48 to be a third-string catcher, but I never got in to catch. Southworth always used to alternate his catching. Masi was a right-handed hitter and Bill Salkeld was the left-handed hitter, and he'd always use those two guys depending on who was pitching against us. If a right-handed pitcher was pitching, he'd use Salkeld at a catcher. But then if they knocked a pitcher out, they'd use Masi, and there was nobody backing up Masi.

So one day he came back down the dugout and said, "In case I need another catcher, you're it." I almost fell off the bench. But I did catch when I was in the service so he must have heard about it. So from that time on if I wasn't playing I'd go down and maybe warm up the pitchers in the bullpen or catch a little batting practice, just for emergency.

If you play the same position day in and day out, the position is easy for you. But if you go from shortstop to second base you've got different places to be in case a ball is hit to a certain area. You have to think to yourself, "If the ball is hit down the line I gotta to be in such a such a position." The same way as in the outfield, you've got to back up the outfielders. If a ball's hit to you, you've got to know where to throw the ball.

The toughest thing I had to do was play five different positions in five consecutive days. The fourth day I played right field and on the fifth day I played third. Coming from right field to third base I felt like I was right on top of the hitter. It was a very odd situation looking at the hitter from way out in right field, then coming into third. My value to a ballclub was that I was a handy guy to have around, I guess.

— *Sibbi Sisti*

We had a lot of speed in the [1954] Oriole outfield, me and Sam Mele, Gil Coan, Chuck Diering. We had a very good club. As a matter of fact, they purchased all of us on the assumption that we still had a couple of good years left in us, that we weren't quite over the hill yet. Because of the fact that we were all major league ballplayers who had experience, we ended up in the first division that first year.

I was very proud to say that I won an awful lot of electrical appliances. They had two contests going in Baltimore, most popular player, and the Oriole of the Week. The Oriole of the Week won an electrical appliance, and I won it seven weeks in a row.

At the end, the most popular would get a Cadillac. We had Don Larsen and Bob Turley working with us. Halfway through the season, I was leading the popular by so many that I thought I had the Cadillac. At the end of the year, Bob Turley had doubled what I had, and I couldn't figure out how until a few years later. He had told all the kids in the park to go in the stands and pull the coupon out of the booklet and put his name on it and stick it into the barrel, and that's how he won.

— *Cal Abrams*

Ellis Kinder was in a room next to Maury McDermott and I. It was a cold night in Detroit, and we were in bed reading a newspaper, and all of a sudden we hear the rattling of the glass window. We figured, well, the wind's blowing pretty good outside, that's the reason for it. When it happened again we looked up and we saw this head looking in the window. It was Ellis Kinder out on this ledge. If he'd fallen from there he was dead. Luckily, it didn't happen. So we opened the window right away and pulled him inside. Got him off the ledge before he fell.

— *Mel Parnell*

When I was hitting all those home runs, we were drawing capacity crowds. We drew as well as anybody. Even as well as Brooklyn, and Brooklyn was the dominating team in the National League in those days. But I was packing them in. That was the only reason. In fact, after my last at bat, everybody would leave the ballpark. They didn't figure I'd get up again.

Of course, baseball was doing very well in those days, after the war. Most of the parks were doing very well. We drew a million five. They didn't break that record until 1960. And that was 1948 or somewhere in there. '49. We drew terrific crowds.

— *Ralph Kiner*

One year, I think it was '56, in an 8-team league, almost every team in the American League had an ex-Yankee as their catcher. Of course, Berra in New York, Berberet, Courtney, Hal Smith, Gus Triandos. So my point is, in those days, if you signed with the Yankees and you went out and had a few years like I had in the minor leagues with the White Sox, everybody in baseball wanted you. "Here's a Yankee, he can't beat out Berra, but he's the next best thing, and look what he did down in Binghamton, or Birmingham," or wherever the Yankees farms were in those days.

And boom! they came up and they gave these guys jobs. Now all of them didn't keep them for a long, long time, but they at least got a half a year toward the opportunity. And of course most of them did pretty well. That's the route I'd take if I had it to do over.

— *J.W. Porter*

Those teams that I played on at Detroit, had we had better bullpens we'd have been tough, because a couple years we led the league in hitting. I led the league in RBI's and Kaline led the league in batting that one year, and we still finished fourth or sixth. *[In 1955 Detroit finished 5th. They led the league in runs scored and hit 6 points higher than the Yankees. Detroit was last in saves with 12. The first place Yankees had 33, the second place Indians, 36; the third place White Sox, 23; the fourth place Red Sox, 34.]* But we had decent starters with

Frank Lary, Steve Gromek, Billy Hoeft, and Ned Garver. We had decent starters. We just didn't have that daily tough bullpen to come in.

— *Ray Boone*

The most enjoyable part of my career was playing for Detroit. I would like to have played my entire career there, but Detroit had other plans. I went to the Yankees for the last part of the '58 season, when they won the pennant. My only regret was that I never played a full season on a really good club.

— *Virgil Trucks*

The Pirates were always good to Bob Friend. I really have no regrets. I had the opportunity to pitch every fourth day. We were all struggling as young kids and were learning how to play as major leaguers, and we made our contributions later on with the ballclub. So I have really no regrets about not going to a stronger club. My record might have been better, but it might not have been. Who knows? I had a great fifteen years with Pittsburgh, and I've stayed here in business. I was in politics here. So Pittsburgh's been pretty good to me.

— *Bob Friend*

We had such a great nucleus of young players after 1959 that were traded away. I really thought, with all those guys — Romano, Battey, Cash, John Callison, so on and so forth, you had a nucleus to be around and maybe win another championship in a couple years.

— *Jim Landis*

Harry Brecheen would buzz anybody; he was a mean pitcher, a tough competitor. We were playing against the Giants and Leo Durocher and Johnny Mize was up. He was in a situation where a home run would have beat Harry. Harry pitched him inside. Mize just stands there and it hits him right between the shoulder blades just below the back of the neck. Mize runs to first base.

Brecheen comes up to hit the next inning. Durocher calls time. He brings in Monte Kennedy, a hard, wild-throwing left-hander. And Leo probably told him, "Get him."

Kennedy hit Brecheen in the right knee so hard I thought he broke his leg. Harry didn't say one word, dropped his bat, ran to first base, and finished out the inning. That poor guy couldn't walk for a week.

And this was the way things were. Everybody protected each other.

— *Chuck Diering*

There was a little bit more camaraderie because there weren't the big salaries. Everything was centered around the thrill of winning and being part of the team and knowing that you were doing your part. Not letting anybody down was an important part of the game. Players stayed together longer on teams; it wasn't as hard to keep up with what uniform they were wearing. Especially the organizations that did real well, like the Dodgers and Yankees and Cardinals — you came up through the organization and then you'd play in the major leagues with the same guys. You spent a lot of time so your personal interests off the field too were closer.

I don't know if a lot of guys get to know each other that well today because after one or two years they move on with somebody else. So that part of the game has changed. I still think the caliber of play that is playing today is as good, except that every time they expand

I think that weakens the league. There are more Triple A players who are playing in the major leagues.

— *Larry Sherry*

Well, when I first came to the Athletics *[in 1943]*, they had a coach by the name of Earl Brooker, and he stayed in the bullpen, he was in charge of the bullpen — and he'd sit down and talk baseball strategy.

But your regular coaches, all they did in those days was kind of direct traffic, you know, around the bases. Oh, if you had a bad day, they'd try to tell you what you were doing wrong, but that was about the extent of it.

I don't fault anybody for it; it's just the way it was. They didn't have specialized coaches to teach you, or work with you.

— *Carl Scheib*

Name the great players of the fifties: Musial, Banks, Williams, Feller ... you can go on and on, and all of them are associated with a single team. Today, look at somebody like Reggie Jackson. Every time you look around he's playing with a different team. It's hard for a fan to really build a relationship with a team or player.

— *Ferris Fain*

Nobody helped me in the minors or in spring training, but that was not uncommon in those days. You were totally on your own. The only person who really helped me was Greenberg when he came over to the Pirates in 1947. *[Greenberg had played his entire career with Detroit, where he led the league in home runs four times, including 58 in 1938. He retired after the 1947 season, after hitting 25 home runs for the Pirates. A Hall of Famer, Greenberg hit 331 home runs and batted .313 in just nine seasons as a full-time player.]* But they didn't have hitting coaches and pitching coaches. And also, when I went to spring training originally with Pittsburgh in 1941 out of high school, they wouldn't even allow me to take batting practice. The regulars wouldn't let you hit. Finally Bob Elliott, who was the star of the Pirates at that time, interceded for me and got me into the batting cage where I could hit with the regulars. Unless somebody like that or the manager would intercede, you couldn't even take batting practice. That's the way the game was played then.

— *Ralph Kiner*

My gosh, we used to get a big kick out of knocking somebody out of a double play. You'd break it up, and if they didn't complete it, you'd get back to the bench and the teammates would all come over and pat you on the back and say, "That's the way to go, nice going." You didn't try to hurt anybody, just broke up the double play.

— *Bobby Morgan*

Most of the time, if you made a mental error, you got fined for it. You could make a physical error, you could have a ball hit right in your hands and you could drop it. You know, it could just bounce out. But that's mechanical.

One good thing about spending a few years in the minors was when you got to the major leagues you were fundamentally sound. When we played the outfield you knew automatically, just like clicking through your mind like a computer, what inning, who the runners were, what they could do, what the situation was, so you automatically knew before the ball was hit what you were going to do with it. And you assumed it was going to be hit to you every pitch. So when the ball was hit through, when it was against the wall, you went back, and you knew where that cutoff man was going to be. You didn't have to turn — and all in one motion, you played the ball off the wall, turned, hit the cutoff man — you've got to hit him right up in his chest where he can just turn and make that — two good throws will get a man much better than one throw that is so damn long there ain't no way in the world you can be accurate, you've got to be lucky. You see what I mean? That's the difference. So two good throws will get him, nail him dead.

— *Pete Milne*

The Chicago Cubs retired my number — oh, the thrill of it! But it was thrilling enough just to get to room with John Vander Meer and to play with Hank Sauer, Frank Baumholtz, etc., etc. I had the good fortune to go to spring training with the Cubs in '49, '50, and '53. And to get to play at Wrigley Field. For the little I contributed it's quite an achievement to realize my uniform is the first to have been retired by the Cubs. I don't even mind that Ernie Banks wore my number 14 after I did.

— *Paul Schramka*

I was around a tremendous group of people. Their faces and names keep popping up into my memory, such as Nellie Fox, Pierce, Rivera, Minnie Minoso. It's just something that's hard to explain, but when you're around a great group of people like that, you'll never forget it.

— *Jim Landis*

The Red Sox were one of those clubs that were going to a youth movement, and I was fortunate enough to be one of those guys, one of the few college graduates that came in. We joined a ballclub that still had a lot of veterans on it. We were kind of the young kids on the block and in those days nobody dared to be very vocal. All we wanted was to be good enough to play in the major leagues.

— *Ted Lepcio*

One thing that stands out in my mind was playing with three Hall of Famers in 1957, who later became Hall of Famers — Warren Spahn, Eddie Mathews and Henry Aaron. They had kind of an awesome team that I had a chance to spend four weeks with, and that's one of the highlights of my career.

— *Bobby Malkmus*

The Milwaukee Braves were near winners in both the years I was there, and they all had one thought in mind, "We gotta win." I thought I was going to help the ballclub win, and they thought I was, and they accepted me as is. That was a marvelous introduction to the team that only heard of Red Murff, and they just took me as one of their own.

I thought it was outstanding, the camaraderie.

— *Red Murff*

If it wasn't for as poor a ballclub as Washington was, I might never have got to the big leagues. I was very lucky. With Pittsburgh I was at the right place at the right time. I only played 22 games, but those 22 games were all-important. I think we won 20 or 21 of those that I came in and finished up or something. You've gotta to be at the right place at the right time.

If you're with somebody else that's got three or four players ahead of you at that position, you're stuck in the minor leagues. I'm just thankful I had the honor to play against some of the great players of all time, and it was fun. It was great.

— *Bob Oldis*

What I treasure most is being with the best ballclub in the best era in the best city. Playing with Hall of Famers and rooming with a lot of them. This is my great reward for what I did and always strived for, being a major league player and ending up with the Yankees. Nothing could have been better than that.

— *Charlie Silvera*

I felt very fortunate to get to the big leagues, and I enjoyed every minute of it. I was always a Cub fan as a kid, being born in Illinois, and then to meet Billy Herman and Billy Jurges and Stan Hack and Charlie Grimm and Gabby Hartnett, and sit down and talk to those guys, and Rip Collins—I was just in awe sitting down and talking to those great players.

And I can remember a lot of times going out East and we'd go into New York and Brooklyn and they were so much better than we were, they'd just beat our brains out. They had some great teams back there, both of them playing against the Dodgers when they had Robinson and Reese and Hodges and Furillo and Snider and Campanella and Newcombe, you know. Just to get on the field with those guys was a great thrill. Even though they'd beat you, you felt honored to be there.

I just feel that when I played, I played with some of the greatest, and against, some of the greatest players that ever put on the uniform. And I think if you look back in the Hall of Fame, who was put into the Hall of Fame from that era, I think there were so many great players there. Not just great players, they were great guys. Down to earth, what you'd really call friends.

— *Elvin Tappe*

I guess I'd have to say the most exciting year I've had was in 1955 with the Giants. They brought me up in the middle of the season, and I finished out that season with the Giants and playing with Willie Mays and that crew, Dusty Rhodes, Whitey Lockman, and all those guys. That was exciting. I got to play regular the short time I was there. Just to watch Mays perform, it was an exciting year. And I did well that year, too, so that helped. *[Terwilliger hit .257 in 80 games.]*

My best year was probably in 1953 with the Senators. I had a real good year. Bob Porterfield won 22 games that year, and I got big hits in three or four of his games, and made some good plays. *[Terwilliger played 134 games that year and batted .252. Porterfield led the league with his 22 wins, losing 10 for the 5th place Senators.]*

— *Wayne Terwilliger*

Frankly, as you look back on the records, I had three great years with the Chicago White Sox. If I had to pick a ballclub that gave me support both in hitting and fielding, I would take the Chicago White Sox. I won more ballgames in any one three year period than with any other ballclub.

I won 20, 19, and 13 for them. Detroit never gave me that type of support. Detroit was always my favorite ballclub, I always loved Detroit. I still do to this day. I have my license plates with my number on it from Detroit. Tiger 22, that's my license plate number. I'll always be a Detroit fan, because I went up with them and I played with some great ballplayers there. I even got to play one year with Charlie Gehringer. I played with Hank Greenberg, Rudy York, Pinky Higgins, I mean, some great, great ballplayers. So they will always stand out as being number one in my life and my career.

— *Virgil Trucks*

I think I won nine out of my last ten starts in 1949. *[Byrne was 15–7 that season.]* They didn't start me the year before until the middle of June or something like that, and I pitched pretty good. I felt rather confident, and I knew I had enough on the ball to get the job done if I could just make them swing at it. We had a real miraculous year that year. It just had to be just plain determination from a team standpoint. Enough of the history had rubbed off on us from the older guys, and when we lost DiMaggio those first 65 games it just seemed like other fellows came through at the right time, and we kept it pretty close. We didn't really know if Joe was going to make it back or not, but it just seemed like almost overnight his soreness in his ankle and heel left him. He had been trying over a period of time to swing a bat and take a little batting practice and that sort of thing, and he just went out there one day and he felt pretty good about it. It's just like the man upstairs decided to let him get well. And he really did pick up the crowd and the pitching staff. It made everybody think, "Well, we've got a real good shot at it now." Of course Charlie Keller was a real good man to have around those days. Lindell and Henrich. We had a pretty good ballclub. Stirnweiss. That was Coleman's rookie year there. And Rizzuto. Yogi. Reynolds. Raschi. Everybody seemed to be doing their bit.

— *Tommy Byrne*

The biggest thrill was being a part of the 1950 Philadelphia Whiz Kids. We were a team and all worked very hard. I remember Roberts winning his 20th game and Sisler hitting the home run to beat Brooklyn. To realize we had won the National League Pennant — there can be no bigger thrill than that. All our teammates were great. I not only respected them, the older I got I realized I loved them.

— *Bubba Church*

One of the things people don't realize is that there were two leagues in the American League, the haves and the have-nots. The haves were New York and Cleveland and Detroit and Boston, and the have-nots were Washington, St. Louis Browns, Philadelphia Athletics, and the Chicago White Sox, before they became the go-go Sox. The Yankees feasted on the have-nots. We'd play them twenty-two times and we'd beat them eighteen, nineteen times. So consequently, the balance in the league was very, very poor. The payroll was so low, though, those clubs could still make money and survive.

That was the one thing, the imbalance in the American League was incredible in those days. The Yankees dominated. What'd we win — fourteen of sixteen from 1949 to 1964. It was just an over-abundance of talent; it all ended up in the same place. I mean, I'm delighted I was in it, but it's not healthy, really. It's better to have more of a balanced league.

— *Jerry Coleman*

Our '49, '50, '51, '52 Cleveland teams would be battling and maybe be a game in front and wind up just a few games back at the end of the season. *[In '49, 8 out; in '50, 6 out; in '51, 5 out; in '52, 2 out].* The Yankees would always go out and get that one guy to put them over the hill. Like a Johnny Sain, Johnny Mize, Enos Slaughter. Guys like this. They would always go over the National League and bring some veteran in to help them out down that last month, that veteran. Whereas in Cleveland we just held on to what we had.

— *Ray Boone*

The Yankees had a pretty good year in 1954 and they weren't even close, they weren't even in contention. Cleveland was a ballclub that was destined to go just as far as they wanted to go. Even the Giants expected us to win the World Series that year. The first two games were the key to the whole thing. They got two real good pitched ballgames, and they beat two of our best pitchers in two tight games. *[The Giants won 5–2 in 10 innings, 3–1, 6–2, and 7–4. Dusty Rhodes drove in 7 of the Giants' 21 runs.]*

Then they got the edge and they got rolling. It's like a roller coaster. You know, you get it moving, just keep going with it. Don't stop. And that's what happened. First of all, the first two games could have gone either way. Had we won either one of those, chances are we would have won the thing. It wasn't overconfidence that beat us because it wasn't that kind of a ballclub. But it was a big surprise when we lost. The Giants were probably more surprised than we were.

— *Art Houtteman*

I'd have to say Cleveland's pitching staff is the strongest I ever saw. I mean, you had Lemon, Garcia, of course Feller was on that club, but he was on the way down. Newhouser was on that club and he didn't pitch much. They had Mossi and Narleski in the bullpen, a tremendous bullpen. And they had Early Wynn. I mean, you couldn't assemble a stronger pitching staff than that. It made it good because you were almost in every ballgame, you never fell out of one. It was fun to play. They were tough.

I don't know how we ever lost. *[Indians went 93–61 in 1955, Kiner's only season with them.]*

— *Ralph Kiner*

Going into Cleveland — that was a tough weekend. You had a four game series in Cleveland you had Lemon, Wynn, Garcia, and Feller. Then they had Narleski and Mossi as their wrap-up guys. I think their fifth pitcher was Art Houtteman. It was a comfortable oh-for-twelve on that weekend.

— *Billy Hunter*

The depth of the pitching staff while I was with Washington probably had more to do with our not winning than anything else. You've got to be strong at catcher, short, second, and in center field. If you're strong there, along with an outstanding pitching staff, you can have a contender. We had some good pitchers. One year, '46 I guess it was, we had four knuckleball pitchers, which nobody likes to hit against — Dutch Leonard, Johnny Niggeling, Roger Wolff, and Mickey Haefner. *[Washington finished 4th — 76 and 78. They were 2nd in batting average and 7th in ERA.]* We had a good pitching staff, but what would happen when you've got that kind of pitching staff, the ballgame would be close, and the catchers have to be pretty good to handle those knuckleballs, and we had a problem with that. Later we had Bob Porterfield, Ray Scarborough, Sid Hudson, Specs Shea, who came from Washington from the Yankees. We had some good pitchers, but not the depth all the way down through the staff that you need in order to be a contender.

— Gil Coan

The White Sox had good pitching when I was there. Billy Pierce was our main pitcher. And when Lopez took over he brought Early Wynn in and he made him his main pitcher. That caused some problems for the club. Bill was very good. Bob Keegan was very good. And Jim Wilson. Turk Lown was a very good reliever, as well as Gerry Staley. Bob Shaw, when they won the pennant, did an awfully good job.

— Ron Jackson

I thought the greatest pitcher we had with the Cubs when I was there was Don Cardwell. He had a live fastball, but he fell in love with a slider, and he threw it too much. Dick Drott had a great arm. Glen Hobbie was a great pitcher. Dick Ellsworth was a good pitcher. All of them had good live fastballs, but sometimes young kids get in these clubhouse meetings and they go over these hitters and everybody says what a great fastball hitter a guy is, and they forget to throw their fastball. They try to become juice ballers and then if they don't have good control, they've got to bring the fastball in, and then they get hit.

— Elvin Tappe

We *[the Pirates in 1960]* clinched the pennant in Milwaukee. That was a big thrill coming back, flying back to Pittsburgh, a big gathering at the airport. Probably the biggest enjoyment I got that year was how the players would get on each other for not moving a player over from second to third with nobody out or missing a cutoff man, or not running hard. They'd get on each other, and Danny Murtaugh, the manager, he'd just take another chew of tobacco and spit it out, 'cause he really had great communication with the players.

But the players got on each other pretty hard to win. And afterwards, when it was all over, and went together and had a beer or something and ate and battled them the next day. It was really a hard-nosed group, with Dick Groat and Don Hoak, Hal Smith, Vernon Law and Bob Friend on the mound. With Elroy we knew if we were one run ahead going into the last couple innings, we had it won. Bob Skinner, Cimoli, those guys. They knew how to play and they did the right things, did the little things to win.

— Bob Oldis

Hank Bauer and I were real close friends, and we had almost identical careers; they called us the "Gold Dust Twins." Hank was a helluva good outfielder. He had a much stronger arm than I did. We could all run. This is something the Yankee ballclub never got credit for. We never hit into ground-ball double plays. Very few. We were a helluva defensive ballclub. When you take in defense, you're taking in pitching, of course. We had Reynolds, Raschi, Lopat, and Ford. There's no better. *[Woodling played 17 years, hit .284 with 147 home runs, 830 RBIs and 830 runs. Bauer played 14 years, hit .277 with 164 home runs, 703 RBIs and 833 runs.]*

— Gene Woodling

I played with Washington in '61 when they were an expansion team and we lost a hundred and Casey brought me to the Mets the next year and I helped them lose a hundred and twenty. As a Met, everywhere we went, we filled the ballpark. It's unbelievable we could play that bad.

— Gene Woodling

I never played in Ebbets Field. I think the guys who lived in Brooklyn or were from the East didn't care for the move to Los Angeles. When we went back to New York, we played the Mets in the Polo Grounds. The clubhouse in the Polo Grounds was in center field. You have to walk from center field all the way to the dugout on the other side. In New York, people came out thirty thousand strong to watch batting practice.

When Snider and Hodges walked in, they booed them all the way from the clubhouse to the dugout. This was during batting practice! It gave me an idea of what it must have been like to play in New York when the Giants and Dodgers were still there.

— Larry Sherry

The Milwaukee Braves could have won four straight pennants. We won in '57 and '58, but in '56 we could have won. We had a one game lead with only three to play, and playing in St. Louis. And we all thought that we were going to be able to win the pennant. But the Dodgers wouldn't lose and we couldn't win a game, and we lost the pennant in the last weekend.

And I wasn't there in '59, but they lost the pennant in a playoff with the Dodgers. It was a period of time when the Braves were as good as any team in baseball. We had four Hall of Famers on the ballclub — Mathews, Aaron, Spahn, and Red Schoendienst.

I just wonder what that team would have made salary-wise if they were playing today. It would be incredible. Just about everybody on that team, with the exception of pitchers, was an All-Star at one time. Crandall was an All-Star catcher and Adcock at first, Schoendienst at second, Logan at short, Mathews third, and Aaron and Bruton and Pafko, guys like that, and Spahn, Burdette, Buhl, Many of those players were All-Star performers.

All of our catchers were good. We had Del Rice and Carl Sawatski. Crandall was an outstanding catcher, an All-Star for several years and might have been one of the best catchers in baseball in his time.

— Ernie Johnson

I started out always wanting to be a Yankee and finish a Yankee. I was traded away in '51, but I did get a chance to come back to them in '54. So in essence I started with them in '43 and I finished with them after the '57 season.

We had some really great ballclubs. Winning was almost everything with the Yankee organization, and everybody tried to help everybody else because we knew we were going to be hitting at everybody's best pitcher every day, to keep us from running away with the pennant. We had some close calls but we won a lot of pennants, and I was fortunate enough to be with six or seven of those teams. *[Byrne appeared in at least four games for eight pennant winners, and he pitched in four World Series.]*

— Tommy Byrne

Well, it was really not a surprise when the Braves moved to Milwaukee. It was a surprise to some people, I guess, the fact that it was one of the first franchises that moved. But sportswriters in that era and radio people will tell you that they really didn't have a big argument when they came to Mr. Perini wanting to move the team because the Braves in 1952 only drew like 289,000 people the whole year. The Red Sox had always been the city's favorite team.

When you draw 289,000, there's just not room for two teams there, and that's why Mr. Perini moved. The timing was a little shocking because they just held a meeting in spring training in '53. We're down there with our Boston Braves uniforms on, and we're pretty close to going back to Boston to start the season, and they just called a meeting and said, "Hey, the team is going to move to Milwaukee."

I think most of the players were happy about the fact that they would be in a city that had only one team. After they got to Milwaukee, the way they were treated reinforced their thoughts about it, because the fans really treated the players great up there.

— *Ernie Johnson*

When I was with the Pirates those five years with Kiner we never did see any left-handed pitchers, unless it was Warren Spahn. Since our power was right-handed, they threw right-handers at us all the time.

— *Wally Westlake*

We had a lot of aggressive guys on the Giants. Before Willie got there in '51 I was in center field. Edie Stanky, "The Brat," was playing second base. He was competitive. He'd turn around and look at me to see if I'd be moving, or if I was going to stand in one spot. That's the way we played. Like John McGraw type of baseball. I'd get mad and tell him, "Just turn around, you SOB, and play second base. I know what I'm doing out here. But that's the way it was, if somebody didn't do something, they'd get after him. "Come on, let's go, shake it up." That's the way we played.

— *Bobby Thomson*

When I went up with the Yankees, I played in left field along with Gene Woodling. He was a left-handed hitter and I was right-handed. Mantle was in center, of course, a switch hitter. Hank Bauer and Irv Noren were in right field. Hank was a right-handed hitter and Irv was a left-handed hitter. That's five outfielders that gave Stengel an opportunity to switch left to right any time he wanted to.

— *Bill Renna*

'56 was the year Cincinnati set the home run record. The feeling was that we were never out of a ballgame. You could go into the sixth or seventh inning three or four runs down and you always felt you were still in the game because we had guys playing and guys coming off the bench that were unbelievable. I mean, they hit the ball. We had Ed Bailey, who could hit the ball out of the park. We had Kluszewski, who could hit the ball out of the park. Wally Post. Gus Bell, Bob Thurman. We had George Crowe, we had Jerry Lynch. We had seven or eight guys that every time they walked to the plate they were always a home run threat. We were about one pitcher short, though.

— *Johnny Klippstein*

The Yankees were definitely professionals. In fact, in the whole organization, they taught you: you keep your nose to the grindstone, you pay attention, you learn your position, and when you're on the field, it's all business and there's no fooling around. In the clubhouse you could fool around, like they normally do, but when you get out on the field and the game starts, why, there's no fooling around on the bench. Sometimes Stengel would be walking up and down the bench and he'd turn around say, "How many outs are there?" So it behooves you to be able to tell him "two outs" or "one out" or whatever. And be right. That's why they had won the five pennants in a row, because they were very businesslike and very professional.

— *Bill Renna*

Some of the guys on the Browns were good upcoming or outstanding ballplayers. In fact, if the St. Louis Browns of 1952 could have been kept together until Turley and Larsen got out of the service — and they were Browns' chattel — we had some guys who could play. We had Vic Wertz. We had Bob Nieman and Roy Sievers. We had Jim Dyck. Willie Miranda came through as a shortstop, and Joe DeMaestri. Courtney could hit, and he hated the Yankees. Even though we finished seventh and we were way out of it, we were just a couple of pitchers away from being a good team.

— *J.W. Porter*

Mantle wasn't the greatest outfielder in the world, but with his speed he could catch up to some of the mistakes he made. He had a pretty good arm, but it wasn't that accurate. We had guys playing in the outfield who had more accurate arms, like Irv Noren. He didn't have a real strong arm, but it was very accurate. We had some other good players in the outfield. We had Bauer, we had Cerv, we had Woodling. Bauer had the best arm of any of the outfielders, plus another guy we had for awhile, Jackie Jensen, who we traded to Washington. Then he ended up an All-Star with Boston. We should have kept Jensen. But you can't keep everyone. We had like seven great outfielders, and you had to get rid of three. But Bauer had the strongest arm, that's why he played right field. And Woodling had the weakest arm, and that's why he played left field.

— *Bob Kuzava*

The best defensive outfield I ever played against, big leagues or minor leagues, was the one Hollywood had in the Pacific Coast League. They had Tom Saffell and Ted Beard and Carlos Bernier. I was a good line drive hitter, and I hit line drives like bullets. Most outfielders couldn't get to them. But it was hard for me to get base hits against these guys 'cause they were all three like deer.

— *Pete Milne*

In 1959 with the Dodgers, I was kind of surprised that we were able to score as many runs as we did. We didn't have a lot of power hitters, but Wally Moon although being left-handed, he hit an awful lot of balls off that screen to left field in the Coliseum. It was like it was made for him, you know. I mean, he would hit the ball off of him inside to left field. They didn't know how to pitch him.

I think the other thing was Charlie Neal, who was not known to be a high-percentage hitter, he probably only hit .240 or .250 or at the most .260, but down the stretch he was coming up with some real big hits. *[Neal, a career .259 hitter, hit a career-high .287 in 1959.]* He hit a couple home runs to help us. John Roseboro, who was also not a high percentage hitter, also started to hit, so it was the little guys who were carrying us, more than the big guys. And that carried over even into the Series. Charlie Neal had a heck of a World Series. *[Neal hit .370, 10–27, with 2 home runs.]*

The playoff — of course the way we won the final ballgame which got us into the World Series — was when Felix Mantilla threw the ball away at first base, which allowed us to score the winning run, so it actually scored on an error. It actually was kind of a sloppy ballgame, but at that point you'll take them anyway you can get them.

—Johnny Klippstein

1962, with the Mets, was my last year in baseball. Casey Stengel was the manager. That was the first year the Mets were in the league. When they were trying to get a team together, they didn't know how to go. They thought, "Shall we go with some young players, some strong legs and some strong arms, and the players with no names, or should we go with the name players and draw a lot of people whether we win or lose?"

So they decided to go with the older type player that had names in the big leagues. They had Gil Hodges, Don Zimmer, Roger Craig, Richie Ashburn, Frank Thomas. New York people knew these players.

Anyway, we outdrew the Yankees that year. We finished last, naturally, because our skills had diminished. Casey just couldn't spur us, like he could the Yankees, because we were all thirty-six and thirty-seven years old, and older. But we enjoyed ourselves. We didn't win many games, but the ballclub had a great year financially because they drew something like a million and a half people.

—Joe Ginsberg

Chapter Seventeen

Endings, Wishes, Regrets and Joys

How does it all end? A line from a T.S. Eliot poem goes, "Not with a bang, but a whimper." So it is with the career of many a baseball player. It often ends with a sense of fulfillment. More often, though, it ends with the belief that it ended too soon, that potential hits or games pitched well were still possible. Often injury brought an untimely end to a career. At other times it was a team's decision that a different player would be of more help. Sometimes it was a player's feeling that his best days were behind him, and that it was time to move on to a different life. Some players are left with thoughts of a career they wished had worked out differently. Outweighing the regrets, though, are their joys of having been able to play in the big leagues.

As in Robert Frost's poem "The Road Not Taken," each player faces a myriad of forks in the road, paths that he must choose between which will forever change the direction of his life. Circumstances beyond his control also send him down certain paths he wouldn't have chosen on his own. Looking back, he might sigh with regret about some segment of those paths, or he might sigh with satisfaction at the fruits that lay along that path. It's always interesting to recall events which could easily have turned out differently; it's fun to speculate on where other "roads" might have led.

One voice rings loudest and clearest of all in those spoken by players of the '50s, a voice that drowns out the regrets. It is the voice that expresses a love of the game, the joy of having been there.

Baseball meant everything to me. I played in an era that I think will go down in history as the greatest era in baseball.

— *Frank Thomas*

In '54 I hit .324 in the C league in Salinas, California. I hit 20 home runs and drove in 102 runs. I went to the Mexico League in '55 and led the league in hitting until the very last day, and then I lost it to a teammate. In '57 I hit .284 with 20 home runs and 102 runs batted in. I thought I would at least get an invitation to spring training with the Pirates, and when I didn't I was really disappointed. In '61, after eleven years in baseball and not getting back to the big leagues I retired.

— *Paul Pettit*

I can almost see it in slow motion, that ball Jerry Coleman hit in the eighth inning of that Yankee–Red Sox showdown in 1949, the last game of the season, with the winner going to the World Series. They beat us 5–2, the killer coming when, with the bases loaded and two outs, Coleman hit a dunk fly ball down the right-field line and I had to go all out. I had to catch it or else, because everybody was running. I missed the darn thing by two inches or so, and I popped all the blood vessels in my left knee. I was in the hospital for 10 days when I got back to Boston. Even Mr. Yawkey and Joe Cronin didn't know I hurt myself that bad.

But the biggest hurt was losing that game.

— *Al Zarilla*

When I retired in 1959 I went on a barnstorming tour with Satchel Paige and the Cubans. The tour ended when Paige quit and when Castro told the Cubans that if they didn't come back to Cuba immediately they wouldn't be permitted back in.

— *Virgil Trucks*

I was traded from the Yankees to the Senators in 1952. There are always ten pitchers on a squad, and I was always about the tenth pitcher, and I had to make a living somewhere, and in the major leagues I made a little more money than I would have in the minors, but what happened was at the end of the '52 season was that the Washington Senators released me.

In the winter Birdie Tebbetts called me. He was going to manage Indianapolis for the Cincinnati and Cleveland clubs. He was looking for a pitching coach, and he thought I might be able to do the job, maybe pitch a little bit, and coach. The money was decent for that type of job, so I accepted it. I went to Indianapolis and we developed Ray Narleski that year for the Cleveland Indians. So there wasn't much need for me to pitch at Indianapolis. We had a good ballclub. So Birdie went to the big leagues in '54 and I went with him and stayed in the big leagues as a coach for twelve years.

— *Tom Ferrick*

Until my arm injury things were going pretty well. In 1949 I led all professional baseball in hitting with a batting average of .446. In 1950 I was named Minor League Player of the Year. *[In three minor league seasons — 903 at-bats — Saucier batted .380.]* Then I hurt my arm in 1951 and only played in 18 games with the Browns. *[When Bill Veeck used the midget Eddie Gaedel as a pinch-hitter against Bob Cain, Saucier was the player pinch-hit for in the first inning, because Saucier was injured and wouldn't have been able to play in the field.]* I was called back to active duty in the Navy in April, 1952. When I was released from active duty in April of '54, I retired from baseball at the age of 27.

— *Frank Saucier*

The Braves released me in the middle of the year in 1954. I was told they would give me my unconditional release and I could go sign with anybody or they could re-sign me as a coach. At that time I was 34, 35 years old, and I figured I wasn't going anyplace. So I took the job as a coach. What was a little bit unusual is that my whole playing career, from 1939 to 1954, I was with the Braves' organization.

— *Sibbi Sisti*

What I treasure most is that I knew that I was a major league pitcher. Forty years after I signed with the Pirates an article came out that mentioned me as one of the top two prospects to ever come out of Southern California.

So even though I didn't have the career I might have had if I hadn't hurt my arm, I thought that was quite a tribute.

— *Paul Pettit*

I played pro ball for seventeen years. I missed three and a half seasons during World War Two. Like many others who had to serve, I missed some of my prime years as a player, being in the service from age twenty-one to twenty-five.

I was proud to have made All-Star teams in the Georgia-Florida League, the Southeastern League, and the American Association. I always played hard and tried to do the little things to help the team, like hit behind the runner with a man on second and no outs, run the bases hard to break up double plays. I considered myself a complete team player. I tried to play the way people like Stanky, Hemus, Dark, Reese, Slaughter and that type played.

— *Pete Castiglione*

It was always such a thrill for me to walk into a big league clubhouse and see my beautiful uniform, with the number seven, hanging in the locker.

I guess I went to the park so early every day because I was afraid that one day it wouldn't be hanging there for me anymore. And sure enough — much too soon, one day it wasn't.

— *Ted Kazanski*

The biggest days of my life in baseball were getting in the World Series with the old St. Louis Browns and playing in the All-Star Game in 1948 with guys like Williams, DiMaggio and that group. It was an honor, because I was almost like a rookie, my second year in baseball. My favorite days were playing with Vern Stephens of the St. Louis Browns and rooming with him with the Browns and Red Sox, and just being fortunate enough to play the great game. To me, baseball's a kid's game, and I enjoyed playing it so much. Where can you get paid for doing something you enjoy so much?

— *Al Zarilla*

I was 26 when I quit baseball and joined my dad in the funeral business.

— *Paul Schramka*

Everybody has a dream or something they want to do. And I wanted to be Yankee and I wanted to finish a Yankee, which I did. I got traded away — I would have like to stayed there from start to finish, but I've got no regrets. I had a few injuries but not enough to slow me down, to keep me from playing. Baseball will always be in my blood, and I'm proud to have participated and I can always say that I did the best I could, so I have no regrets at all. No sir.

— *Tommy Byrne*

I was happy with my career. I missed a few milestones that I wanted to reach. Just like any other player, I always wanted to play in the World Series, but I never made it. I wanted to hit the three hundred plateau in home runs, but I played a lot of games in Forbes Field, which was not a home run hitter's park. I feel that if I'd played in a different ballpark I'd have done that, and if they'd let me play the last two years, I'd have done that. I finished fourteen home runs shy. *[In Thomas' last three seasons he moved from the Mets to Phillies to Astros to Braves to Cubs, never getting much playing time.]*

But baseball has opened a lot of doors in life for me. It taught me competition and how to approach it. It has taught me to get along with people. My baseball career was a dream come true for me.

— *Frank Thomas*

The only regret I have about my baseball career is the sore arm that pretty much curtailed my career. I should have probably been working out in the winter time. I hurt that arm, and then I got bounced around quite a bit. But that's the only bad thing that ever happened to me in baseball.

— *Spider Jorgensen*

I wish I had got traded from the Athletics. My best year was in '48. I wish I had got traded about '49 or '50. We had problems with the pitching staff on our club. You know, a losing club always does. If you'd be a starting pitcher and lose the game, you'd be in the bullpen, and another guy would be in there. And then if he'd lose, well, maybe you'd get back in again. Every year that they kept me in the starting rotation, I had winning years.

Detroit and Boston wanted Eddie Joost and me. They wanted Eddie Joost mainly, but Philadelphia wouldn't let him go so I didn't go. I beat Detroit quite a few times, and I knew liked me a little bit. I was hoping I could go to Detroit.

That was one thing I wanted, just to see if I couldn't do better if I had a better club behind me. Also, I wish we had had pitchers enough that I could have played the outfield. I really think I could have stayed up there awhile longer as an outfielder.

— *Carl Scheib*

I really always loved baseball. When I was at home growing up, I started in these tiny Midget Leagues. I have a brother who's two years younger than I am. We were on the same team back there in the Midget Leagues, and we'd have our uniform on all day long, playing ball. It's was something that I just grew up with. I kept up through Midget Leagues and American Legion ball.

— *Bob Cain*

I started out playing baseball in the little town of Wyandotte, Michigan, then I went to a little Catholic school, played in school, went through an American Legion program, which was beautiful.

Baseball is the greatest game in the world, and I gave it twenty-seven years, seventeen as a player, ten as a scout, and I have no regrets. It's been good to me, I've played in three World Series. Just this little guy from small towns.

I wasn't the greatest pitcher in the world and I wasn't the worst, but there's some great ballplayers who played their whole lives and never got in a World Series. Hey, I thank the good Lord for giving me some ability. Baseball's been good to me and good to my family, so I can say nothing but nice things about it.

— *Bob Kuzava*

The thing I miss most is not the feel of the ball or the size or swing of the hitter or the smell of hotdogs and popcorn, or the tantalizing sounds of the game: the crack of bat meeting the ball. What I miss most is that moment at the start of every game, standing on that green field and looking out at the flag with moist eyes and the feeling of pride in being an American. What I miss most is the daily playing of our beautiful National Anthem.

— *Red Murff*

They say lightning doesn't strike twice. Well, it does. Three times for me. I missed out on World Series shares three years in a row. In '50 we lost on the last day to the Phillies. In '51 we lost in that playoff against the Giants on Thomson's home run. Then in '52 I was traded to the Reds in mid-season and the Dodgers went on to win the pennant.

— *Cal Abrams*

Early in my career I enjoyed my career very much because — and I don't mean it for some big ego or anything — but if you look at the records I was having for about four years in a row I was having some Hall of Fame years as far as driving in runs and hitting home runs were concerned. Then after the '54 season when we moved, I got victimized by two-platooning and I think that cost me a great deal of my career.

I'm not blaming anybody. I'm just saying that you don't produce when you're two-platooned. If you go into the years of '55 through '59, the last five years I played I didn't do as much as I did the first five years I was up there. *[In Zernial's first four full seasons, he averaged 33 home runs a year. In his next four seasons, he averaged 22 home runs a year. In his last two years, playing part-time for Detroit, he hit a total of 12 home runs.]*

— *Gus Zernial*

Of course I regret we came so close to having some great years there at Boston — close to winning a World Series. Close to winning a pennant some other years. Couldn't get quite over the hump. But still, there are a lot more positives than negatives. I'm thankful for my years in baseball, because I think the forties and the fifties is really one of the great eras of the game, with some of the greatest players.

— *Boo Ferriss*

The only regret I have about my career is I wish I could have played better, been more successful, but I have no regrets otherwise. Baseball was good to me, and I enjoyed it. It meant a lot to me and still does. It's a great game and I try to encourage the young fellas to play every chance they get because it's such a great game.

— *Billy Hitchcock*

No thrill was greater than putting on a major league uniform for the first time. I played against Cincinnati in old Braves' Field — went hitless — but it was still a great experience.

I was happy to be in Boston — after all, it was the majors — but I have to admit I was glad when we moved to Milwaukee, only 200 miles from home — Elkader, Iowa — my folks and friends got to see a lot of games.

It was fun to play in front of them and in front of the 30,000 people in the stands, much different from the 2,500 who watched us in Boston. It's not the hits or fielding plays I remember most: it's all the friends I made in baseball, and the feel of that uniform that first day.

— *Jack Dittmer*

I'm so very grateful to God to have been a part of old-time baseball. It has significantly colored my life and made me proud to be thought as one of those ancient breed. I may have sued baseball, but as our Lord says, "I chastised you because I love you."

— *Danny Gardella*

Overall, I'd have to say I had a decent major league career, and there were some real outstanding moments, but I didn't attain the things that I think I should have attained. I'm not saying I'm not the fault that it didn't happen that way, because I was physically sound and I certainly had the opportunity. I didn't work up through the minors, and maybe I pitched as well as I could have. Who knows? But sometimes you're no better than the ballclub you're playing for.

I liked the game and I did everything that was asked of me and maybe a little bit more in some cases. The final thing, when you look at the score or your record, and in your own mind if you haven't done what you had hoped to do or wanted to do. Maybe there is no blame. Who knows?

— *Art Houtteman*

I'm proud to hear my peers, a lot of players and coaches, say my fastball and curve were among the best. Yogi made the comment that I had the best curveball. Some have told me, "Man, I couldn't hit you with an ironing board."

I had good stuff. With the ability I had I should have been a bigger star. That's my one regret, but my only regret, and not much of one really. I had fun. I think we all did back then. We were happy to be there. I'd be happy to do it all again, just the way it was.

— *Don Ferrarese*

I think that in 1946 that if I'd gone to Triple A baseball and put in that year there, it would have helped me a great deal. I think I would have learned a lot more about a better class of baseball before going from Double A, which was the Southern League in a war year, to the major leagues, when all the stars came back from the war. It was tough. *[Coan was brought up to the Senators in 1946 after being named Minor League Player of the Year in 1945.]*

— *Gil Coan*

I have no regrets about my career except that I wish I could have played when I wasn't injured. That's my only regret, but I had no choice about that.

— *Marty Marion*

I was disappointed in not getting to play in the big leagues earlier. I spent eight years in the minors and two years in the Army during the War. *[Malzone was 27 years old in 1957, his first full big league season.]*

— *Frank Malzone*

My oldest son was born in January, 1952, and I enjoyed being with him and my wife during my free time, when we were at home. But staying on the road two weeks at a time, riding trains (instead of flying) and sleeping on a train between cities, made it rough on a 160 pound person playing every day.

I wish I could have been a catcher and only played against left-handers and played

about one half the time. I feel I could have been a much better player. I caught in semi-pro, and some in the minors, but they felt I was too small.
— *Skeeter Kell*

Coming from a one-room schoolhouse in Arkadelphia to pitch in the major leagues was just an exciting opportunity. I was a very, very bashful young man, and of course not having good eyesight I had a few problems. So baseball gave me a lot of confidence and the chance to see a lot of the world. I certainly don't have any sour grapes, because I got to go places and do things out of baseball that I would have never got to do otherwise.
— *Jack McMahan*

Being traded from Cleveland to Cincinnati was a big disappointment, but probably the biggest disappointment I had was with some of those years on the coast, in the Coast League, when my arm really felt good.

I think I was a big league pitcher then. If I'd have had some of those years when I was young, when my arm felt good, I could have started 400 games in the big leagues instead of 209.
— *Cal McLish*

My only regret was that I signed with the wrong team. But as far as the career and playing, boy, not a single regret. What I treasure most is the guys, the guys that I played with and against, and the friendships formed. The people I met, and the travel — it was a real education.
— *Jim Dyck*

I could have been maybe a little smarter out on the mound than I was. Mixed my pitches up a little more maybe, and tried to get them to hit my pitch instead of hitting their pitch. Things like that come to me now, after fifty-six years in baseball.

If I'd maybe done some of those things back then it may have improved my overall record a little bit. Other than that I don't think I would have changed anything.
— *Randy Gumpert*

Any regrets? The only thing that I can think of is that I got too darn old to play. Man, it's fun out there playing baseball.
— *Jimmy Bloodworth*

I evidently belonged there, but there I was, still looking at these guys as my heroes instead of looking at them as me competing against them. But how can you change that? When you're young, that's just the way you feel.
— *Ted Kazanski*

Of course I would have loved to have hit better and stayed longer with the Yankees or Red Sox or played more. But overall I figure I'm very happy with the way it went. I think back now, I seemed to fare fairly well in fielding and everything, and I could throw fairly well, and I ran fairly well, for a big guy. I felt that I probably could have done better had I thought more and got into the hitting more than I did. That's one thing that kind of bothered me, I probably should have considered the count more, or whatever.

If I had it to do over again, I'd probably put more thought and concern into the at-bats instead of going up there and just looking for the ball—I knew it was three and on and two and one and all that, but a little thought given to it, I may have been to do a little better. But I was very happy with what I did.

— *Bill Renna*

I don't have any regrets about my career. Not a one. I played for twenty years professionally, eight years in Triple A, eight years in the big leagues. That's sixteen out of the twenty I played at a very high caliber. I was inducted into the Brooklyn Dodger Hall of Fame with Bobby Bragan.

I played my last five years at Buffalo, New York, in the International League and had a couple real good years there. I thought I was going to get back in the big leagues, but I never got another shot.

I left the big leagues very young, about thirty-two. My first couple years at Buffalo, one year I hit twenty-one home runs, played shortstop. I thought I might get a call back as a utility man, but I never got another call.

I don't have any regrets about that either.

— *Bobby Morgan*

I think I would have pitched longer if Paul Richards had stayed with the club *[White Sox]*. But after I won 16 and lost 9, the next year I came up with a bone spur, in '55, which set me back a couple of months. Then the next year I had hemorrhoids and a fissure. So those things hurt me.

But I was fortunate to do what I did, because I was in the service for three years and was twenty-five, going on twenty-six before I even got started. So that didn't help.

If I hadn't gone in the service, I would like to have tried out at third base, because in college and high school I always played third base or shortstop. I know I could have hit in the big leagues. I wasn't too good a runner, so I might have had a problem there. *[Keegan hit .321, 9–28, in his first big league season, with a career .163 average.]*

— *Bob Keegan*

The only thing I would have liked to have changed would have been to stay there a little longer. Once you're there, you know, and you get a little sample of it, you just hope it will last and last. Each year was a new year, and you had to kind of fight for your position each year. If I could have gotten another year or so, I would have been much happier, but I'm just happy that I got a chance to make it up there.

— *Herb Plews*

I would like to have gotten out of the Yankee organization sooner than I did. They were tough. Cheap. I was 4–1 with Newark one year and making about four hundred and I went in and said, "I need some more money." All you wanted was another fifty, and they wouldn't even talk to you. So then you go back and pout and don't do as well. Cheap. The cheapest organization I've ever been in.

At one time the Newark baseball club was probably as good as a lot of the big league teams. They could tie up a player for years in those days. Now it's tougher to do that. You were just a piece of meat for them, I guess.

— *Bob Keegan*

I have no regrets now about not being a first string catcher. The first couple of years we won the pennant and I'm playing behind an eventual Hall of Famer, so I know I'm not going to beat him out for his job. I understood what my role was and I did it.
— *Charlie Silvera*

If I went back and did it all over again, there's only one thing I might have wanted to change. Probably would have started learning to throw a slider maybe at an earlier point in my career and thrown more breaking balls instead of just fastball, fastball, fastball. I think probably I would have been a little better pitcher before I started relieving.

I really had better success when I became a reliever than I'd had as a starter. I think perhaps if I had tried to work a little more with the breaking balls and change of speeds I probably would have been a better pitcher over that early eight years of my career.

But other than that, I wouldn't do it any different. I'd go back and I'd play for the same money, too.
— *Johnny Klippstein*

The one regret I have is that I never played with a championship team, and it's so much more difficult playing with lousy teams. I mean, it was tough to play when you finished last or seventh every year. That's tough, you know. I regret that.

I loved playing in Pittsburgh, the people were great, and they treated me well there, but not having been part of a good baseball team certainly was very difficult.
— *Ralph Kiner*

I wish instead of being a catcher I would have been an infielder from the time I was a small boy, because really I'd only played about 102 games in the minors as an infielder when I went up to the big leagues. And that's tough sledding. Fortunately, I had Joe Gordon as my second baseman, and he really helped me a lot.
— *Ray Boone*

I always wanted to be a ballplayer. My father really influenced my career. I take great personal satisfaction that I did something in life I really enjoyed. As a result I have lots of present memories and good friends.
— *Bob Keegan*

I had the good fortune to go to spring training with the Cubs in '49, '50 and '53. I was the youngest player on the roster each year. In '53 Hank Sauer broke a finger in spring training so I got to play some. I hit a couple of homers and batted over .300 and made the Cubs roster. I was in the outfield with Sauer, Hermanski, Baumholtz, Jeffcoat, Bob Addis and Preston Ward. Even though I wasn't up there long, it was fun anyway. I was lucky. How many people can say they played major league baseball.
— *Paul Schramka*

My days in the game were not as great as a lot of fellows, but nobody enjoyed going to the ballpark more than I. Baseball was everything to me. Whatever I have I owe to the game. What stands out most of my eleven years in the majors was walking on the field at the Polo Grounds for the first time and realizing I was part of a big league club, then playing against guys like Stan Musial, outstanding in all ways, a real gentleman, one of the best players I ever saw. Sometimes I think baseball has lost the feeling among young people that it had years ago, then I see the crowds it draws and think maybe I'm wrong. That special magic only baseball has isn't likely to ever die.

— *Willard Marshall*

I did what millions of other boys would like to have done, and that's be a big league ballplayer. The game itself was always exciting because no two could possibly be the same.
— *Ken Lehman*

Baseball is a great game whether one is pitching in front of 92,705 fans as I had the chance to do in the 1959 World Series, or playing in the sandlots to empty bleachers. I've been around, played with many teams: the Tigers, White Sox, Kansas City Athletics, Milwaukee Braves, San Francisco Giants, the Cubs and the Mets. I was the first Met pitcher to win four straight games. Then Tom Seaver came along. There's life outside of baseball, but I've enjoyed my life in baseball, not just my pro career but with the amateur teams I've coached, with the kids who love the game, too.
— *Bob Shaw*

I think the biggest thing about my career is that I got the chance to play against all the great players, with and against them. I look back and I think, Geez, I played with and against some of the greatest players that ever played this game, for crying out loud. I didn't do a heck of a lot, but I did little things, you know. I got home runs off Whitey Ford, a Hall of Famer. Don Newcombe. I look back on some of the guys — Jim Bunning. I took Jim Bunning downtown. I can look back at those and I can laugh about it, but I had a great time.
— *Wayne Terwilliger*

I feel I had a great life in baseball. Being one of only 400 ballplayers at the time was something not many young players had a chance to do. It was a dream answered for me. *[Dillinger led the AL in stolen bases three straight seasons.]*
— *Bob Dillinger*

I looked forward to a game every day. I looked forward to going to the ballpark, putting on the uniform. I enjoyed the pregame practice every day. I hated the rainouts, the rain delays. I didn't enjoy the packing and the unpacking for road trips and all that stuff.

But going to the ballpark — playing catch and playing pepper was something that seemed like it was worthwhile. And of course, I really enjoyed watching the ballgame. I loved to watch the hitters hit. I paid more attention to hitters than I did pitchers. I loved to see good plays. I was really a fan.
— *Cal McLish*

I really feel lucky just to have made it to the big leagues. Then, to be on teams with future Hall of Famers and great players will always be my greatest memories. Being with the Cards with Musial, Schoendienst, Slaughter, Gibson. Yankees with Mantle, Maris, Ford, Howard, etc. Cubs with Ernie Banks, Santo, Jenkins, etc.

I recall the day I was pitching for the Milwaukee Braves and relieved in both games of a twinbill in St. Louis. My entire family was there and I won one game and saved another. On the Braves' club were the one and only Hank Aaron, Ed Mathews, Warren Spahn, Torre,

Alou and numerous others. I struck out Musial, Bill White and Gary Kolb to end the ninth winning in the win. My family were even happier than I.

— *Bobby Tiefenauer*

Just being in baseball is what I treasure most. The rest of it is a matter of effort and the way the ball bounces. You get a break or don't get a break, or you're in the right position at the right time. A lot of times it's got nothing to do with you as an individual. It's a matter of being in the right place at the right time.

— *Art Houtteman*

I think I'm very, very fortunate. I was born with club feet and deaf in one ear. Luckily, I had surgery right away that corrected the problems. My mother, when she saw me in the World Series, said my dad had cried because looking at me as an infant it was unlikely I'd ever be able to do anything like that. I have to feel that God was pretty good, giving me a shot to perform at that level.

— *Larry Sherry*

I signed my first contract with the Athletics when I was sixteen years old. I was so young and so innocent, it was just like a dream. You like to play baseball, and the first thought that comes to your mind was that they were crazy to pay you to play baseball.

— *Carl Scheib*

Baseball gave us a chance to experience things we might never have experienced. My wife and danced at the Waldorf Hotel to Guy Lombardo. We saw Henry Fonda in *Mr. Roberts*. We saw Mary Martin and Ezio Pinza in *South Pacific*. We will never forget those times.

— *Bob Dillinger*

More than anything I liked the competition. I look at it now as something I did that only a few get to do. And add to that the memories of players like Banks, Snider, Reese, Hodges. As exciting as it was back then, I think it's more exciting now to look back on it.

— *Randy Jackson*

I was a still a boy in June, 1955, when I signed my contract and joined Baltimore in Detroit, was eighteen and scared, a boy among strangers, among men, caught between my lifetime dream of being a major leaguer and the sense that I didn't really belong.

— *Wayne Causey*

I'm sure the fans remember, better than I do, certain situations I was involved in during the ten years I played on some good Yankee teams. Many books have been written about some of the things that happened on those Yankee teams in the '50s, and I probably contributed to some wins.

But what I did isn't what mattered. My mind was geared strictly on whether we won the game. Nothing else was at all important. Baseball is truly a team sport and no one individual can win or lose any game despite how he plays in it: he can only offer teammates a contribution. Individual moments often elude me; memories of winning stay with me always.

— *Gil McDougald*

There were really great ballplayers at that time. I think the biggest thing is the love of the game. The players would associate with each other. In other words, say you were on the road and we stayed in a hotel. After the ballgame you would go back to your hotel after eating and there might be fifteen or twenty guys sitting around in the lobby talking baseball.

We used to sit around after the game in the hotel and talk baseball.

— *Sonny Dixon*

When I started my pro career, I wasn't even thinking that I wanted to get into baseball that bad. It was still a dream, but you're twenty-nine years old, you say, "Well, that's behind me."

And all of a sudden, you decide, "what the heck? I'm not the happiest person in the world where I am, why not go and try something and see if you can do it?" It was very difficult to go into a program cold turkey like that, at that age, without anything but a guarantee that we'll get you a job this winter so you can make an income for your family.

Of course, the age factor was always there. I think that if I did anything good, I proved that if you have major league talent it will usually get you to the major leagues. I think that's about the only thing I proved, that the major league talent will get you to the major leagues. You may have injuries that will keep you from that, but that's something that's unavoidable.

— *Red Murff*

The first big thing that happened to me was of course just playing the first game in the major leagues. I think that's the biggest thrill that a guy can have. You finally realize your dream, and at the same time you're a little apprehensive about whether or not it's going to work.

— *Ralph Kiner*

I went over to Cincinnati in 1956 as a right-handed pinch hitter, and Birdie Tebbetts was managing. He had Gus Bell in right field, and Smoky Burgess and Ed Bailey catching, and Ted Kluszewski. His lefthanders were good hitters, all of them *[They also had George Crowe at first base.]* I was supposed to be a right-handed pinch hitter, when they'd bring left-handed pitchers in. Or when they were starting lefthanders I was expecting to be in the lineup.

I was over there maybe six or seven weeks. I'd hit off Haddix one time and eight days later I'd go up and get a chance to hit off Spahn. You know, eight days in between swings, and I finally went to Tebbetts and said, "Birdie, you don't need me here. I can't sit on the bench, I have to play. Get me out of here, will you?"

He said, "Well, you're right. I just don't pinch hit for my lefthanders."

He talked to Gabe Paul at that time, the Coast League was like a retirement home for big leaguers, and Gabe said, "I can send you to Seattle." I said, "Do it." From there, for the next five or six years I played regular out in the Coast League, and loved every minute of it. I was making respectable salary at that time. So the longer I played, the happier I was. During that era a lot of players made more in the Coast League than they could in the major leagues. It was a great place to play.

I played a little bit at the beginning of 1961. I lost three years in the service, but those years counted as far as actual playing time, because you're under contract. So I actually played in my twenty-first year of professional ball.

— *Jim Dyck*

Seventeen. Endings, Wishes, Regrets and Joys

Baseball was good to me. I enjoyed it all. I was fortunate to have great players most of my career — many Hall of Famers like Mantle, Ford, Berra, Kaline and Yastrzemski. They made it easy.

I feel proud that I did it my way and was never fired as a manager at New York, Detroit or Boston.

— Ralph Houk

I remember one night in June of 1953; I was 19 years old, I guess, we were playing on a Friday night in the Polo Grounds, and I looked up in the stands and there were like fifty-five thousand fans — it was a full house — and I looked over at the other dugout when I was in the field. It was such a beautiful sight. The field was so green. And the lights and the full house and all these guys in the other dugout that a few years ago I had read about, and now I was on the same field with them. So I kind of said to myself, "Geez, what are you doing here?"

— Ted Kazanski

When I originally wrote letters to the players who graciously gave their time to make this book possible, I did so with the idea that I might write poems based on the moments the players shared. I decided instead that what the players told me was best left unchanged. But perhaps it is only fitting that I include this poem written by the great relief pitcher, Elroy Face.

> Twenty-two years in professional ball.
> Two stand out above them all.
> 1959 was a special year,
> 17 straight wins. I did endear.
> 1960 was a special team.
> We all fulfilled a special dream.
> The Pittsburgh Pirates beat the New York Yanks,
> And to that team my special thanks.

— Elroy Face

Few expressed their pride at having played in the fifties more powerfully than J.W. Porter:
I'm so proud to have been a player in the fifties that I could explode. Oh, I wish I could have played more, done a little better. But I was there. Of all those kids at Oakland Tech who wanted to be, I was the one that was. It's a side room, that American Legion room in the Hall of Fame at Cooperstown, but I'm there. Rollie Fingers is in both rooms. Wow! I hit a homer off Don Larsen the next April after his perfect World Series game. Double wow!

Appendix: The Players

The data below include, for each interviewed player, his big league seasons, primary positions played, the teams played for, whether the player batted/threw right or left, the position-players' batting averages and home runs, and the pitchers' wins, losses, saves, and earned run average.

On several occasions a player was traded from a team and then returned to it; the team is only mentioned once. Each player's major and minor league statistics are easily available elsewhere; this list is merely intended to provide an overview. The first listing is of the players who spoke to me.

Cal Abrams, outfielder, 1949–1956
    Brooklyn Dodgers, Reds, Pirates, Orioles, White Sox
    BL   TR   BA .269   HR 32

Johnny Berardino, infielder, 1939–1942, 1946–1952
    Browns, Indians, Pirates
    BR   TR   BA .249   HR 36

Lou Berberet, catcher, 1954–1960
    Yankees, Senators, Red Sox, Tigers
    BL   TR   BA .230   HR 31

Jimmy Bloodworth, infielder, 1937, 1939–1943, 1946–1947, 1949–1951
    Senators, Tigers, Pirates, Reds, Phillies
    BR   TR   BA .248   HR 62

Milt Bolling, infielder, 1952–1958
    Red Sox, Senators, Tigers
    BR   TR   BA .241   HR 19

Ray Boone, infielder, 1948–1960
    Indians, Tigers, White Sox, KC Athletics, Milwaukee Braves, Red Sox
    BR   TR   BA .275   HR 151

Don Buddin, shortstop, 1956, 1958–1962
    Red Sox, Houston Colt .45's, Tigers
    BR   TR   BA .241   HR 41

Tommy Byrne, pitcher, 1943, 1946–1957
  Yankees, Browns, White Sox, Senators
  BL TL W 85 L 69 S 12 ERA 4.11

Bob Cain, pitcher, 1949–1953
  White Sox, Tigers, Browns
  BL TL W 37 L 44 S 8 ERA 4.50

Andy Carey, third baseman, 1952–1962
  Yankees, KC Athletics, White Sox, LA Dodgers
  BR TR BA .260 HR 64

Pete Castiglione, second baseman, third baseman, 1947–1954
  Pirates, Cardinals
  BR TR BA .255 R 24

Bubba Church, pitcher, 1950–1955
  Phillies, Reds, Cubs
  BR TR W 36 L 37 S 4 ERA 4.10

Gil Coan, outfielder, 1946–1956
  Senators, Orioles, White Sox, NY Giants
  BL TR BA .254 HR 39

Jerry Coleman, infielder, 1949–1957
  Yankees
  BR TR BA .263 HR 16

Chuck Diering, outfielder, 1947–1952, 1954–1956
  Cardinals, NY Giants, Orioles
  BR TR BA .249 HR 14

Sonny Dixon, pitcher, 1953–1956
  Senators, Philadelphia A's, KC Athletics, Yankees
  BB TR W 11 L 18 S 9 ERA 4.17

Bobby Doerr, second baseman, 1937–1944, 1946–1951
  Red Sox
  BR TR BA .288 HR 223

Jim Dyck, outfielder and third baseman, 1951–1956
  Browns, Indians, Orioles, Reds
  BR TR BA .246 HR 26

Del Ennis, outfielder, 1946–1959
  Phillies, Cardinals, Reds, White Sox
  BR TR BA .284 HR 288

Ferris Fain, first baseman, 1947–1955
  Philadelphia Athletics, White Sox, Tigers, Indians
  BL TL BA .290 HR 48

Don Ferrarese, pitcher, 1955–1962
  Orioles, Indians, White Sox, Phillies, Cardinals
  BR TL W 19 L 36 S 5 ERA 4.00

Tom Ferrick, pitcher, 1941–1942, 1946–1952
   Tigers, Indians, KC Athletics, Orioles
   BL   TR   BA .241   HR 20

Boo Ferriss, pitcher, 1945–1950
   Red Sox
   BL   TR   W 65   L 30   S 8   ERA 3.64

Ben Flowers, pitcher, 1951, 1953, 1955–1956
   Red Sox, Tigers, Cardinals, Phillies
   BR   TR   W 3   L 7   S 3   ERA 4.49

Bob Friend, pitcher, 1951–1966
   Pirates, Yankees, Mets
   BR   TR   W 197   L 230   S 11   ERA 3.58

Ned Garver, pitcher, 1948–1961
   Browns, Tigers, KC Athletics, LA Angels
   BR   TR   W 129   L 157   S 12   ERA 3.73

Dick Gernert, first baseman and outfielder, 1952–1962
   Red Sox, Cubs, Tigers, Reds, Houston Colt .45's
   BR   TR   BA .254   HR 103

Joe Ginsberg, catcher, 1948, 1950–1954, 1956–1962
   Tigers, Indians, KC Athletics, Orioles, White Sox, Red Sox, Mets
   BL   TR   BA .241   HR 20

Jim Greengrass, outfielder, 1951–1956
   Tigers, Indians, KC Athletics, Orioles, White Sox, Red Sox, Mets
   BL   TR   BA .241   HR 20

Randy Gumpert, pitcher, 1936–1938, 1946–1952
   Yankees, White Sox, Red Sox, Senators
   BR   TR   W 51   L 59   S 7   ERA 4.17

Dick Hall, pitcher, 1955–1957, 1959–1971
   Pirates, KC Athletics, Orioles, Phillies
   BR   TR   W 93   L 75   S 68   ERA 3.32

Gail Harris, first baseman, 1955–1960
   NY Giants, Tigers
   BL   TL   BA .240   HR 51

Billy Hitchcock, infielder, 1942, 1946–1953
   Tigers, Senators, Browns, Red Sox, Philadelphia Athletics
   BR   TR   BA .243   HR 5

Art Houtteman, pitcher, 1945–1950, 1952–1957
   Tigers, Indians, Orioles
   W 87   L 91   S 20   ERA 4.14

Sid Hudson, pitcher, 1940–1942, 1946–1954
   Senators, Red Sox
   BR   TR   W 104   L 152   S 13   ERA 4.28

Billy Hunter, infielder, 1953–1958
    Browns, Orioles, Yankees, KC Athletics, Indians
    BR   TR   BA .219   HR 16

Randy Jackson, third baseman, 1950–1959
    Cubs, Brooklyn Dodgers, LA Dodgers, Indians
    BR   TR   BA .261   HR 103

Ron Jackson, first baseman, 1954–1960
    White Sox, Red Sox
    BR   TR   BA .245   HR 17

Ernie Johnson, pitcher, 1950, 1952–1959
    Boston Braves, Milwaukee Braves, Orioles
    BR   TR   W 40   L 23   S 19   ERA 3.77

Spider Jorgensen, third baseman, 1947–1951
    Brooklyn Dodgers, NY Giants
    BL   TR   BA .266   HR 9

Ted Kazanski, infielder, 1953–1958
    Phillies
    BR   TR   BA .217   HR 14

Bob Keegan, pitcher, 1953–1958
    White Sox
    BR   TR   W 40   L 36   S 5   ERA 3.66

Skeeter Kell, second baseman, 1952
    Philadelphia Athletics
    BR   TR   BA .221   HR 0

Ralph Kiner, outfielder, 1946–1955
    Pirates, Cubs, Indians
    BR   TR   BA .279   HR 369

Nellie King, pitcher, 1955–1957
    Pirates
    BR   TR   W 7   L 5   S 6   ERA 3.58

Johnny Klippstein, pitcher, 1950–1967
    Cubs, Reds, LA Dodgers, Indians, Senators, Phillies, Twins, Tigers
    BR   TR   W 101   L 118   S 66   ERA 4.24

Bob Kuzava, pitcher, 1946–1947, 1949–1955, 1957
    Indians, White Sox, Senators, Yankees, Orioles, Phillies, Pirates, Cardinals
    BB   TL   W 49   L 44   S 34   ERA 4.05

Jim Landis, outfielder, 1957–1967
    White Sox, KC Athletics, Indians, Astros, Tigers, Red Sox
    BR   TR   BA .247   HR 93

Max Lanier, pitcher, 1938–1946, 1949–1953
    Cardinals, Giants, Browns
    BR   TL   W 108   L 82   S 17   ERA 3.01

Bob Lennon, outfielder, 1954, 1956–1957
  NY Giants, Cubs
  BL   TL   BA .165   HR 1

Ted Lepcio, infielder, 1952–1961
  Red Sox, Tigers, Phillies, White Sox, Twins
  BR   TR   BA .245   HR 69

Don Liddle, pitcher, 1953–1956
  Milwaukee Braves, NY Giants, Cardinals
  BL   TL   W 28   L 18   S 4   ERA 3.75

Danny Litwhiler, outfielder, 1940–1944, 1946–1951
  Phillies, Cardinals, Boston Braves, Reds
  BR   TR   BA. 281   HR 107

Bobby Malkmus, infielder, 1957–1962
  Milwaukee Braves, Senators, Phillies
  BR   TR   BA .215   HR 8

Frank Malzone, third baseman, 1955–1966
  Red Sox, California Angels
  BR   TR   BA .274   HR 133

Marty Marion, shortstop, 1940–1950, 1952–1953
  Cardinals, Browns
  BR   TR   BA .263   HR 36

Tim McCarver, catcher, 1959–1961, 1963–1980
  Cardinals, Phillies, Expos, Red Sox
  BL   TR   BA .271   HR 97

Cal McLish, pitcher, 1944, 1946–1949, 1951, 1956–1964
  Brooklyn Dodgers, Pirates, Cubs, Indians, Reds, White Sox, Phillies
  BB   TR   W 92   L 92   ERA 4.01

Pete Milne, outfielder, 1948–1950
  NY Giants
  BL   TR   BA .233   HR 1

Bobby Morgan, infielder, 1950, 1952–1958
  Brooklyn Dodgers, Phillies, Cardinals, Cubs
  BR   TR   BA .233   HR 53

Red Murff, pitcher, 1956–1957
  Milwaukee Braves
  BR   TR   W 2   L 2   S 3   ERA 4.65

Bob Oldis, catcher, 1953–1955, 1960–1963
  Senators, Pirates, Phillies
  BR   TR   BA .237   HR 1

Joe Ostrowski, pitcher, 1948–1952
  Browns, Yankees
  BL   TL   W 23   L 25   S 15   ERA 4.54

Milt Pappas, pitcher, 1957–1973
   Orioles, Reds, Atlanta Braves, Cubs
   BR   TR   W 209   L 164   S 4   ERA 3.40

Mel Parnell, pitcher, 1947–1956
   Red Sox
   BL   TL   W 123   L 75   S 10   ERA 3.50

Paul Pettit, pitcher, 1951, 1953
   Pirates
   BL   TL   W 1   L 2   S 0   ERA 7.34

Taylor Phillips, pitcher, 1956–1960, 1963
   Milwaukee Braves, Cubs, Phillies, White Sox
   BL   TL   W 16   L 22   S 6   ERA 4.82

Herb Plews, infielder, 1956–1959
   Senators, Red Sox
   BL   TR   BA .262   HR 4

J.W. Porter, catcher and outfielder, 1952, 1955–1959
   Browns, Tigers, Indians, Senators, Cardinals
   BR   TR   BA .228   HR 8

Bill Renna, outfielder, 1953–1956, 1958–1959
   Yankees, Philadelphia Athletics, KC Athletics, Red Sox
   BR   TR   BA .239   HR 28

Mike Sandlock, catcher and infielder, 1942, 1944–1946, 1953
   Boston Braves, Brooklyn Dodgers, Pirates
   BB   TR   BA .240   HR 2

Carl Scheib, pitcher, 1943–1945, 1947–1954
   Philadelphia Athletics, Cardinals
   BR   TR   W 45   L 65   S 17   ERA 4.88

Bob Shaw, pitcher, 1957–1967
   Tigers, White Sox, KC Athletics, Milwaukee Braves
   BR   TR   W 108   L 98   S 32   ERA 3.52

Larry Sherry, pitcher, 1958–1968
   LA Dodgers, Tigers, Astros, California Angels
   BR   TR   W 53   L 44   S 82   ERA 3.67

Charlie Silvera, catcher, 1948–1957
   Yankees, Cubs
   BR   TR   BA .282   HR 1

Sibbi Sisti, infielder, 1939–1942, 1946–1954
   Boston Braves, Milwaukee Braves
   BR   TR   BA .244   HR 27

Bob Smith, pitcher, 1955, 1957–1959
   Red Sox, Cardinals, Pirates, Tigers
   BR   TL   W 4   L 9   S 2   ERA 4.05

Frank Sullivan, pitcher, 1953–1963
   Red Sox, Phillies, Twins
   BR   TR   W 97   L 100   S 18   ERA 3.60

Elvin Tappe, catcher, 1954–1956, 1958, 1960, 1962
   Cubs
   BR   TR   BA .207   HR 0

Sammy Taylor, catcher, 1958–1963
   Cubs, Mets, Reds, Indians
   BL   TR   BA .245   HR 33

Wayne Terwilliger, infielder, 1949–1951, 1953–1956, 1959–1960
   Cubs, Brooklyn Dodgers, Senators, NY Giants, KC Athletics
   BR   TR   BA .240   HR 22

Frank Thomas, outfielder, third baseman and first baseman, 1951–1966
   Pirates, Reds, Cubs, Milwaukee Braves, Mets, Phillies, Astros
   BR   TR   BA .266   HR 286

Bobby Thomson, outfielder and third baseman, 1946–1960
   NY Giants, Milwaukee Braves, Cubs, Red Sox, Orioles
   BR   TR   BA. 270   HR 264

Virgil Trucks, pitcher, 1941–1943, 1945–1958
   Tigers, Browns, White Sox, KC Athletics, Yankees
   BR   TR   W 177   L 135   S 30   ERA 3.39

Tom Upton, infielder, 1950–1952
   Browns, Senators
   BR   TR   BA .225   HR 2

Bill Virdon, outfielder, 1955–1965, 1968
   Cardinals, Pirates
   BL   TR   BA .267   HR 91

Gale Wade, outfielder, 1955–1956
   Cubs
   BL   TR   BA .133   HR 1

Wally Westlake, outfielder, 1947–1956
   Pirates, Cardinals, Reds, Indians, Orioles, Phillies
   BR   TR   BA .272   HR 127

Gene Woodling, outfielder, 1943, 1946–1947, 1949–1962
   Indians, Pirates, Yankees, Orioles, Senators, Mets
   BL   TR   BA .284   HR 147

Tom Wright, outfielder, 1948–1956
   Red Sox, Browns, White Sox, Senators
   BL   TR   BA .255   HR 6

Al Zarilla, outfielder, 1943–1944, 1946–1953
   Browns, Red Sox, White Sox
   BL   TR   BA .276   HR 61

Gus Zernial, outfielder, 1949–1959
    White Sox, Philadelphia Athletics KC Athletics, Tigers
    BR   TR   BA .265   HR 237

    In addition to those 92 players, 31 others generously gave of their time to send me written comments about moments in their careers, and/or their feelings about having played in what is considered by most to be baseball's Golden Age. Forty-seven of the 1,078 items quoted in this book are written comments sent to me by the following players:

Jerry Casale, pitcher, 1958–1962
    Red Sox, LA Angels, Tigers
    BR   TR   W 17   L 24   S 1   ERA 5.08

Wayne Causey, infielder, 1955–1957, 1961–1968
    Orioles, KC Athletics, White Sox, California Angels, Atlanta Braves
    BL   TR   BA .252   HR 35

Art Ceccarelli, pitcher, 1955–1957, 1959–1960
    KC Athletics, Orioles, Cubs
    BR   TL   W 9   L 18   S 0   ERA 5.05

Dave Cole, pitcher, 1950–1955
    Boston Braves, Milwaukee Braves, Cubs, Phillies
    BR   TR   W 6   L 18   S 0   ERA 4.93

Al Corwin, pitcher, 1951–1955
    NY Giants
    BR   TR   W 18   L 10   S 5   ERA 3.98

Roger Craig, pitcher, 1955–1966
    Brooklyn Dodgers, LA Dodgers, Mets, Cardinals, Reds, Phillies
    BR   TR   W 74   L 98   S 19   ERA 3.83

Bud Daley, pitcher, 1955–1964
    Indians, KC Athletics, Yankees
    BL   TL   W 60   L 64   S 10   ERA 4.03

Bob Dillinger, Third baseman, 1946–1951
    Browns, Philadelphia Athletics, White Sox
    BR   TR   BA .306   HR 10

Jack Dittmer, Second baseman, 1952–1957
    Boston Braves, Milwaukee Braves, Tigers
    BL   TR   BA .232   HR 24

Carl Erskine, pitcher, 1948–1959
    Brooklyn Dodgers, LA Dodgers
    BR   TR   W 122   L 78   S 13   ERA 4.00

Elroy Face, pitcher, 1953, 1955–1969
    Pirates, Tigers, Expos
    BR   TR   W 104   L 95   S 193   ERA 3.48

Danny Gardella, outfielder, 1944–1945, 1950
 NY Giants, Cardinals
 BL   TL   BA .267   HR 24

Carroll Hardy, outfielder, 1958–1964
 Indians, Red Sox, Houston Colt .45's, Twins
 BR   TR   BA .225   HR 17

Ralph Houk, catcher, 1947–1954
 Yankees
 BR   TR   BA .272   HR 0

Ken Lehman, pitcher, 1952, 1956–1958, 1961
 Brooklyn Dodgers, Orioles, Phillies
 BL   TL   W 14   L 10   S 7   ERA 3.91

Jerry Lynch, outfielder, 1954–1966
 Pirates, Reds
 BL   TR   BA .277   HR 115

Willard Marshall, outfielder, 1942, 1946–1955
 NY Giants, Boston Braves, Reds, White Sox
 BL   TR   BA .274   HR 130

Gil McDougald, infielder, 1951–1960
 Yankees
 BR   TR   BA .276   HR 112

Jack McMahan, pitcher, 1956
 Pirates, KC Athletics
 BR   TL   W 0   L 5   S 0   ERA 5.04

Jim Pyburn, outfielder and third baseman, 1955–1957
 Orioles
 BR   TR   BA .190   HR 3

Paul Schramka, outfielder, 1953
 Cubs
 BL   TL   BA .000   HR 0

Lou Sleater, pitcher, 1950–1952, 1955–1958
 Browns, Senators, KC Athletics, Milwaukee Braves, Tigers, Orioles
 BL   TL   W 12   L 18   S 5   ERA 4.70

Gerry Staley, pitcher, 1947–1961
 Cardinals, Reds, Yankees, White Sox, KC Athletics, Tigers
 BR   TR   W 134   L 111   S 61   ERA 3.70

Dick Tettelbach, outfielder, 1955–1957
 Yankees, Senators
 BR   TR   BA .160   HR 1

Bob Tiefenauer, pitcher, 1952, 1955, 1960–1965
 Cardinals, Indians, Houston Colt .45's, Milwaukee Braves, Yankees
 BR   TR   W 9   L 25   S 23   ERA 3.84

Joe Tipton, catcher, 1948–1954
    Indians, White Sox, Philadelphia Athletics, Senators
    BR   TR   BA .236   HR 29

Lee Walls, outfielder, third baseman and first baseman, 1952, 1956–1964
    Pirates, Cubs, Reds, Phillies, LA Dodgers
    BR   TR   BA .262   HR 66

Hal White, pitcher, 1941–1943, 1946–1954
    Tigers, Browns, Cardinals
    BL   TR   W 46   L 54   S 25   ERA 3.78

Del Wilber, catcher, 1946–1949, 1951–1954
    Cardinals, Phillies, Red Sox
    BR   TR   BA .242   HR 19

Red Wilson, catcher, 1951–1960
    White Sox, Tigers, Indians
    BR   TR   BA .258   HR 24

Sal Yvars, catcher, 1947–1954
    NY Giants, Cardinals
    BR   TR   BA .244   HR 10

Index

Aaron, Hank 1, 103, 144, 195, 234, 239, 252
Aber, Al 206
Aberdeen, Maryland 7
Abrams, Cal 14, 40, 43, 53–54, 59, 67, 79, 98, 124, 127, 129, 135, 166, 174, 195, 205, 210–211, 227, 231, 247
Adams, Herbie 90
Adcock, Joe 1, 144, 195, 239
Addis, Bob 251
Addison, New York 48
Addison's Disease 199
Agganis, Harry 103
Alabama State League 13
Albany, Georgia 4
Alemeda, California 98
Alexander, Dale 17
All-Star 10, 19, 23, 29, 32, 35, 42, 44, 107, 110, 160, 165, 170–172, 188, 204, 213, 220, 239, 241, 245
Aloma, Luis 17
Alou, Felipe 253
Alston, Walter 80–81, 201, 213
American Association 15–16, 19, 23, 26, 35, 131, 135, 140, 210, 217, 245
American Legion 5–6, 18, 128, 246, 255
Amoros, Sandy 176
Andalusia, Alabama 3, 221
Anderson, Bobby 194
Ankenman, Pat 18
Antonelli, Johnny 92, 200
Aparicio, Luis 103–104, 106, 118, 188
Appleton, Pete 136
Appleton, Wisconsin 4
Arkadelphia 249
Army-Navy World Series 37
Ashburn, Richie 104, 150, 174, 242

Astroth, Joe 130
Atlanta 131
Augusta, Georgia 136
Avila, Bobby 159

Bailey, Ed 197, 240
Baldschun, Jack 200
Baltimore / Orioles 15, 34, 49, 53, 56, 58, 72, 79, 88, 91–92, 95, 100, 135–136, 181–182, 184, 201, 203, 220, 231, 253
Banks, Ernie 1, 96, 103, 194, 233–234, 252, 253
Barlick, Al 44–45
Barnes, Frank 17
Barney, Rex 176
Bartell, Dick 196
Baseball Digest 173
Battey, Earl 232
Battle of the Bulge 37
Bauer, Hank 62–63, 65, 104–105, 173, 175, 177, 179, 238, 240–241
Baumholtz, Frankie 151, 234, 251
Bear Mountain in West Point 10
Beard, Ted 241
Bearden, Gene 173
Beaumont, Texas 9, 69, 199
Bell, Gus 1, 101, 156, 194, 240, 254
Benbough, Ben 126
Bennett, John 214
Benton, Al 130
Berardino, Johnny 110
Berberet, Lou 46, 62, 136, 169, 187, 207, 231
Bernier, Carlos 241
Bero, Johnny 181
Berra, Yogi 6, 40, 63, 96, 100, 105–106, 111, 136, 138, 147, 158, 172, 176, 178, 182, 189, 193, 206, 231, 236, 248, 255

Bessent, Don 19
Bickford, Vern 137
Bilko, Steve 29, 201
Birmingham, Alabama 3, 33, 221
Birmingham Black Barons 16
Birmingham News 221
Bithorn, Hi 98
Black, Joe 106
Blackwell, Ewell 69, 99, 138, 155, 199
Blade, Ray 10
Blasingame, Don 97
Bloodworth, Jimmy 1, 48, 55, 72, 140, 154, 174, 224, 249
Blyzka, Mike 203
Boggess, Dusty 38–39, 45
Bolger, Jim 29
Bolling, Frank 205
Bolling, Milt 50, 75, 90–91, 103, 112, 114, 122, 129, 140, 167, 169, 205, 220–221, 229
Bollweg, Don 132, 175, 180
Boone, Ray 18, 24, 39, 75, 83, 88, 109, 123, 154, 171, 184, 206, 232, 237, 251
Bosarge, Cotton 151
Boston / Braves 10, 20, 34, 46, 49, 61, 99–100, 108, 125, 130, 137, 142, 201, 223–224, 239–240, 244, 247
Boston / Red Sox 3, 6, 10–11, 15, 24, 31, 42, 49–51, 59, 75, 79, 86–88, 91, 96–97, 102, 112, 116–117, 122, 130, 147, 153, 168, 173, 182, 186, 189, 191–192, 199–200, 207, 217, 219, 224, 229, 234, 236, 240–241, 244–246, 248–249, 255
Boston University 103
Boudreau, Lou 18, 21, 61, 75, 77, 81, 122
Bowman, Bob 120

267

Boyd, Bob 183
Boyer, Ken 102
Boyer boys 209
Bragan, Bobby 73, 75, 77, 81, 218, 250
Branca, Ralph 176, 185, 196
Braves Field (Boston) 49, 247
Brazle, Al 19
Breadon, Sam 165
Brecheen, Harry 19, 72–73, 155, 232
Brewer, Tommy 140, 161
Bridges, Marshall 8
Bridges, Rocky 55, 118
Bridges, Tommy 146
Briggs Stadium (Detroit) 49, 56, 58, 84, 87
Brooker, Earl 233
Brooklyn / Dodgers 4, 6, 10, 14–15, 17, 19, 22, 26, 31, 34–36, 43–44, 49, 53–54, 76, 78, 80–81, 96, 98, 100–101, 124, 135, 139, 144, 154–55, 158, 160, 172, 174–181, 184–185, 188, 192–193, 196, 198, 200–204, 223, 231–232, 235–236, 239, 247, 250
Brosnan, Jim 198
Brown, Bobby 106
Brown, Joe 178
Brown, Skinny 91, 100
Bruner, Jack 17
Bruton, Billy 239
Buddin, Don 43, 46, 50, 72, 86, 88, 100, 106, 121, 129, 168, 188–189
Buffalo, New York 7, 19
Buhl, Bob 101, 198, 239
Bunning, Jim 84, 106, 139, 152
Burdette, Lew 1, 106, 137, 143, 149, 177, 198, 239
Burgess, Smoky 39, 106, 254
Burkett, Jesse 142
Burton, Les 34
Busby, Jim 1, 160, 171
Busch, Augie 93
Busch Stadium 49
Bush, George 84
Byrd, Harry 25, 203
Byrne, Tommy 28, 30, 36, 41, 43, 62–63, 66–67, 89, 105, 110–111, 119, 137, 157–159, 176, 206, 223, 236, 239, 245

Cain, Bob 17, 59, 97, 105, 110, 119, 155, 159, 210, 244, 246
Calderone, Sammy 200
Callison, Johnny 200, 232
Campanella, Roy 17, 172, 176, 194, 235
Campanis, Al 34
Canadian-American League 215
Caracas, Venezuela 168, 190–191
Cardwell, Don 238
Carey, Andy 26, 51, 57, 64, 83, 98, 112, 144, 155, 158, 175, 177, 179, 217, 229
Caribbean World Series 183
Carpenter, Bob 211
Carrasquel, Chico 1, 22, 106–107, 160, 189–190
Casale, Jerry 31, 96
Cash, Norm 232
Castiglione, Pete 53, 76, 93, 104, 114, 124, 137, 185, 191, 202, 213, 245
Castro, Fidel 244
Ceccarelli, Art 185
Cedar Rapids, Iowa 98
Central League 198
Cepeda, Orlando 201
Cerv, Bob 241
Chambers, Cliff 19
Chapman, Sam 29
Charleston 151
Charlotte 79
Chattanooga 7, 24, 79
Chicago / Cubs 7, 27, 33–34, 49, 53, 68, 79–80, 93, 95–96, 98, 101, 113, 127, 137, 151, 159, 164, 181, 185, 191, 195, 198, 201–204, 213–214, 222–223, 227, 234, 238, 245, 251–252
Chicago / White Sox 5, 7–8, 17, 22, 24, 31–33, 40, 49–50, 54, 59, 64, 67, 70, 73–74, 78–79, 91, 97–99, 102, 108, 110, 115, 118, 132, 160, 162, 168, 175, 177–179, 181–183, 187–188, 205–206, 210–211, 216, 219, 231, 235–236, 238, 250, 252
Chipman, Bob 99
Church, Bubba 41, 44, 113, 121, 127, 130, 150, 155, 183, 197, 211–212, 236
Churn, Chuck 191
Chylak, Nestor 45–46
Cicotte, Al 161
Cieslak, Ted 24
Cimoli, Gino 238
Cincinnati / Reds 8, 10, 43, 45, 49, 55–56, 68–69, 97–98, 101, 103, 116–118, 138, 144, 146, 148, 155, 179, 181, 184, 187, 191, 193, 196–197, 199, 201, 205, 211, 216, 223–224, 240, 244, 247–249, 254
Class D Alabama-Florida League 3
Clearwater, Florida 86
Clemente, Roberto 103
Cleveland, Mississippi 32
Cleveland / Indians 3, 8–9, 18, 20, 24, 31–32, 37, 49–50, 58–59, 64, 73–74, 76–77, 79, 83, 98, 112, 114, 119, 121, 138, 154, 156–157, 159, 171, 173–179, 187, 195, 200, 202–204, 206–207, 209, 213, 231, 236–237, 244, 249

Coan, Gil 7, 24, 39, 58–60, 71, 135, 138, 144, 171, 173, 215, 219, 225, 230, 238, 248
Cochrane, Mickey 37
Cocoa Beach, Florida 6
Cohen, Andy 153
Colavito, Rocky 140
Cole, Dave 96
Cole, Dick 125
Coleman, Jerry 15, 35, 64–65, 107, 116–117, 146, 167, 173, 177, 216, 230, 236, 244
Coleman, Rip 181
Coliseum in Los Angeles 49, 185, 241
Collins, Joe 107, 175
Collins, Rip 22, 235
Colorado Springs, Colorado 24, 27
Columbus, Ohio 19, 185
Comiskey Park (Chicago) 49–50, 58–59, 84, 90, 98, 219
Conley, Gene 198–199
Conlin, Jocko 40, 100
Connors, Chuck 29, 96
Consolo, Billy 209
Consuegra, Sandy 96
Cooper, Walker 40, 101–102
Corwin, Al 31, 181
County Stadium (Milwaukee) 49, 57, 157, 195
Courtney, Clint 25, 64, 70, 107, 132, 231, 241
Craft, Harry 68–69, 81, 199
Craig, Roger 19, 66, 98, 242
Crandall, Del 97, 101, 194, 239
Crone, Ray 200
Cronin, Joe 148, 168
Crosetti, Frank 63, 107
Crosley Field (Cincinnati) 49, 55–58, 101, 113
Crowder, Red 209
Crowe, George 240, 254
Cuba 244
Cuban League 35

Daley, Bud 172
Dandridge, Ray 35
Dark, Alvin 69, 96, 108, 194, 245
Dascoli, Frank 80
Davidson, Billy Joe 98–99
Dean, Dizzy 188
Delmore, Vic "Deacon" 194
Delta State University 32
DeMaestri, Joe 132, 241
Denver 16–17, 27, 151, 153, 203, 207
Derringer, Paul 146
Des Moines 27
Detroit / Tigers 3, 7, 9, 17, 19, 25, 33, 49, 56, 58, 74, 77, 84, 87, 96, 99, 111–113, 129 136, 138, 140, 142, 154, 160, 172–173, 179–180, 184, 186, 191,

Index

193, 195, 200–202, 205–206, 216, 222, 231–233, 236–237, 246–247, 252–253, 255
Dickey, Bill 62, 105, 180
Dickson, Murry 99
Diering, Chuck 10, 14, 38, 58, 73, 139, 180, 191, 202, 220, 230, 232
Dihigo, Martin 190
Dillinger, Bob 27, 252–253
DiMaggio, Dom 107, 171, 229
DiMaggio, Joe 36, 52, 82–83, 88, 90, 96, 148–150, 157, 167, 173, 227, 236, 245
DiMaggio, Vince 184
Dissinger, Roy 4, 151
Dittmer, Jack 247
Dixon, Sonny 89, 91, 110, 119, 136, 149, 156, 254
Dobson, Joe 108
Doby, Larry 79, 171, 209
Doerr, Bobby 1, 26, 31, 51, 173, 217, 223, 225, 229
Donovan, Dick 1, 70, 108, 125, 177
Dorsey, Tommy 193
Douglasville 97
Drabowski, Moe 94
Dressen, Charlie 32, 70, 75, 78, 106, 168, 175, 187
Dropo, Walt 96, 99, 139, 157, 186, 188, 193
Drott, Dick 29, 238
Drummondville, Canada 165
Drysdale, Don 2, 7, 19, 80, 106, 140, 146, 149, 154, 160, 193–194, 198, 205
Duquesne Club 123
Duren, Ryne 30–31, 162
Durham, Joe 15, 135
Durocher, Leo 2, 33, 44, 48, 68, 75–78, 172, 195, 197, 216, 232
Dyck, Art 19, 35
Dyck, Jim 15, 19, 35, 46, 50, 67, 82, 88, 111, 120, 126, 136–137, 153, 157, 180, 182, 216, 225, 241, 249, 254
Dyer, Eddie 77, 165
Dykes, Jimmy 61, 76–77, 81, 201, 227

Easter, Luke 27, 99, 121, 155, 159
Eastern League 48
Ebbets Field (Brooklyn) 49, 52–54, 57, 68, 98, 139, 175, 185, 195, 213, 239
The Ed Sullivan Show 183
Edwards, Bruce 202
Eisenhower, Dwight D. 85
Elkader, Iowa 247
Elliott, Bob 108, 233
Ellsworth, Dick 238
Embry, Red 31
Engels, Joe 7

Ennis, Del 75, 98, 104, 108, 150, 156, 174, 212, 223
Ermer, Cal 79
Erskine, Carl 137, 149, 155, 175, 180, 192, 230
Essie, Bill 6
Evansville 19
Evers, Hoot 132, 186

Face, Elroy 148, 163, 255
Fain, Ferris 65, 107, 109, 158, 229, 233
Federation League 16
Feeney, Chub 23
Feller, Bob 36, 77, 98–99, 109, 119, 146, 150–151, 153–154, 158–159, 162, 206–207, 233, 237
Felten, Happy 195
Fenway Park (Boston) 49–51, 59, 85–88, 90, 103, 122, 153, 219
Ferrarese, Don 33, 73, 88, 118, 156, 179–180, 211, 247
Ferrick, Tom 22, 37, 83, 114, 119, 141, 156, 159–160, 166, 174, 230, 244
Ferriss, Boo 32, 50, 87, 109, 121, 147, 173, 247
Fingers, Rollie 255
Fitzgerald, Ed 189
Flood, Curt 165
Flowers, Ben 10, 17, 19, 96, 118, 168, 192
Fodge, Gene 29
Fonda, Henry 253
Forbes Field (Pittsburgh) 49, 54, 58, 113
Ford, Whitey 1, 6, 137, 149, 154, 157–158, 161–162, 172, 175, 238, 252, 255
Fort Myers, Florida 125
Fort Worth, Indiana 16
Fort Worth, Texas 23
Fowler, Dick 100
Fox, Nellie 109–110, 115, 139, 160, 175, 234
Foxx, Jimmy 148
Foytack, Paul 84
Franks, Herman 34
Fredricksburg, Pennsylvania 4
Freese, George 29
Fridley, Jim 159, 203
Friend, Bob 1, 16, 53, 92, 104, 114, 117, 125, 127, 151, 157, 163, 171, 223, 230, 232, 238
Friend, Owen 206
Frisch, Frankie 222
Furillo, Carl 129, 155, 176, 179–180, 235

Gaedel, Eddie 110, 244
Galan, Augie 29
Galveston County 5
Game of the Week 195
Garagiola, Joe 6, 95

Garcia, Mike "The Bear" 153–155, 206–207, 237
Gardella, Danny 115, 248
Gardner, Billy 88
Garver, Ned 16, 19, 29–30, 39, 59, 68, 110, 112–113, 121, 136, 143, 146, 152, 160, 168, 181, 227, 232
Gas House Gang 22
Gehrig, Lou 42, 52, 184
Gehringer, Charlie 236
Geneva, Alabama 4, 151
Georgia-Florida League 9, 245
Gernert, Dick 21, 51, 59, 96, 128, 150, 152, 156
Gibson, Bob 8, 77, 252
Gilbert, Charlie 20
Gilbert, Larry 20
Ginsberg, Joe 9, 14, 48, 51–52, 66, 150–152, 186, 191, 196, 202, 206, 242
Glenn, John 88
Globetrotters 160
Goetz, Larry 41, 43
Gold Dust Twins 238
Gold Glove 100, 118
Golden Greek 103
Gomez, Ruben 54, 185
Goodman, Billy 128, 188, 229
Gordon, Joe 73, 77, 81, 251
Gordon, Sid 184
Gorman, Tom 213
Graham, Jack 27
Grange, Red 6
Grasso, Mickey 70, 186
Gray, Ted 180
Great Lakes 37
Green, Fred 45
Greenberg Gardens 113
Greenberg, Hank 60, 209, 233, 236
Greengrass, Jim 11, 18, 28, 45, 48, 54–56, 68–69, 82, 101, 105–106, 108, 114, 116, 118, 123, 126–128, 131, 156, 168, 187, 192, 194, 196, 199, 211, 221, 223
Grieve, Bill 182
Griffith, Calvin 32, 168–169
Griffith, Clark 166, 206–207
Griffith Stadium 49, 52, 58–59
Grimm, Charlie 9, 78, 80, 101, 235
Grissom, Marv 157, 185
Groat, Dick 45, 238
Gromek, Steve 206, 232
Guam 37
Guercio, Ted 203
Gumpert, Randy 52, 71, 84, 90, 108, 129, 147, 160, 168, 249
Gutteridge, Don 209

Haas, Bert 35
Hack, Stan 235
Haddix, Harvey 1, 19, 39, 111, 163, 194, 202, 254

Haefner, Mickey 17, 237
Hall, Dick 1, 7, 25, 76, 106, 116, 141–142, 178
Hall of Fame 37, 39–40, 78, 94, 103–104, 107, 109–110, 114, 117–118, 123, 128, 137, 150, 162, 208, 220, 233, 239, 247, 250–252, 255
Hamilton, Jack 149
Hamner, Garvin 205
Hamner, Granny 174
Haney, Fred 70–71, 181
Hansen, Andy 172, 212
Hardy, Carroll 91
Harridge, Will 206
Harris, Bucky 61, 68, 71–72
Harris, Gail 10, 12, 23, 72, 90, 92, 111, 136, 191–192, 201
Harris, Luman 74
Harshman, Jack 181
Hartford 22
Hartnett, Gabby 235
Hatten, Joe 179, 202
Havana, Cuba 33, 35–36
Hawaii 28, 37, 114, 178
Haynes, Marcus 160
Hazel, Bob "Hurricane" 10, 111
Hegan, Jim 111
Hemus, Solly 194, 245
Hendley, Bob 159
Henrich, Tommy 111, 173, 184, 236
Herman, Billy 37, 235
Hermanski, Gene 202, 211, 251
Herzog, Whitey 207
Hickory, Maryland 7
Higby, Kirby 158
Higgins, Mike "Pinky" 72, 75, 77, 91, 116, 138, 186, 192, 236
Hillman, Dave 29, 195
Hitchcock, Billy 47, 60, 109, 124, 134, 147, 189, 247
Hoak, Don 45, 238
Hobbie, Glen 79, 195, 238
Hodges 31, 44, 66, 155, 176, 188, 195, 203, 235, 239, 242, 253
Hoeft, Billy 232
Holloman, Bobo 130, 182–183
Hollywood (Pacific Coast League) 28, 115, 158, 218, 241
Holmes, Tommy 111
Honochick, Jim 43
Hornsby, Rogers 53, 55, 66–69, 77, 100–101, 120, 131–133, 181, 186–187, 196, 199
Houk, Ralph 16–17, 32, 80, 111, 203, 255
House, Frank 25
House, Jack 221
House That Ruth Built 52
Houston 181
Houston Colt '45s 216–217
Houtteman, Art 7, 18, 34, 56, 154, 196, 206–207, 222, 237, 248, 253

Howard, Elston 203, 252
Howard, Frank 112
Hubbard, Cal 39
Hudson, Sid 39, 42, 52, 71, 108, 140, 142, 166, 207, 214–215, 225, 238
Hunter, Billy 6, 23, 32, 63, 81, 112, 114, 117, 119, 131, 203–204, 237
Hurley, Ed 182
Hutchinson, Fred 68, 160, 194

Indiana, Pennsylvania 6
Indianapolis 26, 33
Indianapolis Clowns 16
International League 15, 18, 23, 220, 250
Interstate League 151

Jackowski, Bill 41
Jackson, Larry 8
Jackson, Randy 23, 41, 53, 100, 104, 161, 165, 188, 203, 213, 228, 253
Jackson, Reggie 233
Jackson, Ron 5, 26, 73–74, 101, 104, 111, 139–140, 162, 167, 218, 238
Jacksonville 87
Jamestown 9
Jansen, Larry 155
Japan 18
Jeffcoat, Hal 251
Jefferson Hospital, Philadelphia 211
Jenkins, Ferguson 252
Jensen, Jackie 1, 72, 112, 229, 241
Jersey City 17, 220
Johns Hopkins 211, 214
Johnson, Connie 136
Johnson, Darrell 32, 203
Johnson, Ernie 34, 70, 79, 156, 177, 201, 239–240
Jones, Sad Sam 188
Jones, Willie "Puddinhead" 112, 174, 197
Joost, Eddie 229, 246
Joplin 35, 209–210
Jorgensen, Spider 28, 35, 75, 116, 125, 130, 155, 179, 205, 246
Judson, Howie 168, 220–221
Jurges, Billy 235

Kaline, Al 1, 112–113, 231, 255
Kallas, Harry 28
Kansas City Athletics 32, 49, 139, 171, 217, 252
Kansas City Blues 35, 227
Kazanski, Ted 21, 23, 41, 46, 70, 80, 86, 95, 108, 146, 161, 188, 217, 245, 249, 255
Keegan, Bob 5, 34, 73–74, 79, 86, 107, 109–110, 140, 145, 162, 166, 188, 222, 238, 250–251
Kell, Frank 6

Kell, George 6, 113, 132, 160, 186, 229
Kell, Skeeter 5, 30, 33, 99, 227, 249
Keller, Charlie 148, 236
Kellner, Alex 140–189
Kennedy, Monte 232
Killebrew, Harmon 1
Kinder, Ellis 122–123, 151, 161, 229, 231
Kiner, Ralph 74, 95, 113, 124, 143, 148, 168, 181, 184, 201, 204, 231, 233, 237, 240, 251, 254
Kiner's Corner 58
King, Nellie 4–5, 13–14, 125, 147–148, 151–153
Klaus, Billy 128, 200
Kline, Bobby 207
Klippstein, Johnny 4, 33, 45, 54, 57, 99, 101, 113, 118, 148, 162, 184, 201, 224, 240, 242, 251
Kluszewski, Ted 101, 113–114, 156, 186, 194
Knapp, Larry 45
Knoxville, Tennessee 17
Kolb, Gary 253
Korean War 10, 35
Koufax, Sandy 9, 19, 150, 154, 159, 185, 205
Kretlow, Lou 98
Kritchell, Paul 11
Kryhoski, Dick 203
Kubek, Tony 85
Kurowski, Whitey 180
Kuzava, Bob 24, 36, 71, 90, 106–107, 111, 113, 118, 125, 138, 143, 145, 154, 162, 166, 168, 171, 173–175, 183, 209, 241, 246

Labine, Clem 1, 23, 161
Landis, Jim 46, 52, 74, 84, 90, 110, 125, 128, 143, 172, 189, 232, 234
Lane, Frank 19, 24, 35, 211
Lanier, Max 19, 48, 56, 77, 165, 216, 224
LaPalme, Dave 158
Larker, Norm 190
Larsen, Don 1, 85, 159, 179, 203–204, 231, 241, 255
Lary, Frank 114, 139, 232
Lasorda, Tom 80
Law, Vern 1, 163, 238
Lehman, Ken 185, 252
Lehner, Paul 143
Lemon, Bob 77–78, 114, 140, 153–155, 160, 187, 206–207, 237
Lemon, Jim 1, 188
Lennon, Bob 4, 20–23, 47, 76, 78, 87, 122, 140, 185, 208, 213, 218
Lennox Hill Hospital 180
Leonard, Dutch 33, 237

Index

Lepcio, Ted 46, 77, 85, 91, 112, 114, 129, 131, 139, 161, 218, 234
Leppart, Don 203
Liddle, Don 20, 22, 34, 45, 78, 93, 102, 112, 131, 139, 149, 162, 176, 200–201
Life Magazine 98
Lima, Ohio 99
Lincoln, Nebraska 25, 27
Lindell, Johnny 44, 99, 114, 158, 236
Little Rock 47
Little World Series 35
Litwhiler, Danny 19, 40–41, 56–57, 59, 69, 108, 111, 115, 128, 223
Lockman, Whitey 97, 129, 235
Loes, Billy 1
Logan, Johnny 1, 193–194, 239
Lollar, Sherman 130, 132, 175
Lombardo, Guy 253
Long, Dale 1, 75, 115, 176, 192, 194, 230
Lopat, Eddie 105, 115, 137, 146, 157, 160, 163, 176, 238
Lopata, Stan 174
Lopez, Al 73–74, 86, 139, 213, 238
Los Angeles (Pacific Coast League) 27, 29, 75
Los Angeles Dodgers 9, 27, 49, 66, 80–81, 111, 159, 180, 184–185, 205, 216, 239, 241
Louisville 31
Lown, Turk 238
Lowry, Peanuts 180
Lupien, Tony 15
Lynch, Jerry 133, 144, 240

Maas, Duke 218
Mack, Connie 61, 166
Maglie, Sal 31, 40, 115, 137, 159, 161, 213
Mahaffey, Art 200
Main, Forrest 99
Majeski, Hank 83, 186, 229
Maldanoldo, Colonel Benjamin 191
Malkmus, Bobby 14, 24, 84–86, 133, 157, 188, 194, 234
Malzone, Frank 9, 50, 97, 100, 115, 127, 129, 138, 141, 162, 215, 248
Manchester, New Hampshire 17
Mansfield, Ohio 20
Mantilla, Felix 242
Mantle, Mickey 1, 32, 46, 54, 58, 82–85, 96, 133, 136, 138, 147, 157, 175, 179, 184, 193, 209, 240–241, 252, 255
Mapes, Cliff 24, 209
Marciano, Rocky 80
Marion, Marty 8, 32, 47, 50, 54, 57, 66, 69–70, 77, 81, 103, 112, 115, 126, 138, 159, 161–162, 180, 210, 248
Maris, Roger 140, 252
Marrero, Connie 96
Marshall, Willard 252
Martin, Billy 1–2, 107, 115–116, 122, 179, 183
Martin, Dean 117
Martin, Laurin 189
Martin, Mary 253
Masi, Phil 8, 61, 230
Mathews, Eddie 1, 144, 177, 234, 239, 252
Mauch, Gene 29, 68, 75, 178
Maxwell, Charlie 1
Mayo, Eddie 78
Mays, Willie 1, 54, 91, 97, 116, 122, 129, 144, 185, 187, 200, 202, 235
Mazerowski, Bill 116–117, 137
McCall, John 92
McCarthy, Joe 102
McCarver, Tim 1, 8
McCormick, Mike 125, 185
McCovey, Willie 184, 201
McDermott, Maury 87, 102, 117, 140, 151, 161, 207, 231
McDonald, Jim 203
McDonald, Mage 212
McDougald, Gil 1, 46, 106, 117, 155, 253
McGowan, Bill 42
McGraw, John 54, 240
McHale, John 204
McKinley, Bill 42
McLish, Cal 27, 68, 70, 75, 77, 155–156, 178, 216, 249, 252
McMahan, Jack 12, 31, 92, 184, 217, 249
McMahon, Don 99
McMillan, Roy 1, 45, 55, 117–118
Meggy, Lou 6
Mele, Sam 175, 230
Memorial Stadium (Baltimore) 49, 53, 56, 58
Memphis 17, 103
Metkovich, George 31
Mexican League 243
Mexico 25, 165
Mexico City Tigers 187
Miama Marlins 79
Miksis, Eddie 202
Miller, Bill 203
Miller, Bob 84
Miller, Stu 118, 192, 203
Milne, Pete 15, 18, 30, 54, 57, 61, 115, 134, 172–173, 220, 234, 241
Milwaukee / Braves 5, 9, 26, 49, 57, 70, 85, 101, 111, 131, 157, 164, 171, 176–177, 184, 195, 198, 200, 204, 234, 239–240, 245, 247, 252
Minneapolis 17, 20, 23, 32, 35, 76
Minnesota Twins 79

Minoso, Minnie 27, 115, 160, 171, 175, 177, 234
Miranda, Willy 118, 203, 241
Mr. Roberts 253
Mitchell, Dale 112–113, 209
Mize, Johnny 96, 107, 175, 232, 237
Mobile, Alabama 23, 103
Montague, Hugh 11
Montreal 15, 34–35, 204
Montreal Royals 185
Moon, Wally 97, 241
Moore, Terry 188
Moreno, Julio 96
Morgan, Bobby 18–19, 93, 117, 126, 149, 174–175, 204, 233, 250
Moryn, Moose 96
Mossi, Don 154–155, 237
Most Valuable Player 18, 23, 110, 125, 220
Mueller, Don 31, 129, 185
Municipal Stadium (Cleveland) 31, 49–50, 58–59
Murff, Red 5, 8, 13, 47, 94, 143–144, 150, 183, 234, 247, 254
Murtaugh, Danny 178, 191, 238
Musial, Stan 31, 69, 82, 85, 91–94, 97, 102, 104, 115, 135, 144, 153, 171–172, 180–181, 194, 202, 233, 251, 253
Muskegon 198

Narleski, Ray 154, 237, 244
Nashville 20–23, 108, 122, 213
National Anthem 247
Neal, Charlie 241
New England League 17
New Iberia, Louisiana 4
New Orleans Pelicans 10
New York / Giants 6, 10, 20, 23, 29, 31, 35–36, 49, 54, 66, 75, 77, 97, 102, 107, 110, 116, 122, 129, 131, 157, 169, 176, 180–181, 196–197, 200–202, 204–205, 218, 220, 223, 232, 235, 237, 239–240, 247
New York / Mets 62–64, 66, 98, 110, 164, 204, 238–239, 242, 245, 252
New York / Yankees 5, 8–11, 15–16, 19, 24–25, 28, 33, 37, 39, 49, 51–52, 56, 62–64, 67, 69, 71, 80, 83–85, 88, 97, 102, 105, 110, 114–115, 117–118, 123, 130, 135, 138, 140, 142, 144, 158, 160, 162–163, 167, 170, 172–180, 184, 186, 188–189, 193, 199, 203, 205–206, 209, 215–217, 229–232, 235–238, 240–242, 244, 249, 252, 255
New York Daily News 172
Newark Bears 15, 250
Newark in the Ohio State League 16

Index

Newcombe, Don 17, 19, 80, 137, 140, 149, 155, 176, 185, 201, 235, 252
Newhouser, Hal 118, 153, 237
Niarhos, Gus 8
Nichols, Chet 26
Nieman, Bob 1, 241
Niggeling, Johnny 237
Nixon, Richard 85
Nixon, Willard 140, 161
Noren, Irv 1, 42, 240–241
Norfolk 10, 35–36
Norman, Bill 201

Oakland 28–29, 35, 126, 134, 180, 204
Oakland Tech 255
O'Brien twins 205
O'Connell, Danny 200
O'Dell, Billy "Digger" 187
Oklahoma City 18
Oldis, Bob 45, 70, 79, 118, 63–164, 235, 238
Omaha 17, 27
O'Neill, Steve 78, 80, 188
Oneonta 215
Oriole of the Week 231
Osborn, Don 183
Ostrowski, Joe 4, 23, 113, 163, 174, 208
Ott, Mel 29
Ottawa 30
Overmire, Stubby 174
Owen, Mickey 16
Owens, Jim 200

Pacific Coast League 12, 15, 20, 26–31, 35, 75, 115, 126, 130, 135, 146, 167–168, 181, 197, 205, 211, 241, 249, 254
Pafko, Andy 191, 202, 239
Page, Joe 121, 171, 176
Paige, Satchel 23, 67, 119–122, 155, 178, 212, 244
Paperella, Joe 40–41
Pappas, Milt 1, 73, 85, 134, 163, 182
Parnell, Mel 11, 13, 42, 50–51, 78, 80, 85–86, 88, 98, 102, 108, 117, 121, 123, 129, 140, 151, 158, 160–161172, 185, 188–189, 193, 229, 231
Passeau, Claude 98
Paul, Gabe 69, 199, 210, 254
Pawtucket, Rhode Island 22
Pennock, Herb 11, 163
Pensacola 36
Perez, Tony 31
Perini, Lou 200
Perkowski, Harry 45
Perranoski, Ron 205
Pesky, Johnny 32, 107–108, 128, 229
Pettit, Paul 7–8, 14, 20, 98, 147, 181, 187, 210, 214, 243, 245

Philadelphia / Athletics 25, 33, 36, 49, 65, 76, 89, 100–101, 130, 132, 140, 143, 182, 186, 189, 209, 212, 229, 236–237, 246, 253
Philadelphia / Phillies 16, 19, 28, 45, 49, 72, 80, 95, 108, 112, 120, 126, 140, 156–157, 174, 178, 183, 188, 191–192, 196, 199–200, 204–205, 211–214, 216, 236, 245, 247
Philadelphia Whiz Kids 236
Philley, Dave 59
Phillips, Lefty 7
Phillips, Taylor 9, 26, 31, 40, 68, 93, 95, 97, 114, 146, 164–165, 198
Phoenix, Arizona 26
Piedmont League 15
Pierce, Billy 17, 64, 102, 135, 140, 162, 168, 175, 177, 189, 234, 238
Piersall, Jimmy 1, 86, 89, 121–123, 191–192, 211, 229
Pinelli, Babe 188
Pinza, Ezio 253
Piper, Pat 95
Pitler, Jake 98
Pittsburgh / Pirates 7–9, 17, 25, 44, 49, 53–54, 80, 99, 103, 108, 113–114, 117, 123–124, 141, 144, 146, 157, 164, 167, 177–179, 181, 185, 201–204, 210, 213–214, 218–219, 223, 232–234, 238, 240, 243–244, 251, 255
Player of the Year 248
Plews, Herb 5, 16, 28, 32, 56, 78, 80, 84, 107, 132, 161, 207, 250
Podbielan, Bud 68, 100
Podres, Johnny 96, 176, 186, 205
Pollet, Howie 19, 95, 101, 126
Polo Grounds 40, 49–50, 53, 57, 75, 172, 180, 192, 220, 239, 251, 255
Porter, J.W. 8, 24–25, 67, 72, 84, 98–99, 106, 120, 126, 155, 181, 231, 241, 255
Porterfield, Bob 172, 235, 238
Portland, Oregon 28–29, 130, 168
Post, Wally 240
Powell, Rabbit 46
Prince, Bob 204
Pueblo 27
Puerto Rico 26
Pyburn, Jim 181

Quincy, Illinois 35
Quinn, John 164

Raffensberger, Ken 193
Ramos, Pedro 70, 86, 134
Ramsdell, Willie 158

Raschi, Vic 105, 123, 157–158, 163, 171, 173, 186, 236, 238
Reardon, Beans 40
Reese, Pee Wee 14, 22, 81, 104, 118, 123, 176, 184, 188, 203, 235, 245, 253
Renna, Bill 15, 42, 52, 64–65, 105, 130, 132, 180, 227, 240–241, 250
Reynolds, Allie 105, 123, 157, 162–163, 172, 175–176, 209, 236, 238
Rhodes, Dusty 20, 191, 235, 237
Rice, Del 100, 215, 239
Richards, Paul 58, 72–73, 78–79, 108, 140, 164, 181, 184, 220, 250
Richardson, Bobby 85
Rickey, Branch 7, 10, 14, 17, 25, 56, 123–125, 144, 166, 204, 210, 218
Rifleman 96
Riggs, Lew 34
Rigney, Bill 197
Rigney, Johnny 37
Ripken 7, 205
Ripken, Cal, Jr. 42
Rivera, Jim 24, 115, 125, 132, 159, 175, 234
Rizzuto, Phil "Scooter" 64, 96, 107, 125, 202, 207, 230, 236
Roberts, Curt 210
Roberts, Robin 126, 137, 139, 151, 155–156, 161, 171, 174, 191, 200, 211, 236
Robinson, Brooks 100, 126
Robinson, Eddie 160, 182
Robinson, Frank 26, 103, 126, 135, 148
Robinson, Jackie 34, 127, 176, 195, 213, 235
Rochester, New York 15, 33, 74
Roe, Preacher 93, 115, 124, 127, 155, 175–176
Roebuck, Ed 19
Rogavin, Saul 223
Rogers, Packy 18
Romano, Johnny 232
Rookie of the Year 23, 25–26, 183–184
Roseboro, Johnny 241
Rosen, Al 27, 138, 171, 184
Roufe, Red 179, 212
Rowe, Schoolboy 37, 140
Rowland, Pants 27
Ruffing, Red 140
Runge, Ed 39, 46
Runnels, Pete 1, 127–128, 188
Rush, Bob 101, 137
Ruth, Babe 4, 50, 52, 54, 133, 184, 189
Rutherford, Johnny 101
Ryan, Connie 197
Ryan, Nolan 5, 119
Ryba, Mike 6

Sacramento 28–29
Saffell, Tom 241
Sain, Johnny 35, 148, 172, 180, 195, 237
St. Claire, Ebba 200
St. Louis / Browns 6, 8–9, 23–24, 30, 32, 37, 39, 42, 49, 54–56, 58–59, 64, 66–67, 77, 112, 119, 121, 126, 132, 137, 143, 159–160, 166–167, 180–181, 200, 206, 215, 219, 223, 225, 230, 236, 241, 244–245
St. Louis / Cardinals 4, 6, 8, 10–11, 15, 17, 19, 22, 28, 33–34, 41, 44, 49, 54–57, 81, 92–94, 97, 105, 115, 118, 124, 126, 135, 142, 165, 178, 180–181, 187–188, 194, 202–204, 224, 234, 239, 252
St. Mary's College 179
St. Paul, Minnesota 35
St. Petersburg 15
Salinis, California 20, 243
Salkeld, Bill 230
Sally League 87
San Antonio 15, 46
San Berardino 146
San Diego 27, 32
San Francisco (Pacific Coast League) 28–29, 115
San Francisco Giants 34, 49, 185, 252
San Joaquin Valley 15
Sandlock, Mike 20, 28, 44, 71, 124, 134, 158, 208, 214, 222
Sanford, Fred 65
Sanford, Florida 207
Santo, Ron 252
Sarasota 86
Saucier, Frank 244
Sauer, Hank 55, 95, 127, 234, 251
Savannah 30
Sawatski, Carl 239
Sawyer, Eddie 72
Scarborough, Ray 42, 238
Scheffing, Bob 29
Scheib, Carl 52, 76, 83, 106, 109, 121, 125, 130–131, 142–143, 145, 167, 169, 216, 220, 226, 229, 233, 246, 253
Schmitz, Johnny 202
Schoendienst, Red 104, 180–181, 200, 202, 239, 252
Schramka, Paul 127, 134, 245, 251
Schulte, Wildfire 184
Schultz, Bob 181
Schuster, Billy 27
Score, Herb 136, 155, 203
Seals Stadium (San Francisco) 49
Sealy Mattress 160
Seattle 15, 28–30, 135, 254
Seaver, Tom 252
Segrist, Kal 203

Seminick, Andy 41, 126, 174, 196–197
Senior Bowl 103
Seton Hall 114
Sewell, Rip 135
Shantz, Bobby 137, 189
Shaw, Bob 74, 87, 99, 105, 110, 149, 165, 177, 238, 252
Shea, Specs 238
Sheehy, Pete 65
Shepard, Jack 148
Sherry, Larry 7, 17, 19, 81, 96, 141, 146, 184, 205, 217, 233, 239, 253
Shibe Park (Philadelphia) 49, 57–59, 83, 193
Shotton, Burt 75
Sievers, Roy 121, 169, 188, 241
Silvera, Charlie 64, 91, 100, 111, 130, 159, 173, 182, 235, 251
Simmons, Curt 99
Simpson, Suitcase 27, 196
Sinatra, Frank 117
Sisler, Dick 113, 150, 174, 236
Sisler, George 137
Sisti, Sibbi 26, 55, 59, 62, 132, 141–142, 222, 226, 230, 244
Skinner, Bob 238
Skowron, Bill 39, 66, 107, 39, 66, 107, 177
Slaughter, Enos 8, 56, 92, 128, 202–203, 237, 245, 252
Sleater, Lou 181, 186
Smalley, Roy 191
Smith, Bob 12, 111, 117, 138, 193
Smith, Frank 193
Smith, Hal 203, 231, 238
Smith, Mayo 16, 33
Smith, Vinnie 39
Snider, Duke 53, 129, 144, 172, 175, 188, 195, 235, 239, 253
Sockem Post 6
Sorianto, Dewey 28
South America 220
South Pacific 253
Southeastern League 2245
Southern Association 7, 22, 24, 135, 151
Southern League 45, 248
Southworth, Billy 26, 69, 230
Spahn, Warren 19, 97, 100–101, 116, 143, 152, 157, 198, 234, 239–240, 252, 254
Spartanburg, South Carolina 17
Speake, Bob 29
The Sporting News 19, 26, 118, 167
Sportsman's Park (St. Louis) 49, 54, 58, 64, 92
Staley, Gerry 73, 128, 178, 181, 202, 238
Stanky, Eddie, "The Brat" 76, 122, 187–188, 196–197, 240, 245
Stengel, Casey 20, 25–26, 40,

52, 61–66, 71, 81, 83, 106, 142, 158–159, 170, 172, 174, 176–177, 179–180, 189, 199, 203, 238, 240–242
Stephens, Vern 59, 72, 122–123, 128–129, 157, 229, 245
Stewart, Dave 180
Stirnweiss, Stuffy 236
Stottlemyre, Mel 128
Strickland, George 213
Stuart, Dick 157
Suder, Pete 189, 229
Sukeforth, Clyde 4, 129
Sullivan, Frank 102, 115–116, 129, 131, 153, 171–172, 199–200
Summers, Bill 46, 187
Surkont, Max 101, 168
Susce, George 8, 129
Susquehanna League 7
Swarthmore 6–7
Swift, Bob 110, 132

Tampa, Florida 223
Tappe, Elvin 27, 29, 38, 113, 148, 235, 238
Tatum, Goose 160
Taylor, Bill 21
Taylor, Sammy 10, 58, 66, 79–80, 94, 101, 139, 194–195, 210
Taylor, Tony 194
Taylor, Zack 110
Tebbetts, Birdie 111, 194, 211, 221, 244, 254
Temple, Johnny 55–56, 186, 196
Terwilliger, Wayne 28, 43, 55, 57, 92, 107, 115–116, 123, 127, 129, 161, 202–203, 222, 235, 252
Tettelbach, Dick 84–85, 207
Texas League 7, 15–16, 18, 27, 69, 135, 168, 199
Thomas, Frank 1, 9, 39, 45, 80, 103, 116, 118, 135, 137, 144, 147, 161, 171, 176, 185, 204, 242–243, 245–246
Thomasville, North Carolina 4
Thompson, Fresco 21
Thompson, Hank 180
Thomson, Bobby 35, 54, 129–130, 163, 167, 181, 185, 200, 227, 240, 247
Three I League 19, 35, 98
Throneberry, Marv 140, 204
Thurman, Bob 101, 240
Tiefenauer, Bob 253
Tighe, Jack 201
Time Magazine 98
Tipton, Joe 24, 61, 130
Toledo, Ohio 15, 33
Torgeson, Earl 115, 130
Toronto 22, 32, 70, 180
Torre, Joe 252
Travis, Cecil 36
Triandos, Gus 203, 231
Triple Crown 84–85

Trout, Dizzy 130, 151
Trucks, Virgil "Fire" 3, 25, 109, 132, 149–150, 160, 179, 183, 185–187, 195, 200, 212, 221, 232, 236, 244
Turley, Bob 1, 121, 158, 177, 179, 189, 203, 231, 241
Turner, Jim 62–63, 130, 158
Tuttle, Bill 113, 191

Umont, Frank 192
Upton, Tom 6, 9, 41, 102, 225

Valenzuela, Fernando 180
Valo, Elmer 130, 216
Vancouver 126
Vander Meer 37, 234
Vargo, Ed 45
Veeck, Bill 24–25, 30, 66–67, 110, 119, 130, 167, 244
Vernon, Mickey 152, 193
Vero Beach 6, 10, 22
Virdon, Bill 54, 102, 105, 178

Wade, Gale 29, 101, 191, 195, 197, 210
Waitkus, Eddie 174, 212
Waldorf Hotel 253
Walker, Dixie 134
Walker, Rube 202
Walls, Joanna 2
Walls, Lee 2, 18, 144, 198, 218, 221
Waner, Lloyd 135
Ward, Preston 251
Warneke, Lon 43–44
Washington / Senators 7, 9, 32, 36–37, 49, 52, 56, 58–59, 70–71, 78, 82, 84–86, 102, 109, 115, 142, 152, 160, 166, 168–169, 175, 177, 186, 188, 190, 205–208, 214–215, 219–220, 225, 234–238, 241, 244, 248
Waterloo, Iowa 24, 98
Waveland Avenue 93
Waycross, Class D Georgia-Florida League 9
Weaver, Earl 63
Weik, Dick 142, 206
Wertz, Vic 153, 171, 225, 241
West, Max 27
Western League 27, 35
Western Michigan University 5
Westlake, Wally 13, 36, 60, 74, 92, 123–124, 176, 204, 225, 240
Westrum, Wes 102, 131
White, Bill 201, 252
White, Hal 179
White, Jo Jo 46
White, Sammy 131, 182, 191
Wichita 26, 164
Wichita Falls, Texas 151
Wiesler, Bob 207
Wight, Bill 17, 100, 152, 206
Wilber, Del 193
Wilhelm, Hoyt 1, 23, 131, 151
Williams, Esther 27
Williams, Ted 36, 72, 77, 79, 82, 85–92, 97, 103, 107, 112, 114, 122, 130, 133, 139, 143–144, 147–150, 155–158, 171–172, 192, 217, 224–225, 227, 229, 233, 245
Williamsport 116
Wills, Maury 195
Wilson, Jim 238
Wilson, Red 8, 191–192
Wise, Casey 29
Wise, Hugh 22
Wolff, Roger 237
Woodling, Gene 20, 56–57, 62, 64, 85, 105, 131, 133, 167, 174, 180, 184, 203, 226, 238–241

World Series 2, 6–7, 20, 24, 42, 51, 62–63, 92, 111, 116–117, 130, 141, 146, 160, 163–165, 170, 174–178, 185–188, 198, 202–203, 216, 237, 239, 241–242, 244–247, 252–253, 255
World War II 1, 7, 12, 32, 34, 36, 118, 245
Wright, Tom 13, 33, 49, 52, 67, 79, 87, 89–90, 102, 168
Wrigley, Phil 164
Wrigley Field (Chicago) 49, 56–58, 95, 98, 101, 234
Wyandotte, Michigan 246
Wyatt, Whitlow 131
Wynn, Early 74, 114, 131, 146, 151, 153–154, 174, 177, 206–207, 237–238

Yankee Stadium (New York) 40, 46, 49, 51–53, 58–59, 65, 83, 91, 96–98, 102, 159, 173, 175, 179, 183–4, 189, 205–206, 215, 220
Yastrzemski, Carl 255
Yawkey, Tom 193, 199, 244
Yokem, Ray 10
York, Rudy 132, 184, 235
Yost, Eddie 85, 132, 160–161, 186, 188
Young, Bobby 159
Young, Cy 93
Young, Dick 179
Youngston, Ohio 16
Yvars, Sal 175

Zanesville, Ohio 24
Zarilla, Al 15, 82, 134, 185, 215, 226, 244–245
Zernial, Gus 65, 132, 135, 209, 247
Zimmer, Don 22, 242

www.ingramcontent.com/pod-product-compliance
Lightning Source LLC
Chambersburg PA
CBHW081158230426
43666CB00016B/2852